THE TROUBLEMAKER

THE
TROUBLEMAKER

Michael Scott and
His Lonely Struggle against
Injustice

ANNE YATES
and
LEWIS CHESTER

Aurum

First published 2006 by
AURUM PRESS LIMITED
25 Bedford Avenue
London WC1B 3AT
www.aurumpress.co.uk

ISBN 1 84513 080 4

10 9 8 7 6 5 4 3 2 1
2010 2009 2008 2007 2006

Text design by Peter Ward

Typeset in Adobe Caslon and Adobe Caslon Openface
by SX Composing DTP, Rayleigh, Essex

Printed and bound in Great Britain
by MPG Books, Bodmin

In memory of Cyril Dunn, the first to try

CONTENTS

Foreword by
Desmond Tutu
ix

Introduction   xi

1	In the End	1
2	In the Beginning	4
3	Irresolute in Africa	9
4	Communist Commitment	15
5	A Passage to India	21
6	Wartime	31
7	Betrayal	37
8	Doing Time in Africa	47
9	Tobruk	57
10	The Herero Connection	74
11	Frog versus Bull	88
12	Homecoming	100
13	Celebrity Status	112
14	Eviction from Africa	127
15	Man about Manhattan	145
16	'Made for Each Other'	157
17	Crisis in Oxford	165
18	Campaigning Clerics	177
19	'A Time to Speak'	186
20	Doing Time in England	197
21	Gunning for the Canon	214
22	Positive Resistance	225
23	Industrial Warfare	232
24	An Indian Eviction	241
25	Losing Touch	255
26	Scott versus the Africa Bureau	263
27	A Suspicious Nature	277

28	Maverick Status	284
29	A Place for Paranoia	293
30	Moving Mountains	299
	Notes and Sources	308
	Bibliography	328
	Index	332

FOREWORD

I NEVER MET Michael Scott in person but that did not stop him making an indelible impression on me. I knew two things about him; two things that made him a quite remarkable human being. Almost everyone certainly in the black community knew about the white Anglican priest who had outraged many in the white community and exasperated his Church officials by what they considered his brazen effrontery of actually slumming it in the black squatter camp of Tobruk near Johannesburg. I was among the many in the black community who held him in a very high regard for what we considered a conspicuously courageous act of solidarity with the poor and downtrodden of our land. I was not aware that any other white person had shown their concern for our plight quite so dramatically.

Then I was also thrilled by how he had managed to place the issue of the Hereros and so South West Africa (later Namibia), on the agenda of the United Nations and so of the international community. These actions, indeed achievements, qualify him eminently for a special niche in the annals of our struggle against injustice and oppression. The project to persuade the UN to act decisively in the matter of the Hereros, in the process frustrating South Africa's machinations to derail it, could have been a full-time occupation for a lesser mortal.

It is amazing that Scott should have had the energy and the ability to have so many irons in the fire. I certainly have found it nothing short of breathtaking that he was able to deal with the plight of farm workers in Bethal to the east of Johannesburg while also participating in peaceful demonstrations about obnoxious laws affecting the Indians in Natal and then going to India because of his concern for the fate of the Naga people, opposing the Central African Federation, and when he was banned from South Africa and South West Africa, heading up the Africa Bureau founded with the help of David Astor, editor of the *Observer*, and others to advance the cause of decolonization in Africa and then being part of the nuclear disarmament campaign. Perhaps there was a danger of him spreading himself too thinly but he did appear to have been endowed with boundless energy though his health was not robust.

Michael Scott was greatly admired for his role in helping to bring independence to Ghana, Zambia, Malawi, Tanzania and of course Namibia. He helped many of us black South Africans not to become anti-white, for here was a white man who cared about us. I am glad he was on our side; imagine if he had been on the other side! He is undoubtedly one of the heroes of our struggle, who contributed to what happened in South Africa in 1994.

Desmond Tutu, January 2006
Archbishop of Cape Town, 1986–96
Awarded the Nobel Peace Prize, 1984

INTRODUCTION

I N JANUARY 1952, with the Cold War at its height, a British
diplomat at the United Nations wrote privately to his political
masters in London, 'One fact is inescapable, Michael Scott is
now regarded as the champion of the poor and oppressed by the non-
white world. Nothing can stop the steady momentum of his
reputation by a growing number of people in a growing number of
countries.'[1] At the time Scott was a priest without a parish, living on
hand-outs.

A few years later, after Scott had achieved a more secure eminence
as Director of the Africa Bureau, dedicated to the end of Empire in
Africa, he was described by an American commentator as 'an
effective, British admixture of Jesus and Gandhi, with more than a
trace of Marx'.[2] On the occasion of Scott's death, in 1983, Bruce Kent,
the organizer of the Campaign for Nuclear Disarmament (CND),
who was then a Catholic priest, wrote of him as 'a great man, wider
and bigger than any dozen Bishops or Popes'.[3]

Despite these accolades, history has not been kind to Scott's
memory. In his native country he is virtually a forgotten man. His two
main places of residence in London bear no identifying blue plaques.
His books are out of print. Aside from a Michael Scott Street in
Windhoek, the capital of Namibia, and a stained-glass window
commemorating him in a quiet Sussex country church, there is not
much to jog any recollection of his existence. Yet, by any yardstick,
Scott was one of the most remarkable Englishmen of his time. There
has never been a priest or peace campaigner quite like him.

Unfortunately for Scott's posthumous legend he was also a lot
more complicated than any number of bishops or Popes. Along with
the admiration he also excited intense antagonism. His apparent
mildness of manner, sometimes mistaken for diffidence, concealed an
iron resolve. His great friend, David Astor, the editor of the *Observer*,
would speak of 'his funny combination of modesty, selflessness and
intransigence, but it takes you a little while to come to the

xi

intransigence'.[4] Never a team player, Scott could rub people up the wrong way. He had what almost amounted to a love affair with India but his connection with that country would end with his being strip-searched and deported.

In the long struggle against white supremacy in South Africa his dealings with his co-warriors were often prickly. His relationship with Canon John Collins, the great fund-raiser for the anti-apartheid cause, was positively bad. Business with Scott could spell trouble for his allies as well as his foes. Friends, even the most intimate ones, often did not know what to make of him.

The man himself abhorred self-disclosure, though he threw out occasional clues. The trouble with moderates, Scott would say, is that they are only moderately against evil. Given this perspective, it was not entirely surprising that he often found himself out on a limb and, on several occasions, behind bars in jail. It did, however, make for an unusual Odyssey which was rendered even more complicated by his personal style: he had a talent, and undoubted taste, for the clandestine. The mystery about the way he operated in relation to public issues also attached to his private life; though celibate, Scott enjoyed close relationships with a succession of attractive women. On all counts – as a man, as a political activist and as an interpreter of the Christian message – Scott defied the conventional categories.

His strangeness has also militated against efforts to write about him. Indeed, it is the main reason why many of those who contributed to the preparation of this book can now only be thanked posthumously.

The first serious attempt to write a full-scale biography of Michael Scott was made by the *Observer* journalist, Cyril Dunn, starting back in the spring of 1974. Working under the patronage of his editor, David Astor, Dunn interviewed Scott many times along with a wide range of his contemporary friends and fellow campaigners. He eventually abandoned the project, confessing himself defeated by the complexities of his subject's personality, though he had no hesitation in saying that there was no other political priest in Scott's class 'for originality, nerve, human interest and sheer uniqueness'.[5] After Scott's death, Astor asked him to have another go. Dunn declined but gifted all his carefully indexed interview notes to a possible successor. A few years later Astor found one in Anne Yates. Like Dunn, she conducted a wide range of interviews but found that her main task was mastering the huge quantity of papers which had been lodged in Rhodes House, Oxford. The Scott Papers, as they are called, fill a hundred large carton boxes, many of them uncatalogued. By the time of her death in 2000, she had managed to extract the essence from this awesome pile and was close to completing a first draft of the manuscript. I was invited to finish the job by David Astor. Then he also died a few months later.

Since Astor's death the project has survived through the generosity of Anne Yates's four children – Elizabeth, Janet, Richard and Nicholas – and with the help of a small grant from the Africa Educational Trust (AET), a charitable organization founded by Michael Scott, which still provides support for the education of thousands of young people in Africa, especially those whose lives have been affected by war and violence.

I am hugely indebted not only to Cyril Dunn and Anne Yates but to all those who encouraged them with information and advice along the way. Some are mentioned in the text and source notes but I cannot claim to know them all, though they all merit my thanks. Of those who were directly helpful to me personally with information about Scott's life and times I am most grateful to Lorna Richmond, Jane Kellock (née Symonds), Enuga Reddy and Denis Herbstein.

I am also beholden to many others who helped the project in a variety of ways. They include: Goolam Aboobaker, David and Josie Adler, Jonathan Aptaker, Guy Arnold, Janine Aron, Pat Arrow-smith, Neal Ascherson, Margaret Becklake, Peter Calvocoressi, April Carter, Judith Chester, Susanne Chowdhury, Vida Comber, Tom Crawley, Robin Denniston, Peter and Elizabeth Dunn, Alex Finer, Oliver Gillie, Wilfrid Grenville-Grey, Vusi Gumede, Peter and Jane Katjavivi, Peter Kingshill, Phillip Knightley, Margaret Legum, Luithui Luingam, Dr Neela Malviya, Pralim Malviya, Linda Melvern, J.P. Misra, Jo Morris, Laureen Morrow, Ernest Morton, Roger Murray, Maurice Nchabeleng, Benedict and Caroline Owen, Bruce and Anne Page, Richard Payne, David and Marie Philip, Michael Randle, Michael Rogers, Katherine Salahi, Ann Slavitt, Colin Smith, Yaw Turkson and Randolph Vigne.

Sadly some of the people who were helpful to me have since died. The most important were Eiluned 'Lyn' Owen, Ethel de Keyser,

Colin Legum, Freda Levson, Fr Aelred Stubbs CR, Anthony Sampson and of course David Astor.

At the Bodleian Library of Commonwealth and African Studies at Rhodes House I was deftly assisted by John Pinfold, the Librarian, and, Lucy McCann, the Archivist, in the reading room and by Tony Hill and Darren Treadwell down among the Scott boxes in the basement. I am enormously grateful to Margaret Lipscomb for sharing the load of the research, particularly in Rhodes House. Carol Heaton, my agent, and Piers Burnett, the publisher, were both models of understanding patience throughout as were my patrons at the AET, Michael Brophy and Jill Landymore.

My warmest thanks, however, must go to Elizabeth Welsh, Anne Yates's younger daughter, who helped constructively at every stage and, even more importantly, maintained faith in the project when many others, myself included, thought it would defy completion.

Lewis Chester
March 2006

CHAPTER ONE

IN THE END

LOOKING BACK on the enigma of his own life as priest, jailbird, and creative troublemaker, the Reverend Michael Scott decided to confront his demons. Though introspective by nature, there were some areas of his own experience he was reluctant to bring to the surface – things hinted at but never fully confessed to another living soul. He had once, some years earlier, been persuaded to consult a psychoanalyst, but the association had been brief. The psychoanalyst had later pronounced him 'fearless as a lion, but unable to look inside himself'.[1] At the age of seventy-five, and dying of cancer, Scott summoned up the will in a letter to one of his oldest friends, David Astor, the former editor of the *Observer* newspaper. Scott told Astor of the urgent need he felt to communicate a dread 'bottled up inside me' for over sixty years. The main focus of this apprehension proved to be the principal at the Southampton preparatory school he had attended as a child. As Scott put it:

> That man was the single most dreaded factor in my life on account of the inner conflicts, bewilderments and fears that he generated inside me . . . His religion appeared to be very real to him and I was never in any position to question it, because it was outwardly so close to the religion of my parents whom I dearly loved. Prayers and religious instruction were always first in the school curriculum. In addition he could often be heard praying and singing all by himself in the school chapel and accompanying himself on the organ. He was very strict and quick to notice any misdemeanour large or small in those whom he particularly favoured with his attention which included vigorous spanking on the bare skin, across his knee . . . Punishment would often be followed . . . by 'making it up' or 'showing there is no ill feeling' with kisses and facial caresses as inescapable as his quite foul breath. Once there was the warning 'One day I shall have to do it all over you from top to toe.'

Scott relates that his main schoolmistress, a Miss M____, seemed to have an instinct for knowing which boys the principal most favoured having sent to him for correction:

> She never seemed to miss any misdemeanour on my part or failure to gain the necessary minimum of 60 per cent for homework which would mean being sent with a note down to him to await a convenient time for his attention in the bathroom . . . I was of course bewildered by this treatment compared to the true affection showed by my parents who taught me the same religion. But I was too ashamed and terrified by it to speak about it to them, and they if they heard I had been punished would joke about it.

Scott makes it clear he regarded the harrowing tension of this period as having a direct connection with the grim intestinal problems that plagued him throughout his adult life. He also saw it as the breeding ground for a mistrustful disposition, which among other things, had complicated his relationships with women friends. 'Sex', he wrote, 'can become an object not of reverence or enjoyment but of fear and perverted preoccupation.' He had no doubt that the abuse had wrought 'permanent damage', which could only be confessed 'now that it's too late ever to be repaired'.[2] In his reply to Scott's letter, Astor wrote commending its bravery and significance: 'This certainly explains much in your later life that must otherwise be mysterious.'[3]

In the appalling annals of child abuse, Scott cannot be counted among the worst victims. Outwardly, the experience seemed to leave him wholly intact. Yet as an education in the nature of hidden oppression it could scarcely be improved upon. The villain of the piece was clearly the ogre of sanctimony embodied by the principal, but he could not have prospered without an elaborate, unquestioning support system, operating within the school and beyond. Crucial to his tyranny was loyal staff work, best exemplified by Miss M____, who seems to have operated as the procuress-in-chief. But the main ingredient was credulity – mistaking appearance for reality – which blinded even those with the best intentions to what was going on. It was this, more than anything, that enabled Scott's loving parents to seem almost oblivious to their son's distress.

Even in the chastisement-happy days of early twentieth-century English private education, children could sometimes find allies against creepy schoolmasters who insisted on fondling them after a good spanking. But like most children trapped in such situations, Scott was rendered powerless by the notion that he himself must be the one in the wrong, and he would prolong the misery with his own reticence. It is evident the boy Scott had a crash course in just how complicated an oppressive system can be, and how difficult it is not to become its accomplice, even in the role of victim.

As a man, Scott buried this aspect of his past deep within his consciousness, but it could never be effaced. Indeed, it seems to be one of the main clues to an extraordinary life that would become almost entirely devoted to the identification of oppression and how best to combat it: non-violently if at all possible, but, *in extremis*, not necessarily. Along the way this seemingly diffident, mild-mannered priest would serve four terms in jail, and incur specific bans for his political activities in South Africa, Nyasaland (now Malawi) and India, leaving in his wake a trail of outraged authority figures. But among the descendants of oppressed people in those countries, and indeed many others, his name still resonates. He is seen as a man who was not merely dedicated but driven to confront injustice. Some regard Michael Scott as a saint.

He was certainly the most paradoxical of men. Scott had no panaceas or easy solutions, and no legions to call on: even within his own church, with which he was most frequently at odds. His politics were almost constantly in flux. Attracted by Communism, he would later angrily reject it. His deep reverence for Gandhian-style methods of non-violent resistance proved no impediment to his enlisting for training as an RAF rear-gunner in the war against Hitler. He was the first English priest to raise the standard of rebellion against white supremacy in South Africa, and later, among the first to advocate negotiation with the supremacists. Though he was tenacious in his chosen commitments, few people have been less hampered by conventional notions of consistency. Even his Christian faith, he would be the first to acknowledge, was fragile and clouded with uncertainty and doubt. His most esteemed friends, David Astor and the philosopher Bertrand Russell, were both atheists.

He was, by common consent, an almost complete 'loner', but one blessed with a unique gift for signposting a way for others out of the consequences of oppression. His personal tragedy, on the evidence of his confessional letter to David Astor, was that he never found a way out for himself.

3

CHAPTER TWO

IN THE BEGINNING

MICHAEL SCOTT was born at Lowfield Heath in Sussex on 30 July 1907, the youngest of three sons. Initially he was something of a disappointment to his gentle, softly spoken Scottish mother, Ethel, who had hoped for a daughter. On the other hand, his arrival into the world seemed to confirm the outstanding male vigour of his father, the Reverend Perceval Caleb Scott. Before taking Holy Orders, Perceval Scott had excelled at sport – playing cricket for Scotland and soccer, as an amateur, for Charlton – and his Christian ministry could be said to be of the muscular variety. He was very High Church, which among many of his Anglican co-religionists suggested a tendency to 'Popery'.

When Michael was four years old, his father obtained a living at St Augustine's Church, Northam, on the banks of the River Itchen. In those days High Churchmen were distrusted to some extent by the Anglican hierarchy and tended to find themselves steered into the less savoury parishes. For the most part they did not much mind this discrimination, even relishing the challenge. Northam, however, located by the Southampton docks, was unusually insalubrious. Then rated the second worst slum in England, it ceded pole position only to the worst parts of London's East End. Its 10,000 inhabitants, packed into an area of half a square mile, lived in dingy streets of back-to-back houses, leading down to the river from which the place had been reclaimed – though not entirely. In winter, when the river flooded, families already living in overcrowded conditions had to cram their existence into the upstairs rooms. When the floods receded the ground floors would be covered with a malodorous slime.

Understandably, these Dickensian conditions found some reflection in the temperament of the people, which was inclined to be uncouth. Those men who had work tended to find it in the docks or at sea. Northam provided many of the crew that went down with the *Titanic*. Children ran wild in the streets without benefit of shoes. And family tensions, usually about the impossibility of making ends meet, would often wind up in the Vicarage, requiring the Reverend Perceval Scott's adjudication and solace. His children became familiar with the sound of 'grown-ups' crying in his study. The Summer Treat, an expedition to the New Forest for local children, had to be organized with military precision, with a special train and a strong police presence. Michael Scott grew up as part of this slum world, but at a remove. The Vicarage, though not princely, was larger than its neighbouring houses and contained evidence of a slightly better than hand-to-mouth existence, along with some traditional solidity. In pride of place in the hall hung a portrait of an illustrious ancestor, John Scott (1784–1867). Said to be the natural, albeit unacknowledged, son of Admiral Purvis, he would serve in Nelson's Navy and later rise to the rank of commander. His son, Thomas Scard Scott, who became a clergyman, was Michael Scott's grandfather. With his father so busy, responsibility for Michael's social counselling fell principally on his shy, unassertive mother. This passage from Scott's memoir *A Time to Speak*, published in middle life, gives some idea of the dilemmas it posed for her and the most sensitive of her three sons:

> I would slip out with some tin soldiers in my pocket to play with those children in the alleyway. I was proud of my little possessions and perhaps I wanted to show them off. I did not see any reason why I should not play with the others. They spoke a little differently perhaps, and some were a little dirtier, but there was not any real difference that I noticed. However, once I was seen playing with them in the street and was reported to my mother, who sent for me in a great state of mind. I was to be punished for 'playing in the gutter'. When I said I didn't know there was anything wrong, my mother looked as though she did not believe me at first but then, after a long searching look, she went away and came back with her eyes all red, and said I would not be punished and could stay up to supper and afterwards get on with my homework. Then I had the feeling that I must have cheated and got myself out of a punishment by saying I could not see it was wrong, and I ought to have known it as otherwise my mother would not have been so upset about it. But there was homework to do, and my mind could not cope with so many difficulties at once.[1]

More succinctly, Scott would later tell one of his would-be biographers, the *Observer* journalist Cyril Dunn: 'The truth is my parents were dreading my becoming contaminated and I suppose I can understand my mother's feelings when I used to come back to the vicarage with words like "fuck".'[2]

The family formula that evolved was that the Scott boys could associate with local children in the church clubs, but not fraternize with them on the streets, where the risk of contamination was deemed to be greatest. Clearly there was a degree of class-consciousness in all this, but not of a spiteful kind. The compassion of Scott's father and mother was never in question at a time when the Church was required to provide much of the social relief that is now shouldered by the state. They were genuinely committed in service to the poorest in the parish. However, they were equally committed to a parallel responsibility of bringing up children who read books, esteemed learning and loved the Lord – all minority interests in the 'real world' outside the front door.

Over the road was a cobbler's shop run by an old man versed in the history of rebellion, going back to the peasant uprisings in the Middle Ages. The cobbler was known as 'the Bolshevik' to Scott's father, but young Michael found opportunities to listen to the old man's tales of working-class and nonconformist struggle. He was introduced to the Chartists and the Tolpuddle Martyrs. It was the beginning of Scott's radical education, though he was dismayed by the cobbler's description of him as having been 'born with a silver spoon in your mouth'.[3]

The experience of being perceived as privileged in an under-privileged world can be hazardous. Scott's red school cap, required wearing on his two-mile walks to and from his preparatory school at Hurst Leigh, afforded a natural provocation. It signalled his difference from the local Northam lads, who would tease him for his resemblance to 'a red top match',[4] when they felt pacifically inclined. At other times they would beat him up. All that can be said in mitigation of this violence is that it had none of the sexually creepy undertones of the violence that Scott was simultaneously experiencing at school. It was, nonetheless, an outstandingly miserable time.

Scott's main consolation through all this was his relationship with his father, and his religion, in that order. He would later write: 'I understood my father and loved him very much, which I had to admit was more than I could ever say about God, hard as ever I tried.'[5] Scott was moved by the pageantry of the actual church, with its wealth of brocade and velvet hangings providing a majestic contrast to the dinginess of its geographical surroundings, but had problems grasping its message. The experience of taking Holy Communion sometimes filled him with wonder and a sense of belonging to God, but more often it left him feeling flat. He would write: 'I had the horrible feeling it did not all make sense but I put away the thought; because if it failed to make sense, nothing would make sense. I would be alone, I would not belong to anyone. And it was terrifying not to belong to anyone in an impersonal world of meaningless suffering.'[6]

Scott formulated for himself what he called 'the question',[7] which was not so much a request as a description of an inward search for some meaning and purpose in life, some existential truth that could accommodate those parts of himself that would sometimes 'impishly mock at the things I believed'.[8] It seems fairly clear that the original formulation was a critical response to his father's simple and direct belief system, though it would later become a key characteristic of what Scott would term his 'religion of doubt'.[9] Any direct questioning of his father's beliefs was unthinkable, though it is very likely in psychological terms that some of Scott's early guilt feelings derived from this unspoken area. When his father collapsed with a heart attack during a game with his children, Scott believed it was his fault.

The certainties that were available at the time were the joy of being coached by his father in the art of wielding a straight cricket bat and the refreshment of life on the water. When the king's yacht, *Alexandra*, came to be scrapped, her twenty-two-foot gig was given to Perceval Scott. With an 'old salt' acting as skipper the family sailed past the shipyards out of Southampton Water into the broad reaches of the Solent. Days of sailing, and excursions to the New Forest, provided a release from the oppressions of Northam.[10]

Perceval Scott also did his duty by his sons to the extent of informing them about 'the facts and mysteries' of life, though Michael initially, and for some time thereafter, found them hard to take in: 'the thought that my own life was the result of what my father described, and the implication that it took place between him and my mother, simply did not bear thinking about'.[11]

The Northam experience, lasting eleven years, would come to an end shortly after the end of the First World War when Perceval Scott's ill-health dictated a family move to a country parish in Suffolk. To Michael it seemed like the escape at the end of 'some dark seemingly interminable tunnel'.[12]

Scott rounded off his schooldays as a boarder at King's College in Taunton, Somerset, an establishment founded in the wake of the Tractarian Movement of 1833, which in turn harked back to the Non-juring days when some churchmen refused to take the oath of allegiance to William of Orange. It was impeccably High Church. It was also strict, but without any of the paedophilic resonances of Scott's prep-school education. The orderly work-hard, play-hard ethos of the place was not uncongenial to Scott, who made good progress with his studies and impressed his father by playing rugby for the school team, and winning his colours.[13]

By his final year, his face had lost some of the cherubic quality that had contributed to his earlier tribulations, but he was handsome in the classical English style, with bold regular features, and, at six foot one inch, one of the tallest boys in the school. There seemed every likelihood that he would delight his father still more by following his elder brothers, Roy and Nigel, into the Anglican priesthood by way of Oxford University. But Michael, with the answer to his 'question' still far from resolved, had other plans, and other problems.

CHAPTER THREE

IRRESOLUTE IN AFRICA

URING THE General Strike of 1926, Nigel and Roy Scott pitched in as volunteers, providing an extra special policeman and railway worker to assist in the cause of saving the country from economic and social chaos.[1] Their younger brother Michael, however, was a notable absentee during those stirring but divisive days, when the organized strength of the working class pitted itself against the resource and mettle of the middle and upper classes, and lost.

Michael Scott's political consciousness was still underdeveloped, but the plain fact of the matter was that he was not in any position to take sides. As the strike began, he embarked, seriously unwell, from Harwich en route for Switzerland and Dr Rollier's Sun Cure Clinic in Leysin. He was diagnosed as having tuberculosis, one of the prime killer diseases of the time.

Scott's precipitous decline into ill-health had started during his last term at school with a series of acute but inexplicable abdominal pains. With his concentration impaired, he had failed one of the subjects in the School Certificate exam, blighting his prospects of a place at Oxford University, and jeopardizing his secret ambition to break with the family's clerical tradition by training to become a doctor. Instead he took a temporary job as a prep-school teacher, while pursuing a correspondence course to repair his exam failure.[2] At the school, he found himself assigned to disciplinary duties and expected to wield 'the slipper', at which point his abdominal pains returned with increased intensity. Admitted to hospital for removal of the gall bladder, the doctors also discovered TB mesenteric glands.[3]

The sun cure at the clinic in Leysin occupied most of Scott's next year. On his discharge the medical advice was that he would be wise to abandon any plans of going to Oxford or of studying medicine in one of the London hospitals. A dry, warm climate was said to be necessary to effect his complete recovery. By way of further recuperation, Scott would therefore spend the next stage of his life in

South Africa's Cape Province, which provided suitably clement weather conditions, and a job opportunity thought to be within his physical compass, which involved assisting in the day-to-day care of lepers. What might have been carefree undergraduate years were, in Scott's case, spent developing an abnormally close acquaintance with human sickness and suffering.

The South African connection arose through one of his father's churchwardens, Henry Engleheart, whose brother was an archdeacon in the Cape Province. Archdeacon Engleheart ran the leper settlement on Robben Island, eight miles off the Cape mainland: a grim location, which many years later would find alternative use as a secure prison for Nelson Mandela and many other African liberation leaders during the post-war apartheid era. Engleheart had also established another centre at St Raphael's, in Faure, to the east of Cape Town, which catered for partially cured lepers who might in certain circumstances be deemed fit enough to return home. This was to be Scott's home and workplace throughout his twentieth year.[4]

The stigma of the disease was still awesomely powerful. People, even close relatives, were inclined to shrink from the disease that disfigured faces, limbs and in some cases, minds. Many families would simply refuse, or say they could not afford, to readmit a leper back into their homes. St Raphael's, in consequence, became an expanding enterprise, obliged to provide nursery schools and the rudiments of community life for those destined never to return home. Scott was expected to help the nurses and teachers in the task of creating this sense of community. Physically, he was well up to the job, but mentally, as he would later recount in *A Time to Speak*, it imposed a huge strain:

> There were some in whom an 'arrested cure' had been effected at an early stage of the disease, others to whom it had come too late to save them from terrible disfigurements. Some were quite young and still had the love of life and beauty in them, yet had to see strangers, and even fellow lepers, shrink away in horror from them. Half the face was beautiful and sensitive and appeared to have the soft bloom of pristine sex upon it, and the other half repellent with the flesh eaten away or the features fixed in a permanent sneer or grin. Some would have only one or two fingers left on one hand, the other would just be a stump.

They would use what fingers or stump they had to sew or make baskets. Some were lame, some were blind . . . [5]

Scott recalled being so moved by the appearance of one sightless victim that he tried to effect a miracle cure of his own, by touch. Finding, inevitably, that it didn't work, he then reprimanded himself for the sin of pride.[6] How, he wondered, could love be reconciled with such cruel processes of nature? It was another of those questions without any clear answer, though its formulation did help to steer Scott in the direction of becoming a priest after all and he decided to acquire the learning necessary to test his vocation.

It has sometimes been suggested the radicalism that prompted Scott's heroic combating of racial discrimination in South Africa after the Second World War had its origin during the period he worked with the lepers. However, this does not appear to have been the case. Scott himself would say that he was 'insensitive about and unaware of' the larger issues of race and the colour bar during much of his first stay in South Africa.[7] There were understandable reasons for this. St Raphael's, by its nature, was an isolated community, and while all its sufferers were black, the staff was interracial. The polarity he found most troubling at the time was not the one between white and black, but that between the sick and the well.

The other significant polarity, more confusing than enlightening – or so it seemed to Scott – was the one that existed between his own jumbled feelings and the extraordinary beauty and order in the natural world that surrounded him. In Northam there had been some direct correspondence between the wretchedness of the environment and his own unhappy interior life, but South Africa posed a more complicated problem. In this new world the environment appeared not only wondrous but also analgesic. Thus:

> I was fascinated by the beauty of the Cape and could always escape my inward doubts and dreads by going off for a walk by myself to somewhere where I could lie stripped in the sun and see the rugged mountains dropping sheer down into the sea, and listen to the cicadas in the tall eucalyptus trees and smell the sweet scent of heath and wild flowers . . . It all had a spectacular and dramatic beauty that may have been misleading . . . [8]

Scott's education in the political realities of South Africa did not effectively begin until he started his course of theological studies at St Paul's College, Grahamstown, in the Cape's Eastern Province. And then only very slowly. St Paul's prepared candidates for ordination in the Anglican Church, as long as they were white. But Grahamstown itself provided a high degree of insulation from the coarser aspects of the country's racial arrangements. In appearance and atmosphere it was like an English cathedral town.

In this comparatively cloistered environment, Scott diligently acquired the learning necessary for his vocation, mastering a wide range of subject matter from the Christian creeds, through the Apostolic Succession, to the Thirty-Nine Articles of Religion. Much time was spent on church history and the analysis of ancient heresies. This would enhance Scott's appreciation of the great schism between East and West that afflicted the Church in the fourth century, and amplify his awareness of the bitterness that attended the Reformation. The scholarly warden, Archibald Cullen, who later became a bishop, impressed Scott with his ability to get behind 'the liturgical form of words' and make the Gospel a vivid present experience. Even so, Cullen's insistence that there should be no discussion of the origin of evil made it hard to deduce how the experience should apply in the contemporary world.[9]

Scott learned more of African realities between college terms when he made deliberate attempts to widen his knowledge of the country. Missionary life interested him and he went on extended visits to two of its outposts: the Society of the Sacred Mission at Modderpoort, near the border with Basutoland (now Lesotho), and the Mission of the Society of St John the Evangelist at Tsolo in the Transkei. At Modderpoort, he was amused by the delicacy of the leisure reading – issues of *Punch* magazine, sent out by a spinster well-wisher from England, with brown paper patches pasted over the ladies' underwear advertisements to prevent corruption of the Fathers. In both places he found evidence of dedication, even saintliness, but his deepest impression was of 'the great gulf' separating the missionaries from the life of the people.[10]

The gulf was less manifest when Scott visited an agricultural community in the Eastern Cape close to King Williamstown. Scott learned from the sheep farmer he was staying with that the area had been plagued by the most appalling drought. As a result every resource of spiritual power in the area, from the Christian missions to the local witch doctors, had been tapped to produce rain. Nobody could be sure whose prayers to the Almighty produced the miracle, but the rain fell, in gigantic quantities, while Scott was there.[11]

On a visit to the diamond diggings at Grasfontein, Scott discovered many of the hopeful diggers, mainly Afrikaners, in the grip of an epidemic of enteric. Such treatment as was available was being carried out in makeshift tents, there being no hospital. Under the tutelage of a local lay reader, Scott carried out the task of washing and shaving men too weak to attend to themselves.[12]

On another vacation, in 1928, Scott explored Johannesburg's predominantly black Sophiatown district, where a small group of Christian workers waged 'a ceaseless, losing battle against disease and disorder'.[13] It was one of the key locations to which Scott would return almost twenty years later, with the battle still conspicuously unwon. From these and other expeditions Scott achieved a good basic grasp of the problems confronting the Church in a segregated society, but formed no precise idea of how he could fit into it.

After two years at St Paul's, with his health seemingly fully restored, Scott decided to return to England to complete his theological studies. Before he left, Warden Cullen took him to one side for a chat about his future intentions. When Scott confessed to having no clear idea of what he wanted to do with his life, an unsurprised Cullen said, in the kindest possible way: 'You have never been able to make up your mind, dear man, and I don't think you ever will.'[14]

Scott, however, was not so irresolute as he appeared to Cullen, or indeed to himself. He had already made what was probably the key decision of his life. That aspect of the Christian tradition which held that suffering in itself had merit had been totally eliminated from his personal creed. Out of the ugliness of the Northam slums, the isolation and despair of the rejected lepers, and the circumstances of his own illness and abuse as a child, Scott had established a bedrock of conviction that there was nothing remotely holy or Christ-like in the condition of suffering for its own sake. Far from being sanctified, it was something that had to be rebelled against. The problem of course, in a world replete with so many forms of suffering, was knowing where and how to begin. Scott was hoping and praying that the act of becoming a priest would show him the way, and was naturally disappointed when it failed to produce the desired effect.

CHAPTER FOUR

COMMUNIST COMMITMENT

THE FORMAL completion of Michael Scott's studies at Chichester Theological College in Sussex led smoothly to his ordination as a priest by Bishop George Bell on the Feast of St Thomas in 1930. Among Scott's first clerical duties was the task of officiating at a burial service at which he lost his footing and slid inelegantly into the open grave, where he was subsequently joined by the first person who tried to haul him out. Full dignity was soon restored, but Scott would later speak of the incident as epitomising the farcical quality of his early years as a priest.[1]

Scott's ministry began with his being licensed to the parish of Slaugham, close to his birthplace in Lowfield. Like many Sussex country parishes, Slaugham managed to blend gentility with sporting enthusiasms, mainly of an equestrian variety. Scott himself would ride – though not hunt – several times a week, astride horses loaned to him by the richer parishioners. His spiritual duties were necessarily combined with a great range of activities featuring dinner and tea parties, tennis and cricket, dances, concerts, and as he put it: 'interminable polite conversation'.[2] For a young man in a hurry to get to grips with the world's pain and problems, it could only be boring. And Scott may well have reflected that of the three sons of Perceval Caleb Scott, he had drawn the shortest clerical straw. Roy Scott, en route to becoming a chaplain in the Royal Navy, was at least affording himself the opportunity to see the world, while Nigel, reckoned to be the most conservative of the three boys as they were growing up, was actually in the thick of social change, working on a slum clearance project in London's depressed King's Cross area.[3]

After two years of Slaugham, Scott was able to move closer to the centre of great events by transferring to a London parish. His first appointment was to St Stephen's in Gloucester Road, South Kensington, where he continued to fret. Part of his restlessness during this period can be attributed to the fact that, unlike most young Anglican priests, he was not married and starting a family or engaged in the earnest pursuit of 'finding a wife'. The combination of long illness and what he saw as the scrambling of his sexual responses in childhood apparently convinced Scott that celibacy was the right course for him. Later in life he would meet a woman who would put this conviction to an extraordinarily severe test, but it seems to have been proof against any assault through his late twenties and early thirties. His good looks, though, could complicate life. A wealthy young Kensington woman – who told him he could always turn to her in time of crisis – cooled in her enthusiasm for him only when he asked if she would mind taking care of two temporarily homeless children. Less veiled was a direct homosexual invitation made by one of his fellow priests in Kensington. This unwelcome approach was among the things that persuaded Scott to seek employment elsewhere.[4]

Although close to the heart of the West End, St Stephen's did not have much to offer in terms of dynamic Christian witness. It was deemed a fashionable church but it lacked animation. Most of those who attended it were older ladies who had seen better days, often in the colonies. They tended to lead sad, self-absorbed lives in which bridge was the recreation and church the consolation. Of the major events in the world, like the rise of Hitler and Nazism in Germany, Roosevelt's launching of the New Deal in America, and closer to home, the great depression that was already engulfing the British working class, Scott's parishioners had little knowledge and scant curiosity. Scott was moved by their plight but felt imprisoned by his circumstance. Far from bringing him closer to a sense of grappling with the world's problems, it seemed as if his vocation was actually taking him further away. This led to a perception, of which he would later write in *A Time to Speak*:

> Gradually, I was becoming aware that over and above the recognized denominations of Christianity, and apart from the innumerable little sects into which Christendom had become divided, there were two kinds of Christianity. There was the religion which was the divine sanction of the *status quo*, and there was the religion which was the divine instrument of change. No doubt all the truth was not to be found in either exclusively.[5]

Scott, however, had no doubt about his being part of the *status quo* apparatus when he dearly wanted to be on the side of change. He would bridge the gap between the two concepts, at least to some degree, by moving a few miles across London to its East End, where animation of all kinds was in plentiful supply. The parish of All Souls in Lower Clapton, where Scott became an assistant priest in 1933, may not have been Scott's Damascus, but it was the first place where his latent energy could be tapped. In appearance, with its mean, overcrowded streets, it was not unlike Northam, though without the flooding. But the main difference was a sense of vibrancy and action, of great issues being at stake. With Mosley's blackshirts attempting to command the streets and counter-demonstrations being mobilized by the Communists and other left-wing groups, politics and their social ramifications were inescapable even for a church that wanted to shelter behind a *status quo*. Among Scott's new influences was a 'Comrade Jim', a retired Covent Garden porter rendered homeless, who was billeted temporarily in Scott's allocated house. When Scott asked him why he made a habit of stuffing his cap with newspaper before going out, Jim explained it was the best way 'to soften the blows of the policemen's truncheons'.[6]

The great debate in All Souls' Church centred on the problem of whether shelter should be offered to the Hunger Marchers streaming down to London from Scotland and the north-east of England as a demonstration against the mass unemployment. Local apprehensions focused on the presumed threat to jobs in the area, and possibly the virtue of its womenfolk. Scott was able to overcome these alarms and the main body of the marchers stopped for rest and refreshment in the local church hall, before their final dignified advance on Westminster. An additional contingent of some thirty women accompanying the march had to be billeted on camp beds in Scott's own house. This caused some raised eyebrows even in the parish, particularly after news leaked that their feet had been washed by the assistant priest.[7]

On a wider political front, it seemed to Scott that Fascism was the great menace of the age, and that the most trenchant opposition to it was being supplied not by the conventional politicians, or by the Church, but by the Communists. He became involved with the Communist Party. The closeness of his involvement is still not totally clear, mainly because Scott himself later wanted it that way. After the Second World War, when his work frequently took him to the United Nations in New York, the main impediment to his going there was the suggestion of a Communist past, which could have prevented his entry into the United States. Scott did eventually write about his Communist association in *A Time to Speak*, published in 1958, but not with any great precision. Late in life, when asked by Cyril Dunn, his would-be biographer, about what had been the exact nature of his CP affiliation, Scott replied: 'I think I may have applied to be a probationer, a novice or whatever it is, but I never heard anything more about it. I think I certainly signed something, which Emile kept himself and which, if he had wanted to, he could have used to put the screws on me.'[8]

The 'Emile' in this context was Emile Burns, a senior full-time official in the British Communist Party organization, and a prolific producer of pamphlets and tracts about working-class struggles, including one on the General Strike. Burns had at one time headed the party's Agitprop department in King Street and was reckoned to be the movement's second most important theoretician, after R. Palme Dutt. This was a very high connection for Scott to make, and through Burns he met other senior figures, among them the party's leader, Harry Pollitt, whom Scott could not help noticing was wearing a fur-lined jacket ('though he said someone had given it to him'). At a grass-roots level Scott was invited to join a cell of the party based at a North London bus depot, which had a reputation for militancy. Though not called on to speak publicly on political issues, Scott's Sunday sermons began to carry more purposeful messages about 'the inseparability of prayer and action'.[9]

The attention he had once devoted to liturgical texts and the Bible was now being directed towards mastery of dialectical materialism and the key Communist texts, among them Lenin's *The ABC of Communism*, Engels's *AntiDuhrang* and Read's *Seven Days that Shook the World*. He also found himself being escorted to any films featuring the Russian Revolution. There was, Scott thought, much in the social conditions of the East End to support a Marxist analysis, even though its message of inevitable class conflict was discomforting to Christian ears. He would later say of this period: 'I struggled to find some means of harmonizing such widely different conceptions of the meaning and purpose of life and found myself in a perpetual state of conflict between these two rival explanations of our situation, two conflicting codes of conduct.'[10]

Scott was inclined to think that Communism's appeal, not only to himself but to many others, owed much to the organized Christian churches losing touch with the poor and underprivileged, and becoming obsessed with their own arcane rituals. The interpretation that Communism might be occupying ground abandoned by the Church was a useful validation for Scott the comrade, but tough on Scott the priest. Yet another degree of tension was imposed by the different expectations of him entertained by his new-found allies on the left. Emile Burns and others in the party's upper echelons seemed content to keep Scott on the books as a 'sympathizer': someone trustworthy, who could be discreetly deployed on carrying messages or money into situations where a more obvious card-carrying Communist might be blocked. The local left-wingers, however, who met Scott on a day-to-day basis were keen to have him leave the Church and throw in his lot with the party full-time.

Scott's main contact among the local Communists was a cabinet-maker called Julius Jacobs, who served on the London District Committee of the CP and was later a Hackney borough councillor. It was Jacobs who lent Scott his copy of *The ABC of Communism*. Jacobs's partner at the time was Jane Orme, who came from an upper middle-class background but was no less dedicated to the cause. Jacobs and Orme spent many evenings with Scott discussing the implications of a Communist commitment. These conversations had a no-holds-barred quality. Orme recalled: 'I was at that time convinced that religion was the opium of the people and that for Michael Scott to be mixed up with it was a terrible waste. I told him so and he took all that extremely well. I used to think it's working – he does see the error of his ways.' In justification of the faith, Scott told her that the supreme act of socialism for him was Christ's death on the Cross, to which she would respond: 'utter nonsense'. Orme and Jacobs justified this badgering on what seemed to them wholly altruistic grounds: getting Scott out of the Church would free him 'to do good things'. They shared a conviction that Scott had qualities of leadership that could be invaluable to the party, and were hugely disappointed when it became apparent that Emile Burns and the other leaders thought otherwise. Orme recalled: 'They just thought he would make a wonderful cover man. They didn't want to use him in his full capacity, but only as a postman. This seriously upset me. I thought they were making a great mistake. I can remember lecturing Emile Burns about it, "Here you have this rounded man who could be of tremendous use, not only as a postman."'[11]

The immediate effect on Scott of being seen as a potential force for good as a Communist activist was to drive him to even deeper levels of introspection about his Christian commitment. One of the ways out of the contradictions that now beset him was 'the religious life', and for a while towards the end of 1934 Scott thought seriously of becoming a monk.[12] The option of praying for a sinful world as part of an ordered religious community existing at a remove from the confusing, front-line action must have been enormously appealing at the time. But only for a very short while. The prospect of poverty and chastity held no particular terrors, but Scott rightly deduced that, in his own particular case, obedience might prove an insuperable problem.

Scott's second plan of escape from what he described as 'the mental and physical strain' of life in Lower Clapton involved going abroad again. This was a more realistic option, since the Anglican Church in the Far East was crying out for able young priests. In February 1935 he sailed from the London docks as a chaplain on an army transport bound for India – but with his Marxist leanings still intact. Before leaving he had told his Communist friends of his readiness to do anything he could to help the cause, provided it did not conflict with his Christian conscience. As India was then Britain's largest colonial possession, with its own strongly anti-imperialist Communist Party organization forced to operate underground, Scott was assured of an interesting, albeit clandestine, future.

CHAPTER FIVE

A PASSAGE TO INDIA

D URING HIS time in India Michael Scott was employed as the domestic chaplain to the Bishop of Bombay, and subsequently as chaplain to the Bishop of Calcutta, while secretly operating as an active agent of the Communist Party. It was a delicate situation, rendered more complex by virtue of the fact that the established nature of the Anglican Church, deriving its authority from the Crown, made it an integral part of British rule and presence in India. The Communists necessarily were among those keenest to chuck the British out.

Scott would describe this 'somewhat equivocal position' as increasing his reliance on God, 'because only God could understand all the conflicting pressures and demands that were made on my loyalties and capacity for action'.[1] However, it was by no means inexplicable in lay terms. Scott was by this time sufficiently versed in Marxist theory to perceive imperialism as a form of exploitative monopoly capitalism that had to be opposed. And while Scott still saw his Christian commitment as being of supreme value, this was by no means the same thing as his commitment to the Church, which he saw as largely failing in its basic mission to relieve the poor and distressed. There was therefore nothing illogical in his using the cover of the Church to advance the Communist interest. It was, nonetheless, both complicated and risky in practice.

The India that confronted Scott was in turmoil. Its position as 'the jewel in the crown' of Britain's far-reaching empire was still essentially unassailed, though attitudes to its possession had been modified by events. Britain still controlled the vast subcontinent through its network of potentates and princes, who did much of the governing – and revenue collection – on behalf of the imperial power. Even those of the most reactionary disposition could be confident that, in an emergency, their authority would be backed by British force. The symmetry of this system, however, was threatened by the broadly based nationalist movements, creating new disruptive loyalties across traditional lines. Some of its manifestations were violent, like the spate of assassinations of British district officers in isolated outposts, but a more disconcerting problem was presented by sheer weight of numbers: particularly those assembled through Mahatma Gandhi's non-violent resistance strategies. In an effort to syphon off some of the militancy, the British government enacted the India Act of 1935.

Under its carefully worded provisions, Indian Ministers, nominated by the British but usually selected from elective assemblies, were deemed fit to hold portfolios in the central government and in the provinces, but only those of lesser status – Health, Education and Transport. All the key departments – Justice, Law and Order, Political Affairs, Appointments and Finance – would continue under the control of the Indian Civil Service (ICS). This measure of power-sharing, or 'dyarchy' as it was called, met with bitter opposition from Winston Churchill and other Tory backbenchers in the House of Commons, who saw it as an assault on empire; but it still failed to appease the Indian nationalists. To the Communists, perceiving that all the real power still resided in imperial hands, the India Act was a sham.

In the polite European society of Bombay, to which the young Michael Scott was obliged to pay his respects, nationalists were seen as ingrates and agitators and generally spoken of with contempt. Gandhi, Scott would recall, was characterized as 'a bowler-hatted lawyer who resorted to Indian dress to deceive the masses into thinking him one of themselves'.[2] Like any other young Englishman with prospects, Scott was not encouraged to question or probe behind the prevailing nostrums of the ruling caste.

Even so, Scott's modest job did provide him with a window on other realities. He would, for example, obtain an early insight into the grim underside of a law-and-order system that allowed detention and imprisonment without trial. Among his tasks was the job of interviewing delegations who came to petition the bishop. Stories of brutality in the prisons would come up with distressing frequency. One case was, he felt, so flagrant that it warranted the bishop taking it up personally by requesting the Governor's intervention. Scott recalled the counsel he received in *A Time to Speak*:

Without giving an answer, the bishop said that he would like to go for a long walk and talk over one or two matters with me. In the course of a long and exhausting climb up a nearby hilltop, he put a number of searching questions to me, all of which were directed towards making me 'face realities'. In the end it came down to the question whether it was not better that a few agitators should suffer in the gaols than that whole tracts of country and innocent villages should have to be laid waste.[3]

Conversations of this character had the effect of increasing Scott's contact with the Communist movement. About the nature of this contact, for the reasons outlined in the last chapter, Scott always remained fairly reticent. Indeed, his own writings on the subject tend to dwell somewhat disproportionately on its comic aspects, suggesting that much of his clandestine work was essentially inconsequential. Sent as an undercover 'postman' to Singapore with £100 to deliver to a stranded Indian delegate en route to the Seventh World Congress of the Communist International, Scott arrived as planned, only to find that his man had been deported back to India. On another assignment, equipped with letters from English comrades to Communist operatives in Tokyo, Scott was obliged to seek out the assistance of geisha girls to help with the essential task of translating the names and addresses into Japanese. When the geishas' suspicions were aroused by his obvious lack of interest in further services, the project had to be abandoned. Another Mission Unaccomplished.[4]

However, Scott's effectiveness as an agent inside India cannot be seriously faulted. The best evidence for this comes not from his own reminiscences but from another remarkable Englishman, Michael Carritt, who worked for the Communists during the same period. Carritt would much later (in 1985) write about his and Scott's Indian undercover experiences in a slim, but wickedly funny, book entitled *A Mole in the Crown*. Further details of their exploits have recently been chronicled by Nigel West, Britain's leading writer on espionage matters. In his book *Mask*, published in 2005, West describes Scott and Carritt as the co-organizers of 'a strong covert European cadre'.[5]

Carritt, as the upwardly mobile son of an Oxford philosophy don, first arrived in India in 1930 set on a formal career in the ICS. After a dramatic introduction – two of the first district officers he worked under were assassinated, while he himself narrowly escaped being shot in an ambush – Carritt soon concluded there were genuine causes for dissatisfaction and that the imperial system he was pledged to uphold was both oppressive and reactionary. Like Scott, Carritt encountered prison conditions at an early stage and found them highly radicalizing. He was also disconcerted by the admiration for Adolf Hitler exhibited in the upper reaches of the ICS.

During a home leave in England in 1936, Carritt made contact with the Communist Party, asking if he could be of service on his return to India. After acquainting Harry Pollitt with his request, Carritt was guided to Ben Bradley, who ran the League Against Imperialism. Bradley equipped him with the credentials necessary for an agent, and told Carritt that if he had any difficulty contacting the Indian Communist leaders (which was quite likely as most of them were fugitives), he should seek out the Bishop of Bombay's house on Malabar Hill, and ask for a certain Reverend Michael Scott. Back in India, Carritt did encounter initial suspicion of his motives when approaching his nominated Indian contacts, so, as instructed, he went to the bishop's house. This is how he described the circumstances of his first encounter with Scott:

> Malabar Hill is an exclusive residential suburb of Bombay, several hundred feet high, very salubrious. It enjoys a fine view of the bay, the harbour and the long sandy coast. This is where the Bishop's residence was. It was not so much a 'palace' as a very large and luxurious colonial-style bungalow with an impressive portico and a vast veranda.
>
> And there I waited for Reverend Michael Scott to rise from his siesta when the heat of the day gave way to a glorious display of evening lights and colour over the city and harbour.
>
> I explained my mission and, for what they were worth, produced my credentials. At first he was sceptical and very cautious, but Ben Bradley's handwriting and the fraternal gift of £80 for the party news-sheet were convincing. But before we could begin to talk the inevitable servant appeared to announce that supper was being served and that ... 'His Lordship the Bishop requests the pleasure of the company of your guest at his table.'
>
> There was no escape ... We sat down to the strangest formal meal

I have ever eaten. There were four of us, Michael; myself; the Bishop, fat, bubbling and jolly; and his wife, tall and thin and who, long ago having lost all hope of this life, was committed to eternal silence. Half a dozen servants fluttered around the table, serving a simple but beautifully cooked four-course meal and filling our glasses with iced water.

After the formalities of preserved fruits and Grace, we excused ourselves, and Michael walked with me down into the sticky heat of Bombay's night. He insisted that I stay over for another night so that we could have a long talk the next day in order to 'put me in the picture'.

Next morning we met, as arranged, and boarded a ramshackle tram that ran northwards from Bombay serving a series of seaside suburbs where prosperous Indians had built little bungalows in the sandhills behind Juhu beach.

I now discovered Michael's romantic addiction to conspiratorial techniques, which he had learned about from reading about the Communist movement in Germany before the advent of Hitler. One of them, which he insisted on operating, was 'tram-hopping', at alternate stations we would descend from the tram and then, as it started to move off, jump on again whilst watching to see if any 'watchers' followed suit.

Juhu beach is endless – or so it seems. It is desolate and deserted; it slopes very gently to the sea so that there are hundreds of yards of foaming rollers always pounding up the shore. And above the water's edge there is always a shining skim of foam lying on the sand . . . and the wind blows a haze of sea spray over the long beach, making it always misty, mysterious and desolate.

Here, where the damp, hard beach joined the soft sand of the dunes, we sat all day whilst I was 'put in the picture'. This involved a description by Michael of the personalities and abilities of the leading Communists, as far as he knew them – Doc Adhikari, the Party Chairman, P.C. Doshi, the General-Secretary, Dange, Ghate, Ranadive and Mirajkar. Then we discussed the possibilities of helping with the production of the illegal news-sheet . . . [6]

The association between the two undercover Michaels became more intimate when Scott transferred to a similar post in Calcutta,

Carritt having preceded him there to take up the position of Under Secretary to the Chief Secretary to the Provincial Government of Bengal. Carritt's position was less exalted than the title might suggest, but it was, crucially, part of the political secretariat. Carritt was therefore in a position to scutinize the flow of 'law-and-order' documents, including the weekly secret reports from the police and district officers. He would also see all the encrypted correspondence with London. Some of this information was clearly of keen interest to activists planning demonstrations and to runaway leaders trying to keep one jump ahead of capture. Mechanisms for supplying it were devised.

The most important Communist in Calcutta at that time was P.C. Doshi, the party's general-secretary, though his fugitive existence meant that he could be seen only on rare occasions. For day-to-day purposes Carritt and Scott made contact with the CP leadership through 'Ahmed', a junior government clerk, whose house in a road leading off Karaya Lane was considered respectable and 'safe'. Karaya Lane itself, however, enjoyed a salacious reputation as a red-light district, with brothels catering for European proclivities. On their joint visits to see 'Ahmed', the security-conscious Scott made a point of parking his car – a jaunty sports model – in Karaya Lane. As he explained to Carritt, it was less likely to attract attention in such a racy neighbourhood. Despite this precaution, it did one day manage to attract the attention of a diligent police officer, who, after checking its licence number to determine ownership, informed the bishop of the vehicle's seemingly inappropriate whereabouts. This led to Scott's being carpeted by the bishop who said: 'it has been reported to me that your car is often seen in a disreputable part of this city. Dear boy, for my sake, if you feel you must go to those places, please take a taxi.'[7]

Scott's good fortune in being mistaken for a clerical libertine naturally helped to keep the lid on his other activities. Although the Communist Party in India was minuscule in comparison with other political groupings, its underground network was wide and it was deemed to have a decisive influence in the All-India Trades Union Congress. It was also strongly placed in the less well-organized peasant congress, the All-India Kisan Sabha. Operationally, the Indian party was defined as being under 'the care and protection' of the British CP, which automatically enlarged the roles of Scott and

Carritt, as the main bearers of secret tidings to and from the United Kingdom.

Censorship of the mail was routine procedure in a country that banned not only the more inflammatory Marxist texts, but also the milder socialist offerings of scholars like G.D.H. Cole and Harold Laski. Scott and Carritt, however, being ostensibly part of the most loyal and trustworthy echelon of society, received their mail unmolested. They therefore became the conduit for messages, policy documents, and a flow of left-wing literature, all much appreciated by the Indian Communists, who felt isolated from the international scene. Carritt and Scott would process some of the literature into 'simple, popular articles' on international politics for the illegal press.

Carritt records that, although he and Scott were technically only Communist 'couriers', their special role had the effect of turning them into 'unofficial advisers' to the Indian movement. They would sometimes find themselves involved in discussions of policy and even tactics. Carritt's impression was that Scott's Marxism was in some ways more orthodox than his own. At one discussion with D.C. Doshi about allocation of scarce resources, Carritt argued that the party should make more effort at engaging the revolutionary potential of the peasantry. Scott, however, more faithful to the international party line that put industrial society in the van of progress, thought that any extra available resources should be concentrated in Bombay, where the textile workers were well organized. It is possible, however, that this difference was more environmental than ideological. Scott had only scant acquaintance with India outside its major cities, while Carritt, as a former district officer, had direct knowledge of the disaffection of the country's rural poor.

In *A Mole in the Crown*, Carritt paints an intriguing pen portrait of Scott in India. No one less like a smooth undercover operator could be imagined. 'Michael', Carritt wrote, 'was, at the best of times a tousled and unkempt individual. In the years of our collaboration and comradeship, I never saw him looking anything other than dilapidated. This, of course, could be (rightly) attributed to his other-worldly attitudes and his sense of relative values.'[8]

Carritt was clearly very fond of Scott, though sometimes exasperated by him. Carritt's idea of fun had a mildly rumbustious quality, while Scott's humour, though by no means deficient, tended

27

to be of a 'dry and clerical' nature. They naturally did not see eye to eye on matters of religion, though Carritt found Scott very ready to criticize aspects of church dogma and ritual. But arguments on such topics were never explored to the limit, as Scott would terminate them with the reflection, 'I couldn't hurt my father.' Carritt was the older of the two, though only by a few months, and the more worldly, but Scott always seems to have operated on a higher level of seriousness. What impressed Carritt most was Scott's resolution and determination, which overcame inner conflicts that were 'tearing him to pieces'.[9]

Aside from Scott, only two other members of the European community in Calcutta knew of Carritt's subversive role. One was John Auden, brother of the poet W.H. Auden, who worked on the government Geological Survey, and the other was Humphrey House, then Visiting Professor of English Literature at Calcutta University. Professor House also features in Scott's recollections in *A Time to Speak*, as 'an amusing friend . . . with a delightful carefree mind'[10] though not as a Communist. But of his closest collaborator, Michael Carritt, Scott makes no mention. This could have been to protect Carritt who went on to become a university lecturer in England, but Scott also showed no eagerness for private reminiscence when Carritt ran into him after the war. From the abruptness of this encounter, Carritt concluded that the delicate subject of Scott's career as a Communist agent was firmly closed.

In spite of this snub, Carritt continued to hold Scott in the highest regard. Interviewed shortly before his death in 1990, he would say of Scott: 'He modelled his life more than any man I've seen on Jesus Christ. He was one of the most dedicated people I've ever seen. He never gave up.' Carritt recalled that, like other left-wingers before him, he had tried to persuade Scott to leave the Church as a way of easing his inner tensions. 'I think now,' said Carritt, 'I shouldn't have done that.'[11]

Scott's main method of relieving his tension in India was unusual. After a period of home leave in 1937, during which he delivered a long report on Indian conditions to the Communist headquarters in Paris and took part in a massive Popular Front demonstration, Scott returned to Calcutta and took up membership of the Bengal Flying Club. The experience of learning to fly over India's great rivers, the

Ganges and the Brahmaputra, Scott would recall, 'gave me a great sense of satisfaction and escape from my dilemmas at that time'.[12] An apt pupil, Scott would soon enjoy the further satisfaction of flying solo.

Another form of release would be developing friendships with other Europeans who viewed India in a progressive, though non-Communist, light – among them the famous Quaker Agatha Harrison, who, as a member of the India Conciliation Committee, tried to keep open lines of communication between the British government and the Indian Freedom movement. Scott was still closer to Charles Andrews, a former priest, who was then involved in solving the problems of Indians recently repatriated from South Africa. Through Andrews – a fervent though not entirely uncritical admirer of the Mahatma – Scott developed his knowledge of Gandhi's non-violent philosophy and strategies. Scott was impressed but did not see it as having any significant application to problems in Europe, where the arms race had broken into a gallop and war fever was mounting by the day. Communism still appeared to him the only force capable of combating Nazism, though the Moscow trials were beginning to reveal some of Stalin's imperfections. Like others with similar convictions, Scott suppressed his doubts:

> I resisted the suspicion that Communism might be leading towards yet another form of organized tyranny. It seemed to me that such an eventuality would spell the end of hope for mankind. So I accepted the suggestion that the evidence of compulsion and liquidation was either exaggerated by Imperialist propaganda or that those measures were made necessary by ruthless attempts at intervention and sabotage.[13]

Any immediate possibility of refining this judgement would be shattered in the summer of 1938 when, driving home from the Bengal Flying Club, Scott made glancing contact with an oncoming bus and spiralled off the road. His life was probably saved by the arrival, shortly after the collision, of an Indian doctor, who was able give him an injection and ensure his rapid admission to hospital. After three months in hospital and a further long period of recuperation at Kasauli, in the foothills of the Himalayas, Scott was accounted fit enough to return to England.[14]

Despite the complexities of his life in India, Scott never gave his religious superiors any cause to question his abilities as a concerned priest. When asked to provide a job reference for Scott in 1939, Bishop Foss Westcott wrote from Calcutta: 'I formed the highest opinion of his character and found him a sincere, conscientious and devoted worker . . . he has real sympathy for those in distress and would be genuinely concerned to do his utmost for them.'[15]

Scott considered his period as an undercover operative in India as being probably the most oppressive of his adult life. Its circumstances certainly were not conducive to any form of spiritual, or even moral, growth, and Scott would write with self-lacerating impatience about 'my duplicity and my impotence' at that time.[16] On the other hand, it did leave a residue of skill. Scott was now thoroughly versed in the art of equivocation, while preserving the straightest of straight faces. And, while this would by no means be the key to his subsequent witness, it undoubtedly helped him out of a few very tight corners.

CHAPTER SIX

WARTIME

WITH THE war clouds gathering over Europe in the summer of 1939, Michael Scott again found himself in the all too familiar environment of a hospital ward. Since his return from the Far East he had worked on a book about his experiences in India, and more stressfully, re-established his contacts with the British Communist Party. The abdominal pains that had intermittently troubled him since his teenage years returned with increased intensity.

Scott spent several weeks in the Hospital for Tropical Diseases, undergoing a variety of tests but with no conclusive results. It was suggested his pain probably had a nervous origin. On his discharge, he was issued with a sheet of dietary instructions, headed with the injunction: 'Avoid undue nervous or physical strain.'

Scott, accordingly, accepted an assignment from the Communists that made any such avoidance deeply improbable. In the months immediately prior to the war, the British CP made a priority of improving its recruitment and organization in the war industries. Scott was asked if he would be prepared to help establish factory groups in the Park Royal area of north-west London, where a number of munitions factories were located. The idea was that these factory groups should eventually supersede the more traditional cells based on streets or neighbourhoods. Scott agreed to help, with the customary provision that he would not be required to do anything that conflicted with his Christian conscience. The work consisted of contacting and assembling workers for meetings, which would then, as he described it, 'be addressed by a party boss with the proper working-class accent'.[1] Scott was not himself required to make speeches, but with twenty factories needing to be canvassed the work was physically demanding. It was also, given the sensitivity of the operation, a clear indication of the CP's regard for Scott's ability.

Scott's own resolution may well have been braced by the renewal of an old acquaintance. For some part of the time he would flat-share in Battersea with Michael Carritt, 'the mole in the Crown', recently returned from India, and Carritt's younger brother, who was also a Communist (a third Carritt brother had been killed in the Spanish Civil War, driving an ambulance for the Friends Unit). Ideologically, they seemed to be all at one, though the Carritt family's abiding memories of cohabiting with Scott tended to dwell on his awesome untidiness and helplessness in the face of household chores.[2]

Scott's work for the Communists in the munitions factories extended up to, and beyond, the announcement of the Nazi–Soviet pact. At first, Scott's impression was that the pact may have been Russia's way of forcing the West to decide where it stood, and was therefore not necessarily a bad thing. And even after war was declared on 3 September, the Communist Party line was that Britain should fight Nazism, regardless of the pact's existence. There was still no serious conflict in Scott's mind. But as the weeks went by, Scott began to perceive the existence of profound confusion regarding the party's stance and aims. He recalled: 'Communists in the army were coming to us and saying, "Look, I've been been drafted down to Dover. Do I pull the trigger or don't I?"' And there would be no clear answers from the party's higher echelons.[3]

Comrades who had spent years building an anti-Fascist popular front found themselves expected to about-face, and effectively undermine people's confidence in fighting the war against Hitler. Scott was now dismayed by a sense of being a cog in a political machine that was going in the wrong direction. With the main prop of his long-term intellectual support for Communism – the fight against Fascism – in the process of being rapidly dismantled, Scott was again taken seriously ill, though this time with more positive consequences.

Admitted to St Luke's Hospital, Fitzroy Square, on Christmas Day 1939, suffering from a complete stoppage of the bowel, Scott was rewarded on emerging from his operation by his surgeon's observation: 'If it's any consolation to you, you have a very rare disease. Nobody knows the cause of it.'[4] Scott had a condition known as Crohn's Disease and almost certainly had been afflicted with it, undiagnosed, for many years previously. While there was little consolation in actually having the disease, there was at least some relief in Scott's knowing that his pain was in not in any way a product of his imagination, but the result of a specific physical disorder.

Though incurable, Crohn's Disease – or ileitis as it is sometimes called – was treatable. Its manifestation is usually an inflammation of the lower part of the small intestine, the ileum, though it can affect any part of the digestive tract. In those days, the principal surgical procedure, known as a resection, involved cutting out the diseased section of the intestine. This would usually relieve the patient's suffering, though the inflammation tended to return, sometimes years later, next to the area of intestine that had been removed. This would necessitate another operation. In Scott's case, his resection operation at St Luke's would be the first of six.

Convalescing at his parents' home in Buckinghamshire, Scott decided his days of working directly for the Communists had come to an end, though there was some regret in the renunciation: 'I still had sympathy with some of their aims and with some of them as individuals, whose courage and devotion to the cause I respected as something greater than I had ever been able to put into any cause myself. In truth I really did not know what to believe myself.'[5]

What he came to believe was that he should enlist, not as a chaplain in the Armed Forces, but as a combatant. His simple reasoning was that it was 'preferable to die fighting Nazism than to submit to it', with the complicating rider that the business of 'exhorting others to fight' was 'abhorrent' in his own case.[6] Essentially, he did not think he could invoke the name of Jesus in the cause of killing people, but he also could not see how the threat to civilization posed by the Fascist powers could be successfully opposed other than by force of arms. With his flying experience, he thought the RAF might be ready to have him.

He discussed the idea with the Right Reverend George Bell, the Bishop of Chichester, who had ordained Scott in 1930, and who enjoyed a deserved reputation as one of the more radical figures in the episcopate. Bell had been sharply criticized in many quarters for being unfashionably early in his indictment of Nazism, and would be even more sharply criticized ten years later for publicly deprecating the Allied bombing of civilian populations. Though clearly apprehensive about where a war in the air might lead, Bell thought Scott should follow the dictates of his own conscience, even if it meant his becoming a rear-gunner on a British bomber.

The next hurdle to be surmounted involved telling his family.

Since his return from India, Scott had enjoyed unusually close contact with his parents, particularly after his spells of illness, but the level of communication with them does not appear to have been profound. He would say at one point in *A Time To Speak*: 'any discussions (on political matters) with my parents only caused them much anxiety'. And he said of his father: 'We always talked openly and frankly except about my hidden life,'[7] which, of course, must have left a great deal unsaid.

When Scott told his parents of his decision to enlist in the RAF, and of the reasons leading up to it, they were shocked and bewildered. To Scott's father there could be no vocation more important than that of being a priest: the idea that his son should voluntarily suspend his priesthood to engage in the world's affairs as a combatant seemed almost sacrilegious. On the night following his son's disclosure of his intention, Perceval Scott had a severe stroke, from which he never fully recovered, though he would live another nine years. Scott's naturally self-recriminatory nature went into overdrive. He did not change his mind, but he did delay his enlistment for a few months while his father made a partial recovery.[8] By way of filling in time, Scott took on temporary parish work in Fulham, supplemented by air-raid warden duties during the early stages of the Blitz.

Scott knew that his age and medical history militated against any chance of his becoming a pilot. But there seemed to be no impediment to his serving as an aircrewman, provided he could get through the medical. In the autumn of 1940 he reported to the RAF depot in Enfield, where he was accorded a remarkable A1 medical rating, before being dispatched to Bridgnorth in Shropshire, for basic training. The intricacies of military aviation and weaponry skills for aircrew would be imparted later at a training centre near Blackpool. Scott had no problem with the technical aspects of the programme, but was unable to disguise the fact that physically he was not up to it. At one physical training session his performance moved his flight-sergeant to bawl out a request for 'a little less reverence and a little more zip'.[9]

Twelve months after his enlistment Scott was discharged as being 'physically unfit for air force service'. His ileitis had flared up and he was obliged to go into hospital again for another painful resection operation. Having failed to kill, or get himself killed, in the business of defeating Nazism, he now had to face another painful reality. After two more brief hospitalizations, occasioned by his slow recovery from the operation, the doctors declared that his chances of achieving sustained activity or anything resembling a working life – in either war or peace – did not look at all promising in Europe. South Africa had seemingly restored him to health once before: perhaps it could do the same again.

South Africa was attractive for another reason that escapes serious mention in Scott's autobiography. Recently released MI5 security files indicate that Scott renewed constructive acquaintance with Emile Burns and other leaders of the British Communist Party. Security intercepts show that Burns's initial idea was that Scott should leave the Church and come and work 'full-time' in the party's propaganda department. Scott, according to the intercepts, rejected this proposal, mainly on the grounds that it would be too upsetting for his family. Burns then became excited at the possibilities in the South African option and communicated this excitement to the party's leader, Harry Pollitt. A record of the intercept, dated 13 January 1943, reads: 'BURNS came in to see HARRY POLLITT. Burns said:- You remember MICHAEL SCOTT. Well, he had an interesting proposition – to look after the souls of the natives in Pretoria. He went on to say that if Scott accepted the job it would be a unique position, and very valuable to the South African Party . . .'[10]

There was no suggestion that Scott should go to South Africa as an official agent of the party, as had been the case in India, but it was clearly understood that his work there would dovetail with that of the Communists. Scott's progress thereafter would be keenly monitored by the CP's leadership in London, and as is now evident, secretly by MI5.

While waiting for a passage to the Cape, Scott resumed his duties as an air-raid warden and acted as chaplain to a convent in Bournemouth, which also ran an orphanage. Scott's duties in Bournemouth were comparatively light, affording time for contemplation – or what he called 'inner disquisition' – about his next course of action. By the time his ship sailed from Liverpool in the spring of 1943, Scott had formed a positive idea of what he wanted to achieve at its final destination:

I began to feel increasingly that, having been spared the kind of fate that had been the lot of too many of my friends and contemporaries, I must use the life that had been given back to me by the skill of doctors and nurses to fight the evils of oppression and injustice which I knew I should find in South Africa – and to fight them with new weapons not inspired by the hatred and fanaticism which Nazism had let loose in the world.[11]

It was in some ways a presumptuous resolve for a sickly young man of thirty-five, carrying a weight of uncertainty and guilt about his political affiliations, and with a somewhat erratic career record to date. But it was, as it turned out, not beyond his capacity.

CHAPTER SEVEN

BETRAYAL

MICHAEL SCOTT's response to South Africa in 1943 is best summed up by Trevor Huddleston, who arrived to start a new ministry in Johannesburg at almost the same time. Huddleston, who would later write *Naught for Your Comfort*, the most brilliant indictment of South Africa's racial policies, resembled Scott in many ways. He was tall, lean, and ascetic in appearance, with his hair close-cropped, and as a member of a monastic order, the Community of the Resurrection, necessarily celibate. There was a key difference, however, which Huddleston would later comment upon as follows:

> Although Michael and I had come from the same English background and the same ecclesiastical tradition: although, within a fairly short time, I couldn't fail to recognize the marvellously rich human resources going to waste through such dire poverty, it took me the best part of four years to understand that it wasn't the symptoms but the disease itself that had to be fought. It took Michael about four weeks . . . [1]

In reality, it probably did not take Scott that long, but he needed time to unpack and settle in. The South African Church Institute in London had assigned him to a post as Assistant Priest at the Pretoria Native Mission, but Scott instantly disturbed the sensitivities of the senior priest there by sitting on the veranda and companionably 'talking to an African priest and drinking a cup of tea'.[2] Subsequent disagreements about African rights (or the lack of them) and trade-unionism led Scott to approach the Bishop of Johannesburg, Geoffrey Clayton, with a request for another job. Clayton obliged by finding him two on the outskirts of Johannesburg's Sophiatown: assistant to the St Alban's Coloured Mission under the Reverend Maurice Clack, and chaplain to the Sisters of the Order of St Margaret's and their orphanage in St Joseph's Home. Scott's home base, thereafter, was a rondavel, a round thatched dwelling, in the garden of St Joseph's. His salary was £354 a year.

Scott had been only dimly aware politically during his first stay in the country, but this time, with the benefit of a thorough Marxist education, he had a good idea of what he was up against. The status of the Union of South Africa within the British imperial scheme of things was that of a self-governing Dominion. Its constitutional arrangements had been devised in the wake of the Boer War, the bitter conflict at the turn of the century between Britain and the Boer Republics. In practice, the answer to the problem of reconciling the two warring white tribes had been provided by their mutual oppression of the blacks. This development was foreseen, even advocated, by Sir Alfred Milner, the British High Commissioner of the time, who had told his political master in London, 'You have only to sacrifice "the nigger" and the game is easy.'[3]

By 1943 the sacrificial process was near completion, with the black population of the country – around ten million – being deployed in a wholly subservient way to its two and a half million white inhabitants. Blacks now owned less than one-fifth of what had once been their land – by far the most ill-favoured fifth. They had no effective franchise as an avenue for political redress, and few political rights. In the House of Assembly, three out of a total of 164 members were said to represent the native population, all three being white. Black advancement beyond the heaviest and most menial type of work was blocked by a rigidly enforced colour bar. Wages for a demeaned black proletariat were uniformly low: those of African miners in the Transvaal had not increased in real terms for thirty-five years. Forced by economic necessity to leave the impoverished native reserves to seek work in the white man's mines, farms and homes, the Africans led a thoroughly dislocated existence, albeit one carefully monitored by the police through the application of 'pass laws'. The regulations governing the Indian and coloured communities were less draconian, but still sharply discriminatory.

The politics of the enfranchised white minority was dominated by the need to mesh the interests of the inhabitants of English and Dutch origin. The interests of other races were incidental to this central concern, although after South Africa's entry into the war on Britain's side there appeared, initially, to be some prospect of progress, if only for the volunteer non-white troops and others involved in the war effort. This proved illusory. General Jan Smuts, the Prime Minister and leader of the ruling United Party, was seen as a liberal figure abroad, but remained ultracautious in matters of racial policy at home. Like others in his party, he was intensely concerned about the electoral threat posed by the rise of the National Party, which was almost pure Afrikaner in complexion and included many of an openly Nazi persuasion. To Smuts's way of thinking, concessions to the 'native cause' would only embolden the Nationalists. He wrote privately and pessimistically to a friend: 'What will it profit this country if justice is done to the underdog and the whole caboodle then, including the underdog, is handed over to the wreckers.'[4]

Some of the consequences of this political inertia combined with impacted social and racial injustice were outlined in one of Scott's first letters home to his parents describing his new surroundings:

Sophiatown is a native township, housing people of all races and colours; African, Indian, Chinese and Coloured who work in the various industries in Johannesburg. They are desperately poor with their little houses or huts patched up with flattened-out paraffin tins and old bits of rusty corrugated iron which blow about and make an awful din when there is a wind, which is often. . . . There are these huge, great mine dumps all around, too – great pyramids of pulverized rocks – all that is left, after the gold has been crushed out of the ore, and when the wind is strong it blows the dust off them as though they were steaming . . .

There is a quite a fair sprinkling of Christians. But many of them belong to queer little African sects which have split off from the parent body, very often on account of the heavy dues they are expected to pay. They have their own little tin church where they dress up in strange but colourful garments, and dance and sing, and pray for hours on end. It is so strange to hear their very lovely singing in harmony coming out of the most dilapidated old corrugated iron building. They have an almost pathetically fervent faith that God will one day come down and put everything to rights for all the oppressed people in the land. I say pathetic because so much of it is deliberate man-made evil.

Johannesburg – with its vast wealth and luxurious modern life – seems very faraway though the lights are blazing along the range of hills that form the Witwatersrand. Here there is poverty, and stench and noise, and all that is bred of these filthy conditions; malnutrition of the children, drunkenness, gambling, venereal disease . . . Sometimes one feels almost overwhelmed by the sum total of the havoc and misery that our so-called civilization has brought upon the African people. Here there are three hundred and fifty thousand of them, miners mostly, separated from their families in the native territories for nine months in the year, to work underground for three pounds a month. So one is brought back to the pressing problem of the age – poverty in the midst of plenty . . .

I had to resign from Pretoria before I had been there a month because I felt so strongly . . . But I hadn't come out from England to be dictated to on such matters of principle. I don't think there is any virtue in the sort of humility which always bows to the authority one usually respects . . .

I expect the people at home who brought me out here are being told what a self-opinionated young cub they had picked on! And probably this is so, but if one hasn't got some pretty strong convictions in all this physical, moral and social mess, I think one would go right off one's rocker. Even so, I haven't that strong sense of evil that some people seem to feel when they come here slumming. They commit murders when they are desperate or drunk and sometimes even children of six are drunk on the streets on that filthy muck they call beer (yeast, pineapple juice, a dash of methyl to give it a kick, and a dollop of boot blacking to add a little tang) – but there is nothing evil about poverty, ignorance, disease and underfeeding.

The evil lies over there where the beauty parlours are, and everything is so nice and hygienic, and people buy and sell to one another with little bits of paper, the products which all these people have created with their hands or dug out of the earth.[5]

It is clear that Scott was finding his own voice on social issues, and as importantly, feeling able to address them within a framework of Christian compassion, rather than Marxist logic. Scott's interpretation of a Christian's duty in this new situation did not, however, coincide with that of his formidable bishop. Geoffrey Clayton, an Anglo-Catholic like Scott's own father, had been the Bishop of Johannesburg since 1934 and had a reputation as a scholar and as an outstandingly shrewd defender of the Anglican Church. In Adrian

Hastings's *A History of African Christianity*, he is rather equivocally, but comprehensively, described as:

> Dry, unemotional, distrustful of populism of any sort – pentecostal or political – an English upper middle-class type who was constitutionally as incapable of identifying with blacks as with women, or with the poor anywhere in his own lifestyle, he was yet able to assess the general situation with courage and very clear judgement, and did not for one moment question that the Church's task – secondary (to the worship of God) but still immensely important – was to speak up for the poor and the weak.[6]

Clayton was a patrician. He was disinclined to meet with African leaders, seeing solutions to 'the native problem' as being a matter for informed discourse between whites. He was against the colour bar, but could only perceive its removal as part of an evolutionary process. He also seemed relatively undisturbed by the *de facto* segregation in his own church. In matters of church conduct he was regarded as a disciplinarian, and he tended to view priests inclined to political action outside their pastoral bailiwicks with particular distaste.

Scott, whose judgement of character tended to lag some way behind his judgement of an issue, initially thought of Clayton as a potential ally. He wrote to his bishop in September 1943 inviting him to come and address a conference of black and white organizations designed 'to draw closer together those whose consciences are moved in the matter of colour bar legislation'. Clayton pointedly, and rather primly, turned down the invitation on that grounds that he would be busy 'confirming' new Christians, while Scott was choosing to spend his time 'conferring'.[7]

Undeterred, Scott pressed on. He established a committee in Johannesburg designed to put pressure on the legislature on race issues, which would later fan out to become a movement called the Campaign for Right and Justice (CRJ). Scott drafted the manifesto for its inaugural conference and sent it to all the Anglican bishops in South Africa. Five replied encouragingly, although in the event none attended the conference. The gathering of some 200 delegates in Johannesburg's Darragh Hall, adjoining the cathedral, passed a variety of combative resolutions calling, among other things, for recognition for African trades unions, a minimum wage of £2 a week, rent control, and no colour bar.[8] Then Scott overreached himself.

To give these issues more international muscle, Scott cabled the British Labour Party and the British Council of Churches with news of the conference decisions, and appended a statement to the effect that 'messages of support had been received from five bishops'. This caused outrage, and Scott was denounced from the upper reaches of the episcopacy for his 'wrongful claim': the bishops' endorsements had extended to the idea of the conference but not to its resolutions, and their publication abroad was deemed embarrassing to the Church. Like the government, the churches viewed race policy as a domestic issue. Clayton, whom Scott strongly suspected was mainly responsible for cooling the initial enthusiasm of his five bishops, accused Scott of 'blundering in', and more eloquently, in a personal letter, warned him against trying 'to tie the church or the diocese to your chariot wheels'.[9]

Clayton's own reforming initiative, *The Church and the Nation* report, produced by a commission he had established two years earlier, was unveiled at the November 1943 Synod. It was in some ways a powerful document, arguing for increased church involvement in social and economic issues, for greater social justice, and for extension of the franchise. But it did not seriously undermine the concept of white supremacy or attempt to represent the interests of other racial groups. The report asserted: 'though there is no final wrong principle involved in the practice of segregation, various evil forms of it are to be condemned'.[10] To a small minority of priests at the Synod, Michael Scott among them, the report's phrase advocating 'a gradual removal of the colour bar' seemed like a perfect recipe for doing nothing.

While the report could not be described as providing 'a divine sanction for the *status quo*', it did not, to Scott's way of thinking, come close to expressing the urgency of the need for change. He, therefore, pushed on with the task of building his own organization, though he would write to Clayton, in what he thought were mollifying terms: 'I feel strongly that what we are trying to do is in no sense contrary to the work of the Synod Commission and the implementing of its Report.'[11] Clayton remained unappeased. Some weeks later, while canvassing for new adherents in the Jewish community, Scott discovered one of Clayton's spokesmen had been putting it about that Scott's Campaign for Right and Justice had been specifically ruled out of order by the Synod. This was not the case, though the bishop's personal disapproval had been manifest.

Clayton's exasperation was probably enhanced by Scott's campaign becoming almost flagrantly newsworthy. Scott would draw into his enterprise a remarkable constellation of characters – too remarkable as it turned out – but genuinely eye-opening in a country long grown accustomed to thinking in blinkered racial categories. As president of his design, Scott recruited Justice F.E.T. Krause, an Afrikaner with an exotic personal history. Imprisoned by the British during the Boer War, Krause had been Judge President of the Orange Free State, making a name for himself by denouncing the pass laws and the police from the bench. As chairman, Scott installed H.E. Wraige, the Archdeacon of Kimberley, one of the few churchmen openly ready to risk Clayton's wrath.

Scott himself served as secretary to an executive committee that was not only multiracial but broadly based politically, and included several Communists and ex-Communists whom Scott thought he could work with, though not for. Within a very short space of time more than a hundred organizations offered their support and affiliation. Outfits that were not, in the normal course of business, prepared to work with each other, found themselves ready to sign up to the CRJ's three main stated objectives:

1) The full and direct representation of all sections of the community.
2) The abolition of all legislation discriminatory on the grounds of colour, sex, and race.
3) The provision of land for the landless peoples of South Africa, and assistance in making the best use of it.[12]

Along with a variety of welfare, teaching, and church groups, the CRJ found favour with more heavy-duty organizations, like the African and Indian Congresses, the African Mineworkers' Union, and among the more left-wing trade unionists in the Trades and Labour Council. Scott also almost miraculously, and perhaps unwisely, enticed the South African government into qualified support of his enterprise. Four cabinet ministers – for Justice, Health and Housing, Agriculture and Economic Development – agreed to preside at a projected CRJ conference on regional planning, which was intended to provide a climax to the campaign's efforts. But there was a condition that Prime Minister Smuts laid down: Scott should, on no account, allow his campaign to form the nucleus of a new political party.[13] Scott made the pledge, seemingly without much effort. Indeed, at the time he saw the CRJ as being beneficial to the interests of the United Party in any electoral contest with Dr Malan's opposition National Party. With the war seemingly almost at an end, Scott thought the CRJ would provide the United Party with the post-war rejuvenation it needed to meet the Nationalist threat.

As the campaign freewheeled through 1944 and into 1945 it developed enough policies and ideas to equip several political parties, while keeping up pressure on the government through deputations to all the principal ministries. Scott's main obsession, however, was not so much with manifestations of injustice as with root causes. He gave most thought to how to offset the malign effects of South Africa's mining-based economy, which was so productive in terms of its yield of precious stones and metals, and so damaging in its deployment of human resources. It was the mining industry that split up families and created the shifting proletariats for which there was no, or only the scantiest, provision. Scott found a kindred spirit in Dr Andre Bruwer, an Afrikaner who had served as an economic adviser to the government, but who was also a man of independent views. Bruwer's thinking had developed from the American experience of the Tennessee Valley Authority and from Lewis Mumford's *The Culture of Cities*,[14] bringing together concepts of social and regional development. On Scott's urging, Bruwer devised a regional planning scheme designed to relieve the over-concentration of South Africa's industrial base. It required serious infrastructure investment, particularly on new railway links, and it was not shy about its intervention in the free market, but it envisaged a mixed, managed economy, not unlike those already developing in Western Europe. It was radical, but hardly Marxist.

Scott, meanwhile, was experiencing acute difficulty with the management of the CRJ. An excellent vehicle for throwing up ideas and the occasional demonstration, it was not seriously roadworthy in organizational terms. On the executive, it was almost impossible to find a common basis for action between the white liberals and the white and black radicals. There were tensions between the Communists and the churchmen, and even greater tensions between the Communists and the ex-Communists. When Archdeacon Wraige resigned, pleading pressure of other business, Scott took over the chairmanship but with a sense of increasing isolation. The campaign was clearly not destined to have a long life, although the end, when it came, was bizarre in the extreme.

It began with what seemed like a golden opportunity. Scott came into possession of a document that exposed the inner workings of the Broederbond, the sinister Afrikaner secret society, dedicated to racial supremacy and 'the Afrikanerization of our public life'.[15] Founded in 1918, the Broederbond had always been shrouded in mystery. According to the document, it had effectively infiltrated all the higher reaches of South African society. In journalistic terms, Scott was in possession of a scoop of major proportions and he was appreciative of its potential. He decided the CRJ should publish the document in pamphlet form, as an illustration of the existence of 'A state within a state'.[16]

Before the pamphlet could be released, Scott was visited by a strange character claiming that the information it contained was his, and not that of the maverick Afrikaner whom Scott had originally presumed was the author. He further maintained that he had originally assembled the Broederbond information as part of a secret commission for the United Party. The stranger's credibility on this point would be buttressed when, shortly afterwards, two senior members of the United Party – Marais Steyn and Henry Tucker – came knocking at the door of Scott's rondavel. They asserted the material constituted part of the government's 'military intelligence' and as such could not be published.[17] Given the uncertainty about the document's provenance, Scott reluctantly decided to veto release of the CRJ pamphlet, a decision he subsequently came to regret.

Arguments about the withdrawn pamphlet and the overall direction of the campaign exacerbated the tensions on Scott's disparate executive. And the idea that the CRJ should effectively throw off the gloves and come out openly fighting as a political party began to seem more seductive to some of its members, particularly those on the left. In order to quell the restlessness, Scott called a meeting at which he reminded those assembled of his original pledge to General

Smuts. He also, incautiously, put his stewardship on the line. He was outvoted, and as he would record later: 'In a mood of black despair I resigned from the campaign I had struggled day and night for two years to build up.'[18]

The first casualty was the long-planned conference on 'The Shape of the Future', scheduled for December 1945, which was to have featured Dr Bruwer's regional plan and actively involved government ministers in its public discussion. Feeling he could no longer give any guarantees on the direction the CRJ might take, Scott released the four ministers – Jan Hofmeyer, Dr Colin Steyn, Sydney Waterson and Dr Henry Gluckman – from their promise to attend and cancelled the event. The second casualty was the CRJ itself, which, deprived of the focus of Scott's leadership, fragmented still further and soon withered away.

Scott's own inquest on the campaign was a shade unforgiving. He would write of feeling 'betrayed' by his own church, particularly by its hierarchy, 'betrayed' by the Communists, whose support had amounted to 'a kiss of death' and 'betrayed' by deficiencies in his own strength of purpose.[19] But this was the language of disappointed expectation rather than real analysis. Scott's enterprise may have fallen well short of its immediate objective, but it still had a ground-breaking significance. With hindsight, it is possible to see the CRJ experiment, bringing together so many mutually suspicious groups in an effort at common cause, did extraordinarily well to survive as long as it did. And while it could not forestall the looming menace of Afrikaner Nationalism, it certainly fashioned many of the ideas and approaches that would later be used against apartheid to great effect. In the light of history, Scott's CRJ had genuinely creative consequences.

Scott's self-reproach was also not well founded. In terms of conventional politics he can be judged to have attempted too much too soon, but for someone intent on the destruction of political conventions that had already lasted far too long, this was inevitable to a large degree. His mistakes were primarily due to impetuosity and overeagerness and not to any deficiency in his objectives. He would certainly have to absorb the lesson that he was never likely to achieve any great distinction as an organization man. But this, as it turned out, was no bad thing.

CHAPTER EIGHT
DOING TIME IN AFRICA

Michael Scott was always sensitive to the charge of being ready to subordinate his immediate pastoral responsibilities to the needs of a public cause, and for good reason: it was largely true. During the more intense phases of the Campaign for Right and Justice, there was no real way of concealing the fact that Scott was a near full-time activist and a spare-time priest. Bishop Clayton noted this with extreme distaste.

There was, however, even in formal church terms, a mitigating circumstance. Those who were obliged to cover for Scott during his abrupt, and sometimes long, absences were also among his most fervent supporters on the wider issues. Maurice Clack, Scott's head of mission at St Alban's, was among the few who saw his assistant priest's outside work as part of his Christian purpose. And while the orphans at St Joseph's Home were appreciative of Scott's storytelling ability, and deeply impressed by his untidiness, they were encouraged to give him space at crucial times. Sister Geraldine Mary, who became Mother Superior, would say that Scott's quality of finding commitment through self-questioning was something that strongly reinforced her own vocation and religious life. When, in later years, their paths diverged, she would always end her letters to Scott *'in corde Jesu'* – 'in the heart of Jesus'.

Outside this immediate circle of those who knew him best, Scott was not popular. Most of his fellow priests, rendered uncomfortable by his actions, viewed him with apathy or varying degrees of antipathy. As always and everywhere, rocking the boat tended to gather limited support. In Scott's case the number of his open supporters in the Church could be counted on the fingers of one hand. Trevor Huddleston, installed as priest-in-charge of the Anglican mission to Sophiatown and Orlando, was a friend, and sometimes confidant, but not a supporter. Huddleston was still inclined to share Clayton's gradualist view of the way ahead, and was rendered 'uneasy' by Scott's campaigning methods.[1]

47

More positive encouragement could be relied upon from Tom Comber, the radical Rector of St Mary's, Jeppe, and from Arthur Blaxall, a saintly old priest who devoted his life to the service of the blind. Both had shown a readiness to criticize Clayton openly in the Synod. But these priests, along with Clack, constituted a mutually approving network, rather than a power base or anything resembling a cabal. Scott naturally welcomed their fellow-feeling and comfort but never went out of his way to achieve consensus, even with intimates. Though accessible, Scott was not by nature inclined to consult others, except his God. His behavioural pattern, already deeply ingrained, was contemplation (his 'inner disquisition'), followed by decision, followed by action, often in an unpredictable direction. Anticipation of his moves was problematic for his enemies and often quite difficult for his friends.

During the early months of 1946, with his hopes for the CRJ now buried, Scott was in a contemplative phase. He became more available for parish routines and may even have given his bishop cause to conclude that the diocese's most determined troublemaker had reformed. Scott's thinking was indeed undergoing some change but not, as it turned out, in a less disruptive direction. Given what seemed like a political impasse, Scott decided that he needed to explore other avenues in pursuit of his objectives.

One of the first results in May 1946 would be a new wave of headlines about priestly intransigence. In an open letter to the Acting Prime Minister, J.H. Hofmeyr, Scott wrote of his intention not to pay his income tax as a protest against 'European bad faith in its dealings with non-European peoples'.[2] And he thought others should follow his lead. Instead of stumping up the £15 he was deemed to owe to the taxman, Scott proposed to send £10 to the African Mineworkers' Union, then gearing up for strike action, and £5 direct to the Department of Justice 'to combat injustice and improve the penal system'. This gesture represented a minuscule blow to the Exchequer, and no great enrichment for the mineworkers – whose subsequent strike was brutally crushed – but it did serve its intended purpose of opening public debate about the legitimacy of the state. It also had the effect of sharpening Scott's own ideas on the subject, particularly in relation to 'the lawlessness of the law'.

Among the commentaries on Scott's action – nearly all adverse –

was one contained in a personal letter from what was considered the highest reach of the liberal establishment. The Principal of the University of the Witwatersrand, H.R. Raikes, writing more in sorrow than in anger, and assuring Scott of his mutual concern for 'the welfare of the non-European population', urged a more careful thinking through of the problem. Scott would then perceive that non-payment of tax was essentially an 'antisocial' action, and that his 'sinning against the Law' in this respect would almost certainly lead him, wastefully and unnecessarily, to jail.

Scott's reply, never published because of Raikes's insistence on the privacy of this exchange, is probably the best summary of his political thinking at the time, and certainly the best clue to his willingness to flout the law more flagrantly at a later stage. He wrote:

Thank you for the courteous way you have expressed your disapproval. I am afraid I find it difficult to see how the standards implied in such expressions as 'antisocial' and 'sinning against the Law' are necessarily and always compatible with our Christian beliefs about the nature of God or man . . . According to our religion, and, so far as I know, to science and nature, we are made subject to one set of laws, while the state in which we live imposes two sets of laws . . .

The Native Urban Areas, and Native Representation Acts, the Land Act and our industrial legislation all combine to deprive the majority of our population of the opportunity of constitutional change, and at the same time artificially obstruct their advance spiritually, socially and economically.

Further, the state, by prohibiting large sections of the people from exercising their natural skills and God-given talents, appears, from a Christian standpoint, to be exceeding the limits of its functions, and opposing the authority of natural justice and the Divine Purpose . . . In point of fact our laws are unnecessarily manufacturing criminals by the thousand every year . . . Living amongst the non-European peoples one can already sense the grave danger in which our society stands from the lawlessness of 'law and order' as in practice applied to them.

At all costs to the individual, a greater sense of responsibility must surely be brought home to those in whom responsibility has been vested. If my proposal appears to you to be a gesture of despair, it is

49

not, I can assure you, through any wish to become a 'martyr'. The thought of gaol horrifies and revolts me.[3]

Within three months of posting this letter to the Principal, Scott would find himself behind bars, though not for the reason that Raikes predicted.

In the summer of 1946, there were serious disturbances in the coastal city of Durban, where there was a large established Indian population, numerically almost equal to the European. Under the recently passed Asiatic Land Tenure and Indian Representation Act, more generally known as 'The Ghetto Act', severe restrictions were placed on Indian commercial and residence rights. Opposition to the Act, mobilized by the Indian Congress, was deliberately modelled on the passive resistance techniques of Mahatma Gandhi, who had pioneered their application in South Africa some forty years earlier, before transplanting them in India.

Scott was well versed in the theory of Gandhi's *satyagraha* (or soul force), but had not, to this point, seen or embraced it in action. The theory which had it that passive resistance could not only confront oppression but also, if correctly applied, achieve a 'release' of goodness in the oppressor, was entirely congenial to Scott. He saw it as being wholly in tune with his Christian belief, in that it seemed to be an expression of love's power to combat evil. Whether it could constitute practical political action in Natal's racially complex situation was not so evident, though India's progress towards full independence of the British empire (achieved in 1947) suggested that it might.

In June, a small liberal Natal-based outfit calling itself the 'Council for Human Rights' asked Scott to act as an observer and to publicize the resistance in Durban. Needing no second invitation, Scott left his parish at short notice to drive to Durban with three other highly motivated companions, none of them churchmen – Dr Yusuf Dadoo, the Communist president of the Transvaal Indian Congress, Bettie du Toit, a militant official in the Food and Canning Union, and Yusuf Cachalia, a young Congress leader. Recalling their mood on the long drive down to the coast, Scott would write: 'We were all rather nervous for each of us had a reputation that was inimical to the mobs at work in Durban, and no one had the least idea how it was going to turn out.'[4]

The passive resistance that Scott observed took a well-disciplined form, at least as far as the resisters were concerned. The main objective of the action was occupation of a triangular stretch of empty municipal land in the centre of Durban, on the corner of Umbilo Road and Gale Street. There was nothing much to covet in the actual location, but Indians were legally excluded from it under the terms of the new Act. This provided it with a symbolic significance. Before each action, the appointed group of resisters was given precise instructions in a nearby church hall. There were no circumstances in which they should allow themselves to hit back if abused or physically attacked. With this lesson absorbed, they were led to the 'resistance camp' on site, where gangs of white youths also assembled, choreographing their own response, which had more to do with releasing aggression than any innate goodness. On the signal of a blown whistle, the white youths piled in, hurling racial abuse as a preliminary to kicking most of the male resisters unconscious. The police did not intervene.

Scott, in his observer and reporting capacity, cabled Prime Minister General Smuts and Gandhi in India, drawing their attention to the conspicuous inaction of the local authorities, which seemed to provide a sanction for mob violence. In his personal capacity, as someone who endorsed the aims of the demonstration, he felt that his 'only possible course' was to join the resisters. Scott wrote of this first direct experience of *satyagraha* in *A Time to Speak*:

In the same way as before the attacks began with a charge and sort of high-pitched hunting cry. The men volunteers were very soon knocked down and lying huddled on the grounds. The girls had not been seriously assaulted. I was dressed in my cassock and they recoiled from assaulting me, just as they were about to do so. Having learned something of the spirit of the satyagrahas by this time, I spoke to them without heat. Two girls came up and started shouting 'Coolie guts' and 'Curry guts'. 'Are you an Anglican? You should be ashamed of yourself, you renegade. If I had known what your religion teaches, I'd never have been confirmed.' 'God would never have had me,' said one. 'He's had me,' said another.

Two men came up and started pushing, expecting I would hit back, but they were bullies and had a frightened look in their eyes for all they had the physical mastery of us.

It was during this episode that I remember one of the Indian girls, a Muslim, saying to me, after many of the men had been knocked unconscious in front of her, 'It's not their fault, they don't know what they are doing.' I don't suppose she had ever read the story of the Crucifixion, but her religion had taught her more than those two girls had found in ours, it seemed.

I felt so sick, and helpless, and ashamed, and yet her remark seemed strangely to reassure me in the knowledge that by standing still there on that particular piece of ground one was enabling something to be done – yes, enabling God to do something – against the dreadful evil power which was manifest in that sadistic mob. I knew Zenab Asvat was right, they did not understand. Far more responsible were the religious leaders who preached the colour bar under the sign of the Cross in South Africa, and the statesmen and politicians who in season and out of season played upon the racial prejudices of the people.[5]

For Bettie du Toit, who stood alongside Scott through this particular resistance, the most abiding memory was of Scott's face and her own being covered with spit.[6]

The demonstrations continued with the police becoming much more actively involved, arresting people in large numbers, not under the new Act, but mainly for 'trespass'. Each time the resisters were arrested and released, pending hearing of their case, they would return to the 'resistance camp', until their next arrest. Scott spent the early weeks of July rotating in this fashion, while back in Johannesburg his bishop fumed. Clayton finally sent Scott what amounted to an ultimatum, demanding that he must be back in his own district, 'and ready to resume your work, not later than Saturday 20 July'.[7] Scott must have known this was serious and that his job could well be at risk, particularly in view of the fact Maurice Clack, his friend and protector at the St Alban's Mission, had recently been moved on, to be replaced by the Reverend Harry Leach, who had been one of Clayton's chaplains.

On Friday, 19 July, one day before the bishop's deadline, Scott led another batch of resisters to the camp and was again arrested for trespass. Charged with four offences of trespass and one of riotous assembly, Scott was sentenced to three months' imprisonment. In all, some 2000 resisters were sent to prison in the course of the demonstrations. No charges were preferred against their assailants. In a statement to the magistrate's court, Scott deployed his knowledge of St Paul's epistle to the Colossians with maximum effect:

> With regard to the personal reference to myself from the bench, and the surprise that was expressed at my association with people of another class, namely my fellow prisoners, I must first disclaim any such superiority of class or intelligence as that suggested, and to state further that my religion knows no colour bar. It recognizes no artificial barriers of race or class, indeed, it must challenge any conception of racial inferiority for there cannot be 'Greek or Jew, circumcision or uncircumcision, Barbarian, Scythian, bondman or freeman, but Christ is all and in all.'[8]

Scott's obdurate witness to this proposition and consequent imprisonment was inescapably national news, in India almost as much as in South Africa. He was almost instantly accorded heroic status in the Indian media. Aside from Father Satchell, who headed the local Anglican Indian mission, Scott was the only white priest seen as being actively supportive of the Indian cause. Yusuf Kat, the Urdu poet who drew cartoons for *The Leader*, created a widely reproduced image of Scott in his cassock under the banner 'I am my brother's keeper'.[9] The publication *Indian Opinion* devoted a special supplement in praise of the Durban resistance, illustrating the feature with a photograph of its three main heroes: Scott with Yusuf Dadoo and Monty Naicker, the Congress leaders for Transvaal and Natal respectively, both also imprisoned. Among the telegrams of support sent to Scott in Durban jail was one from an Indian pacifist, saying simply, 'Heartiest congratulations'.[10]

The tone of the white South African response was, predictably, less congratulatory. The *Sunday Express* was representative in reporting that most of the white clergymen in Johannesburg disapproved of Scott's action, which seemed to lead to 'encouragement of lawlessness'.[11] The newspaper earnestly counselled that clergymen should 'preach tolerance rather than take any action which broke the laws of the country'. Nevertheless, there were slivers of encouragement for

Scott. The Reverend Harry Leach, whom Scott had presumed was a fully committed ally of his disapproving bishop, was publicly quoted in defence of his absentee assistant priest, asserting: 'He has gone to gaol as a protest against unjust laws . . . Many people who do not know him well have judged him falsely.'[12] He even indicated that Scott's post at St Alban's could still be open to him when he came out of jail.

Scott did his time in Durban prison, with a few weeks' remission for good behaviour. He sewed mailbags, scrubbed buckets and cleaned latrines but acknowledged that his time behind bars was easier than for most inmates, partly because he was white, partly because he was a priest, and partly because he would spend three weeks in the prison hospital. In a prison that housed almost a thousand convicts, non-Europeans outnumbered Europeans – from whom they were segregated – by a ratio of thirty to one. Characteristically, Scott would write more graphically about their plight, than he would about his own. Thus:

> The cells of the non-European section of the gaol were so crowded that at night the floor space was entirely covered with the forms of prisoners lying alternately head to foot with room only for a pail of water and a latrine bucket . . . Non-European prisoners were made to strip naked in view of all of us and perform the most grotesque antics so that the warder could satisfy himself that nothing was concealed between the legs or toes or anywhere else on the prisoner's body . . .

Of the ritual of corporal punishment, an enormously popular form of correction with the South African prison authority, Scott would write:

> Non-European prisoners were marched to the other side of the court-yard leaving their clothes in heaps on the ground outside the hospital, and were made to wait in line along the wall of a shed on the opposite side of the prison yard. The warders who were to inflict the punishment would pass the time of waiting by practising their strokes in view of the waiting prisoners, with a cane about four feet in length. Then one by one the prisoners would enter the shed to be tied to a triangular frame and undergo their sentence. Sometimes there were screams,

sometimes there were not; but always, when the victim emerged from the shed, he would be hardly able to stand . . .

From the chief warder, who complained about being overwhelmed by pressure of numbers, Scott extracted an interesting confidence. The warder said: 'The vast majority of natives are not criminals at all. They are perfectly law-abiding natives really, but they happen to have infringed some regulation under the network of pass laws. It's not the prison you want to reform but the laws.'[13] At that time an African could be required to carry up to nine passes, ranging from 'permission to seek work out of the Reserve', through 'a night pass after 11 p.m.' to 'a residential or site permit'. Failure to produce the appropriate pass on demand by a police officer could lead rapidly to jail. Criminal convictions of non-Europeans for the pass law violations ran at around 800,000 in 1945.

During his term in prison, Scott was allowed no form of association with the non-white resisters, though he would provide a voice for all the inmates by writing a detailed memorandum on prison conditions for the Penal Reform Commission. Scott also had time to reflect on his own condition, asking of his actions: 'Was it just a futile gesture of a rather eccentric clergyman, as I was told people were saying outside, or more maliciously but no less possibly, a piece of self-righteousness and exhibitionism?' Scott's readiness to ascribe the worst motives to his own actions were, however, impeded by a strong sense of the 'rightness and logic' of what he had done, and more importantly, by an apprehension, almost amounting to a revelation, that God endorsed it. His answer to his own question, therefore, was: 'There was something infinitely greater than myself in what was being worked out and if it made me look ridiculous that didn't matter.'[14] Scott did not come out of prison a changed man, but he came out with an even stronger sense of purpose.

In what sometimes seemed like a one-man crusade over the next year, Scott was regularly portrayed as a self-righteous, egotistical exhibitionist, or by more kindly critics, as a ridiculous eccentric whistling for the moon. However, the notion that Scott actually sought this lonely eminence at the outset does not accord with the facts. The best evidence of this is a letter written to Scott many years later by Tom Comber, one of his small network of white priestly supporters, in which he said: 'I can never forget that day at Doornfontein mission house, when you invited me to go to Durban to join with the Indians and "non-violent action." I declined on the grounds that I had a parish, services to take, and sermons to preach. Fair enough. I had not your guts.'[15]

CHAPTER NINE

TOBRUK

WHEN MICHAEL SCOTT came out of prison on 23 September 1946 his reception committee consisted of two friends from his Campaign for Right and Justice days: Leon Levson, a successful Johannesburg photographer, and his wife Freda, a witty and talented writer, who published under her maiden name of Troup. After a brief conference at the prison gate, they all agreed that the first item on the agenda should be lunch, which became a gastronomic epic.

Each course at the nearby Indian restaurant would, Freda recalled, be followed by Scott's asking the waiter for repeat helpings 'with that beatific smile he knew how to turn on'. She logged Scott's overall intake as two soups with naan bread, two large fish platters, two substantial meat curries, and two puddings, before he went on to 'demolish' a large pile of sweet buns. He ate, she said: 'like a man who did not know where the next meal was coming from'.[1]

Despite Scott's abiding intestinal problem, there was probably some wisdom in this proceeding. Scott's knowledge of where the next meal was likely to put in an appearance became increasingly sketchy in the ensuing weeks, as it became apparent that Bishop Clayton was not keen to renew his employment at St Alban's, or indeed anywhere else in the diocese.

Clayton, for his part, did not see how he could allocate a situation to a priest likely to absent himself from his parish for outside political work at no – or very little – notice, particularly when the outside work constituted defiance of the law. Scott, on the other hand – now seized with the idea that the passive resistance to injustice in South African society was something that could and should involve not just him but the whole church – was not able to give any guarantees of future good behaviour likely to appease his superior. Their differences were expressed in a correspondence of rising testiness, with Scott trying to edge Clayton towards radicalism, and Clayton trying to edge Scott towards conformity, with neither having any discernible success. In the end, Scott efficiently burnt his last available boat by writing, 'difficult as it is having no means of livelihood or sphere of work recognized by the church . . . I would rather face what this may entail than submit to the misuse of authority.'[2]

There was a compromise, albeit a rather lopsided one. Although Clayton refused to allocate Scott a salaried position, he was granted a general licence that allowed him to continue to work as a priest in the diocese on a locum basis, getting paid as a freelance. In economic terms this did not amount to much. Few parish priests were ready to welcome Scott as a locum, while Scott himself narrowed his options by refusing to preach in any church that had an explicit or implicit colour bar in place, which included a high proportion of Anglican establishments. Effectively, Scott was out of work, a situation with one redeeming feature as far as his relations with the South African government were concerned: his unwaged condition meant he could no longer be deemed to owe any tax.

Aside from occasional locums and some paid articles for the press, Scott was forced to rely on his own modest savings and the generosity of friends and supporters, who fortunately were now numerous, though mainly outside the church. Among the radical element in white South African society – people like the Levsons – Scott was already being seen as a vital instrument for change. Among African leaders, like Nelson Mandela, the rising young star of the African National Congress (ANC), he was perceived as 'a great fighter for African rights',[3] while many people in the Indian community were convinced that Scott could walk on water. Few of these admirers could be deemed wealthy, but they did represent a deep reservoir of hospitality.

In Johannesburg, the Levsons provided a home for Scott's fast accumulating mass of books, pamphlets, and reports – and frequently for Scott himself. The Levson household was bookish as well as being political. Freda was born in Pretoria but educated in England, graduating from St Hugh's College, Oxford, before teaching in Cambridge for a while. She described herself as 'not churchy', and remembered Scott as a polite, if sometimes eccentric, house guest, given to the consumption of endless cups of tea along with sweets carried concealed about his person ('though he would always give you one'). He had a good sense of fun and a nice line in humour, mainly self-deprecating, often prompted by his extreme forgetfulness.[4]

He was very attractive to women, but, Freda recalled, had no special girlfriends – 'not interested, never had the time'. However, despite her testimony on this point, Scott's level of emotional immunity to the opposite sex may have been less profound than she imagined. In the final stages of the war, Scott's Crohn's complaint led to his being hospitalized under the care of Dr Loswell Braun, Head of one of the Medical Services at the Johannesburg General Hospital. Shortly before his discharge Scott made a proposal of marriage to Margaret Becklake, one of the junior house doctors on Dr Braun's team. The recipient of this proposal, who went on to become a distinguished epidemiologist, is now in her eighties. She remembers the offer – 'although deeply sincere it was probably as much of a surprise to Michael as it was to me'. She interpreted it as, 'perhaps the desperate search of a sick man for stability in a world of turmoil'. She was not his doctor but saw Scott regularly as the member of staff with responsibility for checking patients' charts and medicines. After his release from hospital they met once for tea at his rondavel at St Joseph's, where the proposition dissolved as a result of her feeling not yet ready to make a commitment. They never met again. Her impression of Scott at the time was that 'he was driven by a sense of guilt at not being a part of the fighting war against Nazism. As a result he drove himself to the very limit, physical and psychological, in an attempt to atone.'[5] Scott himself never seems to have discussed the circumstances of his proposal with any of his friends, not even with the Levsons. It seems likely that he interpreted the episode as an impulsive moment of weakness, though it is also strong evidence that some part of Scott's complicated make-up craved a more conventional existence.

Some of Freda Levson's white acquaintances thought Scott 'egotistical', though she never detected the slightest evidence of this at close range: 'he was moved to do the things he did – but not through personal publicity seeking'. But allowances, she felt, had to be made for the fact that Scott's absorption with the task in hand was such that he never kept up with people in a conventional social sense: 'When you were doing something with him, you were the best of friends, then he'd be off doing something else with another cast of best friends.' This could upset people, especially when combined with Scott's seeming unpredictability, but no offence was intended. 'Some people thought he was directed by voices, like Joan of Arc. But I always found him entirely logical, though he certainly used people.'

One of the Levsons' closest family friends – who proved most eager to be used – was George Norton, the son of a Krugersdorp baker, who worked as a missionary in Zululand. Norton was physically the opposite of Scott: small, round, and puckish. He was also a fund of jocular stories, not all of them entirely proper, which provided a cheerful complement to Scott's more reticent wavelength. When in Johannesburg, the two men took to going around together, making a duo that excited comparisons with Robin Hood and Friar Tuck.

Scott would also find himself welcome at Johannesburg's Kholvad House, where the Indian Congress maintained a flat with Ismail Meer, then a law student and later a legal adviser to Nelson Mandela, as its caretaker. Scott was given the key of the door and could always rely on being well fed by the Pahad family, who lived nearby, and who, according to Meer, 'treated him like a son'.[6] Meer also usefully acquainted Scott with a kind-hearted pawnbroker, who undertook to let him 'borrow' back any articles of value he might wish to hock.

Though a welcome guest in many quarters, Scott's quality of personal generosity, linked with absent-mindedness, could create predicaments. Arthur Blaxall, the radical priest who ran the Blind Institute at Ezenzeleni, in Roodepoort, would recall the time when Scott stayed in the small rondavel he maintained for visitors to his community. As Scott was away for several days on political business, Blaxall decided to lodge another friend in the rondavel who complained next day of having all his clothes stolen. Scott was promptly located. He explained he had decided to stay away longer than anticipated and nipped back to pick up all his clothes when no one else was about. 'Michael,' said Blaxall, 'you not only took your clothes but the clothes of my friend. Will you bring them back?' 'But I gave them all away,' said Scott.[7]

From December 1946, Scott solved his accommodation problems in an entirely unexpected but spectacular fashion by becoming South Africa's first and only white 'squatter' in a shantytown called Tobruk, outside Johannesburg. In doing so he was perfectly aware that he was breaking the law, though he was confident of scriptural authority for his civil disobedience. He would later write in *A Time to Speak* that

Jesus did not content himself with mouthing generalities about the brotherhood of man:

> He saw that the power of evil had to be challenged even if it expressed itself through the authority of the State . . . His arrest and conviction on the charges of treason and blasphemy were in accordance with the law of the land. There is surely a sense in which it is true to say that He disregarded the law, and even that He deliberately incurred the penalty of disobeying it.[8]

Of all Scott's political and religious actions in South Africa, his initiative in the first five months of 1947, which involved identifying with and sharing the lives of the country's poorest and most demeaned African inhabitants, was the one that most captured the imagination. It was, as even his enemies were bound to concede, brave almost beyond belief for a white man to go and live where heavily armed white cops in large numbers feared to tread. According to the novelist Nicholas Monsarrat, who was one of the few white people prepared to visit Scott at his new address, Tobruk 'was the most awful place I had ever seen in my life'. Monsarrat's first impression of conditions there, later related in his autobiography, *Life Is a Four-Letter Word*, was as follows:

> Most of the huts were a pitiful patchwork of corrugated iron, rusty old oil drums, planks and barrel staves; some were hessian shacks, with walls of cardboard cartons, floors of trodden cow-dung, and a leaky bucket for sanitation. The 'streets' had grown out of the tracks which criss-crossed the hillside; they were rutted, littered with refuse, and served as open drains for slow-moving sewage. Filthy goats, half-starved dogs, coal-black innocent children patrolled them in company, like some nightmare army of mixed conscripts. Over all was a corrosive smell of fouled earth and wood-smoke and excrement; and over that a choking, enveloping ochre dust, a pall which was the true pall of defeat and death.
>
> I followed Michael Scott as he made his rounds: sick at heart, proud to be with him. For there was no doubt of his stature in this terrible place; as soon as he came into sight, a crowd gathered, and the word 'Scott . . . Scott . . . Scott . . .' exploded in whispers all around us . . . Michael plodded on, up one filthy street and down another, in his

dusty cassock and cracked boots he might have been a latter-day Christ on the Mount of Olives, compassionate, wise and observant, suffering for all who suffered. But he was an angry Christ also.[9]

Scott's anger with the situation had some justification. Tobruk was one of several outlaw communities that had 'squatted' on vacant municipal land on the hills overlooking Johannesburg, eloquent evidence of the city's inability, or unpreparedness, to provide adequately for those attracted to the area by the need for work. Its name, intentionally ironic, was borrowed from the Tobruk to the far north, where the South African troops had fought bravely but had been eventually overrun in 1942 by Rommel's tanks, and many of its original inhabitants were ex-servicemen. More recently, it had provided an unofficial overspill facility for the adjacent teeming locations and townships in the Orlando area. Tobruk's 17,000 inhabitants lived beyond the law and beyond the provision of any municipal services. Those who were not sick on arrival rapidly became disease-prone in an area without any water, other than supplies physically lugged from outside locations. On the highest political level, the city and central government spent much time and effort blaming each other for a housing situation that had spiralled out of any semblance of control.

Scott's introduction to Tobruk came via the African section of the Springbok Legion, a radical group that originated in South Africa's wartime army, and which maintained close links with the African Mineworkers' Union and the Communist Party. The Legion was persuaded that the unofficial form of law and order in Tobruk was breaking down and in need of repair, and that the city authorities needed to be more urgently alerted to the dire conditions there. Scott undertook this ambitious assignment for a secular stipend of thirty shillings a week. Once again, he was embarked on an enterprise that would enjoy Communist support, but this time he was very much alone, which probably enhanced his effectiveness.

At first, it was thought Scott would work with Samuel Komo, a Zulu and ex-soldier, who ran Tobruk's unofficial 'administration' with the assistance of a fraternity of 'guards' and 'police'. Scott went to live in Komo's 'yard' but their relationship soon foundered. Komo and his men, it appeared to Scott, were essentially part of the problem not the solution. There would soon be disagreements over the methods used by Komo's 'police' to collect 'subscriptions' for practically non-existent services, like refuse collection and security. To Scott it seemed akin to extortion, verging on gangsterism. He was also unimpressed by the brisk trade, which seemed to be sanctioned by the camp's leadership, in 'Ethiopian passports' – documents in which the Lion of Judah declared that This His Beloved Subject was exempt from South African pass laws. These bogus documents, like medieval indulgences, were not cheap, retailing at five shillings apiece. In *A Time to Speak*, Scott reported:

> I was asked to convey a demand for a constitution and a proper system of accounting. This demand was at first met with sullen acquiescence, but the same night an ominous sound was heard. The Zulu war cry, with its rhythmic cadences, is unmistakable. Louder it grew as motor-lorries containing bands of Zulu braves approached the camp. They were uncontested by the camp guards and, stamping the ground and beating their drums and clashing sticks with one another, they danced down the main street and took up their position in the square, challenging all who were disloyal to the chief (Komo) to fight it out. No one took up the challenge; but the next night, when the visitors had retired to their own camp again, the chief's hut was surrounded and only my last-minute intervention saved him from a severe thrashing.[10]

Komo left Tobruk but kept dissension alive from a neighbouring township. In the brief power vacuum a new camp committee was created with Scott as its temporary chairman, and more orderly procedures were instituted for the accounts and the provision of rudimentary services. Scott also started a school. Then Komo returned. This time it was Scott who beat a strategic retreat, but only a short distance away to the insecure precincts of the Congregational Church of Christ, run by a more pacific Zulu called Theophilus Mtembu. Scott shared one all-purpose living room with Mtembu, his wife, and many children, and a brown-and-white chicken tethered to a table leg. His sleeping arrangement was a flapping sackcloth shelter, attached to the sackcloth church.

With Scott and Komo at loggerheads over Tobruk's governance, things became progressively more unpleasant. Scott's school was disbanded by an emboldened Komo, who had one of its teachers marched away in handcuffs by his 'police'. Not long afterwards, it was only Mtembu's physical intervention that saved Scott from being clubbed to death with an iron bar, wielded by an unknown assailant lurking at the door of the church. Then other persons unknown torched the Congregational Church of Christ, which, along with Scott's personal shelter, burnt rapidly to the ground.

Scott and Mtembu were able to find creative refuge in nearby Orlando West, where Nelson Mandela lived with his first wife Evelyn and their baby son in more fireproof circumstances in a house equipped with a cement floor and a tin roof. Their visit made a substantial impression on arrangements in the Mandela household, which Mandela would later describe in *Long Walk to Freedom*:

> Our house was tiny and Scott slept in the sitting room, Dlamini [Mandela's name for Mtembu] and his wife slept in another room and we put all the children in the kitchen. Michael Scott was a modest, unassuming man, but Dlamini was a bit hard to take. At mealtimes he would complain about the food. 'Look here,' he would say, 'this meat of yours, it's very lean and hard, not properly cooked at all. I am not used to meals like this.' Scott was appalled by this, and admonished Dlamini but Dlamini took no heed. The next night he might say, 'Well, this is a bit better than yesterday, but far from well prepared. Mandela, you know, your wife just can't cook.'
>
> Dlamini indirectly caused the situation to be resolved, because I was so eager to have him out of the house that I went to the squatter camp myself and explained that Scott was a true friend of theirs, unlike Komo, and that they should choose between the two. They then organized an election in which Scott triumphed and he moved back to the squatter camp taking Father Dlamini with him.[11]

Scott's troubles with Komo and his gang was only one aspect of his problems. On 13 February 1947 he was summoned to appear in court to answer the unwieldy charge of being in breach of regulations prohibiting residence in a location or native village without the permission of the Minster of Native Affairs, with the concurrence of the Johannesburg City Council. At this point Scott was struggling to contain an outbreak of smallpox in Tobruk, and trying, against the opposition of several local witch doctors, to establish a vaccination programme. Scott's new-found friend George Norton was alerted to this crisis, and managed to persuade the court that Scott's continued presence in Tobruk was essential on public health grounds. The case was adjourned, but reactivated as soon as the smallpox outbreak was brought under control. On 25 March, Scotti, listed as being 'of no fixed abode', was convicted under Section 9(8) of the Native Urban Areas Act and received a suspended sentence of a £5 fine or fourteen days in prison. Scott immediately lodged an appeal and returned to Tobruk.

Evidently alarmed by Scott's increasingly dangerous circumstances, Bishop Clayton wrote to him in April expressing some sympathy and making a proposition: 'I recognize that you are living in Tobruk shantytown because you believe that your duty lies there and I cannot but admire your courage . . . Tobruk obviously cannot last for much longer. I understand that your financial resources are nearly at an end. I have no right to meddle in your private concerns . . .' Clayton, nonetheless, offered 'financial help' to facilitate Scott's prompt return to England, concluding with the sentiment: 'I should have thought that for your own sake it was most desirable that you should have a period during which you would not be the centre of public interest.'[12]

Clayton was right in assuming Tobruk could not last much longer, as the Johannesburg city fathers were now gearing up a massive operation to close it down and remove its inhabitants to the new township of Moroka. He was wrong, however, in assuming that Scott was looking for a way out, though most of his savings had indeed expired as a consequence of having to find £100 out of his own pocket to finance a squad of emergency sanitation ditch-diggers during the smallpox outbreak.

Scott's objective in making conditions in Tobruk more widely known was handsomely achieved, but inevitably through the medium of making himself much more widely known. The image of a lone white priest championing the interest of the most downtrodden blacks was manna to the journalistic trade. Without Scott, Tobruk was just another story about one of many catastrophically poor communities in South Africa. With Scott there was human drama writ large, and of course the opportunity to take pictures excellently suited to the black and white newspapers and magazines of the day. One of the most effective picture displays featuring Scott's efforts in Tobruk appeared in the influential American magazine *Ebony*.

Closer to home both the *Sunday Express* and the *Rand Daily Mail* ran prominent articles devoted to the same subject matter, as did *Inkululeko*, the Zulu newspaper.[13] *Inkululeko*'s comment, in April 1947, on the official efforts to evict Scott was:

No wonder this man of high Christian principle must be debarred from living in Tobruk shanty-town. His Christian faith is too strong for the city council which, despite its 'Christian' protestations, believes not in brotherhood of the many but in slavery for Africans. Were there more such as he, we would have less quarrel with the church in this country.

A group of Johannesburg journalists, aware of Scott's fondness for a substantial curry lunch, entertained him at intervals at the city restaurant 'The East African', emerging afterwards with the satisfied look of reporters who had been fed 'good copy'. Scott also became adroit at prompting interest in Britain, supplementing the work of the news agencies by sending his own reports direct to the *News Chronicle*, *Manchester Guardian*, and the *New Statesman*. Scott also used a movie camera, one of his last and most prized possessions of any value, to some effect. Later, combined with film from other sources, his Tobruk footage would feature in a documentary entitled *Civilization on Trial in South Africa*.[14]

In correspondence with his parents, Scott would tell them not to worry. This injunction, however, given the public news about his activities and whereabouts, was not always efficacious as Mrs Scott's letter to her son, dated 29 April 1947, indicates:

You say don't worry and I do try very hard indeed not to and to remember you are in Our Father's hands, but I am only human and I love you so much it's very difficult – but perhaps this is just a little bit of the Cross I am allowed to bear. I keep thinking of Our Lady and how her dear son said to her 'Wist ye not that I should be about my Father's business.' That is what you are doing my most beloved boy. I wish I knew if you had been put in prison again. I do hope not though I suppose even that would be better than that awful slum.[15]

While Scott could be confident his work in the shantytown was publicly clarifying the secular issues that divided South African society, his private relationship with his own church became even more confused. In Tobruk he assisted in the affairs of Mtembu's nonconformist church, offering prayers for the dead: mainly babies who expired at a rate of one a day, helping to maintain South Africa's unenviable record for abnormally high infant mortality. But he was also involved with a small group of Anglicans who were among the most reliable helpers in his organization of a general welfare programme. Keen to reward their support, Scott wanted to celebrate Holy Communion with them, but felt he needed the permission of his bishop. Clayton replied to Scott's request on 28 April, saying that he had discussed the matter with the priest-in-charge of the Orlando area, who happened to be Trevor Huddleston, and that 'He [Huddleston] is not willing that you should celebrate Holy Communion in Tobruk shantytown.'[16]

Scott, it appeared, had inadvertently put Huddleston on the spot. Despite their political differences, the two men were now very close. For some time past Huddleston had formally acted as Scott's 'confessor', the priest Scott went to as a penitent for counsel and absolution. Even so, Huddleston had responsibilities that made it difficult for him to give sympathetic consideration to Scott's request. Father Hunter, who was the minister at the Holy Cross church, just outside Tobruk, was opposed to any rival ministry taking shape in the actual shantytown, reasoning that Tobruk's Anglicans could walk to his church. As the man in overall charge, Huddleston made what seemed at the time like the most feasible bureaucratic decision, siding with the incumbent Hunter against the freelance Scott.

This was not a major event in church history, or even in that of Tobruk, but it did have historical significance in that it led to the longest exchange of private correspondence between Scott and Huddleston on an issue that touched them both deeply. In many histories of South Africa the names of Michael Scott and Trevor Huddleston are yoked together, as being among the few white churchmen accepted as 'honorary blacks' by the African people. There is some logic in this, as both men came to be seen as not merely supporting African causes but as specifically identifying themselves with their struggle – Scott through passive resistance and his work in Tobruk, Huddleston through his opposition to the racist Bantu Education Act and his campaign against the forced removal of the black population from Sophiatown. However, the original distance between their perceptions of a Christian's duty in an unjust society was wide indeed, as their correspondence shows. On 18 May, Scott, still smarting at the decision preventing the celebration of Holy Communion in Tobruk, wrote to Huddleston:

> It does seem to me that there is a lack of understanding of the real significance of Tobruk and of what I was trying to do there. I cannot reconcile myself to your point of view in forbidding me to minister to the people there in the camp. I don't think you appreciate how deeply I feel about the whole matter . . . I am of the opinion that you yourself have been misled by the expression of opinion of others [This was a thinly veiled reference to Bishop Clayton and his entourage]. There is obviously a very fundamental difference of outlook and I do not see how I can bring myself to submit to what appears to me to be a misuse of authority and discipline . . . I must thank you for all the help you have given me in the past but I am afraid at the risk of hurting your feelings I must look elsewhere for counsel and absolution.

Huddleston wrote back on the following day in terms that suggested he was more concerned with Scott's mental and spiritual balance, than with any details of their disagreement:

> My dear Michael, Thank you for your letter. I am not in the least hurt that you should wish to go elsewhere for your spiritual direction, but I am deeply sorry and distressed that you should feel yourself so misunderstood.
>
> As you have written so frankly I propose to do the same, trusting you to accept what I say in all charity.
>
> 1. You seem to have reached the stage where every issue which affects you is seen as some fresh occasion for 'persecution.' This is a very dangerous state of mind to be in, and it is wholly unjustified by anything that the Bishop or others in the Church have said or done. I say this without qualification for I believe it to be true.
>
> 2. Although you seek counsel and advice from others, the ultimate authority in every case is the forum of your own conscience. This I believe to be contrary to true Christian experience within the church. 'He learnt obedience by the things which he suffered.' But you rebel against any kind of obedience which seems to conflict with your own 'conscientious' ideas. You talk about 'a misuse of authority and

discipline' – but on your part you do not appear to be ready to live under any authority or discipline except your own . . . Surely, surely you should at least consider whether you may not be wrong in some respects, and not simply say that you are being misunderstood.

I am absolutely convinced that for your own soul's sake you must get away from all this intense living on a crisis, and that you must make a decision about your future and abide by it. At the risk of everything you should take the path of obedience for a while – obedience that is, to authority outside yourself: you should take 'the hidden life' and absolutely forswear the glare of publicity (which is not sought deliberately, I am sure, but is nonetheless damaging for that): above all you should devote yourself to one job for a considerable time.

These may seem very hard words. I cannot help it. I would be untrue to myself if I did not say what I think. I am not questioning your sincerity or courage for a moment. In these I lag far, far behind you. But I write this because I truly love you and would do anything in my power to help you. Yours affectionately, Trevor Huddleston CR.

There was nothing remotely feigned about Huddleston's concern for Scott's welfare, but his letter's avoidance of any specifics about the role of the Church in South Africa almost ensured that it would miss its mark. After three weeks of silence, Huddleston wrote again saying, 'I suspect that you are angry with me for my last letter to you but I should be very sad to feel that you did not wish to have anything more to do with me on account of it.' He urged Scott to let him know how he was feeling and what he was planning to do. Scott replied on 20 June:

My Dear Father, No, I am not angry with you at all. That would be very silly . . . But you should not deceive yourself that I am suffering from a persecution complex . . . You hold an official position. You are responsible to an institution and a community. Your actions and even your outlook is influenced by your responsibilities and loyalties you have chosen. Some of these are not always compatible in the extremely sordid system of social and economic and moral arrangements which obtain in our time and age. That is why we are propelled hither and thither and even find ourselves moving in opposite directions perhaps.

These are some of the reasons why I have still great hesitancy about joining a [religious] community. I think they tend to take possession of people and the conflict of loyalties sometimes obscures certain things which have to be known and understood and acted upon . . . I must follow the indication that God gives me. I hope one day this may bring us closer together again.[17]

No precise indication of Scott's intentions was mentioned. But in the aftermath of Tobruk, Scott lost very little time before venturing into another lion's den, though of a somewhat different sort.

Although Scott's church could find no particular use for him beyond facilitating his entry into the political purdah of a monastic order or equipping him with a one-way ticket back to England, there was a rising clamour for his services by an ever-widening circle of secular acquaintances. There was no man in South Africa it seemed better at 'highlighting' an issue. With this in mind, the left-wing *Guardian* newspaper directed Scott's attention to the Bethal area of the Eastern Transvaal, long notorious for its grotesque labour conditions. Bethal provided a reasonable illustration of what was meant by black Africa's ironic condensation of its history, which ran along the lines, 'The white man had the Bible and we had the land, now we have the Bible and the white man has the land.' In fact, the white settlers retained a firm grip on the Bible as well, but their reading of it, through the medium of the Dutch Reformed Church, managed to confirm their notions of divinely sanctioned racial superiority.

Bethal was the centre of an extensive farming area producing maize and potatoes. The farmers were white, principally Afrikaner, while their labourers were almost uniformly black, many of them immigrants from Nyasaland hoping to make it to the big money city of Johannesburg. A significant number of farmers solved their labour problems by 'recruiting' immigrants in the border area with what were effectively press-gang methods. The 'recruits' would then be required to work all hours of the day, for exiguous pay, and live in conditions resembling those in prison. During their non-working hours they were kept in compounds, frequently locked in, and poorly fed. Floggings, beatings, and killings of those trying to escape were common.

Scott went to Bethal, accompanied by Ruth First, a bright young *Guardian* reporter, and found conditions there even worse than he had been led to believe. In one compound, he wrote, 'there were three or four mattresses amongst about fifty men, and no blankets . . . Many had no boots . . . All maintained that they were very roughly treated by the foremen, . . . were always being cursed at, and very frequently beaten with sjamboks.'[18] It was a similar story in other compounds, and Scott's memorandum on his visit, suggesting 'near to slavery' conditions, was taken up and published, in edited form, by the influential *Rand Daily Mail*. The newspaper followed up Scott's disclosures on 28 June 1947 with a powerful editorial indicting the area's 'rule of the sjambok', which seemed to have displaced the rule of law. In Bethal there was outrage and uproar. There was also some perturbation in the government, anxious to stay on-side with the powerful white farmers' voting bloc and keen to present a national image of civilized standards to the United Nations, which had recently opened for business in New York.

In an overheated atmosphere, Scott's restrained and painstakingly factual memorandum began to appear like a gross slur on the national character. The white farmers' union in Bethal brought matters to a head by requesting Scott's attendance at a public meeting, where he could be questioned about his findings. To the alarm of Scott's friends he accepted the invitation, knowing that his reception would at best be hostile. To the angry farmers, Scott – as a man who had not only eaten with but gone to live with 'natives' – was an object of profound disgust, regardless of his views on agricultural labour relations.

Scott's meeting with the farmers in Bethal Town Hall on the evening of 9 July was short but exceptionally nasty. The account of the occasion in the next day's *Johannesburg Star* ran under the three-deck headline: 'Pandemonium Reigns When Reverend Michael Scott Tries to Address Farmers'. It reported:

As Mr Scott rose to speak shouts and boos came from every part of the crowded hall. One man rose and appealed to the meeting to allow Mr Scott to speak, 'Don't be afraid, let him speak, we can fix him later,' he shouted.

'We won't let him speak,' shouted back the crowd, 'Let him go to his coolies.'

Mr Smit [President of the Bethal branch of the Agricultural Union, who chaired the meeting] assured the audience that Mr Scott had promised not to be long, and pleaded with them to let him have his say. 'Not a word,' shouted the crowd.

A suggestion was made that the meeting should vote on whether Mr Scott should be allowed to speak. A man in the crowd called out: 'Let him speak in Afrikaans or not at all.'

'If he can't speak in Afrikaans let him speak in Kaffir,' called another voice, and another added a few moments later: 'Or in coolie.'

Some of Scott's prepared address did get delivered, though little of it could be heard above the baying and catcalling.[19] He never did manage to reach his conclusion, based on his research into the Ministry of Agriculture's official regulations, that dairy cows were far better protected by law in terms of living space and sustenance than were compound labourers. Before this insight could be imparted, the meeting had effectively been taken over by an Afrikaner woman in the audience who virulently insisted Scott had insulted Afrikaner motherhood, her own three sons, and the entire nation. While this tirade was being uttered there were demands for Scott to stand up while the lady was speaking, which he sensibly did. The mood was unsubtly changing from nasty to ugly. Obviously fearing a riot, or something worse, Scott was urgently detached from the proceeding by a police officer and led out through a side door into the street where a high-powered police car was waiting with its engine running, ready to whisk him away.

Once again, Scott was making banner headlines in a way that horrified Clayton and the as yet unradicalized Huddleston, but this time he did find a measure of church support. Although some African clergy were privately supportive of the ANC, their stance in public tended to be one of watchfully preserved neutrality on political issues. Paid much less than their white clerical brethren, they were not encouraged to entertain ideas far above their station or to thrust their heads above any parapets. Scott was, therefore, particularly pleased to encounter, among the letters of commendation for his efforts, one from the Interdenominational African Ministers' Association, expressing, 'appreciation of the unique courage you are having of championing our African people in the Bethal area'.

Though given to self-criticism, Scott does not appear to have been much affected by the reservations about his conduct expressed by Clayton and Huddleston. This was not because he was now, just turned forty, suddenly possessed of a profound lust for personal publicity:

though, unlike his church superiors, he saw it as potentially useful.

Scott's robustness at this time was almost certainly due to his finding full expression for the key elements in his complicated make-up – his detestation of man-made suffering, his independence of mind, his Christian belief, and his not inconsiderable cunning. And while he could be described as a man without any discernible career prospects, he was also a man who was now thoroughly confident of his path, which in his case was more important.

Subsequently, when the accumulating injustices in the South African system persuaded Trevor Huddleston to follow much the same path, Scott's former 'confessor' was generous in his own repentance. Almost ten years later, in his best-selling book, *Naught for Your Comfort*, Huddleston wrote of his early contacts with Scott: 'To my shame, I did very little to help him. Somehow it took me a long while to wake up, and it is good to be able to apologize publicly now for an apathy I cannot excuse.'[20]

There may, however, have been one aspect of Huddleston's original criticism of Scott that touched a nerve. This was the suggestion that Scott needed to devote himself 'to one job for a considerable time'. There was no denying the episodic nature of Scott's progress to date. He was a brilliant illuminator of areas of cruelty and injustice, but there was a question mark over his powers of commitment to any single cause. At the root of many of his problems with his white colleagues in the Church was their sense of being in it for the long haul, while Scott seemed to be passing through, leaving them to pick up the pieces after his inspired disruptions. Even Scott's secular friends tended to see him in the role of creative maverick rather than of an enduring ally.

Only time could prove that Scott did indeed have quite remarkable powers of endurance and tenacity of purpose, but an opportunity was afforded by the turbulent events of 1947, when, to use Scott's own words, he became 'the straw at which desperate people clutched'. The most desperate of all were a tribe called the Hereros, which wanted Scott to redress the effects of a colonial history of unparalleled brutality. By taking them on, Scott acquired one job, among many others, not just for the 'considerable time' recommended by Huddleston, but effectively for life.

CHAPTER TEN

THE HERERO
CONNECTION

ONE OF THE principal aims of South African government policy after the war was a massive expansion of its frontiers by annexing the territory of what is now Namibia, then known as South-West Africa. Scantily populated and thought – correctly as it turned out – to have huge untapped riches in terms of natural resources, it was seen as ripe for the taking. The reason why South Africa never did manage to achieve this aim is explained by the complex interaction between an impoverished tribe called the Hereros, the Reverend Michael Scott, and a fledgling United Nations. In later years the phenomenon of 'world opinion' being invoked through the UN against South Africa's racial policies became commonplace, but it was Scott who was among the first to mobilise it in pursuit of a specific cause. Scott's white supremacist critics would suggest he had opportunistically sought out and exploited the Herero issue as a way of discrediting the Union in the eyes of the world. All the evidence, however, indicates that it was the Hereros who originally found Scott and chose him to represent their cause, though, as a matter of necessity, it was by one of history's more circuitous routes.

Of all the tribes in Africa, the Hereros could be said to have suffered most from the white man's scramble for possessions on the continent. A proud and independent cattle-droving people accustomed to ranging wide with their herds, they were soon at odds with the German settlers who came in the late nineteenth century to establish themselves on tribal land reclassified as part of Germany's imperial empire. It is sometimes suggested that racism was an unintended by-product of imperialism, which in many instances may have been true. But Germany, possibly because it came late into the colonial business, was in many ways more clear-sighted about its fundamental nature. Paul Rohrbach of the German Colonial Office, writing shortly before the turn of the century, would convey its racist aspect in terms that could hardly be bettered by the architect of the Third Reich. Thus:

> The decision to colonize in South-West Africa could after all mean nothing else but this; namely, that the native tribes would have to give up their land on which they had previously grazed their stock in order that the white man might have the land for the grazing of his stock.
>
> When this attitude is questioned from the moral law standpoint, the answer is that for nations of the *kultur* position of the South African natives the loss of their free national barbarism, and their development into a class of labourers in service of and dependent on the White people, is primarily a law of existence in the highest degree. By no argument whatsoever can it be shown that the preservation of any degree of national independence, national property, and political organization, by the races of South-West Africa would be of a greater or even of an equal advantage for the development of mankind in general, or of the German people in particular, than the making of such races serviceable in the enjoyment of their former possessions by the White race.[1]

Armed with a philosophy that allowed them to loot, oppress, and subjugate for the 'development of mankind in general', the German settlers were among the more aggressive colonists, but they were in no way exceptional. What was exceptional was the degree of resistance encountered even among tribesmen schooled in Christian notions of eternally turning the other cheek. To the Hereros, and other tribes in the area, Europe's 'civilizing mission' seemed to consist mainly of land seizure as a preliminary to forcing people into uncongenial work down the mines and on settlers' farms, supplemented by forms of justice that verged on lynch law.

In 1904 the Hereros led a rebellion that was put down with terrifying ferocity. German troops, under the command of General Lothar von Trotha, were licensed to kill indiscriminately. Trotha's infamous Extermination Order, which dictated the terms of the massacre, ran:

> I, the great general of the German troops, send this letter to the Herero People. Hereros are no longer German subjects . . . All the

Hereros must leave the land. If the people do not do this, then I will force them to do it with great guns. Any Herero found within the German borders with or without a gun, with or without cattle, will be shot. I shall no longer receive any women or children; I will drive them back to their people or I will shoot them. This is my decision for the Herero people.

The Great General of the Mighty Kaiser.[2]

Trotha's principal military accomplishment had been to encircle the Hereros in a way that forced them to flee with their families eastwards into the barren wastes of the Kalahari desert, sealing off all waterholes against their possible return. In addition to those killed in action, almost half the tribe died of hunger and thirst in the desert. And the momentum of extermination was still relentlessly maintained. In his classic history, *The Scramble for Africa*, Thomas Pakenham records, 'for months German patrols encountered the remnants trying to break back to the west [out of the desert], walking skeletons to be shot and bayoneted as a matter of course.'[3]

Before the rebellion, the Herero population was 80,000. By its close there were around 15,000 in South-West Africa, many in prison labour camps where almost half died in captivity. Some 5000 Hereros miraculously survived the ordeal in the desert to find refuge in the British Protectorate of Bechuanaland. In 1905 Trotha's achievement in wiping out three-quarters of one of Africa's most spirited tribes in what must rank as the most brutally degrading episode in African colonial history was duly recognized by the Kaiser, who awarded the general the Order of Merit for devotion to the Fatherland.

The surviving Hereros were understandably not displeased with the outcome of the First World War, when Germany, as a consequence of its defeat, was stripped of its colonies. Genuine hopes of restoration of Herero lands were entertained when South-West Africa was accorded the status of a Mandated Territory by the newly formed League of Nations, which was supposed to usher in a new era of international concern. Original responsibility for the territory's mandate was vested in His Britannic Majesty George V. Article 22 of the League explicitly stated that the well-being and development of peoples 'not yet able to stand by themselves in the strenuous conditions of the modern world' should be 'a sacred trust of civilization'.[4]

These fine words, however, were undermined by Britain's decision to entrust the administration of South-West Africa to its next-door neighbour, the Union of South Africa, then a British dominion. When South Africa took over administration of the mandate, German settlers were allowed to retain their property, while past promises concerning the restoration of tribal lands were conveniently forgotten. In 1925 the Union forced the Hereros out of some of the few areas which the German administration had left them. They felt they had no choice about moving on. In an earlier, more famous engagement, bombs were dropped on the Hereros' neighbours to the south, the Namas, to put down what was called the Bondelswart 'uprising', which grew out of a dispute over territorial boundaries and payment of a tax of £1 a dog. With the native population efficiently reminded of the power at the disposal of those administering 'the sacred trust', South-West Africa was developed along lines that paralleled those of its more muscular neighbour, with a colour bar, vestigial African rights, and an indigenous population being shunted around to suit the convenience of new waves of white settlers from across the border.

By 1947 the Hereros had their movements, and those of their cattle, restricted to eight 'reserve' locations. These were widely scattered districts assigned for native occupation between the vast tracts commanded by the white settler farms, devoted principally to sheep. From the Herero standpoint, the experience of being governed as part of a Mandated Territory scarcely surpassed the overt colonization that had preceded it. Far from dismantling old injustices, it had effectively compounded them, making the prospect of any redress more remote than ever. They were appalled at the idea that South Africa should, in effect, have its maladministration rewarded by outright possession of their country. There also did not seem to be very much they could do about it, until the appearance of Michael Scott.

While the South African diplomats at the United Nations in New York were trying to establish their country's right to a free rein in South-West Africa, Scott was receiving his first Herero history lesson in Serowe, Bechuanaland, where he was a guest of Tshekedi Khama, the Regent of the Bamangwato tribe. After a few days of social niceties, Scott discovered the real purpose of his invitation. Tshekedi Khama, Scott later recalled, spoke as follows:

> We have some people here; they've been here ever since I was a small boy. I remember them arriving from across the desert and my mother being deeply distressed because of their utterly starving condition, barely able to crawl. She'd told me how they had been treated by the Germans. It is one of the most vivid recollections of my life. My father gave them some land and they've been with us ever since. And now they want to come and see you.[5]

Among the Hereros who came to see Scott was the tribe's elderly Paramount Chief Frederick Mahareru, whose life in exile was dictated by the tradition which held that a tribe with its chief still at liberty could not be considered defeated. Mahareru produced copious recent correspondence from Herero leaders in the reserves inside South-West Africa, expressing desperation at the prospect of their becoming South African subjects. One such letter read: 'The heritage of your father's orphans is about to be taken from them; and because we cannot speak with one voice, as we are scattered all over the country, our heritage may therefore fall to that side for which we have no liking. '[6]

As their conversations developed, it became apparent that Scott was being perceived as the 'one voice' that could make a difference. Tshekedi Khama's motives in bringing together Scott and the Herero issue were not entirely disinterested. For some time past, Tshekedi had been recognized as one of the most forceful and adroit black politicians in southern Africa. Pre-war he had caused an international incident by ordering the flogging of a dissolute white man who had persistently molested black women. Deposed from office by the British, he was rapidly reinstated as a result of a popular consensus, even among whites, that in this instance the proposed punishment fitted the crime. Despite his pugnacious record, Tshekedi was seen as being an enlightened leader by British officials in the territory, and outside Bechuanaland as a champion of black rights by politically active Africans. Tshekedi, nonetheless, exercised his authority with a sense of being politically on a knife-edge.

Bechuanaland, like the two other Protectorates sharing frontiers with South Africa, Basutoland and Swaziland, was a High Commission territory administered directly by the British government. Historically, they had never been conquered, having been ceded voluntarily to Britain by their tribal chiefs seeking protection from Afrikaner invaders. To a large degree tribal structures had been maintained intact, and Africans in the Protectorates, though poor, enjoyed a much higher level of liberty and responsibility than their repressed brethren inside South Africa. The government of South Africa made no secret of the fact it was keen to absorb these territories into its own frontiers. Indeed, such a development had been envisaged as a possibility in the Schedule to the South Africa Act of 1909.

Tshekedi was conscious of being confronted with an early form of 'domino theory' – if South-West Africa was allowed to disappear into the maw of South Africa, the Protectorates were unlikely to be far behind, as maintenance of their status could scarcely be ranked among Britain's top imperial priorities. Impressed by Scott's efforts in Tobruk, Tshekedi felt he might be the man who could prevent the toppling of the first domino by championing the Hereros.

In Johannesburg some of Scott's sophisticated liberal acquaintances were at first surprised by what seemed like a new excursion into the complexities of tribal politics. But as the issues became clear, there was much good-humoured rallying around, some of it expressed in verses composed by Freda Levson and two of Scott's missionary doctor friends, Anthony and Margaret Barker:

> Michaelis Scotius, Anglican
> By the Four Freedoms swore
> That the House of Mahareru
> Should suffer wrong no more.
> By UNO he swore it,
> His cassock hitching up.
> He begged forgiveness for his sins
> And stuffed his rucksack full of tins,
> Two billycans, one cup.
>
> He waved Tot Siens to Bethel,
> Sala Kahle to Tobruk,

Farewell and Hail to Durban Gaol,
His friends and home forsook.
He bought a 3rd class ticket
South-westward turned his face
To gather facts and evil acts
Before the world to place.[7]

The third-class ticket took Scott to Windhoek, the capital of South-West Africa. He went there, shortly after his meeting with Tshekedi and Chief Mahareru in Serowe, with a view to detailing the Hereros' grievances, if possible in the form of a petition that could be presented to the United Nations. He was met by a group of young Herero activists, the Red Band, and equipped with a guide, Berthold Himumuine, a student teacher who became Scott's interpreter. Satisfied that Scott was a messenger from the exiled Chief Mahareru, the Red Band agreed to take him to meet the most senior Herero chief in the Territory, Hosea Kutako, then living in the Aminuis Reserve.

To go to the reserve, Scott needed a permit issued by the Native Commissioner. The issue of this permit would later become a cause célèbre when Scott's campaign on behalf of the Hereros went public, with the South African authorities insinuating that it had been obtained by trickery or stealth. There were some modest grounds for this insinuation. Scott, in conversation with the journalist Cyril Dunn, would later acknowledge: 'I didn't tell him [the Commissioner] exactly why I wanted to go. I just said I'd seen the Hereros in Bechuanaland and thought it would be interesting to meet their relatives. I said the Hereros in Bechuanaland had thoughts about coming back to South-West Africa and I was interested to learn what the South-West Hereros thought.' Neither at the time, nor later, did Scott feel any significant guilt about this deception. As he also told Cyril Dunn, 'in this contest with South Africa everything was so heavily weighted against us I felt we were entitled to take any advantage we could. It is surprising how many people do allow the South Africans to lay down the law about what is right or wrong. They are the usurpers.'[8]

After a long, bone-shaking lorry drive through the bush, Scott arrived at Chief Hosea Kutako's kraal in Aminuis around midnight, and was initially taken for a white trader who had lost his way. He would recall, 'As this was explained to Hosea his first look of incredulity slowly gave way to an expression which perhaps I will never be privileged to see again.'⁹ With his mission fully understood, there was almost instantaneous rapport between Scott and Kutako, who had trained for the Lutheran priesthood before he became a tribal leader. Kutako told Scott he had already approached the Territory's South African Administrator, requesting permission to send Herero spokesmen to the UN, or alternatively, leave for the UN to send a Commission to conduct its own referendum in South-West Africa. He had been bluntly told, on both counts, that as the Hereros had no government they could have no recourse to the United Nations.

The issue of a referendum was important. According to the official South African delegation at the UN, the Territory's native 300,000 inhabitants and 38,000 whites favoured incorporation in the Union. This was claimed on the authority of an alleged referendum conducted shortly after the war. From Kutako, Scott learned at first hand that this exercise had little to do with democratic process, but was essentially a manipulated poll of tribal headmen who were for the most part employees of the administration, dependant on its favours, and with no real grasp of any alternative. No attempt was made by the 'polling' authorities to outline the malign effect on land rights likely to be produced by full alignment with the Union's system of land laws. The chiefs were also given the firm assurance, which some considered decisive, that incorporation would not 'remove them from the shadow of King George of England', though it could now be seen that such an assurance had no validity, when the South African opposition party – soon to be the Nationalist government – had declared republican aims. Even one of the Native Commissioners involved in this exercise described it as 'an absolute farce'. The Hereros had made their profound distrust of the enterprise known at the time, and other tribes in the Territory – the Namas, the Berg Damaras, and many of the Ovambos – had since come to share their view.

With the help of his interpreter, Scott took detailed statements covering the range of Herero grievances and 'the fraud' of the referendum, before journeying back across the Kalahari to Serowe, where the actual Herero petition was finally drafted in consultation with Tshekedi Khama and Chief Mahareru. It called for the return of lands, reunification of the tribe within one tribal area, and re-establishment of their tribal organization.[10] In August 1947 Scott made a second visit to the Territory for the witnessing and signing of the petition by the Herero chiefs and fifty leading members of the tribe. Because of restrictions on movement, signing took place at three locations: Windhoek, Okahandja and Gobabis. Scott also received supporting statements from the Nama people, led by David Witbooi, from the Berg Damaras, and from leaders of the Windhoek Ovambos. To avoid problems with the permit-issuing authorities, Scott pitched his tent outside the perimeter of the actual locations, making his visit, technically at least, within legal bounds.

The signing of the petition in Okahandja was a solemn, ceremonial occasion, which Scott recorded on film. Chief Kutako's extempore prayer, as he stood, hat in hand, by the graves of his ancestors, became part of Scott's submission to the UN, and much quoted in his statements and sermons thereafter:

> You are the Great God of all the Earth and the Heavens. We are so insignificant. In us there are many defects. But the Power is yours to make and to do what we cannot do. You know all about us. For coming down to earth you were despised, and mocked, and brutally treated because of those same defects in the men of those days. And for those men you prayed because they did not understand what they were doing, and that you came only for what is right. Give us the courage to struggle in that way for what is right.
>
> O Lord, help us who roam about. Help us who have been placed in Africa and have no dwelling place of our own. Give us back a dwelling place. O God, all power is Yours in Heaven and Earth. Amen.[11]

Scott's formal commission from Chief Kutako was to take the Herero petition, with the supporting documents, to the United Nations and, additionally, to make the Hereros' views known to the British government, which seemed resolved not to offend South Africa in any way. Expenses for the trip were assembled in the form of contributions from the Hereros, which were necessarily nominal, and by an airfare provided by the Council of Human Rights in Durban and the Council of Asiatic Rights in Johannesburg. In addition to representing the Hereros, Scott also planned to publicize the plight of the Indian minority in Durban, many of whom were still serving prison sentences as a result of the passive resistance campaign. Scott also informed Bishop Clayton of his plans to go overseas, if only temporarily, and was rewarded with a useful and not ungenerous letter to present to prospective contacts in New York:

> This is to introduce you to the Reverend Michael Scott . . . a priest of good standing in the Diocese who has resigned his pastoral charge in order to devote himself entirely to non-European interests throughout South Africa. He does not go to America as the representative of the Church: he is acting on his own responsibility: but he has the respect and goodwill of many churchmen as a man of great courage and initiative.[12]

Scott's original plan was to be at the UN in time for the start of its second General Assembly in late September, but he found himself kicking his heels in Johannesburg for six weeks waiting for a United States visa that never arrived. Scott suspected his application had encountered some obstruction at an official level, and he was not wrong. Many years later, when US official documents were declassified under the Freedom of Information Act, it showed that on the basis of reports from Johannesburg, Washington already had Scott listed as 'a troublemaker'. This listing was accompanied by a Justice Department note on his file making the dismissive point, 'There will always be people like Scott who feel they have business with the United Nations but in fact have no official connection.'[13]

Scott had no knowledge of this impediment at the time, but sensed the need to be on the move. He flew to London, where he could at least – as he thought – discharge his subsidiary duty by presenting the Herero case directly to the Commonwealth Relations Office. But in London the CRO gave Scott short shrift. In lofty fashion, he was told that he could not possibly be seen, as 'the matter of the petition was the concern of a dominion government [i.e. South Africa]'.[14]

Baffled and near broke, Scott called on the Indian High Commission for help, where fortunately his reputation as a fighter for Indian rights in South Africa had preceded him. Discussion of his difficulties there would, after several complications, lead to positive consequences. The upshot was that Sir Maharaj Singh, leader of the

Indian delegation at the UN, appointed Scott as his personal adviser, thus giving him a tenuous UN accreditation that enabled him to obtain a limited visa from the American embassy. Scott was finally on his way, though not without apprehension, recalling in *A Time To Speak*: 'I felt it was a serious matter to go outside one's own nation in an appeal to the nations of the world. But it seemed now as if the only hope for the African people was an appeal to the conscience of the world.'[15]

Finding the YMCA in New York more expensive than expected, Scott's initial thought was to pitch a tent in the grounds of Lake Success, where the original UN did its business in a maze of hangar-like buildings. But another church contact, possibly touched by Clayton's unexpected character reference, led to Scott's becoming the house guest of Sartell Prentice, the administrative secretary of the Commission of Churches on International Affairs, who lived close by at Port Washington, Long Island, in a roomy, white colonial-style house. With his base secured, Scott ventured forth, far too late for the start of the UN session, but soon enough to cause serious trouble.

He had already presciently sent a copy of the Herero petition to the Secretary-General. And the Indian delegation had arranged for its circulation to all the other delegates on the key Trusteeship Committee, popularly known as the Fourth Committee, in which all fifty-one member states were represented. This in itself gave the Herero case a head start. On being elevated into the category of an official document (A/C. 4/94:95:96:97) by the Fourth Committee's acceptance, the petition, with its pages of supporting documents, automatically became something of substance that had to be taken seriously.

The UN was still evolving its procedures, but it was already clear there would be no automatic transfer of trusteeship rights and obligations that had been valid under the League of Nations. Essentially, they had to be renegotiated through the Fourth Committee. When the Charter of the United Nations was implemented in October 1945, it was generally accepted all the Mandated Territories should be placed under a UN International Trusteeship system, and that the administering powers should accept the obligation to provide annual reports on progress, hopefully towards self-government and eventual independence.

In practically all cases this was a formality. Britain accepted that Tanganyika, the Cameroons, and Togoland should be placed under UN trusteeship; Belgium pledged likewise for Ruandu Urundi; Australia, similarly for New Guinea; New Zealand the same for Western Samoa; and the French accepted that those parts of Togoland and the Cameroons under its mandate should also come under UN responsibility. Only South Africa held back, insisting on the basis of its 'referendum' that these laborious international procedures were quite unnecessary in the special case of South-West Africa. Given that General Smuts was regarded as one of the architects of the UN, and that the victorious powers who dominated the United Nations regarded South Africa as a valued wartime and strategic ally, its diplomacy commanded considerable respect, particularly in relation to a far-off Territory about which most delegates knew little or next to nothing. And while a majority of the committee was disinclined to grant General Smuts his full heart's desire by allowing outright annexation of South-West Africa, many seemed ready to give South Africa what amounted to a free rein in the Territory, by going along with its fall-back position. This, in essence, would be to allow South Africa to maintain the status quo by continuing its administration 'in the spirit of' the mandate of the defunct League of Nations.

In pursuit of this objective South Africa had – albeit under protest – submitted a report on its administration of the Territory to the Fourth Committee. To Scott's way of thinking this was a miserably inadequate document. In an early letter to his friends in Johannesburg he described it as being replete with 'errors and downright lies', but he went on to conclude glumly that 'pussyfooting' by the great powers on the issue was leading many delegates to contemplate the report's routine acceptance, if only out of 'gratitude for small mercies'.[16]

The report, however, provided Scott with his opportunity as a lobbyist. Scott was not allowed to address the Fourth Committee in person, but he could, through his connection with the Indian delegation, privately canvass all those involved in its deliberations. Suddenly and mysteriously committee members from obscure Latin American countries began asking cogent and penetrating questions about a remote part of Africa wholly beyond their acquaintance. The mystery for the South African diplomatic contingent would rapidly be cleared up by the intelligence that they had previously been seen gossiping with a tall, untidy man wearing a dog collar in one of the UN's many corridors.

By priming individual delegates from the smaller nations with information about the Hereros, the bogus 'referendum' and the Territory's malign experience under the mandate, Scott was able to ensure a rough ride for the South African position stated in the report. The ultimate response of the Fourth Committee was to put fifty further questions to the South African government exploring its past actions and future intentions in relation to South-West Africa. This did not in itself represent victory, but it was undoubtedly a radical change of scenario: from a bold assertion of its unequivocal right to the Territory only a year earlier, South Africa was now very much on the back foot, defensively having to explain its stewardship. And what had once seemed like a tedious legal wrangle over mandate and trustee procedures had, through Scott's intervention, taken on the aspect of a dramatic crusade to save a people.

Scott's unpopularity with the South African delegation knew no bounds. Variously described as a 'crackpot' and a 'traitor', he also featured in a South African police dossier discreetly circulated among members of the international press, which listed all his earlier brushes with the law and sneeringly described him as 'a reserved, eccentric type of man with fanatical views, financially poor and of no fixed abode'.[17]

The effect of this kind of denigration was that it actually made Scott appear more, rather than less, significant. This was particularly the case in a city nourished on cinematic heroics featuring a lone guy from the sticks who comes to town and creates havoc among its more pompous citizenry. In the *New York Daily Post* on 30 December 1947, a feature writer tellingly translated the put-down in the police dossier as essentially conveying the message that Scott 'was a reckless friend of the helpless and a quite unorthodox saint'. To the experience of being outmanoeuvred by Scott in committee, South Africa could add the ignominy of losing the battle for sympathy in the press.

In his personal relations with the press, Scott comported himself with some skill, having good one-liners ready for even the most intrusive inquiries. To a question about his celibacy, Scott deftly explained: 'I have refrained from marriage feeling I could not serve two masters.' To a question about his left-wing credentials: 'I am not a Communist, but Communists have contributed to good causes and I am not ashamed to be in their company.' And to the charge that he always carried revolutionary literature with him wherever he went, he readily pleaded guilty: 'It's my favourite reading,' he told one New York reporter, 'the Lord's Prayer and the Beatitudes.'[18]

CHAPTER ELEVEN

FROG VERSUS BULL

HE NEWS of Mahatma Gandhi's assassination by a Hindu fanatic on 30 January 1948 was the first blight on Scott's return to South Africa after his exploits at the United Nations. It seemed to Scott as if a light that 'offered a bearing to mankind'[1] had been extinguished. Although Scott himself never claimed to be an outright pacifist, he had already concluded that Gandhi's *satyagraha*, combining as it did the elements of love, creative purpose, self-sacrifice and non-violence, ranked in importance with the message of the Christian Gospel, offering a way out of the cycle of violence that bedevilled the human condition. It could, of course, also be concluded that the Mahatma's end pointed up the message that in a violent world, exponents of non-violence could expect no quarter.

In many ways, the year following Gandhi's death would prove the most difficult of Scott's campaigning life. After the high-profile adventures of 1947 with Tobruk, Bethal, and his witness at the UN in New York, as its peaks, came the less well illuminated test of Scott's endurance and strength of purpose while he was losing ground in almost all directions. For the events of 1948 would firmly establish that it took more than the sound of trumpets to bring the walls of social and racial injustice tumbling down. Indeed, in many of the areas to which Scott turned his attention, they appeared to be mounting higher and higher.

Scott spent two frustrating and often fearful months camped in a dry river bed, three feet from the rickety fence that marked the perimeter of the Windhoek location, waiting . . . and waiting for permits that would allow him to hold a meeting in the location and visit the scattered outlying reserves. For Scott the most urgent responsibility was to report to the Hereros and the other tribes on events at the United Nations. The South African authorities in Windhoek, however, detecting no such urgency, efficiently tied up his multiple applications in red tape. Aside from one four-hour session in Gobabis, where, after promising not to hold a public meeting, he was given leave to communicate briefly with Chief Kutako, Scott was allowed no official contact with the UN petitioners.

Scott's time under canvas was not entirely wasted. One of the more poetic official reports on his activities noted that individuals made their way stealthily in and out of the reserves for meetings with Scott, 'elusive as buck slipping into the shadows'. Scott himself would recall sleepless, but constructive nights:

> Awakened by the sound of a low whistle, I would lift up a flap of the tent and find there half a dozen black faces, peering inquiringly through the bush. Holding their sticks and their hats, they would say there was a matter which they would like to speak about. And by the light of a hurricane lamp wrapped in a blanket, under the lee of a bush, I would record their statements.[2]

Through these night-time contacts Scott would learn that many of the tribespeople he made contact with on his earlier visits had been called in for interrogation by the Criminal Investigation Department (CID). He would also glean the useful intelligence that the large Ovambo tribe to the north, which had not experienced German occupation and had suffered least under the mandate, was beginning to share the radicalism of the tribes in the south. Unlike the Hereros, Namas and Berg Damaras, all directly subject to European law in what was called the Territory's Police Zone, the Ovambos had managed to maintain their own system of tribal laws, but now they too were becoming more prone to economic exploitation by white mining and farming interests. Of the Hereros' determination to fight on through the United Nations, with Scott's assistance if possible, there could be no doubt, though Scott found it difficult to convey the intricacy of UN procedures, still only sketchily known to himself.

The clearest message to his tent was of the rising white anger at his 'interference', graphically expressed by correspondents in the local press: 'We declare he is a danger to us,' said one. 'He has traffic here again. The chances are he will again without a thorough study of conditions, express all sorts of prejudices . . .' In the opinion of another, 'the appearance of Reverend Scott at any place has caused nothing but bad feeling between the Europeans and the Coloureds . . .' Another counselled, 'It is indeed necessary that the Reverend Scott should start with improving his person as his appearance is miserable . . . ' Scott's attempts at bringing pressure to bear on the South African authorities was seen by one writer as mimicking the actions of 'an ambitious frog in front of a bull'.[3]

Although many of the comments were couched in terms of heavy sarcasm, there was no mistaking the underlying, and sometimes not so underlying, menace. In a letter to one of his support organizations, the Council for Human Rights in Durban, on 25 March, Scott wrote: 'The Afrikaans newspapers have gone to excess in the expression of resentment, and one, "Die Suid-Wester", published an open threat to drive me out with a rifle. Since the position of my camp was advertised, the threat might have had serious results . . . Needless to say I did not leave.'[4]

When it became obvious no permits would be issued through the administration in Windhoek, Scott returned to Johannesburg and wrote directly to General Smuts, requesting his intervention. Some weeks later he received the Prime Minister's evasive reply, saying he was unable to see his way to assisting Scott in a matter that should be left 'entirely to the discretion of the Administrator of South-West Africa'.[5] Smuts was also displaying a less than wholly cooperative relationship with the United Nations. In May 1948, South Africa duly furnished rudimentary answers to the fifty questions posed by its Fourth (Trusteeship) Committee, but pointedly accompanied them with a firm statement that they were given voluntarily, and should not be taken as recognition by South Africa of any obligation to transmit information to the world body.

Scott encountered a similar hardening of attitudes when, urged on by his Indian friends, he was drawn into the resistance against the boycott of Indian traders in the small platteland towns of the Transvaal. In what was an election year, the Indians felt particularly vulnerable as a target of Nationalist rhetoric. One Nationalist candidate, confident of finding support from white voters for his views, stated in his manifesto: 'The dregs of India came here half a century ago to work the sugar plantations . . . the coolie is not an inmate of this country but a usurper and an exploiter. Millions of people have recently been shifted in Europe to solve racial problems. Why can we not shift 250,000 coolies?'[6]

The immediate aim of the boycott led by white farmers in the

Transvaal was to dislodge the Indians who had set up stores in the small country 'dorps' as well as the big towns. An aspect of this campaign was the fostering of racial animosity between the Indian traders and their African customers. Scott toured a number of platteland districts, interviewing white farmers and trying to convey the idea that the country was being disgraced by a campaign which could only exacerbate its racial tensions. In *A Time to Speak*, he would describe one such interview with a farmer, who considered himself one of the more humane employers in the district in that he never flogged his 'boys', and only had cause to give them an occasional beating. The farmer also made it clear, with an enormous family Bible immediately to hand, that scripture guided his thoughts, which Scott described as being as follows:

> The 'coolies' were out of place in the country. They were always making trouble for the government and it wasn't right that they should have all the trade with the white people in the district. The Farmers Co-operative was the proper trading organization for the farmers to patronize. He would like to see all the 'coolies' sent back to India. The Natives and the whites would get on better. The Indians were doing a lot of propaganda in the country about breaking down the colour bar for Non-Europeans. That of course was impossible. The Lord in His wisdom had made people of different races and nations. The different people He had distinguished by different colours. It was therefore not right to want to mix them all up. And for a people like his own, living in a continent like Africa, it was right that they should cherish what had come down to them and had been preserved by their forebears.[7]

Scott refused to regard such encounters as trying to achieve verbal dialogue with the deaf, but they cannot have been other than dispiriting. And the mere fact of his later being proved right, when in the wake of the boycott campaign a series of ugly riots involving conflict between Africans and Indians took place in Durban, was not much in the way of consolation.

Nor was there much to console on the broader political front. Shortly before the general election, which was of course for whites only, Scott was invited to preside over the opening session of what was called the 'Votes for All' People's Assembly. The invitation was a clear measure of Scott's standing and prestige with South Africa's huge unenfranchised population, and very much in line with the principle of cooperation between the races, which he had pioneered through the original Campaign for Right and Justice. It had been made possible by what was called 'The Doctors' Pact', signed by a trio of Congress Presidents: Dr Xuma of the ANC, and Dr Dadoo and Dr Naicker of the Transvaal and Natal Indian Congresses. These three, in alliance with the Communist Party, had combined to present what was meant to be an inspirational united front of South Africa's voteless majority. In his opening address, Scott advocated a coordinated movement in the country: 'to break the bondage of narrow prejudices, crippling laws and false doctrines which threaten to destroy its soul and reduce it to a desert of sand and gold'.[8]

Scott was, nonetheless, dismayed by the absence of several key ANC figures from the conference. The reason for their non-appearance, it transpired, was a background dispute over the campaign's leadership, it being defined as a principle by some of the higher-ranking ANC members that their organization could only openly involve itself in campaigns that it clearly led. Scott wrote to the ANC leader, Chief Albert Luthuli, more in sorrow than in anger: 'It really is very unfortunate that every move towards unity amongst Non-Europeans seems to lead to dissension. It makes it very difficult to know how to act for the best, sometimes.'[9]

In answer to one of many calls for his help Scott went to neighbouring Basutoland where the executive members of Lekhotla la Bafo (Council of Commoners), a small but well-established rural resistance movement, had been arrested and charged with murder. They were accused of torching the Roma Mission College, causing a fire in which four African children died. Also charged was a young Indian who had taken part in the passive resistance in Natal. It was alleged that he had loaned his motor lorry to those plotting the arson attack. Relatives of the accused maintained the charges had been fabricated with a political motive by the police, who were mostly white South Africans. Lekhotla la Bafo was noted for its fierce opposition to any moves by South Africa seeking to incorporate Basutoland into the Union.

Scott's own suspicions were aroused after a meeting with the Roman Catholic fathers at Roma. They said the fire had its origin on the second storey, an unlikely starting point for an outside arsonist attack. They had also assumed it was caused by a short circuit until the police arrived many weeks later. Scott was able to make the case of interest to Frans Boshoff, a left-wing Johannesburg lawyer, who had previously undertaken the defence of striking miners charged with treason. Under Boshoff's expert scrutiny of the evidence, the case collapsed. Subsequently, the man who was to have been the chief prosecution witness was convicted of the crime.[10]

Scott and Boshoff had less success in trying to evaluate one of Basutoland's much grimmer realities at that time. During their inquiry into the Lekhotla la Bafo affair they discovered that some sixty people, including several tribal chiefs, were in prison under sentence of death after having been convicted of involvement in ritual murders. There could, it seemed, be no better illustration of the fact that man's inhumanity to man knows no racial frontiers. Yet there were a number of peculiarities about this apparent outbreak of cannibalistic savagery, which entailed the eating of a victim's body parts before he was finally dispatched. The principal problem was finding some explanation as to why this gruesome ritual should have been revived after so many years in abeyance.

In pursuit of answers, Scott made it his business to interview a range of missionaries, lawyers, and tribal chiefs, in and out of Maseru prison. One suggestion was that it was the result of intratribal competition, which led contenders for high office to enhance their 'manhood' through ancient superstitious ritual. Another was that the crimes were the consequence of a plaiting of witch doctors' nostrums with a perversion of Christian doctrine relating to the sacrament of the Body and Blood of Christ. Yet another – most favoured by the convicted and those closest to them – was that the crimes were 'manufactured'. It was alleged that persons otherwise deceased had been deliberately disfigured posthumously by South Africans employed as officials by the British authority to create a theatre of 'ritual murder', with the dark motive of discrediting and 'framing' those chiefs and tribespeople who opposed the plan to construct a military road through their tribal territory to link with roads in the Union. There was, in fact, no explanation that did not seem other than incredibly far-fetched.

Scott went on taking statements with Boshoff and another Communist lawyer friend, Jack Levitan, but with a mounting sense that 'the whole affair was altogether beyond me'. All he could do in the short term was send a cable to the Commonwealth Relations Office in London, asking for a stay on any executions and some form of official inquiry. The CRO did eventually send an anthropologist to Basutoland with a brief to investigate ritual murders in the territory, but only after many of those convicted had been executed. And the anthropologist's report was not particularly illuminating. All that can be said with any certainty is that the rate of ritual murders declined after construction of the military road.

Scott's readiness to investigate and, where possible, intercede in the multiple problems arising in southern Africa inevitably took a mental toll. He often felt worn out and unequal to the tasks that presented themselves. And while his strength of purpose held up, his energy level often sagged: 'It was all very well for the Good Samaritan,' he would say of this period, only half joking, 'but what if the whole road was littered with the victims of a decaying social order?'[11]

He had not given up hoping for some kind of accommodation with his Church, but there was to be nothing but discouragement in that direction. It appeared very much as if the Church had given up on him. Midway through 1948, his request to do low-paid 'native work' was rejected by the diocese. He wrote to a member of the hierarchy: 'Naturally I am worried about the position. I have no means of livelihood and have been living on the hospitality of kind friends,' adding, with a mild touch of bitterness, that he was puzzled by the suggestion of there being, 'No native work available for me when there are 350,000 African miners and 100,000 squatters whose problems I know and amongst whom I lived and learned to love. They are in somebody else's "district" I'm told. Yet many of them told me they have never seen a priest in their hut since I left Tobruk.'[12]

The kind friends who supported Scott in Johannesburg were principally Leon and Freda Levson, along with the ebullient George Norton, when he was in town, and Scott's close allies in the Indian Congress. On the road or in the bush his personal economy was, if anything, slightly less fragile in that Scott found it difficult to spend money, even if by chance he had any. Esther Levitan, who accompanied her husband and Scott on their travels around Basutoland, remembered Scott being overwhelmed with generosity in even the poorest and most remote villages: 'They kissed the hem of his cassock, greeted him as a holy person.'[13] Refreshments in the huts would follow. Although money was clearly one of his concerns, Scott does not seem to have been much impeded by considerations of personal poverty. Even at the worst times he appears to have expected that his needs – relatively small since he had given up smoking, and had never acquired the taste for more than an occasional beer – would somehow be supplied, and that clothes absent-mindedly mislaid could easily be replaced.

A similar free-wheeling attitude influenced his relationship with Communists. Although Scott, in consequence of the Nazi–Soviet pact and what he saw as left-wing disruption of the Campaign for Right and Justice, was now inclined to be distrustful of Communism as a creed, he was always quite ready to work with individual Communists and use their expertise when required. This was partly through necessity, since any major multiracial initiative inside South Africa almost automatically involved the CP, as it was the only significant political grouping that treated whites and blacks on an equal basis. But it also appears to have been based on affection and genuine regard for individual members of the party. Boshoff and Levitan, the left-wing lawyers who helped Scott in Basutoland, were also good friends. Scott also admired the journalist Ruth First, who had worked with him in Bethal and later wrote expertly about the Hereros and the complexities of South-West African politics, and whose tragic destiny was to be blown up by a letter bomb posted by the South African security service.

Scott's loose relationship with the CP was also not disagreeable to its more hard-line membership. Rusty Bernstein, a resolute activist in Johannesburg, though he was later acquitted of sabotage at the Rivonia trial, would write admiringly of Scott's role in South Africa in the late 1940s in his autobiography *Memory Against Forgetting*: 'His parish,' Bernstein wrote, 'seemed to be all of suffering humanity, and his motivation a deep sense of outrage against cruelty and injustice,' though he would add the careful afterthought, 'He was close to the party in political spirit and on friendly terms with many of us, but a loner by temperament, ill-suited to the rules and disciplines which party membership would have demanded of him.'[14]

The major event of 1948, which also tended to minimize niceties of political difference on the left, was the general election in May, from which the Nationalist Party emerged victorious, though with a minority of actual votes cast. Under the new leadership of Dr D.F. Malan, a former Dutch Reformed Church minister, South Africa was now officially a society dedicated to the separate development of racial groups and minimal contact between them – the policy known as apartheid. It would take some years to cobble together the succession of repressive legislative acts, giving *de jure* force to all the de *facto* discrimination of the past, but the effect of the government's more belligerent racial outlook would become almost immediately apparent in Scott's prime area of concern. When Scott approached the new administration with a renewed application to visit the Herero reserves, he cannot have been hugely surprised by its prompt rejection.

Although Scott could be crafty in terms of tactics, he was for the most part punctilious in explaining his fundamental objectives, especially to his highest-ranking opponents. On the firm Christian principle that you should hate the sin but not the sinner, Scott held fast to the rule that in any preliminary to serious hostilities over an issue of principle there should be a genuine appeal to an opponent's better nature and willingness to compromise. Even to Dr Malan's. Scott perceived an opportunity when Malan announced his intention of making an early visit to Windhoek, with the aim of reassuring the white community there. Scott wrote to Malan requesting that he should also meet with a deputation from the Hereros and himself, with a view to their obtaining official sanction to put their case before the British government and the United Nations. Scott elaborated:

> In one of many possible ways there must surely be discoverable a just and amicable solution of a problem which has been exercising the conscience of the civilized world for a very long time. From all the evidence it seems as though the Hereros have many of the symptoms of a dying people; and this must be a reflection more upon the rulers than the ruled. In making these submissions I can assure you that I have no other purpose than to assist the cause of justice towards a people who in the past have been most grievously wronged.[15]

Malan's blunt response, channelled through the Ministry of External Affairs, was, 'The Union government do not consider themselves accountable to the UN, to the governments of the United Kingdom or the British Commonwealth in respect of the administration of South-West Africa . . . it is not possible to recognize the possession by you of status to represent the Hereros or any other tribe in the Territory which would justify your being received . . .' Eric Louw, the Minister of Economic Affairs, echoed his master's voice in October by insisting that 'South-West Africa was to all intents and purposes part of the Union and would continue to be so.' He also solicitously warned members of the Foreign Press Association to guard against 'an agitator who is often more concerned with the interests of Moscow than the causes of the natives he professes to espouse'. There was no mystery about the identity of the 'agitator'.

In essence, the new Nationalist government had decided that its interests in South-West Africa would be best served by a vigorous assertion of sovereignty rather than any quest for compromise. The nature of this intention became clearer still with the framing of one of its first legislative acts. This introduced a constitutional change that gave whites in the Territory eight seats in the South African parliament – a move that was also calculated to provide a useful boost to the Nationalist Party's slim overall majority. The evidence that South Africa was ready to defy the United Nations, not to mention Michael Scott, was palpable.

The Hereros' response to these developments was to assemble through public subscription what was, by their standards, the prodigious sum of £430 – the wherewithal needed to finance another Michael Scott mission to the UN, which was scheduled to hold its next General Assembly meeting in Paris in November. As was the case with his first foray into international politics, there were movement problems. At the airport, Scott was asked by a South African immigration officer, acting on instructions from the Department of the Interior, to give up his passport. He managed to retain it, but only by opting out of the flight. His instinct told him that his chances of unfettered travel were much better across an overland border. After a painful journey across Central Africa that combined long jolting car journeys along rutted roads with two short-haul charter flights, Scott would eventually surface in Paris, too late for the committee hearings on South-West Africa, but some days before the full General Assembly met.[16]

Happily for the cause, Scott's extrovert friend George Norton, on leave of absence in England, had been apprised of the delays besetting the Hereros' main champion. Though less well briefed than Scott, he had gone on ahead to Paris and managed some assiduous lobbying of delegates on the Fourth (Trusteeship) Committee while it was in session. He would later say that the use of Scott's name was particularly helpful in his contacts with the Uruguayan, Danish, Norwegian, Polish, Indian and Czech delegates to name but a few. With Scott finally on the scene, the two priests went round together on a final burst of lobbying before the General Assembly session.

According to Norton, their impact on Paris was considerable both in and out of the main event. In a characteristically mischievous letter to the Levsons back in Johannesburg, Norton reported that they were both in good spirits, and that things were going reasonably well, though their intense and excessively handsome mutual friend sometimes needed guidance on local customs:

> Michael and I after trying to dig out the Philippines delegates from the Ritz Hotel (near the Opera) refreshed ourselves at the famous Café de la Paix. Tea!! Waiting for an underground Metro afterwards a lovely young French Mademoiselle pushed the feather of her chic hat into Michael's face. He didn't take the tip. Later another one of obviously doubtful character deliberately banged into Michael and looked back to discover whether he had taken note. He didn't realise the significance of all this until I explained.[17]

Reporting on the UN proceedings in Paris, the *Manchester Guardian*, one of the British newspapers that had been primed by Scott with occasional articles and information throughout the year, was impressed by 'the bland effrontery' of Eric Louw, who led the South African delegation.[18] Louw's argument was that the UN's stance on South-West Africa represented unwarranted interference in the domestic affairs of a member state. The UN, nonetheless, reaffirmed its polite request that South Africa enter into a trusteeship agreement by an impressive forty-three votes to one, though the actual resolution was described by Mrs Pandit, the Indian delegate, as 'lifeless'.[19]

Scott was also less than thrilled. It was encouraging that the UN was not ready to give up on South-West Africa, but he was becoming acutely aware of just how wide the gulf could be between large moral majorities in the General Assembly and realities on the ground. As far as those were concerned the Hereros still had nothing to show from their appeal to world opinion.

But the most dismaying aspect of the occasion for Scott was Britain's heading of the list of abstainers on the vote. Reasoning that South Africa was unlikely to mend its ways as long as it could rely on the British government's tacit support, Scott decided to change his schedule and accompany George Norton back to London.

CHAPTER TWELVE

HOMECOMING

THE BRITAIN TO which Michael Scott returned in December 1948 was still sentimental about its empire. Children in its schools, even in the worst slum areas, were drilled into reeling off the names of the large areas of the globe coloured salmon-pink on the classroom wall maps. This encouraged appreciation of the empire's scale and panoply, but not a great deal of understanding of its detailed administration. It all seemed quite magnificent, but very strange and far away, particularly when – well in advance of the first wave of immigration from the West Indies – there was not very much in the way of first-hand testimony to go on.

There were British people with relatives who had gone to live in Africa, but intelligence on the settlers' grapevine was partial, usually along the lines of Africa being a wonderful place, only marred by problems with the natives. And while there were few open advocates of white supremacy, the idea that Britain was exercising a benign role as far as the world's more backward peoples were concerned was not uncommon. The word 'Commonwealth' was becoming more general currency, but the main imperial sporting jamboree, ranking second in importance only to the Olympics, was still being glorified in 1950, as it had been pre-war, as 'The Empire Games'. So there was some pride, as well as sentiment, in empire. Even so, outside the narrow confines of the academic world, there was not much in the way of curiosity about it among ordinary citizens of a Mother Country intent on binding its own wounds after the ravages of a long and terrible war.

British politicians were not unconcerned about imperial issues, but what with post-war austerity, the need for social reconstruction, nationalization and the Russians being so awkward, the plight of a tiny African tribe could hardly be expected to loom large on the national radar. With his hands full at home, Clement Attlee, the Labour Prime Minister, was not inclined to complicate his life by too much unorthodoxy in other directions. If South Africa – an esteemed strategic ally and Commonwealth partner – wanted South-West Africa, he saw no reason to put obstacles in its way. Nor, until Scott raised the Herero standard, did other leading politicians.

In taking on the British government and a great weight of public indifference, Scott was not friendless. There was, particularly after Indian independence, a rising appreciation of the possibilities for change in Africa, though interest in it tended to be confined to readers of the *News Chronicle*, the *Manchester Guardian* and the *Observer*, the more liberal organs of the day. The more studious among them were already, to some degree, familiar with the unconventional activities of a priest called Michael Scott. So, while there was no fanfare at his homecoming after almost six years abroad, Scott was known by reputation, and even revered, in some quarters.

The Quakers were instantly hospitable. Within a few days of his arrival in London, Scott was at home in the Friends' International Centre in Tavistock Square. Fred and Dorothy Irvine, recently back from Ghana, put him up in their warden's flat, where a spare room doubled as his bedroom and office. Within a few more days, Scott was further equipped with a support group, consisting of three prime activists: John Fletcher, retired from the Friends Service Council, and Esther and Gordon Muirhead, pacifists not long back from Red Cross welfare work in India. They called themselves 'the three musketeers', with Scott, by implication, as their dashing D'Artagnan. More formally, they constituted the executive of the Michael Scott Committee, committed to raising funds for his efforts, fixing his speaking engagements, helping with his reports and keeping track of his laundry. George Norton was the group's official adviser and unofficial court jester. To plot the way ahead they met once a week for a free lunch at Emil's restaurant near St James's Park Station. Emil, a Fletcher connection, had been Albert Schweitzer's treasurer in Britain. Norton reported on these benign developments in letters and postcards to the Levsons and other friends back in Johannesburg. To preserve security, Norton encoded Scott's name on the postcards as either 'Miriam' or 'The Archangel'.[1]

There was a certain gaiety to the proceeding, but it could hardly be considered part of the political mainstream. Pacifism had been a powerful influence in the Labour Party some years prior to the war, but the rise of Nazism and the horror of the Holocaust had put an end to all that. And while respect for the Quaker tradition of public service and independence of mind still ran deep, few politicians looked to the Friends' International Centre for serious guidance. On the other hand, the Centre's extreme cosmopolitanism, deemed highly unusual in those days, served to keep it in an informal political loop of some influence. Peace and civil rights workers from all over the world would meet there, creating a rich admixture of colours and creeds. When Lady Cripps, the wife of Labour's austere Chancellor of the Exchequer, Sir Stafford, was minded to take an interest in African politics, her first move was to ring Dorothy Irvine at the Centre to ask if she could organize a meeting 'with some nice Africans'.[2]

Scott was thoroughly at home in this environment, but restless for opportunities to advance the Herero cause. This would inch forward through a meeting at the Centre with Agatha Harrison, the peripatetic champion of the Women's International League for Peace and Freedom, who had been close to Gandhi and who had known Scott quite well in pre-war India (though not about his Communist affiliation). They had a lot to discuss, aside from old times. Harrison was herself an official UN observer, and as exasperated as Scott by the British delegation's voting record, supporting South Africa on every issue or abstaining. Harrison urged Scott to develop personal contacts with those in high places to supplement his campaigning efforts.[3] On a practical level, before flying off to Delhi, Harrison also cracked open the door that led to Scott's audience with Philip Noel-Baker, the Secretary of State for Commonwealth Relations. With the date set, Scott directed his efforts to assembling the strongest possible delegation.

At the meeting with Noel-Baker in March 1949, Scott was able to demonstrate the connection between the Hereros' predicament and South Africa's increasingly malign racial policies. In asking for a change in Britain's stance at the UN, Scott maintained he was only requesting that his country should come into line with emerging world opinion. There was satisfaction to be had from this encounter in that Scott was finally able to deliver on his promise to Chief Hosea to make the Herero case directly to the British government, but there was rather more cause for disappointment. Noel-Baker and his officials were polite but non-committal. Scott was also distressed by what he saw as the weakness of his own delegation. Although Scott's application was backed by two radical MPs – Tom Driberg (Labour) and Frank Byers (the Liberal Whip) – and by representatives of the Anti-Slavery and Aborigines Protection Society, plus a number of fringe organizations (mostly on the left), support from the ranks of his own church was conspicuously absent. This was not through any want of trying on Scott's part or on that of Esther Muirhead, his secretarial 'musketeer'.[4]

A few weeks earlier, in January, the news had broken that Dr Malan had refused to meet a deputation of churchmen concerned about the direction of his government's apartheid policy. Organized by the Christian Council of South Africa (CCSA), the religious leaders wanted to express the voice of all the recognized churches in South Africa, except the Dutch Reformed Church. Malan had thus, at a stroke, managed to snub the Anglican Church of the Province of South Africa, along with the country's Presbyterian, Methodist, Congregational and Baptist Church organizations. Sensing an opportunity, Scott put Esther Muirhead to work on the task of typing high-speed letters to all forty-one Anglican bishops in Britain, asking them to consider some form of joint representation on behalf of their discountenanced church brethren in South Africa.

Scott had grounds for optimism. George Bell, the Bishop of Chichester, recently appointed chairman of the World Council of Churches, had previously indicated, in the course of 'a quiet talk' at the Athenaeum, that he was ready to mobilize episcopal opinion on Scott's behalf. There seemed no better time than the present with Malan's obduracy affording what Scott perceived as an issue capable of 'rousing the conscience of Christendom'.[5]

Unfortunately for Scott's design, the South African churches showed a marked disinclination to accept Christendom's assistance, letting it be discreetly known through the CCSA that 'any outside assistance would be rather embarrassing at this time'.[6] This effectively silenced Scott's British bishops before they had even given voice; and as a knock-on effect, persuaded Bishop Bell reluctantly to withdraw from Scott's delegation to the Commonwealth Relations Office, for which he had been originally cast in the leading role.

Scott had little difficulty in divining that his problem had much to do with the influence of his old antagonist, Geoffrey Clayton, who, some months earlier, had been consecrated Archbishop of Cape Town, the highest Anglican post in Africa. Clayton had been in touch with Bishop Bell immediately prior to his backing out of Scott's delegation. Although communication between them had long since lapsed, Scott wrote Clayton a letter, questioning his intervention. Clayton wrote back frostily to say that he did not think that 'intervening' was the right word: 'I have merely given my views as and when requested to do so. The church in this country must not allow itself to be regarded as an English outpost. That way disaster lies.'[7] The idea that South Africa's white-led churches could, unaided, put the country's racial house in order was still some considerable way from being dead.

Scott was also frustrated, indeed bemused, by the apparently thoughtful suggestion of the British Conference of Missionary Societies that the solution to the Herero problem might be to regroup the entire tribe in the British Protectorate of Bechuanaland. The idea of shunting African populations around for the convenience of a white minority would soon become a norm in southern Africa, but Scott angrily opposed it from the outset. He allowed his anger to rise towards boiling-point in a pamphlet entitled *Christianity Must Overcome Racialism.* That part of it which concerned what he described as the 'paramountcy' of African land rights has a resonance in southern Africa to this day. As he saw it, the issue of who owned the land was one 'from which the "race question" cannot be separated'. Of the official church response to what Scott regarded as the crisis of the age, he said: 'In England it seems as though Christians are lacking in leadership on the important question of race relations in the light of Christian belief concerning the Nature of God, the Universe, and Man.'[8] As was the case in South Africa, Scott was already exhibiting a capacity for discomforting his church elders. And, as in South Africa, most of his consolation would be found in more secular society.

Scott's spirit was lifted on 26 March when the rafters of the Friends International Centre echoed with Paul Robeson's amazing voice. The American singer had been enlisted as the accompaniment to an international gathering of peace workers concerned about racialism in South Africa. The conference eased Scott's sense of isolation and encouraged further initiatives. With the assistance of Tom

Driberg, Scott persuaded thirty-five members of Parliament to sit tight through a private screening of his film *Civilization on Trial in South Africa*. It was rough and poorly edited but still had a strong impact. The circle of informed interest in what he was up to was slowly widening. Even so, Scott and his committee were becoming aware that if there was to be another leap forward, it was more likely to occur in New York than in London. Everything pointed in the direction of the United Nations. And this time Scott could go there with an enhanced status.

On his first visit to America, Scott had made contact with the International League for the Rights of Man, a New York-based Non-Government Organization (NGO) with a wide reach. Scott had got on well with its energetic chairman, Roger Baldwin. Though no churchman, Baldwin saw Scott as capable of making a unique contribution to the UN by focusing its attention on the plight of subject peoples who had no clear avenue for redress. Under US government immigration rules, his organization was permitted one official observer from abroad to attend at the UN. In the summer of 1949, Baldwin's League appointed Scott as its overseas observer.[9] This scarcely placed Scott at the commanding heights, but it at least ensured his presence in some kind of official capacity, though his visa would again be highly restrictive.

Scott's first duty as an observer was to attend meetings of the Human Rights Commission's Committee on Racial Discrimination. This was a role he found interesting, but not central to his main objective, which was to present the Herero case orally, on the record, in a way that would command maximum attention. There were a number of impediments to this plan, some of which were indicated in the newsletters circulated by the 'musketeers' in London on the basis of his letters home. The August 1949 issue of the Michael Scott Committee newsletter reported:

7.6.49 He arrived in USA on a visa limited to work with UNO i.e. New York and Lake Success.

20.6.49 'There is a good deal of sympathy shown by delegates I have interviewed so far and assurances that it (the issue of UN Trusteeship for South Africa) will be brought up again.'

24.6.49 'I am under restriction here – strong pressure having been put on the US State Dept. by S. Africa it seems not to allow me facilities here and the bank would not allow me any dollars (I finally heard from SA to that effect). I feel pretty badly about this but strong means are being taken in SA to prevent people coming here so I feel I ought to put in as much work as possible while the going is good.'

9.7.49 'It does not seem as though there is going to be any full discussion of SWA in the Trusteeship Council (the body in charge of administering the Trust territories), as the Colonial Powers seem intent on referring the question to the General Assembly. SA would, of course, like the whole subject to be dropped.'

29.7.49 'I may be able to stay on till the Assembly and Fourth (Trusteeship) Committee meets. The World Federation of UN Associations has endorsed the request that I be allowed to make an oral submission to the Fourth Committee, I believe, and it will get the backing of some delegates. But there are strong attempts being made to prevent my being allowed to stay on here I'm told.'[10]

Scott would be obliged to presume on the hospitality of Sartell Prentice, his loyal Long Island friend, for another three months before 'The Question of South-West Africa' came up, as the last item on the Fourth Committee's agenda. With his expectations being raised and lowered, almost by the day, the delays drained his reserves of emotional and nervous energy. He was further demoralized by receipt of a letter from Ambrose Reeves, Geoffrey Clayton's replacement as Bishop of Johannesburg, which informed Scott that his general licence to preach had been withdrawn. The reason given was his long absence from the diocese, though Scott would perceive it as a pointed disowning of his activity at the UN.[11]

In this grim period, Scott wrote his poem *Satyagraha*, which gives some indication of his state of mind at the time:

The spirit of the Lord is nowhere to be seen
Is lost in the night among the stars in their courses.
Is sightless and soundless, but is seen by the hearts desirous of light.
It gleams as a diamond on the dew of the morning.
To the eyes of desire of the truth, the spirit of the Lord is visible,
But nowhere to be found and kept.
Nowhere to be held, possessed, but discerned by the heart's desire,

Hidden from the hater, and the lover of his life, the prejudiced,
The knowers of all knowledge and the teachers of all truth.
The spirit of the Lord is voiceless . . . [12]

The poem goes on for six more verses, in which the light often seems to be on the losing end of its struggle with the powers of darkness. Scott saw it as an affirmation of faith, though it was evidently of a faith stretched to its ultimate limits.

As the days passed, with Scott's memorandum of application to speak mouldering in the files in the Secretary-General's office, there seemed to be an increasing likelihood of its staying there gathering dust, along with the earlier petitions and supporting documents from the Hereros and other tribes. When the general debate on South-West Africa began in the UN's Fourth Committee, the main argument centred on whether it was really appropriate for anyone to speak on the subject at all. Britain and France, the big colonial guns on the committee, endorsed South Africa's 'hands off' position, arguing that it had no juridical obligation under the UN charter to make itself answerable to the United Nations. The smaller powers, however, regarded the matter as unfinished business. They insisted that South Africa was defying the UN by continuing to evade its Trusteeship procedures, which had been reaffirmed in Paris only a year earlier. In the heat generated by this controversy, the name of 'Michael Scott' was mentioned on several occasions. This would lead to a request for general distribution of all Scott's official documentation. On application to the Secretary-General's office, this was promptly supplied. From then on it seemed a very short step to a request that Scott be allowed to elaborate on the documents, by appearing in person before the committee.

In ambulatory terms it was indeed the shortest of steps, with Scott sitting expressionless at the back of the conference chamber through every word of the proceedings. But for the UN it represented a huge stride into the unknown. There appeared to be no provision in the UN charter, or among the organization's precedents, that allowed an individual citizen with no official status to give openly hostile evidence against a member state. There was no problem about Scott's availability to speak, but should he? Was it safe or sensible to transform a UN lobbyist into an open witness? What were the implications for the future of allowing such witness? Would it imply recognition of the right of unrepresented minorities to appeal to world opinion over the heads of their own government? And if so, where would that all end? Debate on these questions over the next week would contribute to some of the most acrimonious argument ever heard at the UN. If Scott was heard, it was suggested, it would be akin to the opening of Pandora's Box. It could open the door to the 'dissidents' of Kashmir seeking to blast the Indian government, to 'troublemakers' from Jamaica aiming to embarrass Britain, and to Arab 'fanatics' from Algeria and Tunisia eager to indict the French.

South Africa's spokesman, Gerhard Jooste, was insistent that in no circumstances should Scott be heard. Britain and France backed him up. According to the British delegate, the act of allowing Scott to talk presented a danger of 'the whole African continent climbing on the back of this procedure'. The United States, earnestly seeking compromise, suggested that Scott should present his statement in writing. But the tide among the smaller nations, with India, Mexico, Guatemala, Pakistan, the Philippines and Haiti in informal alliance, began to turn in Scott's favour. When the great powers persisted in questioning Scott's credentials as a suitable witness, the Mexican delegate upped the moral stakes by declaring: 'Jesus Christ was crucified because he could not provide credentials proving he was the son of God.' The man from Haiti, in similar vein, said: 'This holy man has come to give us light.' The delegate from Belgium, who opposed Scott, did a magnificent job of undermining his own case with the statement: 'There is something deeply moving in the presence of a man who has the love of his underdeveloped brethren and is moved by love for those people. The fact that a white man may enjoy the confidence of men of another colour to this extent should not make us despair of human brotherhood.'[13]

Eventually, by twenty-five votes to fifteen, with six abstentions, it was agreed that Scott should be granted an open hearing before the full committee. In a last-ditch attempt to save the day, South Africa tried to get the decision deferred, to be 'pronounced on' by the full General Assembly. This was ruled out of order. When a sympathizer leaned over to congratulate Scott on this outcome, he gestured towards the crestfallen Gerhard Jooste with the words: 'Don't crow. I'm sorry for that South African fellow.'[14]

There would be no reciprocal sensitivity. There was no sign of a South African presence when, on the morning of 26 November, Scott presented himself before the committee, resplendent with a new dog collar purchased specially for the occasion by Sartell Prentice and in a suit that showed faint signs of having been pressed. On expressed orders from its government, the South African delegation 'boycotted' the event. By all contemporary accounts, they missed a compelling occasion.

Scott spoke in a low, unemotional voice. Rhetorical flourishes were not his style, nor were they required to present a case that had been honed in his mind for over two years. The simple recitation of the Herero story, encapsulating as it did all that was worst in colonial history, needed no embellishment. Much of the address would be taken up with gently leading his listeners from von Trotha's massacre, through the land seizures and humiliations inflicted by the 'pass laws' and other restrictions, to Malan's resolute crushing of contemporary hopes. Scott then skilfully broadened the case to encompass not just the Hereros, but subject peoples everywhere. Thus, South Africa's initiative in South-West Africa was dryly described as 'taking its dishonourable place in the record of means whereby the indigenous populations of the world have by treachery and deceit been deprived of their lands and natural rights'. Scott had no doubt that the churches had contributed to this record, commenting on the familiar African phenomenon of native peoples being converted to Christianity, and subsequently being subjected to unChristian acts by their colonizers. The question now being posed, Scott suggested, was whether the UN should act as a cover in a way that allowed this history of betrayal to be perpetuated, or whether it should create 'a turning point' by living up to its own highest ideals. He finished by reciting Chief Hosea Kutako's prayer, which in the context, seemed as applicable to the UN as much as to the Almighty: 'Oh Lord, help us who roam about. Help us who have been placed in Africa and have no home of our own. Give us back a dwelling place. God, all power is yours in Heaven and earth. Amen.'[15]

Scott's speech, which lasted for just over an hour, was heard in what one witness described as 'a hush rarely experienced at this headquarters of international sophistication, tinged with cynicism'.[16] The calm deliberateness of Scott's presentation lent added weight to the sense of the UN being politely but firmly challenged to do its moral duty. There was, on the day, an almost tangible feeling of uplift. Everyone present was aware that something special had occurred. 'This weekend has seen something new and unique happen to the Parliament of the World,' wrote Stanley Burch in his dispatch for the *News Chronicle*. Burch went on, happy to supply some of the hyperbole missing from Scott's delivery:

> To some of the delegates – Britain among them – 'a very dangerous precedent' has been established. To others, the United Nations have found their soul . . . Black tribesmen of South-West Africa, who for decades have been dumb under the white man's rule have smashed through the cleverest opposition on earth and have presented their story of suffering, and their petition for redress to the United Nations . . . The trumpets should be sounding for Michael Scott today in the kraals, the shanty-towns, the leaky tin huts and the shabby Negro churches which sent him to Lake Success.[17]

Things could not be expected to remain on this exalted plane, nor did they. Shortly after making his speech, Scott learned that the South African diplomats were putting it about in the UN lobbies that his whole story had been 'cooked up' and that he had never in fact been in South-West Africa. In rebuttal, Scott produced clips from his film *Civilization on Trial* that showed him conferring with Herero leaders. For the benefit of a few doubting delegates, Scott organized a private screening with the assistance of the UN's technical staff. He would then find himself ludicrously accused by the South Africans of using UN equipment for unofficial purposes.[18] But the best evidence of how bad the South Africans could be at the art of losing would be provided by its Prime Minister. In a belligerent statement released to the international press, Dr Malan accused the UN of 'interference mania':

> The principle having been accepted that agitators, and what is more agitators of the Scott type we all know, can obtain entrance to its council chambers, bypassing a country's own legal government, there seems to be no limit to interference any more. The way has become open for wide incitement and the creation of unrest from outside. Today South Africa is the prey of this conduct. Tomorrow it will be others . . .

Malan was further moved to make the ominous assertion, 'Really the concern of the United Nations about the Aboriginal population has reached such farcical heights that the Union government will eventually be compelled to protect Aborigines from their embrace,' before concluding with the implied message that apartheid was here to stay: 'South Africa, fortunately, still has sufficient independence and self-respect to refuse to commit national suicide on the instructions of whoever it might be.'[19]

Scott, who had just received news from England of his father's death, was further saddened by Malan's outburst. But in a perverse way it actually underscored the measure of his achievement. The UN, seemingly unaffected, stayed steady on course. In December the General Assembly reinforced the request for South Africa's compliance, and adopted Scott's suggestion that the issue of South-West Africa's constitutional status be referred to the International Court at the Hague. Confident of the legal force of the case against South Africa, Scott was flooded with 'an enormous sense of relief'.[20] He felt that his own task was fulfilled and that the Herero's cause could now be advanced more efficiently by the international experts. This perception, though hugely therapeutic at the time, was premature.

CHAPTER THIRTEEN
CELEBRITY STATUS

THE PROFILE OF Michael Scott published in the *Observer* on 4 December 1949 while its subject was still at the United Nations in New York was laudatory in tone, verging on the hagiographic. After bracketing Scott with David Livingstone and Albert Schweitzer as being 'among the few Europeans who have ever succeeded in crossing the barrier of suspicion that separates Black from White in Africa', the article focused on his 'strikingly handsome face that has something about it of the saint and something of the rebel'. Of Scott in action, it observed:

> He is totally uncompromising where he believes the principles of justice and humanity are involved, and he is unmoved by considerations of what may or may not be regarded as practical, even by his supporters . . . He is careless of food, clothes, and all material pleasures. For some years now, since he resigned from his Johannesburg parish he has had no regular income, and has lived and travelled on the alms of those who wish him well: he has lived exiguously.

It is sometimes suggested, on the measure-it-don't-read-it principle, that there is, in the long run, no such thing as bad publicity. But the good stuff is detectable almost immediately, and there could be none better in what was the strongest and most liberal quality Sunday newspaper of the day. Scott had been accorded what amounted to front-rank celebrity status, and with it a new level of opportunity.

There was no time like the present for capitalizing on such exposure, or so it seemed to members of Scott's Quaker support group, who had supplied the *Observer* writer, Terry Kilmartin, with most of the information for his article. They were therefore eager to set up a round of public appearances, press conferences and speaking engagements for him as soon as he got back to London. Scott, to no one's very great surprise, had another idea. On his return from New York, he would spend a day in Buckinghamshire, visiting his recently widowed mother, before flying off to India, well beyond the reach of his personal publicists.

Scott spent Christmas in Sevagram, the ashram which was Gandhi's home during the last years of his life, along with ninety other leading peace campaigners from thirty-five countries around the world. All the main categories of religious belief were represented at a conference that was first suggested in Gandhi's lifetime, with the idea that he should be its chairman and guide. By the standards of the UN it was a pleasantly informal and loosely structured event combining homage to Gandhi's memory with leisurely inspection of all the peace mountains that had yet to be climbed. Although it did not, as one of the organizers put it, 'waste time passing resolutions to go into government waste-paper baskets',[1] discussion roamed over the world's main friction areas: the nuclear arms race, US–Soviet relations, India–Pakistan, Palestine and, increasingly, Africa. Scott was very much at ease in the company of people who saw their own, and his, immediate problems in a global context. No clear-cut solutions presented themselves, but there was inspiration to be had in finding common principles of action across such a diverse range of faiths. Scott felt the form of worship devised for the occasion – combining hymns, chants, and sacred songs of East and West – reached beyond the confines of institutional religion in a way that expressed humanity's search for the divine.

In Sevagram, he began drafting the first chapters of *A Time to Speak*, evolving his central line of thought, which clearly indicated that he was not among those Christians who comforted themselves with anticipation of a Kingdom of Heaven on Earth: 'Just as there is no beginning to the story there is no ending. There is only a continuous struggle to affirm what is true, to deny what is untrue, to resist what is evil and to discover what there is of goodness and beauty in a world where their opposites seem often to be mightier than the forces of creation.'[2] But even someone inclined to see both history and the future in terms of permanent struggle occasionally needs rest and recreation in the present. And Scott found some for a few weeks in rural India.

The Indian detour was, with hindsight, good preparation for the trials to come. For the next two years Scott campaigned and worked on two continents (Europe and America) while his heart always seemed to be in a third (Africa). Though firm in his objectives, Scott often fretted about his angle of approach, about how to be in the right place at the right time with the right kind of support. Life suddenly became much more complicated. In South Africa at least, for all its perils, Scott knew he was in the right place.

It was always his intention to return to South Africa, if his church would have him. In March 1950 he vaulted the first hurdle when Bishop Bell restored Scott to the ranks of licensed priesthood by issuing him with the authority to preach in the diocese of Chichester.[3] As a priest again in good standing, Scott wrote to Bishop Reeves in Johannesburg asking for restoration of his South African licence, but to no avail. Scott heard on the clerical grapevine that Geoffrey Clayton, Reeves's superior, had dismissively described Scott as 'a freelance', a characterization designed to put him out of bounds.

In search of a compromise, Mother Geraldine Mary proposed that Scott should be allowed to use the convent attached to the St Joseph's Home orphanage as his base, but Reeves squashed the notion in a letter to Scott in February 1951: 'I thought I made it plain in previous correspondence that I would only be prepared to grant a Licence if you were engaged in full-time work for the church in the diocese and I have no such work to offer you.' Mother Geraldine Mary was distressed by what she described as the 'cold caution' of her bishop's response, though as a new man in post fresh from England, Reeves was obviously feeling his way. Many years later, after he had been seriously radicalized by the excesses of apartheid, Reeves told several people that he was 'sorry' about the way he had handled Scott's application.[4]

Scott's internal wrangling over what should be his geographical place in life would eventually be stilled in November 1951 by the South African government declaring him a prohibited immigrant. This prohibition also extended to South-West Africa, which remained firmly under the thumb of the Union, regardless of what the UN might say. As Scott had been out of the country for three years, the South African government could officially reconsider his status. Scott automatically appealed against the decision, but he would never be allowed to set foot in South Africa again.

The time spent before his prohibition had not been wasted. Indeed, Scott's activities in this interval almost certainly contributed powerfully to the decision to ban him. On his return, refreshed, from Sevagram, Scott made it clear that he wanted to extend the range of his concerns well beyond the specific plight of the Hereros. At his request the National Peace Council, with the support of Kingsley Martin, the distinguished editor of the *New Statesman*, funded a conference on the theme of racialism on the African continent with a view to finding constructive economic and social solutions. Out of this conference was born the African Relations Council,[5] essentially the 'three musketeers' in more modern attire, with flanking support. John Fletcher became Treasurer, with Esther Muirhead as Secretary, under the chairmanship of the Reverend Henry Carter, who also chaired the World Council of Churches Standing Committee on Refugees. The new Council, drawn from over twenty voluntary associations, provided Scott with his desired enlarged sphere of operation.

Through the spring and early summer of 1950, Scott undertook an intensive round of public-speaking engagements. According to the staid, establishment newspaper *The Times*, reporting on his April address at the Central Hall, Westminster, 'Scott had no difficulty in holding the attention of several thousand people.' The writer noted that his appearance was 'youthful and ascetic' and that his voice was 'calm and dispassionate', though the mildness of the speaker's manner 'belied the grave warning of the effects of the colour bar in South Africa'. The most compelling part of his speech, however, for what was in the main a law-abiding audience, was the development of his concept of 'the lawlessness of the law'. Apartheid, he maintained, was 'obstructing the natural, social and economic development of all races, the white races included'.[6] In this circumstance Christians had to challenge, and, if necessary, accept the penalty of unjust laws, rather than acquiesce in them.

Scott took the same message to Birmingham, Manchester, Liverpool and Bristol, and on to the academic uplands of Oxford and Cambridge. Journalist Guy Ramsey was also moved to comment on Scott's neglect of basic tub-thumping skills: 'No one less like a walking conscience, or firebrand or a crusader could be imagined.'[7] Scott's oratorical effects were produced by his presence and his ability to engage an audience's finer feelings, at least for most of the time. After making his main points, Scott had a tendency to ramble. On the issue of African development, Scott's imagination had been fired by a radical proposal to dam the Okavango river to irrigate the Kalahari desert. It became his dream of a kind of Tennessee Valley Authority for Bechuanaland, which he was always eager to share, along with precise estimates of the cubic capacity of the amount of water involved.[8] Scott's advisers gently indicated that this was perhaps one of the less riveting parts of his address, and might even be left out. But the Okavango flowed on.

Scott's fame or notoriety, depending on one's perspective, was enhanced by his persuading the publishing house Faber and Faber to bring out *In Face of Fear: Michael Scott's Challenge to South Africa*, in April 1950. The book's author was listed as Freda Troup (Freda Levson's maiden name), though large tracts of it consisted of direct quotations from Michael Scott, and it was produced under his overall guidance. According to the publisher's note on the jacket sleeve: 'The story has been written for Scott by Freda Troup, a South African friend and colleague. She has had access to all Scott's papers and has checked his facts and figures throughout.'

The papers were the ones that Scott had been obliged to leave at the Levsons' family home in Johannesburg before his unconventional exit from South Africa, and Freda Levson would use them to excellent effect. Her startling but undeniably arresting opening paragraph ran: 'One hundred years ago South Africa was like a carcase filled with maggots. People were pouring into the country from every side, devouring the land and looking for more . . .'

Having set the scene, she went on in dramatic style to detail the stories of Scott's adventures in southern Africa. It was a feisty and informative read, marred only by two relatively minor sins – one of commission, the other of omission – though it is difficult to be sure whether they were attributable to Freda Levson or her mentor Michael Scott. The first was the book's almost painfully determined effort to present Scott as a 'simple' essentially uncomplicated man, when it bristled with evidence to the contrary. The second was the omission of any mention of Scott's long Communist affiliation, though other less significant aspects of his earlier career were covered in some detail. Indeed, the suggestion that he might ever have had any partisan political leanings was dismissed rather scornfully. This was misleading though there was a mitigating circumstance.

Evidence from recently released security files suggests that even those most thoroughly acquainted with Scott's earlier Communist affiliation were inclined to view it as being of decreasing relevance. MI5, which had carefully monitored Scott's exploits through the 1940s to the extent of sharing intelligence with the South African security authorities, was now close to giving him a clean bill of ideological health. Its security appraisal of Scott, which was forwarded to 10 Downing Street in May 1950 marked 'secret', reported:

In South Africa SCOTT has devoted himself wholeheartedly to the cause of the coloured communities and has in this respect fulfilled the expectations of the Communist Party. It is believed that he did initially establish and maintain contact with the South African Communist Party, but that later he became isolated from them. When he was in England in 1947, 1948 and 1949 he received considerable assistance from the Indian League and the National Council for Civil Liberties, both 'progressive' organizations, in which Communists have been well represented, but although he received some publicity in the Daily Worker, he had little or no contact with Communist Party leaders, who were naturally anxious to exploit him for their own ends. Although there are indications that SCOTT's increased public prestige had made him difficult of access to officials of the British and South African Communist Party, it is possible that his earlier contacts with them may at any time be renewed.

The lingering element of doubt suggested by the last sentence would be overridden by a follow-up security report on Scott drafted in March 1951 and circulated as 'Top Secret' in the upper reaches of the Foreign Office and the Commonwealth Relations Office. This read:

Although the [Communist] Party has been eager to exploit his [Scott's] reputation, there is no evidence that he has taken the initiative in enlisting their support. Indeed, while the Party's campaign against the South African Government's anti-Communist legislation has increased the value of his name to them during the last six months, there are signs that he himself is deliberately avoiding contact with the party, who consider him to be 'most peculiar' and under the influence of Quakers.[9]

Scott's new-found celebrity in Britain had no discernible impact on his personal style. His modest needs in terms of living space were still supplied by the Quaker centre, though finding room for his fast-ascending mountain of papers was becoming a problem. His personal untidiness continued to amaze. Esther Muirhead was thrilled to acquire a second-hand Savile Row suit large enough to fit him, but noted sadly that Scott rapidly managed to customize it into dishevelment. He still habitually bulked out his pockets with an emergency supply of sweets. The big change for Scott was not so much in himself as in the attitudes of others towards him. People wanted to be associated with him, sometimes in the nicest possible supportive way, sometimes with a view to taking him over. Through 1950, detection of the motives of those making the keenest approaches became one of the key concerns of Scott's Quaker entourage.

Their vigilance sometimes verged on the ridiculous, but it proceeded from their intense admiration of Scott and desire to protect him. John Fletcher's response to any criticism of Scott, actual or implied, was, 'I trust him completely. His virtue controls me.' Esther Muirhead, who functioned as Scott's laundress as well as his secretary, thought he was en route to becoming 'a holy man'[10] – though one who would probably always need some motherly assistance. What they lacked in glamour was more than made up for in terms of commitment and industry. Then glamour in the person of Mary Benson arrived on the scene.

Benson, then aged twenty-nine, was an emancipated South African who worked with the film producer David Lean in New York. One of her compatriots sent her a copy of the Scott profile in the *Observer*, and she decided, on impulse, that she wanted to render her services to his cause, and that she would do so on her next trip to London. She had undoubted skills. During the last stages of the war she had been a captain in the South African Defence Force, the first woman to rise to that rank. She had served as personal assistant to a series of Allied commanders in Algeria and Italy, subsequently transferring to the UN Relief and Rehabilitation Administration, for which she worked in Athens and Vienna. In the United States she had held down a number of responsible production jobs in the film industry, and had displayed aptitude as a scriptwriter. Having grown up in Pretoria, she was well acquainted with human complexity, racial and otherwise. Her father, a Christian Scientist, earned his living as a hospital administrator. She was currently unattached.[11]

Benson's application to become one of Scott's assistants caused something close to consternation among the Quakers, partly because there was indeed a looming vacancy for which she was undeniably well qualified. With George Norton planning to return home soon, the recruitment of another South African-born helper made perfect sense, as the practical overseas experience of most of the Quakers was mainly in India. And with the UN still claiming much of Scott's attention, additional Stateside experience could not come amiss. The underlying worry about Benson was that she seemed too good to be true, unless, of course, she was an undercover spy for the South African government.

A meeting was arranged on the neutral territory offered by the British Film Institute, with the ostensible purpose of discussing editing improvements to Scott's documentary *Civilization on Trial*. The two protagonists were accompanied by 'seconds' – Mary Benson by the film-makers David Lean and Clive Donner; Scott by a full muster of 'musketeers', Fletcher and both Muirheads, with Norton also in puckish attendance, though he was the least concerned about any possibility of Scott succumbing to feminine wiles: 'Thank God, he's not God,' Norton would say of his great friend, 'He would have created everyone neuter for sure.' At the BFI encounter, the Quakers could not help noticing the stylishness of Mary Benson's 'New-Look' coat, and the fact that its occupant seemed lively and attractive. Their suspicions were not allayed.

The next stage of the vetting process would be tea with the Michael Scott committee. Benson was required to answer a number of pointed questions. Was she truly committed to the cause? Or did she have some other motive? Had she come to run off with Scott? Each member of the committee warned her of 'the special nature of this dedicated man'. There was, she should be aware, no room for a woman or any kind of destabilizing influence in his life. Benson emerged from the grilling on probation, deemed sufficiently trust-worthy to be given the thankless task of sorting out the huge packages of documents Scott had shipped back from the United Nations. But she was still not in the clear.

Scott decided she was probably a spy. In a state of agitation, he asked for all his papers back. They were returned in neat bundles, all organized, cross-referenced and catalogued. At this point Scott suppressed his doubts, and Mary Benson was on the team.

A more comprehensive threat to Scott's Quaker power base was presented by Canon John Collins, one of the Anglican Church's more turbulent priests. Collins had started an idealistic evangelical movement in Oxford just after the war, and it had shown remarkable staying power. Called Christian Action, it attracted a wide following across class barriers. Politically it was on the left, and was not afraid to cause offence, particularly on domestic issues. It would mobilize a campaign against capital punishment that was genuinely brave for its time. As a canon of St Paul's Cathedral, a few yards up the road from Fleet Street, Collins was geographically well placed to advance his various causes. He was also exceptionally good at it, to the detriment, some felt, of his churchly activities. Like Scott, Collins was not popular with many in the upper reaches of the Anglican hierarchy.[12]

Collins had some scant knowledge of South Africa, but his real interest was kindled by Scott's address at the UN and by *Cry, The Beloved Country*, a novel of extraordinary intensity about life in Johannesburg written by Alan Paton. Liberal South Africa being a comparatively small world, Paton also happened to be on friendly terms with Michael Scott, and in separate circumstances, with Mary Benson. Collins organized a lecture tour for Paton in Britain, but he had bigger plans for Scott. These came to fruition shortly after what Collins described as Scott's 'magnificent and prophetic'[13] Central Hall speech (which had been sponsored by Christian Action). In the face of some solid opposition on the Christian Action executive, Collins won the organization over to the idea of establishing a Race Relations section. He offered Scott the job as its first Director. In some ways the skills of Scott and Collins did seem complementary. It was possible, in the abstract at least, to envisage the reticent Scott as the brilliant original backroom thinker, while the ebullient, outgoing Collins commanded the front of house as the great implementer and publicist.

It was not, however, Scott's vision. And the threat of a Collins take-over bid would pass quickly. The reason Scott gave for turning Collins down was that the concept of a race section was too wide for him personally, as he wanted to maintain a steady focus on Africa.[14]

But it is possible that this was more of an excuse than a reason, and that Scott already sensed he and Collins were not destined to get along. He could not have foreseen, however, just how unpleasant relations between them would become.

The Quakers eventually lost control of their champion, but by a route that nobody could reasonably have anticipated and with, as it turned out, only a mild degree of bitterness and remorse. As part of his general duties, John Fletcher would try to arrange meetings for Scott with leading journalists, with a view to improving coverage of his activities. One of Fletcher's neighbours in Hampstead, the *Observer* journalist Bob Stephens, offered to fix up an encounter with the paper's editor, David Astor, who had already expressed an interest in meeting Scott, regarding him as 'a hero of our time'. It was routine stuff but, as it was the prelude to what became the most important connection in Scott's subsequent life, it is worth recounting first impressions, as Astor remembered them in a radio interview:

> Bob [Stephens] brought him [Scott] into the office together with an imposing bearded Quaker called John Fletcher and they came in and sat down in a row in the *Observer* office and I was immediately struck by the fact that Michael was the last one to speak. Everybody else talked bar him. I was very taken with him. It's hard to describe his silence because it – he had a great presence and a great sense of – of – can't say certainty, but a certain kind of authority. It takes you some time to discover how he does work, his funny combination of modesty, selflessness and intransigence, but it takes you a little time to come to the intransigence.[15]

The interesting aspect of this impression is that Astor might almost have been describing himself. As an editor, he was known for his rather hesitant, self-effacing style and for allowing other people to have an apparently dominant say, but also for his ability to make hard decisions and stick resolutely by them. Despite their different backgrounds, Astor and Scott were remarkably similar personality types: both listeners with manners that masked their strong sense of personal direction, and almost, but not quite, concealed wills of iron. Astor's atheism was no impediment to their almost instantaneous rapport as kindred spirits. Although there were no immediate developments at their first meeting, Astor would soon make it clear to Scott that he had plans for him in which he might, or might not, be interested. Meantime, he urged Scott to keep well, and if possible, keep out of South Africa, where he could only get himself locked up.

Astor's ability to make things happen was considerable. Unlike most up-from-the-ranks Fleet Street editors, Astor came to his eminence with an extensive range of personal political contacts and an exceptionally large quantity of money. His father, Waldorf Astor, was a multimillionaire mainly through the inheritance of large tracts of New York real estate, while his somewhat overbearing mother, Nancy, was undyingly famous as the first elected woman candidate to take her seat in the House of Commons. David imbibed the atmosphere of high politics and high finance from the cradle, though he seems to have been deeply uncertain about where it all might lead. Not unlike Scott, it had taken Astor a while to find his direction. After dropping out of Oxford, he drifted, often out of work, for several years before the war. At the commencement of hostilities he was interviewed for a post in the Special Intelligence Service (also known as MI6), and turned down. His war service in the Royal Marines was, nonetheless, distinguished, while his rapid post-war rise through the executive positions on his father's newspaper was seen to be on undoubted merit. His father's faith in him was mani-fested by his allocating 49 per cent of the *Observer*'s shares to his son. Astor's ability to attract and keep ace writers, of whom George Orwell was the most notable, was widely admired. Ideologically, Astor shared Orwell's strong opposition to Communism. But he was determinedly liberal in most respects, particularly on colonial issues. He was an early advocate of the controlled decolonization of Britain's possessions in Africa.

Like most serious Sunday papers, the *Observer* was well connected to government in both its visible and invisible aspects. Many journalists had actually been in the intelligence services during the war, so there was nothing strange about there being some traffic in favours between the newspapers and the secret world. However, too close an understanding was rarely good for newspapers, and probably not of much benefit to the nation's secrets. David Astor discovered as much when, by way of being cooperative, he allowed himself to be persuaded to offer a position to Kim Philby, who would work for the *Observer* out of Beirut. It was, of course, an unpleasant surprise to

Astor (and indeed to MI6), when Philby was subsequently unveiled as the Soviet superspy of the century.

Despite his privileged rise, Astor was very well liked by his journalists, though few could refrain from repetition of 'the mortgage story'. This was occasioned by Astor's having to ask a fellow *Observer* executive what exactly a mortgage was. The executive duly explained, adding that most people on the paper had one. 'My God,' Astor is alleged to have exclaimed, 'do you mean that all my staff is in debt?' Astor was also notable for being an unfashionably early enthusiast for psychoanalysis. His personal analyst was Sigmund Freud's daughter Anna, and journalists in trouble would find themselves gently steered in the direction of therapy as an alternative to seeking the more traditional consolation of excessive drink.[16]

There could be no doubting that if Astor became seriously involved with Scott he could position him in a much higher league than the Quakers could ever aspire to. And Astor was indeed serious. He wrote to Patrick Gordon Walker, Noel-Baker's successor as Secretary of State for Commonwealth Relations in the Labour government, about the need to assemble front-line, politically bipartisan support for Scott, with the idea of establishing a proper platform for his unique witness on African matters. The problem, as he saw it, was that Scott's current entourage was too marginal, 'chronically oppositional and crankish' and fringed with 'near-fellow-travellers'. Astor also maintained that Scott was 'aware of their futility'.[17]

Unfortunately for any plans in relation to Scott, long- or short-term, he became very ill, as his Crohn's Disease condition flared again. Opinions differed as to the precipitating cause, ranging from frustration over the agonisingly slow progress of the Herero case at the UN to tension arising out of the tug-of-love over his person between the Quakers and Astor, but it is likely that renewed extended acquaintance with the English climate was explanation enough. In the latter part of 1950, Scott would undergo another resection operation for obstruction of the lower bowel. He then dragged himself to the UN in time for its General Assembly, only to collapse again. A scheduled visit to see Tshekedi Khama in Bechuanaland also had to be cut short through illness.

Early 1951 would see him hospitalized at the Radcliffe Infirmary in

Oxford, as his operation wound opened again. On his discharge he was advised to avoid any stressful activity for at least another six months. Part of his convalescence was spent at David Astor's country home in Sutton Courtenay, near Oxford. Astor helped Scott maintain his interest in current affairs by inviting personalities in the media and academic world to come and see him there, among them the austere Lord Reith, head of the BBC, and the more engagingly outgoing Margery Perham, a fellow of Nuffield College, Oxford, who was one of the country's leading experts on Africa. Perham became a close friend.

The most impressive thing about Scott throughout this period was his absolute determination to keep the Herero cause alive. His prime concern through 1951 was to coax petitions out of church and left-wing organizations in support of the case for direct contact between the UN and African leaders in South-West Africa. When Mary Benson wrote to Scott urging him to take it easy, Scott wrote back, with some irritation:

> I think we should have an understanding that evaluation of things which seem to me to be of importance in relation to the health question are something which really only I can decide . . . Now is a crucial time when I must do what I can or lose all I have attempted to do in the past years . . . I cannot be protected from the consequences of my own actions and it is better for you not to try even from the goodness of your own heart.[18]

Although the precise thought is unexpressed, it seems likely that Scott's urgency was prompted by the idea that he might not have long to live.

In November 1951, Scott was at the UN again, this time meeting more conveniently in Paris. Scott received the news of his banning from South Africa while in Paris, but there were intriguing developments in other directions, though he was not aware of them at the time. Scott made a habit of trying to be on good terms with members of the British delegation, even though they tended to be on the wrong side of any vote in which he had an interest. One delegate who was particularly affable was the youthful Lord Tweedsmuir, son of the author John Buchan, who wrote *The Thirty-Nine Steps*, among many other thrilling tales of espionage and Empire. Agatha Harrison called him 'the nice Lord Tweedsmuir', and he and Scott had a number of long and pleasant, but seemingly inconclusive, chats.

Tweedsmuir, however, was coming to an interesting private conclusion, which he would impart in one of his diplomatic dispatches to the Commonwealth Relations Office in London. As he saw it:

> One fact is inescapable, Michael Scott is now regarded as the champion of the poor and oppressed by the non-white world. Nothing can stop the steady momentum of his reputation by a growing number of people in a growing number of countries . . . If we could find some crusade for him to follow which would be parallel to our ideas he would be a tremendous source of strength to us. If we are regarded as perpetually opposed to him our cause will suffer heavy moral damage.[19]

There does not appear to have been any direct communication, either telephonic or telepathic, between David Astor and Tweedsmuir, but they were clearly both thinking on much the same lines.

The actual business at the UN provided a new test of its ability to impose its will on South Africa. The International Court of Justice at the Hague, which constituted the legal arm of the UN with fifteen judges elected by the Assembly and Security Council, had done its job of deliberating on the South-West Africa question in a way that kept the issue topical and lively. While it accepted that South Africa could not be forced to place the Territory under UN Trusteeship, it also maintained that the League of Nations mandate could not be modified unilaterally by South Africa, and that it was therefore obliged to report regularly to the UN on the progress of its stewardship under mandate conditions. In practice, it meant the UN was still very much involved in what happened in South-West Africa, while the South African government continued to maintain that it was none of their business. The Malan regime did not accept the court's ruling, which, in the interests of speed, had only been advisory and therefore not binding. Nor did it accept Scott's modest proposal that the tribal chiefs Hosea Kutako, David Witbooi, Nikankor Hoveka and Theophilias R.K. Katjiuongua be allowed to testify directly to the United Nations.

Armed with his weight of petitions from what he described as 'interested organizations' in Britain, Scott did a brilliant job of persuading the Fourth Committee to issue official invitations to the tribal leaders. The invitations were coupled with a request to the South African government to facilitate their 'prompt travel'. Mary Benson, meanwhile, on a visit to her parents in South Africa, was re-routed to the Old Location at Windhoek, to assist the chiefs with their departure formalities and help maintain their resolve.

Anticipation of a breakthrough was high, though Margery Perham wrote to Scott in Paris with words of warning:

> My dear Michael, When you disappear into the whirlpool of the United Nations I know that sooner or later I shall see the results in my newspaper. I never expected to see such dramatic results as there have been . . . My only fear is that without Mary [Benson] to help you, you are almost certainly doing all you can to kill yourself by strain and overwork.[20]

Scott's health remained intact, as did the resolve of the chiefs. But it was not enough. On 9 January 1952, Chief Hosea Kutako cabled the UN with a regretful apology – they had been refused passports by the South African authorities. There was no way they could come.[21]

In the glum aftermath, Lord Tweedsmuir tried to comfort Scott with the notion that he had, after all, 'won a symbolic victory'. But Scott was hard to console. The only bright thought he had was that his edict of banishment from South Africa might prove to be less serious than he imagined, and that it might even soon be relaxed. In his official report on this conversation, Tweedsmuir dryly noted: 'I told him nothing in the world is more improbable.'[22]

CHAPTER FOURTEEN

EVICTION FROM AFRICA

ICHAEL SCOTT was one of history's more unusual heroes in that his main concern was to promote heroism in others. In part this can be seen simply as preaching the need for people to live up to the best in themselves and their beliefs: 'If politics is the art of the possible,'[1] he told a Catholic group in 1951, 'religion is the art of the impossible.' But it can also be interpreted as an invitation to others to share the weight of expectation loaded on his own shoulders, which sometimes seemed too heavy to bear.

What was described as Scott's 'one-man mission' on behalf of southern Africa's poor and dispossessed had transformed a seemingly ordinary priest into an extraordinary celebrity. But fame was a by-product of Scott's witness, not its purpose, and could even, conceivably, be its impediment. It is in the nature of shooting stars that they quickly disappear without trace. There was no doubting the strength of Scott's resolution, but the same could not be said for the public's attention span. With the Herero cause stalled at the UN, and Dr Malan tightening the screws of apartheid in South Africa, Scott was in danger of becoming an esteemed, but essentially marginal, voice. The fact that this never happened is a tribute to David Astor's skill as an organizer, and to his capacity for generosity as a friend.

In April 1952 Scott finally loosened his links with his Quaker support group, in which he was inescapably the lone charismatic star of the show, and merged his endeavours with a phalanx of leading experts and academics assembled by David Astor in what was called the Africa Bureau. It was intended that Scott, as the Bureau's first Honorary Director, should be *primus inter pares* (Astor described it as 'a vehicle for Michael'[2]), but the Bureau's aim was to be part of the political mainstream, which did not preclude dissent but certainly implied taking 'the art of the possible' very seriously indeed.

The cast list of those involved was like a roll-call of the liberal establishment. Flanking Scott as the Bureau's first chairman was Lord Hemingford, a Conservative peer recently returned from the

Gold Coast (later Ghana), where he had served as head of a teachers' training college at Achimota. The executive committee included Arthur Creech Jones, who had been Secretary of State for the Colonies in Attlee's Labour government, John McCallum Scott, a leading Liberal, and Lady Elizabeth Pakenham, wife of the former Labour minister, Frank Pakenham. The Bureau's headed notepaper listed no fewer than nine Honorary Presidents: Sir Maurice Bowra, Vice-Chancellor of Oxford University; the Very Reverend Principal John Baillie of Edinburgh University, and a former Moderator of the Church of Scotland; Professor Arthur Lewis, West Indian Professor of Political Economy at Manchester University; the Reverend Professor C.E. Raven, Warden of Madingley Hall, Cambridge; the Reverend Dr W.E. Sangster, Moderator of the Methodist Church; the Right Reverend J.L. Wilson, Bishop of Birmingham; Isaac Foot, a Liberal politician; James Crawford, representing the trade-union interest as President of the National Union of Boot and Shoe operatives; and Miss Mary Attlee, the former Prime Minister's sister, who had spent much of her life engaged on welfare work in South Africa.

There was also a third, and somewhat more significant tier of what were termed 'advisers' to the Bureau. These included Margery Perham, who also regularly advised the government on colonial issues, George W.W. Greenidge of the Anti-Slavery Society, Colin Legum, a South African journalist who wrote on African affairs for the *Observer*, and Astor himself. The Secretary of the Bureau was Mary Benson.

There were no other survivors of Scott's original entourage, though its break-up was achieved relatively painlessly. The Muirheads returned to welfare work in India. John Fletcher moved on to further campaigns with John Collins's Christian Action movement and generously told acquaintances that Astor's platform for Scott's work was better than anything he had been able to devise. George Norton, having already overstayed his leave in Britain, went back to his mission in Zululand. As the man who could be guaranteed to make Scott laugh[3] and take himself less seriously, Norton was probably the greatest loss, though the separation of the two priests seemed likely to be only temporary at the time. Sadly, it was rendered permanent a year later when Norton drowned while swimming off the Durban coast.

Astor provided the start-up costs for the new operation, which included premises at 69 Great Peter Street, above the office of the Society for the Propagation of the Gospel, and handily close to the Houses of Parliament. He also, crucially, settled an annuity on Scott of £1,000 a year (about £19,000 in today's money) to cover his living expenses, and would make a similar arrangement in respect of Mary Benson. There was still no marked effect on Scott's lifestyle. Though he would move out of the Quaker Centre it would be into the circumstance of having no fixed abode. When not staying with friends he would live in cheap bed-and-breakfast establishments, mainly in the Bloomsbury area, and occasionally, when working late, resort to the office couch. But possession of the annuity did have the effect of giving him a degree of independence from the organization of which he was now the director.

The declared aims of the Africa Bureau had a deeply uncontroversial ring to all but the most blimpish imperialists. They were, as stated in its first annual report:

> To inform people in Britain and elsewhere about African problems and African opinions thereon, and to convey to Africa accurate reports on events and attitudes in Britain that concern them.
>
> To help peoples in Africa in opposing unfair discrimination and inequality of opportunity and to foster cooperation between races.
>
> To promote policies for furthering economic, social and political development of all communities in Africa and especially the establishment of responsible self-government in countries where this does not exist.[4]

The Bureau's members were keenly aware of the need for change in the direction of self-government but were at the same time concerned to avoid the possibility of any violent change that might create opportunities for Communist advance. Aside from public education in African realities, the Bureau placed special emphasis on the need to provide African leaders and petitioners with effective support when they came to Britain. The year 1952 saw the beginning of the Emergency in Kenya in an effort to combat Mau Mau terrorist activity, and Scott often reflected that things in that colony might have been rendered much less dangerous if the Kikuyu delegation which came to Britain in the 1930s had not been given such short shrift by the political establishment of the day.[5] The Bureau was resolved that there should be no similar, damaging brush-offs through the 1950s.

The ethos of the operation was best conveyed by *Attitude to Africa*, a Penguin Special inspired by David Astor, with Scott and Colin Legum among its main contributors. Addressed to a popular audience, it reminded the electorate of Britain's continued direct responsibility for fourteen states in Africa, all in the process of transition or likely to be so in the relatively near future. It went on to argue, 'One of the greatest problems for Western statesmanship today is to anticipate, control, and guide the forces of nationalism and social revolution in Africa, so that the inevitable transition towards political autonomy and more industrialized economy may come with as little friction and upheaval as possible.'[6] This responsible outlook, combined with the Bureau's authority, would provide Scott with access at the highest level. It was said of Oliver Lyttelton, who became Colonial Secretary in the Conservative government that returned to power under Winston Churchill's leadership in September 1951, that the sight of Michael Scott entering his office would prompt him to say, 'Ah, here's my conscience walking through the door.'[7]

There was an undoubted nobility of purpose about the enterprise. But an objective observer might reasonably have deduced that another English rebel was being chloroformed in the time-honoured manner by accepting the warm embrace of the ruling class. The stated aims of the Bureau were certainly in line with Scott's beliefs, but they also seemed capable of achievement without him. Organization had never been Scott's forte and at the age of forty-five he was highly unlikely to develop any talent in that direction. On the other hand, Scott's unique qualities – his independence of mind and capacity for personal witness – did not appear likely to be over-exercised as part of an essentially bureaucratic structure. However, they soon found a means of expression.

At the heart of Britain's colonial policy at the time was the move to establish the Central African Federation, yoking together the interests of three British territories: Southern Rhodesia, Northern Rhodesia and Nyasaland. To its advocates, who were strong on both sides of the House of Commons, the federation idea was seen as being progressive in economic and political terms. To its critics, like Scott, it was seen as likely to extend the concept of white supremacy still further, in much the same way as the formation of the Union of South Africa had done early in the century.

Opposition on the ground was particularly intense in Nyasaland, where there was only a vestigial white population. People there saw themselves as being dragooned into submission to the white settlers who dominated the discriminatory political structures in the other two territories. A number of Nyasa chiefs came to London and petitioned against the federation proposal, with Scott's assistance but without success.[8] In March 1953 a motion in the House of Commons setting up the Federation was carried by 304 votes to 260. Although enabling legislation still had to be passed, Federation was now regarded as a done deal. All that remained was for Southern Rhodesia to deliver its verdict on the change in a referendum, and there was little doubt of its being favourable, with fewer than 500 Africans deemed eligible to vote in an electorate of over 40,000. Oliver Lyttelton, the Colonial Secretary who so esteemed Scott's 'conscience', was among those keenest for the Federation's success, seeing it as the possible model for another federation of Britain's colonial possessions in East Africa.

In April, Scott, acting on the basis of his earlier pledge of support to the Nyasa chiefs, but without consulting the Africa Bureau executive or its advisers, flew out to Nyasaland to offer assistance with a last-ditch stand against federation. It was not long before reports picking up on the outrage expressed in the predominantly white local press filtered back to London. On 16 April an editorial in the *Nyasaland Times* lamented, 'We find we can no longer hold to our old respect and regard [for Michael Scott]. The most shocking section of his address was when he ventured to draw a parallel between the martyrdom of the Lord Jesus Christ and the condition of our Africans in Nyasaland . . . This peripatetic Don Quixote is, for the people of Central Africa, a most unreliable guide, philosopher and friend. He might even prove to be their enemy.'

Opinions differ on whether Scott inspired or merely supported the passive resistance campaign against the imposition of federation. Scott would certainly maintain that he only provided support, though Mary Benson, who accompanied him at some of the public meetings in

Nyasaland and in neighbouring Northern Rhodesia, was of the opinion that his support sometimes shaded into outright advocacy.[9] The scope for civil disobedience was unusually wide, especially in Nyasaland, where many of the chiefs had official duties as 'Native Authorities'. Refusal to follow agricultural, forestry and veterinary laws, boycott of legislative and other councils, and, most importantly, refusal to collect taxes could all come under the heading of passive resistance.

When eighty-three chiefs openly expressed their readiness to defy the new Federation, the colonial authorities decided it was time to move against the opposition's leaders. One of them, Philip Gomani, the Paramount Chief of the Angoni, was Scott's host in Lizulu. Gomani had issued a circular to his people advising them to 'take a holiday as far as the payment of taxes are concerned'. Scott was with Gomani, who was a sick man recently out of hospital, when the police came to arrest him. Scott would later write, in a pamphlet entitled *African Episode*, about the events of that evening:

> The chief sat with his wife and counsellors round one of the fires . . . The people were all exhorted not to resort to any acts of violence, no matter what happened, or how provocative the police might be if they came. There was no hatred or anger in his voice as he appealed to God, to Jesus Christ and to the Queen to behold the plight of his people and to take pity on them in their fear and trouble. The police raid was expected any moment . . .
>
> Suddenly everybody was alert as a young boy came running with the news that police cars and trucks were arriving. The people cleared a passage for them and the leading car drew up at the chief's house, the others remaining at some distance. . . .
>
> There was much confusion and delay. Then one of the African leaders asked that Chief Gomani should be allowed to address his people and explain what was happening, or that someone else should do so [the 'someone else' in this instance seems to have been Scott himself]. But the police emphatically refused to allow this.
>
> By coaxing and persuasion the argument was carried on with the chief moving in the direction of the front door. Eventually the police emerged on to the veranda and tried to force a passage through the crowd to the car.
>
> When the chief had been brought to within a few feet of the car,

the police commissioner, apparently thinking it might be impossible to get him into the car, blew his whistle and the police began to launch a tear gas attack. (It afterwards transpired that the African Askaris refused to make a baton charge). The tear gas was thrown amongst the crowd, who did not know what it was, and believed it to be poisonous. They scattered and the chief was hustled into the car and driven away. I followed on foot and found that it had been stopped some way down the road, and that about ten Africans were pushing it in the opposite direction to where the driver intended to go. Then someone opened the car doors, and the chief was carried away on their shoulders to a small hut in a nearby village . . .

It was decided to take the chief into Portuguese territory, where many of the chief's tribe reside. As dusk fell, he was lifted on to one man's shoulders, and the whole party, including his wife and two sons, set off across country to the Mozambique border, which was crossed some time after midnight . . . [10]

The daring of the chief's escape prompted a rapid official response. On 28 May Scott was declared a prohibited immigrant and immediately deported. There was no obligation to provide a specific reason, and none was given. Chief Gomani and his sons were handed over to the Nyasaland police by the Portuguese authorities a few days later, though Gomani would die before he could come to trial.

Meanwhile, Scott's adventures in Nyasaland had created alarm on the Africa Bureau executive. On 29 April, in his absence, it had passed a critical resolution noting that 'one of the functions of the Bureau was to interpret African opinion in this country, rather than to advise Africans on how to deal with certain questions'. On 14 May, still in Scott's absence, the criticisms became more explicit. The minutes recorded that:

> Mr McCallum Scott expressed grave concern both about Michael Scott's departure without prior consultation with the executive and about the advice he appeared to be giving the Africans according to newspaper reports. He felt that if the Africans were determined to continue resisting federation and if the Bureau decided to support this line he would be obliged to resign.

Arthur Creech Jones, a critic of Federation who had written a pamphlet entitled *Challenge, the Fallacy of Federation*, was supportive of Scott's objectives but troubled by his methods. He expressed the worry: 'Our responsibility was to interpret African opinion to the British public, and to give information regarding African opposition but if it were identified with that opposition now that the Federal Bill has been passed the Bureau would be awkwardly placed.'[11] The minutes also recorded that the chairman, Lord Hemingford, regretted not referring Michael Scott's intention of 'thinking of going to Central Africa' to the Bureau's executive when he had first heard about it. Hemingford said that his original impression was that Scott was going there to help the Africans 'cool' their disappointment at the inevitability of federation.

In serious trouble with his executive, Scott would also experience flanking fire from the ranks of the advisers. Margery Perham, an admirer of Scott, but often an exasperated one, wrote to him from Nuffield College on 30 June:

> My difficulty has always been that I never quite understand your views about your duty in these matters. I know you go straight ahead without bothering whether people on the sidelines agree or not; at the same time it makes it difficult for me to come out 100 per cent in your defence. I do agree that we have done a great wrong to Nyasaland, but as a practical, or, as you would say, a compromising person, I believe we should do all that is possible under federation.[12]

Despite her private reservations, Perham displayed commendable public unity. She also penned a letter to the *Spectator* (published on 17 July) in which she praised 'the speed of decision, logic and courage' exhibited by Scott in Nyasaland. The Bureau's executive also backed off from a full confrontation with its director. At its meeting on 14 July, at which Scott was asked to explain himself, he broadened the argument by making a powerful case for passive resistance as the most constructive alternative to violent change in Africa. The minutes recorded Hemingford's accepting that passive resistance was compatible with Christianity but he was worried by Scott's statement to the Bishop of Nyasaland that it was 'necessary to Christianity'.[13] There were evidently bruised feelings, but no resignations.

Scott also managed to muddy his new-found reputation for ideological soundness with the security services. When the Africa

Bureau was first established, MI5 reported in a message to the British security liaison offices in East and Central Africa: 'We have nothing to indicate that the Bureau is of security interest or that it is likely to be a vehicle for Communist designs,' and that, 'in any event, we do not consider that the Reverend Scott's case is of any particular security interest at the moment.'

In the wake of his visit to Nyasaland, however, there was a flurry of resumed interest in his security file. A message to London from the Security Liaison Office, Central Africa, in Salisbury, Southern Rhodesia, accused Scott of doing 'incalculable harm to good race relations in Nyasaland' and concluded with a lament: 'What a pity his Bishop cannot make him settle down quietly somewhere to the "cure of souls".' Another message indicated the Director of Intelligence and Security in Kenya had declared Scott a Prohibited Immigrant in his bailiwick, apparently out of support for his exasperated Central African colleagues. In London MI5 tapped a telephone call between Scott and Dr Hastings Banda, a G.P. in Harlesden who was already being spoken of as a possible eventual independence leader in his native Nyasaland. The intercept failed to uncover anything that could be deemed Communist-inspired, but it did yield the intelligence that Scott, with Banda's backing, was keen to draw the United Nations into Britain's colonial affairs.[14] This cannot have been welcome news from the British government's point of view.

In October 1953 Scott elevated anxiety levels at the Africa Bureau yet again by raising the issue of federation at the United Nations, with the assistance of the Indian delegation. Claiming to speak for eighty-three tribal chiefs in Nyasaland, as well as Northern Rhodesian African leaders, Scott asserted that federation would obstruct progress and reinforce racial barriers. An angry Lord Hudson, representing Britain on the Fourth (Trusteeship) Committee, said in response that any opposition to the Federation at the UN raised 'in acute form the question of the extent to which it would still be useful for Britain to cooperate in this work'.[15] Lord Hudson refused to clarify his remarks, but several delegates interpreted them as a threat by Britain to walk out for the first time in the history of the UN if the matter was pursued.

Under Article 73 of the Charter, Britain had to report on its non-self-governing territories, but the UN had only very limited powers of scrutiny compared to those it exercised in relation to the Trusteeship territories and South-West Africa. The British government was firmly of the view that federation was a domestic concern. And, what was more, David Astor and Mary Benson, Scott's two closest allies, felt the government had a point. They both felt it was impolitic of Scott to goad the British delegation over federation when the main objective at the UN was to line up opposition against the more manifest evil of apartheid. By now Scott had successfully upset every significant echelon of the Africa Bureau.

At this stage, however, concern over Scott's tactics was subsumed by the need to rally round the chief, who suddenly came under virulent attack. In a speech, reported in the *Rand Daily Mail* on 1 November, Sir Godfrey Huggins, the first Prime Minister of the new Central African Federation, referred to what he said were the consequences of Scott's visit to Nyasaland. He was accurately quoted as saying: 'The Reverend Michael Scott's bag as a result of his visit was eleven dead. That isn't bad for a peaceful missionary.'

The deaths referred to had occurred not long before in disturbances in the Cholo area, where there had been long-standing tensions over land rights and the 'thangata', rent payable by Africans on private estates. By the time these riots took place, Scott had long gone, as his public press statement in response to the charge made clear: 'At the time of the deaths of eleven Africans I was five thousand miles away having been deported without trial from Nyasaland more than two months previously. I asked for an opportunity to face any charges that might be made against me through some judicial process. This was refused.'[16]

In much the same way as he had previously written to Dr Malan, Scott followed up his public response with a private letter to the new Prime Minister, seeking reconciliation of their viewpoints. Unlike Malan, Sir Godfrey favoured it with a comparatively lengthy, and not entirely unfriendly, reply. Between its lines, however, there was the clear message that the rapid advances towards self-government already taking place in West Africa were unlikely to be matched in the Central African Federation. Sir Godfrey wrote:

Dear Mr Scott. Thank you for your letter. Perhaps I gave you credit for more than you had earned seeing you were not the only responsible

European who, probably unknowingly, helped to set off trouble in Nyasaland. When you first took up the Native African cause I considered you were on a good wicket but since then you, who should know the African, have adopted an irresponsible attitude possibly the result of your knowledge of the Natives in South Africa who have been in contact with Europeans for some 300 years.

In Central Africa (so-called) there are still only a handful of Europeans, more than half of whom have migrated here since the war, and our Natives are not so sophisticated as the Union Natives, although, even there, attempts at passive resistance do not always remain orderly. I have no hesitation in saying that anyone who urges passive resistance on our Africans is urging them to riot. There is no such thing as passive resistance as far as our people are concerned. They understand obedience and violence and nothing between the two. I have no doubt this will change with time and education.

A few of the Native leaders are well educated wise men but most are self-seekers and far from wise. When the masses wake up they will see through the latter type, in fact they are already doing so.

I am sorry I had to make a scapegoat of you, who started well, and were not influenced by political considerations, but now you are mixed up with people who are a great menace to the peace and advancement of all the people in this part of the world.

The African will come on, there is no doubt of that, and he has already advanced more rapidly than the Georgian working man in England. We must, for the sake of all of us, see that the process is evolutionary, not revolutionary, and if we achieve that object we shall be blessed and produce one of the happiest countries in the world. There are faults on both sides but if they are not magnified by outsiders I have great hope for the future . . .

Meanwhile I would draw to the attention of you and your associates Cromwell's famous letter to the General Assembly of the Church of Scotland on August 3rd, 1650: 'I beseech you, in the Bowels of Christ, think it possible you may be mistaken.'

Alert to the possibility of further dialogue, Scott wrote back to Sir Godfrey, politely requesting a lifting of his banishment order as a preliminary to their meeting personally. But this time the Prime Minister replied more tersely: 'I am very sorry but there is no possibility of your being admitted to any part of the Federation of Rhodesia and Nyasaland at least until the Africans have come to realise that the setting up of this Federation will operate in their benefit'.[17]

The Africans never did manage to come to such a realisation. And with the passage of time it became clear the evolutionary processes of Central Africa entrenched white interests in a way that brought it ever closer to the stern apartheid practices of the South. This development was not lost on the Africa Bureau's executive which soon came to share Scott's militancy on the subject of the Central African Federation.

In South Africa, meanwhile, the politics of cooperation between the unenfranchised races that Scott had attempted to pioneer, but almost despaired of ever being achieved, was actually taking place. On the morning of 26 June 1952, the same day as the Africa Bureau's opening press conference, there was a significant development at Port Elizabeth railway station, where a party of thirty-three protesters deliberately made their way through the 'Whites Only' entrance. As they were arrested and marched away to jail, they sang freedom songs interspersed with chants of 'Mayibuye Afrika!' ('Let Africa Come Back'). They were giving the first public expression to the Campaign for the Defiance of Unjust Laws, whose lineage could be traced directly back to Scott's earlier acts of defiance.

Under the direction of Nelson Mandela, then national president of the ANC's Youth League, Africans, coloureds, and Indians partici- pated in a national campaign against the raft of racist laws passed by the Malan government. Among the prime targets were the Population Registration Act, grading all South Africans according to race; the Group Areas Act, creating the foundation of residential apartheid; the Bantu Authorities Act; and the regulations governing the pass laws, along with the Suppression of Communism Act. Over the next six months 8500 people took part in a protest movement that involved deliberately going to jail for defiance of racially dis- criminatory laws. Although white participation was limited, it was not insignificant. Those arrested and imprisoned as 'defiers' included Scott's biographer Freda Levson (Troup) and Bettie du Toit, who had been at Scott's side during the passive resistance campaign in Durban. None of the unjust laws was repealed, but by the end of the protest Mandela was able to report that the ANC's membership had shot up from some 20,000 to 100,000.

The Defiance Campaign also had an impact in Britain, where the Africa Bureau was trying to widen its base of operations. In 1952 the Scottish Council for African Questions was established with committees in Edinburgh, Glasgow, St Andrews and other centres. In January 1953 the Manchester and District Council for African Affairs would come into existence, finding its support, according to a report in the *Manchester Guardian*, 'in the Christian churches, the Liberal Party and to some extent the Labour Party'. The Sheffield Africa Committee and the Buxton Africa Forum were founded a few weeks later. April saw the beginning of the Tyneside Africa Council, and similar bodies later sprang up in Leeds, Oldham, Birmingham, Cambridge and Bolton. Although not formally part of the Bureau's structure, the regional councils usefully contributed to its funds and provided forums for its front-line speakers. Communication between them was to be facilitated by the Bureau's regular publication, *Africa Digest*, focusing on the latest issues. The general indifference to African questions that had characterized the immediate post-war period was now a thing of the past.

The Africa that confronted the Bureau and its assorted satellites was still almost entirely a European preserve. South of the Sahara only Ethiopia and Liberia – founded on the west coast by freed American slaves in the nineteenth century – could be classed as independent. And while burgeoning nationalist sentiment throughout the continent gave rise to a general impression that an unscrambling of Africa could not be long delayed, the colonial powers, initially, appeared to be in no great hurry. Of the four major ones – Britain, France, Belgium, and Portugal – only Britain in West Africa had devised a phased plan for the transfer of power to indigenous populations.

In many places it was the existence of strongly entrenched white settler populations that impeded any transfer of power. This was true of the Arab north, as well as the black south. Mediterranean Africa saw independence granted rapidly to Tunisia and Morocco, while Algeria, with its large French settler community, would provide the theatre for a long and bitter civil war. Among the British colonies, the Gold Coast (later Ghana) and Nigeria were early candidates for independence, mainly because there were, outside the colonial administration and trading structures, few white faces to be seen. In East Africa things were more problematic. Kenya had a large and wealthy white farming community, which was eager to exert influence over neighbouring Tanganyika and Uganda (in much the same way as the Southern Rhodesian settlers had managed to extend their influence over Northern Rhodesia and Nyasaland through federation). The thrust of official British policy in these situations was to try to achieve momentum towards self-government on the basis of 'partnership' between the races, though Central Africa's Sir Godfrey Huggins rather devalued the term's coinage when he memorably described federation as exemplifying 'the partnership between the horse and its rider'.[18]

One of the Africa Bureau's continuous tasks would be the scrutiny of the various 'partnership' proposals to see if they contained, as they often did, legislative and executive mechanisms likely to ensure white domination after independence. In Kenya's case, this concern for the future would combine with contemporary worries about brutality in the detention camps introduced as part of the Emergency. Scott was himself a great letter-writer on these subjects, mainly to *The Times* and the *Manchester Guardian*, and he would encourage letter-writing campaigns by the various African Councils to their regional papers as a way of influencing local MPs. One of the first of many publications issued by the Bureau, written by Adrian Hastings, a former Catholic missionary, was entitled *White Domination or Racial Peace?*.

On these issues Scott was to the left of the Conservative government but not out of kilter with a growing weight of liberal opinion. His more individual contribution would be shown in his unusually high sensitivity to traditional forms of African organization. Scott was no tribalist. As a churchman, he was proud of the efforts made by David Livingstone and other early Christian missionaries in combating the slave trade in Africa. He had no time for witch doctors and little sympathy for superstitious beliefs that invested inanimate objects with spiritual power. But where, as was frequently the case, tribal organization had evolved along consensual, even democratic, lines Scott believed it could provide a nucleus of cohesion in what was bound to be an uncertain future. Scott was also persuaded that in a continent which was, beneath the colonial veneer, still in many respects an enormous patchwork of tribes, provision and respect for minority interests were essential to the independence process and the prospects for peace thereafter. These attitudes would inform the Bureau's reaction in 1953 to the expulsion from Uganda of the Kabaka, ruler of the kingdom of Buganda. The Kabaka, with his ruling council, the Lukiiko, was seen by the colonial authorities as being a key impediment to progress towards unitary self-government in the colony. The Africa Bureau assumed leadership of a campaign that equipped the Kabaka with the best legal advice in London that ensured his return home, albeit with reduced powers.[19]

The Bureau also found itself deeply immersed in the tribal politics of Bechuanaland, in a way that touched directly on Tshekedi Khama, the Regent of the Bamangwato tribe who first introduced Scott to the Hereros, though the prime focus would be on his nephew, the young chief elect, Seretse. The complex events surrounding these characters would be entertainingly fictionalized in Nicholas Monsarrat's novel, *The Tribe That Lost Its Head*, but the plain facts needed scant embellishment for dramatic effect. During much of the action Monsarrat worked as a press officer in the British High Commission where, as part of his duties, he edited the intelligence newsletter TERGOS (short for 'Territories' Gossip').[20]

While studying law at Oxford University, Seretse Khama met, fell in love with and married Ruth Williams, the daughter of a retired British Army officer. In response to rage expressed in South Africa at the prospect of sharing a border with a black chief married to a white Englishwoman, the British government, then still Labour, cravenly exiled Seretse. At the time Malan's administration was on the verge of introducing its cherished Prohibition of Mixed Marriages Act.

Seretse's banishment exacerbated the problems among the Bamangwato, who were already divided over the merits of the marriage. Tshekedi, who had been Regent since Seretse's infancy, was among those who felt the marriage should not have taken place without his consent.[21] Conflict in the tribe resulted in Tshekedi also being exiled and he would follow his nephew to London where Scott's help was enlisted. Scott's role was to bring about a degree of reconciliation between uncle and nephew and to exert pressure on the colonial authorities to revoke their banning orders. In her biography of Tshekedi, published in 1960, Mary Benson described how he and Scott went about their lobbying in Westminster and Fleet Street:

> They would emerge from the Bloomsbury Hotel like moles, one short and thickset, the other tall and thin and, heads down, minds intent, they would hurry along weighed down by briefcases bulging with memoranda. They were quite unaware, for instance, that the Festival of Britain was on and were astonished when eventually they were driven along the Thames to see its lights.[22]

With the formation of the Africa Bureau, Scott was able to bring bigger guns to bear, involving both David Astor and Margery Perham in the lobbying process, though it would take several more years before Seretse and Tshekedi were free to return to their homeland and participate in their tribe's affairs. Tshekedi, who had been appointed one of the Africa Bureau's Honorary Presidents while in London, died soon afterwards but Seretse would assume leadership of the whole country when it became independent as Botswana in 1966. In his book, *The First Dance of Freedom*, Martin Meredith saw this development as presaging one of Africa's few happy endings: 'Botswana, under Seretse Khama,' he wrote, 'provided a rare example of a multi-party democracy, where elections were regularly contested and political life was free from corruption; his death, in 1980, was mourned by his countrymen.'[23] There would be no comparable felicitous outcome as a consequence of the Kabaka's return to Uganda. Independence there would be the prelude to ruthless abrogation of Buganda's autonomy by the first prime minister, Milton Obote, and the imposition of one-party rule, out of which would grow the monstrosity of Idi Amin.

Scott's other early initiative at the Bureau, to which he attached great importance, was to set up trusts which looked to the future of Africa. The African Development Trust was set up primarily to assist St Faith's Mission Farm near Rusape in Southern Rhodesia. An imaginative, multiracial enterprise, it had been established by Guy Clutton-Brock, an independent, Scott-like character who had been a probation officer in London's East End. Scott had briefly considered setting up something similar himself ('a kind of ashram') after his banning from South Africa, but settled instead for writing about

Clutton-Brock's effort. His article appeared in the *Observer* under the headline 'A Practical Hope for Africa'. After a few years the African Development Trust would be merged into the Intermediate Technology Group, set up by E.F. Schumacher, the radical economist and author of *Small Is Beautiful*, whose thinking Scott admired.[24]

The African Protectorates Trust, launched on royalties donated by Freda Levson (Troup) from her book *In Face of Fear*, was geared to establishing scholarships for bright Africans from South-West Africa and the High Commission Territories (Bechuanaland, Basutoland and Swaziland).[25] Its first scholar was intended to be Berthold Himumuine, Scott's interpreter on his first contact with the Hereros. Margery Perham secured him a place at Oxford University, but the South African government refused to issue him with a passport, an act which would earn it the censure of the UN's Fourth Committee. Himumuine would die before there could be any second thoughts. Scott later expanded the idea by setting up an Africa Educational Trust (AET) to provide scholarships for Africans in other countries, with Professor Alexander Carr-Saunders, a former director of the London School of Economics, as its first chairman. The AET, which went on to absorb the African Protectorates Trust, survives and provides scholarships for Africans to this day.

The development of the Bureau's activities was reflected in the expansion of its staff, though its modest premises made six people a crowd likely to violate the local authority office density regulations. Originally it was thought that Mary Benson's ability to understand Scott's near-indecipherable handwriting would confine her to the office. But she was able to pass on this skill to Jane Symonds and Lorna Richmond, two able young Englishwomen, and free herself for other activities. Jan Green, described by Scott as having 'a genius for inspiring theatre people to give their talents for a cause they believe in',[26] organized the charity events that contributed to the Bureau's funds. Of the volunteers who often worked in the office the most important were Ernest and Beth Morton, friends of Scott from his Quaker Centre period. A Jewish refugee from Nazi persecution in Germany, Ernest served in the British Army during the war and later, like his Scottish wife, became a Quaker. The Mortons, who lived nearby, also provided an added service by allowing Scott to hold his frequent 'off the record' meetings in their flat.

As a boss, Scott was not a hard taskmaster in the conventional sense but he was enormously hard to follow. Like Gandhi, he believed 'a votary of truth is often obliged to grope in the dark'.[27] But the process could create problems. Scott's habit of making decisions after 'inner disquisition', whilst well suited to a lone operator, did not always choreograph well with organizational needs. There was nothing uncharacteristic about the dance he led his executive committee over his Nyasaland intervention. It came to be regarded as the norm. Mary Benson wrote of her boss's style in committee: 'If others disagreed with his point of view, he did not argue and might even nod sympathetically. Not unnaturally they assumed his silence signified assent, but often, no sooner were we back in the office than he followed the course which he had originally decided.'[28]

While he could present a case effectively, Scott rarely showed an inclination for actually arguing one against opposition. Personal confrontation was not his style, though personal pursuit of objectives was, even if it meant bypassing what his fellow committee members thought was a decision. Meetings with the executive and 'advisers' could be long and wordy but often seemed to stray from the point. Some thought this was an aspect of Scott's prodigious absent-mindedness, but his patron David Astor did not labour under any such delusion, at least not after Scott drew his attention to a cartoon which he said illustrated the way he operated. It depicted a fox eluding the pack, leaving the hounds streaming off in the wrong direction.[29]

There was no question about Scott's being the life and soul of the Africa Bureau, but he was also its principal source of exasperation. Perhaps fortunately for the orderly dispatch of routine office business in London, he was often away, leading another life in New York.

CHAPTER FIFTEEN

MAN ABOUT MANHATTAN

ENTRY INTO THE land of the free and the home of the brave
was never a simple business as far as one of its more regular
visa applicants, the Reverend Michael Scott, was concerned.
And it would become even more complicated during the
McCarthyite era: the witch-hunting, 'reds-under-the-bed' period
that disfigured and disrupted every aspect of American public life
from its government to its motion picture industry.

This feverish period was labelled 'McCarthyite' after Joe
McCarthy, the egregious and energetic Senator for Wisconsin, but it
also owed a great deal to Patrick McCarran, the Senator for Nevada,
who was one of history's first UN-bashers. At one of his Senate
judiciary subcommittee hearings, McCarran elicited what he thought
was sound testimony to the effect that several hundred subversives,
including Moscow-trained terrorists, were roaming America under
the auspices of the UN. The testimony was later discredited but
McCarran, undaunted, moved on. In 1950 he devised the Internal
Security Act as a weapon against what were seen as the machinations
of an international Communist conspiracy. Though opposed by
President Truman, who thought it mocked the Bill of Rights, it won
majorities in both the House and the Senate. With the United States
at war in Korea, it was a bad time for legislators to appear in any way
'soft' on Communism.

The impact of the Internal Security Act was brought home to
Scott when applying for a visa to attend the UN in New York in the
autumn of 1952. In addition to responding to the routine inquiries,
Scott was asked to make this affirmation:

I solemnly swear that I am not a member, nor have I ever been a
member of the Communist, Nazi, Fascist, Falange or any other
totalitarian party or any section, branch, subsidiary, affiliate or sub-
division of such party in any country. Furthermore I have never been
affiliated with any such organization.[1]

145

The official guidance to those who felt unable to take such an oath was that they might be 'excludable' (i.e. still eligible for a visa) if they provided names, dates, and particulars related to the suspect organizations of which they were currently, or had previously been, members. Scott refused to take the oath, or give 'excludable' particulars, and publicized his reasons in the New York press: 'I am not a Communist,' his statement read, 'but I cannot undertake to give on oath a full and truthful statement on all these questions which, having regard to all their moral and legal implications, cannot be considered fair questions.' The oath procedure, he argued, amounted to 'a screening process by the US authorities on those attending the United Nations', which violated an earlier agreement between the UN and the US government, providing for 'free access to the United Nations for those having accreditation to it'.[2] It was, of course, a response that spared Scott the embarrassment of raking over the Communist affiliations in his own past, but it was also an undoubted issue of principle, appreciated as such within the Secretariat of the UN, already in the grip of a major 'red scare', and by a broad spectrum of American liberal opinion.

Scott effectively won his argument with the visa authorities, and with his accreditation to the International League for the Rights of Man (ILRM) still intact, was allowed in to attend the UN, though under tight conditions. The UN itself, however, was given a gruelling time by McCarran's Senate Internal Security Subcommittee, with flanking assistance from a New York Grand Jury, directed by Roy Cohn, the Assistant District Attorney who later became Senator McCarthy's unsavoury Chief Counsel. By the end of 1952 some thirty-eight alleged 'UN subversives' had been identified. These were American nationals working in the UN Secretariat who had refused to answer questions about their supposed Communist ties, often by pleading the Fifth Amendment. Though no criminal charges were brought against any of them, most lost their jobs. According to Linda Melvern in *The Ultimate Crime*, her penetrating book about the United Nations, the generalized charges of subversion and espionage that brought them down amounted to 'a cruel hoax', designed to cover up the fact that UN personnel were being weeded out for having radical convictions: 'the very reasons that drew them to work on such an experiment in internationalism in the first place'.[3] Several

The Reverend Perceval Caleb Scott, Michael Scott's father. *Lorna Richmond Collection*

Michael Scott (left) with his brothers, Roy (sitting) and Nigel. *Lorna Richmond Collection*

Michael as a prep-school boy with his pet guinea pig. *Lorna Richmond Collection*

Hosea Kutako, chief of the Herero tribe in South West Africa (now Namibia). *Charles P. Channon*

Cartoon tribute to Scott in *The Leader* for his support of the Indian civil disobedience campaign against South Africa's restrictive 'Ghetto Act' which led to his imprisonment in 1946. *The Leader*

Tshekedi Khama, the exiled Regent of the Bamangwato tribe in Bechuanaland (later Botswana), pictured in England with Michael Scott and Scott's mother, Ethel. *Lorna Richmond Collection*

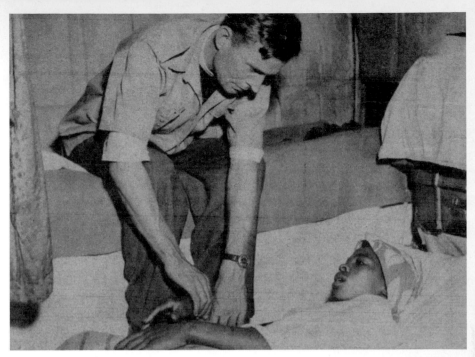

Scott with a smallpox victim in Tobruk, the shantytown on the outskirts of Johannesburg, where the official South African health and sanitation authorities feared to tread in 1947. *Photo News*

Scott inspects what remains of his living quarters in Tobruk after the neighbouring church – also made of canvas – was gutted in an arson attack. *Rand Daily Mail*

The apartheid cabinet of 1948: prime minister Malan (seated, third from left); his successor as premier, Hans Strydom (seated, second from right); Eric Louw (standing, third from right). *National Archives of South Africa, Cape Town*

Rev. Michael Scott: "You chose white, I think?"

Captioned 'You chose white, I think', this cartoon, featuring Scott playing chess with Eric Louw, the apartheid government's Minister of External Affairs, appeared in a Pretoria newspaper in 1958. *The Pretoria News*

Scott with Tshekedi Khama and Mary Benson lobbying against the British government's exiling of Tshekedi and his nephew, Seretse, outside the House of Commons in 1951. *Lorna Richmond Collection*

Scott and Mburumba Kerina petitioning on behalf of South West Africa at the United Nations in 1956. Though effective together in public, they were often privately at loggerheads. *United Nations*

En route to protest at a nuclear missile base under construction outside Swaffham, Norfolk, in December 1958. Marching in the front rank with Scott are two young civil disobedience campaign leaders, April Carter and Michael Randle. All three went to jail. *Austin Underwood*

Scott and the philosopher Bertrand Russell leading a 'sit-in' protest against nuclear weapons on the pavement outside the Defence Ministry in Whitehall in February 1961. *Lorna Richmond Collection*

Nagaland welcomes Scott's peace mission. *Lorna Richmond Collection*

Scott on parade in 1966 with the leaders of the Nagas resistance movement, all wearing their best suits in anticipation of an audience with India's prime minister, Mrs Indira Gandhi. *M. Aram*

Nelson Mandela made an undercover visit to London in 1962 while on the run from the South African police. Here the fugitive ANC leader takes in the sights with two of Michael Scott's ablest helpers, Freda Levson (centre) and Mary Benson. *Leon Levson*

Scott's long-term friends and allies.
Left, George Bell, Bishop of Chichester,
who originally ordained him. *Lorna Richmond Collection*

Centre, Lorna Richmond, who worked at the Africa Bureau and later lived with him.
Lorna Richmond Collection

Right, David Astor, the editor of the *Observer*, who set up the Africa Bureau. *Getty*

Three leaders of the World Peace Brigade march get involved in construction project in Dar es Salaam in 1962. The American activist, Bill Sutherland, wields the pick, while his compatriot, Bayard Rustin (face obscured by the pick) leans on his shovel, and Michael Scott monitors progress. *A.J. Muste Memorial Institute*

Michael Scott making his last appearance before the United Nations in 1982, still petitioning on behalf of the Herero people and Namibia. *United Nations photo 160,777/Milton Grant*

of those dismissed were among Scott's closest allies in mobilizing the case against South Africa at the UN.

Despite these complications, Scott was not unhappy in the United States. Although his London friends would speak of him almost invariably having a hard time in New York, there were aspects of his existence there which benefited his health and general well-being. Some of these, ironically, were largely due to the restrictions dictated by his custom-built visas. He could not, for example, as in London, increase his risks of self-neglect by being of 'no fixed abode', or with his licensed movement limited to a few city blocks, indulge in any exhausting country-wide activity. Nor could he dissipate his energies, at least outside the UN, by following any tangential cause that might take his fancy. His visas routinely excluded any public speaking, a prohibition that extended to his speaking into a dictaphone, if it could be amplified or relayed.

He was in some ways more isolated, but Scott's talent for attracting an impromptu gaggle of supporters and protectors remained intact. Indeed, there were occasions when he needed protection from the protectors. Stanley Burch, the journalist who wrote up all Scott's early triumphs at the UN for the *News Chronicle*, later recalled of their association, 'There were some strange, determined folk surrounding Michael . . . While appreciating her Herculean efforts, he got immensely amused by one burly female who repeatedly proclaimed, "The World is on the March." . . . My wife and I rescued him when we could from his redoubtable disciples – particularly the women – who of course doted on him and wanted to be his spiritual sister or mother or aunt, and do things like driving around Long Island for weekends . . .'4 In America, as was originally the case on Scott's return to London, the Quakers were among those most prominent in this early entourage, acting as cheerleaders and often donating useful stenographic skills.

When the UN was located at Lake Success, Scott was securely based at the Long Island home of Sartell and Agnes Prentice. Later, when the UN headquarters moved to Manhattan, Scott lodged at the General Theological Seminary on 21st Street and 9th Avenue. Of the society there, Scott would write to Mary Benson in October 1952, 'The people here are very friendly and not too solemn. We have little ecclesiastical laughs at one another and our peculiar versions of

Anglicanism and Christianity. A learned doctor had asked me to go and see for myself a church called "All Angels" or I wouldn't believe it possible. The ladies choir he says all have lipstick to match and he wonders if they all use the same one.'[5]

He soon found even more solid grounds for appreciating the seminarians' company, as an antidote to the cult of 'smear and fear' in the political culture: 'There is at the Seminary,' he wrote, 'a refreshingly vigorous Christian culture growing in opposition [to McCarthyism] . . . To me, hedged about with so many restrictions that I did not know whether I could dictate a letter on to a disc without contravening my visa restrictions, it was very refreshing to hear their conversation at High Table. Truly in the best American tradition . . . '

Though obliged to keep his head down with regard to domestic politics, Scott's informal relations in New York, with both its churchmen and its civil rights leaders, seem to have been very much better than those he enjoyed in London. This may have been because his expertise on African matters was less open to challenge, but the more important reason seems to have been that Americans were more inclined to view their politics in terms of human rights and moral issues. They spoke Scott's language in a way that many English leaders, mired in the nuances of constitutional and imperial tradition, did not. And while there was concern about race issues in Britain, there was something very different about the attitudes of American civil rights leaders, both black and white, in their response to racial problems in the country's Deep South, namely a real sense of urgency that would soon manifest itself in the astonishing witness of Martin Luther King Jnr. All of this chimed with Scott's outlook and temperament. So, in some ways, did his comparative immunity from bureaucratic cares in London.

Mary Benson came out to New York occasionally, but her visits tended to be fleeting, sometimes specifically related to concerns about Scott's health as was the case in 1950, when he had to be hospitalized after collapsing at the UN shortly after a Crohn's Disease resection operation. David Astor also stopped by in New York to see Scott when en route to business in Washington. But for the most part Scott operated out of range of the day-to-day concerns of his Africa Bureau, there being no telephone in his room at the seminary.

The city was kind to him in other ways. Once, when stopping to buy a soft drink, Scott turned round to discover that his bag containing his UN credentials and other key documents had disappeared. As it was a Puerto Rican neighbourhood, Scott sought the assistance of a local Roman Catholic priest. The priest put out the word through the local schools that papers designed to help poor people in 'the big UN building' had gone astray. Next day, two young Puerto Rican boys volunteered the bag with the story that they had found it, with the papers all strewn about, by the railway track. But it had been raining, and the papers were bone dry.[6]

For more formal organizational back-up, Scott came to rely on Bill Johnston, who set up a small but enterprising group called 'Episcopal Churchmen for South Africa'. Johnston took on the task of meeting Scott's massive demand for copies of his memoranda designed to sway delegates at the UN. He also extended Scott's range of potentially useful contacts to Elizabeth Landis, an expert on South African law, and Daniel Bernstein, a wealthy Scarsdale businessman philanthropically disposed to assist liberal causes. Both became enduring friends. According to Johnston, New Yorkers took to Scott very readily, though it sometimes took them a while to figure out how he was taking them: 'it took five years for us to get on first name terms, and another five before he put the "t" in Johnston.'[7]

Scott's reserve, when not expounding on the subject of Africa, was the source of some good-natured amusement to his American friends and efforts were sometimes made to extend his capacity for 'small talk'. The most imaginative initiative of this sort was made by the renowned travel writer John Gunther, who had earlier made Scott's acquaintance at the *Observer* office in London while gathering supplementary material for his book *Inside Africa*. Following the meeting, Gunther had penned one of the most attractive portraits of Scott: 'He is a tall, extraordinarily handsome man shy to the point of inarticulateness, gentle and as innocent in some respects as a child flying a kite, but also a zealot, a fighting idealist stubborn and tenacious to the last inch in what he believes to be right . . .'[8] At a cocktail party in uptown Manhattan, Gunther manoeuvred a situation in which the shy, personable priest was left alone in the adjoining vacant library with the shyest and most retiring of movie queens. Gunther checked back twenty minutes later to see how the chemistry between them had developed. He found Michael Scott and Greta Garbo both deeply engrossed, at opposite ends of the room, reading books.

Being at a loss for words was no problem at another party, where Paul Robeson insisted on being introduced to Scott, who took the opportunity of telling him that his singing in *Showboat* and *Porgy and Bess* represented 'the very life and soul of the African people'. Robeson, no less complimentary of Scott's efforts, sought his advice on how to get money raised at his concerts through to worthy causes in South Africa. In truth, Scott never became an adept party-goer, but there were other ways of relaxing. He loved the theatre, and was thankful that much of Broadway fell within the restricted limits allowed by his visas. On the other hand, he regularly lamented that the city's major outdoor playground was, for him, almost permanently off limits. 'I was always dying to know,' he said, 'what went on in Central Park.'[9]

At the serious business end of Scott's affairs, much revolved around Roger Baldwin, the Director of the International League for the Rights of Man. The ILRM was Scott's sheet anchor as far the UN was concerned, guaranteeing his place there, and Baldwin was Scott's first point of contact for unravelling any visa problems. Baldwin also organized fund-raisers on Scott's behalf, advised on presentation at the UN (usually in the direction of greater concision) and introduced him to a wide range of radical acquaintance. Some of them, like Norman Thomas, the veteran socialist, and Walter White of the National Association for the Advancement of Coloured People (NAACP), were drawn into the business of exerting pressure on the authorities to ease Scott's visa restrictions. Occasional 'waivers' were sometimes granted allowing him to visit churches and to preach in hitherto forbidden zones of the city.

The network of Scott's friendships extended to Bayard Rustin and A.J. Muste, both leading figures in the civil rights movement, to Bill Sutherland, the lively, wisecracking co-ordinator for the Peacemakers group in New Jersey, and to an up-and-coming Methodist radical called George M. Houser, all of whom, like Scott, had served prison sentences for peaceful protest early in their careers. Scott's example prompted Houser to set up 'Americans for South African Resistance' in support of the 1952 Defiance Against Unjust Laws campaign in South Africa.

In 1953, Houser extended the compliment by establishing the American Committee on Africa (ACOA), with the assistance of Roger Baldwin and Bill Sutherland. ACOA, which became the main popular engine for advancing liberal ideas about Africa, bore many of the hallmarks of the Africa Bureau, though it developed a more plangent style. Its first regular publication, *Africa Today*, was edited by Keith Irvine, son of the Quaker couple who had first offered Scott shelter at the Friends International Centre in London. In his autobiography, *No One Can Stop the Rain*, the gregarious Houser would write of Michael Scott, 'I never met a more dedicated person.'[10]

Scott also met and influenced the young radical Allard Lowenstein, who would later write a forceful book on conditions in South-West Africa, entitled *Brutal Mandate*. Lowenstein's admiration for Scott verged on hero-worship, though, like Baldwin, he could sometimes be puzzled by the apparent convolutions of his mentor's thought processes. Lowenstein said of his last briefing by Scott before his departure for South-West Africa: 'He asked me a series of questions so twined about with conditional clauses that I wasn't entirely sure what I had agreed to for several weeks after I had answered them . . .'[11]

In 1952 Scott was accorded the accolade of a profile in *Time* magazine, though its hard-nosed conclusion was at best equivocal: 'It seems he will be defeated in the end and pass, among politicians, for a failure. But it is likely that he will be remembered by millions of vote-less Africans as one Christian who cared enough to do something.' Another profile, published in *The Christian Century*, was more upbeat, and more congruent with Scott's own outlook. It commented that Scott had been led to the international stage by his recognition of 'the supreme worth of truth and the priceless value of public opinion in matters of human rights'.[12] In May 1953 the *Chicago Defender* informed Scott that he had been placed on its Honour Roll 'for symbolizing the best in American Democracy',[13] though it also felt obliged to regret Scott's inability to attend 'the Honour Roll luncheon' due to his visa restrictions.

For all his appreciation of the American spirit, Scott fought shy of the Americanization of his own cause. He would, however, acknowledge being tempted when his heightened public profile attracted the attention of Madison Avenue. The Harold Oram Organization, a reputable public relations outfit, offered to 'professionalize' his southern African concerns in a way that rendered them more appealing to the American general public. The attractive aspect of the offer, from Scott's viewpoint, was that the PR company was prepared to send out its ablest staffer to South-West Africa to improve communication with the Herero chiefs. However, prospects of success in the United States were thought to be conditional on two basic premises: anti-Communism and a favourable disposition to Catholicism, since Catholics were regarded as the section of the population most interested in 'world problems'. If these conditions were accepted, it was thought that sufficient funds could be generated to make a campaign self-financing. Scott recalled spending 'sleepless nights' wrestling with the issues raised. He was not disposed to be pro-Communist, still less anti-Catholic, but he arrived at a sense that high-pressure 'packaging' of his ideas could be counter-productive. 'In the end,' he would say, 'I rejected the proposal, believing that the case had an inherent worth of its own which should give it the necessary momentum.'[14]

There was no alternative, as he saw it, to patient lobbying of sympathetic individual delegates on the UN's Fourth Committee, to shoring up their resolve and to supplying them with written memoranda on points that might be useful to them in debate. Although he was rarely at liberty to speak, unless requested to do so as the formal representative of the Hereros, his scope for influencing events was still wide. Outside the Secretariat, Scott was regarded as the main initiator of ideas and tactics relating to South-West Africa. He was also able on occasion to contribute to the wider concerns about South Africa. Between the 1952 and 1953 General Assemblies, Scott gave formal evidence on behalf of the ILRM to the UN Commission on Racial Discrimination in South Africa, and, under Baldwin's guidance, was more succinct than usual. Of apartheid, he would say, 'the ugly menace that had grown up under cover of lofty phrases cannot protect the short-term interests of white or black . . . it may lead to the debacle of so-called Western civilization in that continent.'

Aside from influencing delegates, Scott made a point of developing relationships with key people in the Secretariat charged with steering the UN's business. Francoise Dony, the Belgian head of the UN's Non-Government Organization section, was an early ally. Scott was also close to Enuga S. Reddy, a young Indian official, already showing a precocious talent for coordinating the efforts of the smaller nations against entrenched white interests in Africa. Scott's most creative association, however, was with Jack Sargent Harris, one of the Secretariat's more mature high-flyers. In *The Ultimate Crime*, Linda Melvern describes Harris as being Scott's 'natural ally'.[15] He was certainly the most intriguing one.

An academic anthropologist in peacetime, Harris was recruited into the intelligence community and trained as one of the first secret agents by the Office of Strategic Services (the wartime precursor of what became the CIA). He then rose to become head of America's intelligence network in South Africa. After a short post-war stint as an assistant professor at Chicago University, Harris received a call from his old OSS colleague and friend, Dr Ralph Bunche, asking him to come to the East Coast to join him at the nascent United Nations. Bunche, who would later be awarded the Nobel Peace Prize (the first black man to be so honoured), was then immersed in the problem of sorting out the UN's Trusteeship arrangements. Harris worked with him and, in this context, became friendly with Michael Scott. The friendship with Scott would later be strengthened by their discovering that Harris's wife, Shirley, had been a school friend of Mary Benson in Pretoria, a happy coincidence that would lead to a revival of Benson's childhood nickname of 'Pixie'.

Harris was in a position to move the machinery of the UN at its highest level, though he would say that his dealings with Scott essentially involved teaching him 'how to weave through the bureaucracy of the Secretariat'.[16] There can have been few abler tutors, and Harris was properly credited with guiding the moves in the elaborate waiting game that led to Scott's famous first UN address in 1949. There seemed no reason why their informal creative alliance should not endure through the 1950s. But there would be another unexpected twist in Harris's extraordinary career. He was among the UN personnel summoned to appear before McCarran's Senate Internal Security Subcommittee in the autumn of 1952, and among those who in answer to the question 'Are you a member of the Communist Party?' invoked the constitutional right to silence enshrined in the Fifth Amendment.

Although it was known at the time that 'pleading the fifth' was not invariably a defence tactic, but often a way of avoiding follow-up questioning designed to drag old friends and acquaintance through the mire, the plea alone was sufficient to warrant dismissal from the UN. Harris became the highest-ranking member of the alleged 'subversive' group bounced out of their UN jobs by its beleaguered and frightened Secretary-General, the Norwegian Trygve Lie. Encouraged by Scott, Harris contested the decision through an internal tribunal established by the UN. A year later, in September 1953, he secured a formal admission that he had done nothing in violation of UN staff rules, and along with eleven other victims of the McCarran 'purge', was awarded substantial damages. 'Dear Pixie,' the Harrises wrote to Mary Benson in London on 6 September 1953, 'Since the [tribunal] decision was announced, Senators McCarthy, Jenner, Wiley *et al* have indignantly declared that not one penny should be awarded to us. More nonsense ahead.'[17] In the event, the damages were paid in full, but Harris never did get his job back.

Scott's own correspondence with friends in London tended to dwell on the difficulties of achieving progress at the UN. It was probably this, combined with Scott's description of New York in *A Time to Speak* as exemplifying 'the harsh metallic clutter of our civilization'[18] that gave rise to the impression among his London connections that Scott always had a rough time there. But, in point of fact, the business of commuting to New York once or sometimes twice a year seems to have answered some underlying need in his restless make-up. And once there, the combination of focused activity at the UN, easy companionship at the seminary and fellowship with a peer group of essentially like-minded civil rights activists, appears to have done him a power of good. Far from draining his energies, New York often provided a boost. Serious personal problems did occur there, but these were usually a consequence of his arriving in a depleted condition from exertions elsewhere.

This was very much the case in 1954. As Scott saw it, the UN's deliberations on South-West Africa, though now intensive, were not getting anywhere, at least in terms of what was actually happening in the Territory. The various committees set up to scrutinize its affairs seemed to spend much of their time agonising over the precise extent of their jurisdiction. So while procedural progress of a sort was being made, it was sometimes hard to detect. Describing his frustration at this time, Scott would say to the journalist Cyril Dunn, 'I was eating my heart out because none of this seemed to make the slightest bit of difference to the African condition. All this debating was going on and the costs were fabulous, but one couldn't show that conditions had improved at all.'[19]

Within the Secretariat there was a presumption that matters could be improved by seeking further advisory opinions from the International Court at the Hague. The problem with advisory opinions, however, was that while they were legally authoritative, they were not legally binding. If the South African government chose to ignore them, the UN did not have the power to compel it to comply. In the summer of 1954 Scott came to the view that only a compulsory judgment by the International Court, which could take several years to achieve, was at all likely to bring the South African government into compliance. Unlike advisory opinions, compulsory judgments could, at least in terms of legal theory, be enforced, by economic and military sanctions if necessary.

After consulting Sir Herscht Lauterpacht, Professor of International Law at Cambridge University, Scott formulated a new plan of action. Professor Lauterpacht's view was that Liberia and Ethiopia – the only two black African nations represented both in the League of Nations and at the UN – were the countries best placed to launch a formal action against South Africa at the International Court. This was the prelude to Scott's making two exhausting diplomatic forays – one to Addis Ababa to see the Emperor Haile Selassie, the other to Monrovia to pay his respects to Liberia's President Tubman. Scott attempted to persuade the heads of state of the potential benefits that might flow from their taking on the behemoth of white supremacy to the south in the arena of the International Court. In both cases, the response was friendly but guarded. They were ready to act but only if they could be assured of substantial support from other countries.[20]

The consequence of this intercontinental activity would be Scott's arriving in New York in late 1954 in a jaded and disorientated condition. His health was an immediate concern to his friends there; some thought him on the verge of nervous collapse. Matters were not much improved by the fact that the United Nations was going through one of its more acrimonious phases.

Writing to Mary Benson on 12 December from the General Theological Seminary, Scott described the proceedings at the UN as degenerating into 'a racial brawl', with the nations split 'in a very ugly manner, with the Communist, Muslim and Asian countries on the side of opposition to apartheid and Christian and European countries on the side of South Africa.' The whole business was, he said, 'like living through a mental and spiritual bombardment . . . nerve wracking and exhausting.' He promised to be back in London soon, signing himself 'frantically yours'.

From New York, Scott went on to Canada, which was emerging as a useful potential ally at the UN. In Ottawa, he had fruitful but tiring talks with two government ministers, before going on to Montreal, where, with a sense that his health was fast deteriorating, he sought medical advice. Told that his condition was probably psychiatric, Scott was put on a new medication, cortisone. Still feeling groggy, he wrote to Mary Benson on 30 December, announcing that he would be home very soon: 'It will be wonderful to see you,' he wrote, 'It seems ages. I can't cope with all this alone again.'[21]

To its recipient, the letter might have been seen as an expression of yearning for togetherness. But in reality it was the beginning of the end of one of history's more poignant and unusual love stories.

CHAPTER SIXTEEN

'MADE FOR EACH OTHER'

I T MAY NOT have been love, but it was certainly fascination at first sight. In her autobiography, *A Far Cry*, published after Michael Scott's death, Mary Benson wrote of her first meeting with him at the British Film Institute back in 1950: 'he was not strictly handsome. Perhaps his face revealed the two sides of his nature, one austere, the other mischievous, but he radiated spiritual strength and the overriding impression was one of beauty.' She also noted that his gaze was 'piercing', while his handshake was disconcertingly limp, from which she deduced that he was 'extremely shy'.[1]

There is no parallel description by Scott of Benson's initial impact on him, but as one of his first impressions was that she was probably a spy, there must have been some element of fascination about the encounter for him as well. One of the Quaker chaperones present on that occasion would later comment, a shade regretfully, that it looked as if Scott and Benson were 'made for each other'.[2]

And so, for a long time, it must have seemed to them too. Almost from the outset, their collaboration on what they called 'The Work' was seen to be wholly beneficial, with Benson providing the practical qualities that were sometimes deficient in Scott. It was this combination that persuaded David Astor of the importance of keeping them together when assembling the elements of the Africa Bureau. Astor was no matchmaker, but he had a keen sense of what constituted a good working relationship.

Benson's skills were by no means confined to secretarial activities. She was a very good writer, and seen as having an improving effect on Scott's more prolix, often convoluted, prose style. Astor had tried to sharpen Scott's journalistic efforts by supplying him with copies of George Orwell's old *Observer* articles as models, but it was Benson who really learned from them. She was brave, as her mission on Scott's behalf to the Herero chiefs exemplified; not that she was in danger from the Hereros, but consorting with them made her a prime focus for hostility among Windhoek's bigoted whites. She was expert at picking up the threads of initiatives left dangling by her boss on his frequent trips abroad. She was diplomatic, excellent at smoothing executive feathers ruffled as a consequence of Scott's unpredictability in committee. And she was politically astute, efficiently steering the Bureau away from head-on collisions with John Collins's Christian Action movement, which was often seen as a threat to its independence. She was, in short, a capable and clever woman, and, much to her credit in those pre-feminist movement days, she knew it. She had a high opinion of herself, but not an inflated one.

The exact point at which the working relationship shaded into romance is not clear, but on Benson's side it does not seem to have been long delayed. While helping Scott organize the material for his autobiography, one of her first serious tasks, she broke off to write to her friend Alan Paton. She told him that after all the agonizing years of uncertainty, she had found her purpose in life. Paton, evidently concerned to keep her feet on the ground, wrote back, 'You've clearly been bitten by the bug of holiness, one of the most powerful diseases imaginable.'[3]

Benson, however, stayed aloft and would soon let it be known that she was 'in love' with Scott. She was some way from being the first woman to express such a sentiment, but Scott, now into his forties, was, for all his apparent diffidence, well versed in the art of shaking off or deflecting any unwelcome attachment. Celibacy was his ultimate armour in such situations. But in Benson's case he appears to have tolerated, perhaps even welcomed, the efforts made to pierce it.

Benson would see her feelings as being to a large degree reciprocated during Scott's convalescence at David Astor's country home in the spring of 1951. She recalled Scott saying at that time: 'You have no idea what your coming into my life has meant,' and insisting that he would always want her companionship. He could not imagine the future without her and believed they were capable of creating 'an ideal relationship' together.[4] Their connection moved on to a new plane of intimacy. Benson said in *A Far Cry*:

> We seemed a perfect team. So evident was his dependence on me, his sharing of intimate anxieties and of profound thoughts, that I brushed off the warnings that he could not have anything 'personal' in his life. I could not help assuming that his feelings in time would respond to

the physical attraction I felt for him, just as he had come to look forward to and collect the brief letters I tucked into his pockets whenever he was feeling unwell or depressed.[5]

Benson's openness in these matters, contrasted with Scott's extreme reticence, led some of their acquaintance to conclude that Benson was pushing too hard. However, it is clear from the correspondence between them that Scott attached enormous importance to the relationship, and was not put off by Benson's emotional motivation. If, as sometimes happened, the flow of letters from Benson was interrupted, Scott would evince extreme disappointment. And while many of the letters, designed to keep Scott acquainted with Bureau affairs while he was abroad, were business related, it is evident that Scott fell for Mary Benson, at least as far as he felt capable of falling.

It's just possible that some of the unhappiness they had in store could have been headed off if Scott had been able to bring himself to confess the source of his sexual reluctance, located in his abuse as a child. But he did not, perhaps could not, and the relationship moved on with the signals between them becoming ever more confused, though outwardly they presented an admirable picture of togetherness. Elizabeth Pakenham commented on how fortunate the Africa Bureau was to be represented by such 'a lovely pair'.[6]

Benson's love was not blind. She was among the first people in the Bureau to detect an element of paranoia in the Director's make-up. Unlike other admirers, she was not inclined to see Scott as saintliness personified, and, blessed with a good ear for nuance, she detected that many of Scott's more oblique observations were less than charitable. Once, when asked to describe the nature of Scott's humour, she replied: 'Let me think – what's the nice word for malicious?'[7] She also had reservations about Scott's frequent use of the impersonal pronoun 'one', instead of 'I', which to some implied selflessness, but which might also imply an avoidance of firm personal statement. In fact, she had a far better insight into Scott's psychological quirks than did most of his overly reverential acquaintance. But Benson never wavered in her estimate of Scott's uniqueness, which was manifested through 'his universal love': 'a revolutionary power, austere and enduring, yet deep down very emotional, fighting for truth and justice for the weak and the dispossessed'.[8] Benson's engagement on the same causes encouraged her in the notion that a more personal love would naturally find its way. This was probably a mistake, but an understandable one.

Periods of frustration were discounted when they were punctuated by 'days luminous with shared happiness'. They stayed for a weekend at a lonely house on the Suffolk coast, and 'ambled through reedy marshes, hardly talking but listening to the larks and the gulls, smelling salt on the breeze until we came to a pebble beach and plunged into the deliciously cold sea . . . We laughed a lot, though I can't remember at what.'[9] In a letter to a friend in 1954, she talked of now 'trying hard to bury my little hope but the damn thing perks up from time to time – he is so terribly sweet and thoughtful – insisted on seeing me all the way home last night, and this morning brought potted white hyacinth and some mimosa . . .'[10]

Benson also thoroughly immersed herself in Scott's belief system. She was baptized in the Anglican faith in December 1953, with Margery Perham as her godmother, and soon after confirmed by George Bell, the bishop who had officiated at Scott's ordination. One of her first Holy Communions was taken with Scott at Westminster Abbey. No doubt these initiatives had highly spiritual motives, but Benson's exasperation seems to have been increased by their failure to bring her significantly closer to Scott. Although the tone of affection was never absent from her letters to him, occasional notes of irritability would obtrude. She began to see the downside of her role as Scott's unofficial consort, particularly in relation to other women. She wrote to him:

> Their only real interest in me is that I'm close to you – me as myself, as a personality with a life of my own, doesn't exist for them! Isn't it queer. I suppose it's the particular half-saint, half-teasing symbolic brother, or son, or lover character that you become for so many women – I can think of about fifteen offhand. It's a mixture of something very good and very neurotic.[11]

The mixture of good and neurotic of course also applied very much to the central relationship, with Scott unable to comprehend that a Platonic relationship, however 'ideal', could never be satisfying to Benson, and Benson failing to appreciate the severity of Scott's sexual impediment. Through most of their romance, Scott lived in a series of small hotels and bedsitters, occasionally staying with Benson who lived with a friend in a Belsize Park flat. The courtship on Benson's part, pursuit of an 'ideal relationship' on Scott's, therefore involved a long nomadic round of restaurants, cafés, cinemas and waiting in the rain at bus-stops. Tiring of this enervating routine – 'a love that ended at 10.30 every evening' – Benson saw only one possible solution to the problem: they should get married. She therefore popped the question, and went on popping it almost incessantly. In *A Far Cry*, she frankly recalled her descent into almost uncontrollable shrewishness:

> Marriage became the theme of obsessive nagging on my part, but Michael simply continued to reiterate that there could be nothing personal in his life. But what could be more 'personal' than the confidences we shared? And clearly he did care. The very word 'personal' drove me to a frenzy of frustration which left him drained and bewildered, while I felt sickened at dragging this good man down into a banal desire for marriage, for sex – a word never uttered between us.[12]

The word was certainly uttered, however, in conversations between Benson and many of her, and Scott's, closest friends. By 1954, partly to ease her own tension, and perhaps to put more pressure on Scott, Benson had taken to talking about her predicament widely, to the point where 'Whither the Scott–Benson romance?' ranked second only to 'Whither Africa?' as a topic among those interested in the contemporary affairs of the Africa Bureau. Benson opened her heart to both David Astor and Colin Legum, the *Observer* writer most closely connected with the Bureau. Another confidant was Bishop George Bell. Benson also sought the opinion of Mother Geraldine Mary, Scott's close friend from Johannesburg days, now living at a convent in East Grinstead. South Africa was also drawn into the debate through Benson's contacts with Trevor Huddleston. Perhaps most unwisely, she also touched on the subject with Bishop Ambrose Reeves, the man who had withdrawn Scott's licence to preach in Johannesburg.

Benson's feedback from these confidants was not entirely negative, though most advised bringing the situation to a point of decision. To Benson's surprise, Mother Geraldine Mary seemed to be the one most ready to envisage a Mills and Boon possibility that the course of their true love could eventually run smooth. Astor, however, probably the most psychologically acute person of those she consulted, and by now the one best acquainted with both parties, was pessimistic. He asked Benson to consider the possibility that her fixation on Scott might be part of a neurotic drive to achieve 'the unattainable'. In support of this view, he would observe that two of Benson's previous love affairs also came in the category of being doomed from the outset, both being with older married men. Astor also saw Scott's celibacy as an intrinsic aspect of his 'specialness', and one that he could not risk losing.[13]

Though by no means convinced of these arguments, Benson did act on what seemed to be the consensus of her advisers. She brought matters to a head. When Scott returned to London in January 1955 to resume desk duties at the Africa Bureau, after a series of tiring journeys in Africa and North America, he clearly had a calming resumption of 'the ideal relationship' in mind. Benson, however, had her ultimatum ready. She told Scott that she intended to quit the Bureau and return to South Africa in the summer, unless he had a better idea. Scott's initial response, according to Benson, was to look dazed before muttering resentfully: 'How could you take possession, then throw it all away – don't throw me away.'[14] By this, she construed, he meant 'The Work' as much as himself. In any event, it resulted in sullenness on Scott's part and acrimony on Benson's, which subsequent conversation failed to dissolve.

On 30 January, Benson made the diary entry: 'Talked with M and was driven to a moment of blind anger . . . Having a few months ago said he did feel something physically for me and was that wrong? – He expresses complete surprise that I feel things physically for him . . . I wish I knew what to do . . . Bashing of head on wall can't go on.'[15]

Physical contact between them had never amounted to much more than hand-holding in movie shows when the lights were low, and walking arm-in-arm down streets where Scott could be confident of not being recognized, but the ungluing of their relationship was scarcely less painful than if they had been torridly engaged lovers from the start. Though the exchanges of harsh words would bring some clarification, it was not of an encouraging kind. When Benson angrily demanded to know if Scott wanted her to forgo her wholeness as a woman for God's sake, or for his own convenience, Scott cryptically responded with the bleak beatitude: 'Blessed are they that are eunuchs for Christ's sake', but refused to elaborate.[16]

In April, with the threat of her departure for South Africa still intact, Benson wrote to Scott in a way that blended the animosities of a woman scorned with the tenderness of regret, the rage of a shrew, and a glimmer of seemingly inextinguishable hope. It was clearly her last stand:

> I'm sorry things are so skew. The situation becomes quite intolerable at times and what particularly irritates me then is your doleful voice saying you miss me or it's a long time since you saw me or would I come out, etc. when it is entirely your own fault that things are this way. Then I really feel it would be a great deal better if I deprived you of my company entirely and perhaps you'll make up your mind just what you want. As it is you have things the way you want (provided I'm in a good humour) and see me when you want to and for as long as you want to. Every now and then there are dark hints that you have been thinking things over and we could talk them over but somehow that never comes to much. I have come to the conclusion that I do not want to spend the rest of my life alone and that if it is possible, and someone I care enough about wants to marry me, then I want very much to be married . . . We've been together for over five years now in which we've shared almost every possible problem, as well as a certain amount of joy. But I feel old and tired now and can't go on. You say I was made to laugh, well I was also, like every human being, made to love and be loved, and I do not understand a love between a man and a woman that is not whole. I can understand a very spiritual friendship (but ours is much more than that), or a teacher–pupil kind of affection (which was what I once thought we might have), or a physical affair, or just ordinary friendship. But none of those applies to us. Of course I don't want to put us in a category, but I don't know where I am. Sometimes I think I should give up hoping, and should once and for all make the clean break I'm always contemplating and threatening, and that marriage is quite out of the question for you and so repugnant that it would be your undoing. Then something deep within me rejects that utterly and affirms that what is natural and beautiful and part of the holiness of love between men and women, cannot but enrich you . . . [17]

There does not appear to have been any direct reply to this letter, possibly because Scott, as a result of complications related to his new medication for Crohn's Disease, was again seriously unwell. By June, coincidentally the month originally scheduled for Benson's departure, he was an in-patient at the Middlesex Hospital and about to get into the most serious trouble of his entire adult life.

CHAPTER SEVENTEEN

CRISIS IN OXFORD

O NE OF THE few sensual pleasures Michael Scott allowed himself was sunbathing in the nude, possibly because it could be classed as having a therapeutic quality. It seems likely that Scott first experienced its beneficial effect at the Sun Clinic in Switzerland, where, while still a teenager, he was treated for suspected tuberculosis. Subsequently, when working with the leper community in South Africa, he would often find opportunities to get away to a place of privacy where the sun's energizing properties could be experienced to the full.

In later life, pressure of work combined with more limited sunshine made this pleasure less readily available, but it was never entirely out of reach. Not far from David Astor's country home at Sutton Courtenay, where Scott was a frequent guest, there was in Oxford, as late as the 1960s, a short stretch of the River Cherwell where male sunbathing in the nude was not merely tolerated but almost *de rigueur*. Known as Parson's Pleasure, it was a sequestered bathing area, screened by tall bushes and adjoined by the tumbling waters of a weir.[1]

On the bank by the weir there was (and still is) a set of rollers: metal tracks along which punts could be dragged before launching them again in the higher stretch of the river. When these were encountered by punts coming upriver, any women passengers, in those days more commonly known as 'ladies', were obliged to disembark and make their way on foot around the herbaceous fringes of the male territory in a way that decorously preserved segregation of the sexes. Further upstream was 'Dames' Delight', where women could swim unencumbered by any masculine presence, though they were not encouraged to sunbathe unclothed.

The ambience at Parson's Pleasure was relatively demure, even scholarly. Much of its clientele was drawn from the ranks of senior members of the university. C.S. Lewis was very fond of the place, so too was Maurice Bowra, the Warden of Wadham College and one of the Africa Bureau's platoon of eminent Honorary Presidents. Bowra, indeed, was an important figure in its folklore. On one occasion a punt laden with ladies who had failed to disembark went by, causing consternation among a group of naked dons standing on the river bank. All the dons threw themselves down flat on their stomachs, with the exception of Bowra, who remained standing while calmly wrapping a towel round his head. When the crisis was over and the ladies' punt had disappeared upstream, he explained: 'I like to think I'm known around Oxford by my face.'

Among undergraduates, Parson's Pleasure was naturally a source of much amusement and ribald comment, but incidents associated with the place were comparatively rare. As long as the male bathers stayed within the confines of the area's bushy surround, and the women disembarked at the rollers as required, there was not much cause for complaint. When complaints were made, they tended to be against sunbathers who, either deliberately or inadvertently, failed to observe the geographic conventions. One such sunbather, in early July 1955, was the Reverend Michael Scott, who was arrested and charged with indecent exposure, before being returned to the ward of the Middlesex Hospital, from which he had strayed.[2] From the hospital, Scott telephoned David Astor to say he was in trouble and needed help.

Of all Scott's acquaintance nobody knew better than David Astor that such a charge spelled utter ruin for Scott's reputation as a moral witness on the subject of Africa, or indeed on anything else. If the charge was publicized in any way, his campaigning days would effectively be over, and so, very likely, would be those of the Africa Bureau. The fact that the alleged offence was essentially victimless, and, given the specialized nature of the crime scene, not much of a deviation from the prevailing norm, did not matter. The popular press, which absolutely adored fallen vicar stories, would make mincemeat of his case. Scott would become a laughing stock, and such people rarely manage to retrieve any public reputation no matter how glowing their record of earlier achievement might be. Astor knew all this in his capacity as an experienced newspaper editor, and Scott, even in a disorientated condition, must have been similarly aware of the probable consequences.

On the basis of his conversation with Scott at the hospital, Astor formed the opinion that 'he had been guilty of nothing worse than adverse reaction to a drug'. This conclusion would guide all his subsequent elaborate actions, designed to keep Scott's alleged crime a closely guarded secret.

The background, as Astor understood it, was that Scott had first been admitted to the Middlesex suffering from depression and sleeplessness. He had also been experiencing weird sensations and bad dreams that he suspected might be connected to the cortisone treatment he had embarked on in Canada six months earlier. As an in-patient at the hospital, he had been given further substantial doses of cortisone and 'a pretty powerful sleeping drug', the combined effect of which, Scott maintained, 'had me in a state of unbalance, I suppose in a daze'. This was the condition he was in when he wandered off to Oxford and Parson's Pleasure.

In Astor's view, there were some grounds for thinking that the hospital could, and perhaps should, have exercised closer supervision of an evidently disturbed patient. During his visit, he witnessed a senior doctor giving Scott what appeared to be an unnecessarily severe moralistic lecture about his 'antisocial behaviour'. Astor felt that the doctor's theatricality on this point was excessive, and possibly put on for his benefit to mask some deficiency in Scott's actual care. In the highly charged atmosphere at that time this impression could have been a product of Astor's own worries or even a projection of his need to find someone or something to blame other than his close friend. But any hesitation Astor might have had on this score was removed when one of the junior doctors quietly drew him to one side, and advised him that Scott might fare better in a less censorious medical environment. Astor recalled the young doctor saying to him, 'He [Scott] is done for here.'

At this point Astor decided to act on his instinct and have Scott, along with his case notes, transferred immediately to the York Clinic, part of the psychiatric unit located at Guy's Hospital. He felt reasonably confident of his friend receiving less judgemental treatment there, if only because Astor himself had helped establish the clinic shortly after the war and had provided it with funds. At Guy's, Scott was slowly weaned off the cortisone in conditions of near isolation, with no visitors allowed for several weeks. He began to show a marked improvement. Even so, the head psychiatrist, David

Stafford-Clark, proved reluctant to get involved in any complications relating to Scott's prosecution.

At the time, Astor was working on the hopeful presumption that an authoritative medical opinion acknowledging that Scott's earlier care had been either inadequate, or even misconceived, could result in the charge against Scott being quietly dropped. Once again, it was a sympathetic junior doctor who clarified matters, telling Astor that there was no real prospect of obtaining such an opinion, as if things went wrong it risked the possibility of the profession's worst horror: doctors being called to testify against other doctors in open court about a specific treatment. With the case against Scott looming, he advised Astor to forget about seeking assistance in the medical world and to look instead for other ways of helping his friend.

The other way found by Astor involved the recruitment of an Oxford solicitor who had excellent connections in the police force and was versed in the rhythms of the local magistrates' court, with particular reference to the times when the local reporters were likely to be either having a break or at their most somnolently inattentive. Under this solicitor's adroit guidance, Scott's case was heard and concluded with the minimum fuss and maximum speed. Charged under his rarely used forename of 'Guthrie' and without the identifying prefix of 'Reverend', Scott attracted no outside attention. As the case was of negligible interest without knowledge of the accused man's real identity, it went unreported. Thanks almost entirely to Astor the secret of Scott's offence was preserved intact, and would stay preserved for the rest of his life.

The explanation for the Oxford incident remains elusive. Scott's offence could be viewed merely as an accident waiting to happen, an almost inevitable consequence of what can occur when a notoriously absent-minded man develops a passion for nude sunbathing. The problem with this interpretation, however, is that Scott himself never seems to have subscribed to it. Though reticent about the whole subject, he acknowledged that, though in a dazed state, he was aware of doing something that caused offence. Astor's personal theory, perhaps unsurprisingly, given his fondness for Freudian analysis, put the emphasis on sex. As he saw it, the cocktail of drugs Scott had ingested had somehow released his long-suppressed sexual drive in a way he could not control. This could be a sufficient explanation in that

Scott, after being weaned off the cortisone, did not go on to become a serial offender (though he continued to enjoy nude sunbathing). However, if that had been the whole story, Scott almost certainly would have expressed anger or at least fretfulness at the circumstances that led to his humiliation. But Scott seemed remarkably equable about this, as indeed he appeared to be about the whole episode.

Between the time Scott left hospital and the hearing of his case, he lived with the Astors. Both Astor and his wife Bridget were astonished by the serenity of Scott's demeanour through what they conceived must have been a nerve-wracking period. Scott was detached in a way that almost suggested the crisis was something that was happening to somebody else. This apparent indifference to his fate was seen by the Astors as a mark of Scott's stoicism. But it may also have reflected an odd sense of relief at the idea of his reputation crashing to the ground. For a while, all his heavy concerns, ranging across the planet from the Hereros in the South to Mary Benson in the North, must have suddenly seemed weightless, all demonstrably beyond his ability to cope.

He was now finally, and inescapably, having 'the complete rest' that all his earlier doctors had so unavailingly prescribed. It is probably true, as Astor surmised, that the incident at Oxford represented some kind of assertion by Scott's buried subconscious against his normally ironclad conscious will, but the assertion may not have been motivated by sex so much as by the need to force an outcome that would give his entire system a complete break. In non-psychoanalytic parlance, he just needed to stop the world and get off. If only for a while.

THROUGHOUT THE crisis, Mary Benson's contribution to Scott's well-being, and to maintaining the secret, was considerable. With Scott in hospital, she abandoned her plans for a rapid return to South Africa, and became involved in the delicate task of keeping Scott's family and closest friends informed about the progress of his treatment, without alluding to the Oxford incident. As Scott's mother and two brothers lived outside London, her task was a shade easier than might have been the case if they had been close by, but it was not without its hair-raising moments.

One such moment occurred early on when Scott's brother Nigel decided to come up to London from his parish in Somerset to check on his brother's progress in Guy's Hospital. He was unhappy to be refused access to Michael, and the doctor's explanation for this refusal seemed evasive. On his return to Somerset, he wrote to Mary Benson telling her of his unrewarding experience at the hospital and stating his impression that he was being kept 'in the dark'. Benson wrote back to him in mollifying terms:

> I'm sorry you have been v. worried, and felt the doctors were being cagey. I haven't gleaned very much either . . . they are insisting on complete purdah while they watch him and consult each other . . . But the reports are that he is progressing and is wanting to go on having a rest. I think he at last realises how much he has needed it all these years – I reminded him before all this happened he had gone almost non-stop for thirteen years, with only occasional breaks during which he worked anyway, or fretted about it, and he never convalesced properly after his frequent illnesses . . . Let me know if there are any questions that I can put to the doctors that didn't occur to you . . .

Benson added the homely detail that his brother was 'reading Agatha Christie and listening to the radio'. It was a minor literary master-piece, combining friendly and concerned informativeness with near total obfuscation. Nigel Scott wrote back to Benson to say that as a result of her letter, 'I feel happier about Michael now.'[3]

Benson's skill in this area was also deployed in keeping Scott's now considerable contingent of American friends up to date with developments. The main response in New York to news of Scott's incapacity as a result of a mystery illness was one of self-reproach. The new American Committee on Africa (ACOA) and Scott's old support system, represented by the International League for the Rights of Man, both vowed to do better by him in future. An appeal for funds, launched on Scott's behalf, announced:

> Last year some of us, his friends, became alarmed at the state of his health, largely brought about by the conscientious way in which he insisted on doing work which others were not able to do for him . . . A man of his unquenchable spirit should not, in a country blessed with abundance as ours is, have to impair his never adequate health for lack of money to provide a minimum office set up.

The signatories, calling themselves 'Volunteers for Michael Scott', were Roger Baldwin for the ILRM, the Reverend Donald Harrington for ACOA, Bishop James Pike of the General Theological Seminary, A.J. Muste and three of Scott's women helpers, Lydia Zemba, Lovina Marlowe, and Winifred Courtney.[4]

At the time, it was by no means certain Scott would be in any position to benefit from this fund-raising effort. But with the court case behind him, he recovered his public poise with extraordinary rapidity. He was in New York again in November 1955, answering the call of the United Nations to speak on behalf of the South-West African tribes. With the South African government continuing to block any indigenous representation from the Territory, Scott was still its prime spokesman in the world forum.

There would, however, be no recovery for the Scott–Benson romance, though their relationship was easier than before. Having ceased to look for the impossible in each other, they could be affectionate in a more relaxed way. Benson also made it clear that she really would be moving on, but not in a way that involved threats or ultimata. On Astor's advice, she had already embarked on a course of psychoanalysis. She later described the experience as 'like wading through black mud',[5] but it appears to have been genuinely helpful in her case.

In January 1957, she returned to South Africa to a job worthy of her mettle, helping to run the Treason Trial Defence Fund. Established in response to the South African government's legal onslaught that resulted in 156 of its leading opponents – Africans, Indians, coloureds and radical whites – winding up behind bars, accused of high treason, the fund supported the families of the accused and paid for the legal expertise necessary for their defence. It was a job that distanced Benson from Scott in more ways than one. Two of Scott's least favourite characters among what might be described as the clerical radicals were Bishop Ambrose Reeves and Canon John Collins. But Benson came to respect them both: Reeves in his capacity as director of the Defence Fund in Johannesburg, and Collins in his role as principal supplier of the Fund's money, raised through his appeals in Britain. And they all did a highly effective job. Over the course of several years all those accused of treason were acquitted.

Benson was scarred by her romance with Scott, but seems to have healed in a way that made her stronger than before. She achieved fulfilment as a writer. Her biography of Tshekedi Khama, published in 1960, was the prelude to an important history of the African National Congress, *The African Patriots*, which became a standard work of reference on the movement. Some of its information was supplied by Nelson Mandela in clandestine interviews with Benson while he was on the run from the South African police as the country's most wanted man. She went on to write biographies of Albert Luthuli, the ANC's Nobel Prizewinner, and of Mandela himself – books that helped keep the ANC's battered image alive during the many years its leadership was in prison and exile. Forced to flee South Africa, after being placed under house arrest there, Benson returned to England.[6] She would see Scott occasionally as a member of the Africa Bureau's executive committee, but their old intimacy was never resumed. People sensed an awkwardness between them. She never married.

IN THE spring of 1955, sometime in the frantic period between Benson's first threat to leave him and the indecent exposure incident, Scott too consulted a psychoanalyst. Once again, Astor was the go-between. He asked his own analyst, Anna Freud, if she would arrange some sessions for his friend. At that time both he and Scott were persuaded that his recurrent illnesses had a psychological cause. Anna Freud put Scott in touch with a male psychoanalyst. Scott went to see him once, but never again. In conversation with Astor later, Anna Freud said the psychoanalyst had described Scott as being 'fearless as a lion, but unable to look inside himself'.[7]

It is difficult to gauge what Scott's personal feelings were on the subject. He never wrote about or discussed the experience in any detail. However, with analysis or almost any kind of therapy the biggest decision is seeking it in the first place. It represents an acknowledgement on the part of the client of the need for help and healing. So why did Scott, after making such an acknowledgement, baulk at the first fence?

He confided to Mary Benson that he was disappointed in the psychoanalyst's ability to 'understand the spiritual side'.[8] This was very likely true, but sounds much more like an excuse for quitting than an actual reason for doing so. Even at his unhappiest, Scott cannot have been foolish enough to go to an analyst for spiritual enlightenment, and what analysis had to offer could not seriously disturb his own line of expertise. By this time Scott's own religion was thoroughly demythologized and his most fundamental commitment, to the cause of human justice, hardly required a spiritual component. No amount of analysis was likely to shake Scott's central convictions.

However, there was a crucial aspect of Scott's experience that was crying out to be explored in analysis. As is evident from his last letter to Astor, mentioned in the first chapter of this book, since his childhood Scott had 'bottled up' inside him a dread that stemmed from his sexual abuse at his prep school. And this episode, he was secretly convinced, was directly related to both his intestinal and sexual problems in adult life. This may or may not have been the case, but it is certain that Scott could only begin to repair the emotional damage done by communicating the circumstances of the abuse either to those closest to him or to a therapist skilled in this area. Yet even at a time of great tension, on the verge of almost total break-down, Scott never communicated it, not to Benson, nor Astor, nor to the psychoanalyst.

Some clues as to why Scott should choose to remain 'bottled up' can be found between the lines of his autobiography, *A Time to Speak*. One of its characteristics is a pronounced filial piety. As a child he sees his father as all-powerful, almost godlike, and strong in the faith. His mother is gentle and understanding. However, the nature of the abuse, as Scott would later describe it, went on for months, possibly years. During all this time Scott lived at home, returning every evening from the purgatory of school to the bosom of his caring family. To his parents' failure to protect him, Scott was never to attach any blame. Even in the final letter to Astor he says: 'I was too ashamed and terrified by it to speak about it to them [his parents] and they if they heard I had been punished at school would joke about it.'[9] Scott would only concede to himself the fact that his reticence at the time of the abuse was to a large extent due to the circumstance of his abuser, the headmaster, conspicuously sharing the same High Church religious outlook as his adored father, who was also the headmaster's friend.

Any analyst confronted with this story would almost certainly have deduced that Scott did, in reality, blame his parents for their failure to understand his suffering, through what he regarded as the most dreadful period of his life. And that at some level he wanted to punish them for this failure. This impulse, however, could not be expressed at any conscious level, partly because the young Scott's developing faith prevented it. The repressed feeling was therefore internalized as a guilt to add to the pain of the abuse and the pain of his stifled anger. Small wonder that Scott's stomach seemed to be tied up in knots.

Scott's ambivalence about his parents is suggested by his extreme personal reaction to his father's heart attack and his subsequent stroke. In both cases Scott experienced overwhelming feelings of guilt when no blame could reasonably be attached to him. Some would see this as an indication of Scott's extreme sensitivity. But such feelings often unravel in therapy more revealingly as blocked anger. People feel guilt when harm comes to someone even when it's not their fault because they have secretly or unconsciously not wished the other person well. It would certainly appear the anger Scott felt in relation to his father was much more deep-seated than he wished to acknowledge, and that their differences over interpretation of the Christian message may have been one of its milder external symptoms.

Scott's feelings for his mother were also complicated. Some insight into their relationship emerges from the letters between Mary Benson and Scott's brother Nigel, after Scott was admitted to Guy's Hospital. Nigel expressed what was obviously a general family complaint: 'We are always hearing odd rumours about Michael from all sorts of sources and it does make things rather difficult when we know practically nothing direct.' This was particularly distressing for their mother, whose information about her son's health was liable to come 'from someone who may be a complete stranger'.[10] This could be construed as benign neglect on Scott's part. He did not want to worry her. But it cannot be construed as open communication.

Scott's relationship with his mother, like that with his father, exhibited an underlying tension. He felt bad about not doing enough for her, but was often impossibly busy in other directions. Esther Muirhead, Scott's Quaker secretary, whose admiration for him verged on idolatry, confessed to being 'mildly shocked' by Scott's priorities when his father died after long illness. At the time Scott was experiencing his first major triumph at the United Nations. Afterwards he stayed on at Lake Success for a while before going on to an ashram in India, fitting a one-day visit to his recently widowed mother in between. After Scott's speedy departure for India, Esther Muirhead visited Mrs Scott to alleviate what was a lonely Christmas and found her 'ill, old and very sad'. Muirhead's glum conclusion was that Scott, 'like other great men', had 'a blind spot' where his family was concerned.[11]

This is not to suggest Scott did not genuinely love his parents on a conscious level, or that they did not love him. But the rage and distrust that stem from the feelings of impotence of an abused child will demand expression in some form. The consequence is often antisocial behaviour, sometimes by extending the contagion of abuse. Or, in cases where the guilt is deeply internalized, mental breakdown and sometimes suicide. Scott's remarkable accomplishment was to transform the pain of his dire experience into creative energy. His abhorrence of suffering and his righteous anger at authority figures who seemed to be causing it, or allowing it, can all be seen as first being shaped by his experience as an abused child. Unable to free himself from the consequences of his own abuse, Scott later found a high degree of fulfilment in freeing others. This must have relieved his inner tensions, but such tensions, unless directly addressed, never really go away.

Scott had psychological problems, but they were not insuperable. Disentangling the abuse-sourced, neurotic overdrive from his genuine convictions and feelings would have taken time and patience but the process was unlikely to have imperilled his basic personality or his commitment. It is tempting to imagine that Scott could have untied his psychological knots had he, like Benson, been prepared to 'wade through black mud'. He could, perhaps, even have spared his friends the huge embarrassment of the Oxford incident, which, with hindsight, seems almost like a primal scream against the frustrating contradictions in his own nature. As it was, Scott's brief encounter with analysis must at the time have seemed like yet another threatening pressure on his already frayed nervous system.

Unfortunately, therapy, like religion, rarely works miracles. Given the relentless, driven pace that Scott had established for himself, he was almost certain to have some kind of crack-up or major crisis. Nor is it likely that analysis would have changed him overmuch in the long term. He was not far short of fifty, and already set in his unorthodox ways. On the other hand, it might have helped him feel better about himself, and might even have eased some of the regret he was to feel in old age.

When Scott was almost seventy and the *Observer* journalist Cyril Dunn was interviewing him with a view to writing his biography, the subject of Mary Benson came up. In response to Dunn's probing, Scott initially produced a rather wooden, seemingly well-rehearsed, version of events. She had fallen in love with 'The Work' and, through that, 'rather tragically' in love with him. But there had never been any question of his being able to compromise his commitment by marrying: for him, it had only ever been a 'Platonic' relationship. Later on in the interview, Scott would return to the subject on his own initiative, speaking in a more relaxed way. He would then reveal that he still derived comfort from rereading her letters; that he recalled their days together through the early 1950s as being 'halcyon' ones when 'things were simple, happy and straightforward'; and that he and Mary had 'a very close affinity' that made them 'in every way suited to each other'.[12]

Knowing that Benson was then living in London, Dunn summoned up the courage to ask: 'Why don't you marry her now?' Scott's response was to sit quietly, leaving the question hanging, unanswered, in the air. He then struggled up from his chair and stumbled out of the room, in an effort, Dunn thought, to conceal the fact that he was crying.

CHAPTER EIGHTEEN

CAMPAIGNING CLERICS

MICHAEL SCOTT's long absence through illness in 1955 had no noticeable effect on the expansion of his reputation in Africa. Among poor black Christians in the Central African Federation, there was a grass-roots campaign to have him appointed the next Bishop of Nyasaland.[1] Among the rich white settlers in Kenya, Scott's fame was enhanced by his inclusion in 'the Mau Mau Boogie', a catchy tune with a flexible lyric elaborating on what might happen on safari in pursuit of big game. The verse allocated to Scott ran:

> Turn him over Big White Chief
> Look at name on handkerchief
> 'Oh my God, look who we've shot
> We've shot the Reverend Michael Scott!'

> Chorus: 'Kee, kee Kikuyu.'[2]

In establishing the Africa Bureau, it had always been David Astor's intention to extend Scott's influence beyond the impacted problems of the continent's south to the north where the old colonial arrangements seemed to be in flux. There could be no doubt that his influence was growing, and success overseas bred a modest expansion at home. In early 1956 the Africa Bureau moved to more dignified premises, occupying four large rooms at Denison House in the Vauxhall Bridge Road, where visiting African liberators could be received in some style and the staff – now seven – could finally enjoy some legroom. Though a major step up from previous locations, Denison House was not intimidating. Among the Bureau's closest neighbours in the building were the Anti-Slavery Society and an outfit called The Evangelical Electrical Company, which specialized in the provision of neon signs for churches with a populist outlook.

The illumination provided by the Africa Bureau was of a somewhat different order. Its main mode of operation placed an emphasis on discretion, sometimes even secretiveness. The Bureau had rapidly become the first point of call for Africans aiming to navigate the corridors of power in Westminster and Whitehall, and while this could be combined with requests for publicity, very often confidentiality was deemed more appropriate. As the unofficial bridge between the British government and emergent African movements, the Bureau was naturally hampered by the fact that many of the movements' leaders, like Kwame Nkrumah in the Gold Coast (later Ghana) and Jomo Kenyatta in Kenya, were in jail. Despite this constraint, the Bureau's staff were able to develop a range of fruitful contacts with lieutenants of the imprisoned leaders in both East and West Africa. In the case of Kenya, the Bureau worked closely with Tom Mboya, who played a crucial role through the Mau Mau Emergency period and in the protracted constitutional negotiations that led to his country's independence. Indeed, most of the territories that would eventually achieve independence across the continent, from Ghana to Tanganyika, would later express gratitude to Michael Scott's Bureau for its discreet assistance through the 1950s in keeping open a line of communication with the colonial power.[3]

Along with this backdoor diplomacy, the Bureau maintained a steady flow of pamphlets and policy statements about Africa designed to meet the rising level of public interest in its affairs. One of the more influential policy statements, published in 1956 and written by Scott himself, was entitled 'Nationalism can be led but not driven'. It laid emphasis on the need for British policy to avoid 'head-on collision with moderate nationalist leadership', which might have the effect of driving it in a Communist direction. Full independence should be the ultimate objective but there had to be an awareness of the dangers of 'splinter and minority groups tending to break away and the dominant group in the new state resorting to undemocratic practices to enforce their rule'. In the meantime, all policies should have as their general aim the abolition of 'forms of loaded franchise and political power based on religious or racial prejudice'.[4]

These radical, but hardly revolutionary, sentiments more or less reflected liberal thinking on the end of Empire in Africa. Envisaging the end of apartheid was a more baffling problem. Indeed, the impetus towards decolonization in the north of the continent only seemed to entrench white supremacist ideas more deeply in the south. And the South African government's skill in portraying itself as a bastion against Communism effectively placed it beyond the reach of conventional political leverage. Policy-makers in London and Washington might deplore the racial attitudes exhibited in South Africa, but they were averse to any destabilizing of its regime if it seemed like handing Moscow an advantage in the global struggle.

In the absence of outright political pressure by the powers that could actually make a difference, moral witness against apartheid assumed an unusually high degree of importance. The most effective witness by far came from churchmen, if not from the organized church. In Britain the conspicuous opposition coalesced round three Anglican clerics: Michael Scott, Canon John Collins of St Paul's Cathedral and the militant monk Trevor Huddleston, who returned from South Africa in 1956 to become the Community of the Resurrection's Master of Novices. In the general histories of apartheid, they are very properly yoked together as pioneers – the men who persuaded their church, and ultimately their government, of the urgent need for racial justice in southern Africa. They were not, however, remotely comfortable comrades.

Relations between them were often prickly, and in the case of Scott and Collins there was a serious antipathy that later developed into damaging differences over policy. The *New Statesman* journalist Mervyn Jones, who got to know both men well, would say that Collins found Scott exasperating and 'distinctly Savonarola', while Scott 'simply hated' Collins.[5] The reason why two men sharing the same Anglican faith and priestly function, and with similar aspirations for South Africa combined with a common reverence for Mahatma Gandhi, should arrive at such a pitch of animosity is not entirely clear, but there are some clues.

There was the obvious difference in style. Scott was seen as the poor priest, immersing himself in the suffering of others, with little regard for earthly possessions or personal appearance. On meeting Scott for the first time Diana Collins, the canon's wife, formed the impression of 'a kind of holy vagabond'[6] who had recently been sleeping in his suit. Collins, in contrast, seemed thoroughly at ease with all the high bourgeois values. He was a *bon viveur*, with a love of fine wines, and indulged a touch of sartorial flair when not arrayed in his cassock. The four Collins sons went to Eton. Nobody could accuse Collins of being ascetic, still less a saint. Nor did he exhibit much public evidence of suffering for the cause. In fact, he seemed to rejoice in his role as its leading fund-raiser. The *Observer* writer John Grigg would say of him, not unadmiringly: 'Spiritually John Collins belonged in the Stock Exchange.'[7]

Differences in style, however, were probably less important than the key differences in their backgrounds. Though the younger by two years, Scott could consider himself much the more experienced in terms of grass-roots activity. Against Scott's record of more than a decade in foreign fields sharing the causes of the dispossessed and being ready to go to jail for his beliefs, Collins's actual on-the-ground experience was confined to two months in South Africa in 1954: first, enjoying the hospitality of a wealthy South African businessman, and then as the honoured guest of the ANC. When asked his impression of South Africa, Collins called it 'a pleasant madhouse',[8] which may well have sounded a shade frivolous in Scott's austere ears. And although both men served in the RAF during the war, there can have been no bonding on that score. Scott rejected the idea of becoming a padre because he could not square his Christian conscience with the idea of blessing others to go into battle. Collins served as a padre attached to Bomber Command.

Underlying Scott's attitude to Collins there seems to have been an emotional response that can occur when an experienced front-line soldier contemplates the rise and rise of an officer permanently based in HQ, or when a coalface worker finds himself being leapfrogged up the pit hierarchy by one of the office staff: not jealousy, and certainly not envy, but a certain kind of puzzled resentment. And seen through this optic, Collins's relatively modest human imperfections were greatly magnified, even distorted.

The Africa Bureau staff were encouraged to think of Collins as something of a buffoon, possibly even a dangerous one. Scott suggested that Collins's rhetoric on the subject of South Africa, which was of the aggressive, sometimes highly personalized variety, was more likely to exacerbate divisions than advance the cause. Collins managed to enhance his reputation for provocative utterance when, in the course of a sermon at St Paul's, he preached:

Let us sympathize with Dr Malan. Let us be charitable to him – this poor wretched man, hag-ridden with fear. We know that only love can cast out fear; but as well expect a man with *delirium tremens* to discover in his heart the love to destroy his illusion of pink elephants, as to hope that the Nationalists, whose hearts are full of fear, can rid themselves of the illusion of white supremacy.

The difference in Scott's and Collins's linguistic approaches was most neatly encapsulated in their response to the news that the South African government had refused the Herero Chief Hosea Kutako permission to come to England to preach at St Paul's Cathedral. Scott's observation for the record was: 'Dr Malan let his political creed come before his Christianity.' Collins was quoted as saying: 'He spits in the face of Christendom.' It was of course the Collins remark that got the headline.[9]

Problems of rhetoric were aggravated by organizational concerns. The Africa Bureau and Collins's Christian Action managed to achieve a tenuous degree of cooperation in support of the 1952 Defiance of Unjust Laws campaign in South Africa, but this was not successfully replicated. In 1954 the two organizations came very close to a public falling-out over how to provide assistance for Huddleston's stand in Johannesburg against the racist Bantu Education Act, designed to downgrade education for the country's black population. Christian Action was also seen as being ham-fisted in its approach to problems in Bechuanaland, and specifically to those of Scott's friend Tshekedi Khama. There were also regular disputes about how to synchronize appeals and publicity campaigns that tended to be interpreted inside the Bureau as evidence of Christian Action trying to take over its turf. These differences were not aired in public, but by 1956 the two organizations were barely on speaking terms.[10]

It was therefore a major embarrassment when shortly before his return to England, Trevor Huddleston contacted both Scott and Collins to suggest a united front. Huddleston was eager to find a platform from which he could express his views on the evil of apartheid and that, he thought, would best be provided by the Africa Bureau acting in concert with Christian Action. At that time Huddleston had an international reputation that would be burnished still further by his brilliant book *Naught for Your Comfort*. His dramatic opposition to Bantu Education and to the population removals that had extinguished Sophiatown, the most vital non-white community in the Johannesburg area, had made him famous around the world. He was being recalled by his religious community, though it was thought that the real reason for his return was to head off his probable arrest by the South African authorities. His homecoming wish, therefore, had the quality of a command.

Finding themselves obliged to confer about the Huddleston plat-form, Scott and Collins danced a minuet of disagreement.[11] Collins naturally thought he should speak on this occasion; Scott thought he shouldn't; Collins, on reflection, thought maybe they should both speak; Scott thought neither of them should, and so on. Eventually, the art of compromise came to everyone's rescue, and Christian Action was allowed to dictate the terms of the main event at the Central Hall, Westminster, in April, while the Africa Bureau celebrated its 'homecoming' for Huddleston at the House of Lords in June. This was a more low-key occasion but not without significance in that it provided an early impetus for protest action against apartheid in sport and the arts. [12]

Scott had a lot of time for Huddleston, who was invited to serve on the executive of the Africa Burea, but they were less than bosom friends. Huddleston apologized to Scott for having had reservations about Scott's early militancy in South Africa, both verbally and very handsomely in print (in the text of *Naught for Your Comfort*). Yet there was a residue of reserve on both sides. Scott saw Huddleston, for all his radicalism, as being essentially an organization man. He was inclined to remind those who exhibited excessive admiration for Huddleston's 'charisma' that he had not actually broken any laws or gone to jail. Huddleston, on the other hand, saw Scott, for all his inspirational qualities, as someone who was never likely to show promise as a team player. Huddleston was also inclined to perceive the better qualities in Collins, while Scott was most appreciative of the worse. At one point David Astor was moved to take the three priests to dinner at the Waldorf in the Strand for an informal 'peace conference' designed to improve the level of cooperation between them. His feeling was that the presence of Huddleston would help to moderate the friction between Scott and Collins. It was, he would later recall, not one of his more successful dinner parties.[13]

As was the case when he was essentially a lone campaigner, Scott looked outside the ranks of his fellow churchmen for intellectual stimulus and advice: to academics, some politicians, and some of the more thoughtful journalists. Scott never showed more than a limited talent for delivering quotable sound-bites, but he was much esteemed by journalists in the quality press for his ability to predict where the next big story was likely to break. This applied not only to Africa, but to parts of the world presumed to be outside his normal areas of competence, like South-East Asia and the Middle East. Colin Legum acknowledged that Scott's early warning system often provided him with an edge over his journalistic rivals. Within the Africa Bureau, Scott's ability to foresee political disruptions two or three years in advance was viewed by some as evidence of his prophetic power. Legum, however, favoured a more prosaic explanation. Scott's ability to predict, he thought, was due to his ingrained habit of thinking globally, his constantly refreshed knowledge of the horse-trading between nation states at the United Nations, and his rampantly suspicious mind.[14]

The value of a suspicious mind was to be amply confirmed by the events of the Suez crisis which inspired the *Observer*, in a famous leader written by David Astor and Dingle Foot and published on 4 November 1956, to attack the British government for its 'folly and crookedness'. Although there seemed a likelihood of untoward consequences resulting from Egyptian President Nasser's nationalization of the Suez Canal Company, few anticipated that it would take the form of a secretly planned invasion by British and French troops in support of an Israeli attack on Egypt, giving grave offence to the United Nations and, more significantly, to the United States. It would all end in fiasco, and in premature retirement for the British premier, Anthony Eden. But it was a rough time politically and journalistically, with David Astor and the *Observer* having to take extreme heat from the still considerable section of British society attached to the ideals of gunboat diplomacy.

Scott asserted his position vigorously in the press, writing to the *Manchester Guardian*: 'Britain will have failed in her historic role unless it can be clearly demonstrated that the course pursued by our government is not one which has the support of the British people.' But he also played a more discreet role in the protection of Astor's back by assembling what was informally known as 'the group', not to be confused with 'the Suez Group' which consisted of mainly right-wing politicos who favoured the invasion. The composition of Scott's group was an interesting reflection of the people he saw as his most useful friends at the time. The key politicians in the group were the Liberals Jo Grimond and Lady Violet Bonham Carter, and a dissident Tory, Sir Edward Boyle MP. The press was represented by Richard Scott of the *Manchester Guardian* and Lord Altrincham, better known as the *Observer* writer John Grigg, along with a clutch of editors: Ian Gilmour (the *Spectator*), Donald Tyerman (*The Economist*), and Stephen King-Hall (the *National Newsletter*). It also included Scott's chairman at the Africa Bureau, Lord Hemingford, and Peter Calvocoressi, a commentator on international affairs who worked as a code-breaker at the top-secret Bletchley Park establishment during the war, and who would later become Hemingford's successor as chairman of the Bureau. The only churchman of any significance seems to have been Canon H.M. Waddams, who was general-secretary of the Church of England Foreign Relations Committee, under the chairmanship of Scott's closest clerical friend, George Bell, the Bishop of Chichester.[15]

This informal group would fragment and dissolve with the passage of time, but David Astor was certainly appreciative of its supportive existence throughout the crisis. And, while the trading of favours was not central to their relationship, he may well have felt that Scott was going out of his way to pay him back for his own efforts during Scott's personal crisis in the previous year.

In many minds the Suez crisis represented the end of empire, in that it could be seen as sapping the martial will required to sustain the imperial idea. Even so, it was probably an accident that it should have occurred so close to the events leading up to the first major independence celebration in British Africa, when the Gold Coast became Ghana in a way that unleashed a surge of pan-Africanist enthusiasm. Thomas Pakenham, in *The Scramble for Africa*, writes of Ghana's emergence as sending 'a drum call for freedom echoing from village to village and coast-to-coast.'[16]

In recognition of the Africa Bureau's contribution to the country's evolution, Scott and Lord Hemingford were invited to attend the independence celebrations as personal guests of the new Prime

Minister, Kwame Nkrumah, recently released from jail sporting a cap bearing the initials 'PG' (short for 'Prison Graduate'). At the thanksgiving parade in the stadium at Accra on 6 March 1957, the eve of Independence Day, Scott was conscious of much of the history of Britain and Africa being brought 'vividly into focus'. He would write of it in *A Time to Speak*:

> Just in front of me a Welsh voice could be heard singing 'Thy Kingdom Come O God'. It was Jim Griffiths, former Secretary of State for Colonies, now representing Her Majesty's Opposition. On the dais was the Governor, soon to be Governor General, Sir Charles Arden Clarke . . . standing next to the Prime Minister, Kwame Nkrumah . . . It had required some courage and humility to take a man [Nkrumah] out of prison and appoint him Prime Minister of the country. Following an older pattern of colonial rule the procession demanding his release would have led to repression in the name of 'law and order' and the Fleet would have steamed into the harbour to show the flag. Now the British cruisers were there with all their flags flying in honour of the representative of the Queen, the Duchess of Kent, and the birth of a new State in Africa . . . Away to the left the Union Jack was flying for the last time over Christiansborg Castle, where the slaves were kept injured and terrified after the slave raids before being shipped across the Atlantic.[17]

From Ghana, Scott travelled on to Nigeria where he was also received as an honoured guest as the country celebrated an advance in its self-governing status, though it would be another three years before the Federation of Nigeria achieved full independence. Scott's time in West Africa, however, was cut short by the news from England that his mother was very ill. Her death in the summer of 1957 furnished much of the material for the last chapter of the book that, in his rare leisure moments, Scott had been writing since the beginning of the decade.

'When I left her for the last time,' Scott wrote, 'to go to a meeting in London, which she would not have wanted me to miss, the caress of her fingers was so weak it could hardly have depressed the last note of the Chopin Nocturne she played so tenderly at Northam.'[18]

CHAPTER NINETEEN
'A TIME TO SPEAK'

THE PUBLICATION in 1958 of Michael Scott's autobiography *A Time to Speak* by Faber and Faber in England and Doubleday in the United States naturally extended awareness of his message on both sides of the Atlantic. If anything, the American reviews of the book were more fulsome than those published in his native land.

The *New York Herald Tribune* headlined its review 'On Four Continents: This Anglican priest has fought the good fight', before going on to say in the text, 'The story of how a diffident priest, moved by his religion as both a spiritual resource and a social force has sought to grapple with the problems of colonialism and racialism, is one of the personal, moving epics of this generation.' Homer Jack, writing in the *Progressive*, said:

> Scott is an effective, British admixture of Jesus and Gandhi, with more than a trace of Marx. As Gandhi was a strange combination of saint and politician, so is Michael Scott. He has the prophet's scorn for injustice, but he has the lobbyist's patience also. He can be a mediator as well as an advocate. . . . Michael Scott is a new type world citizen . . . an Anglican clergyman without a church, but with the whole African continent as his parish.

The *St Louis Post Dispatch* also picked up on the Gandhian influence in its review, headlined, 'A Dangerous Man'. It explained: 'He [Scott] is a dangerous man, as Gandhi, whom he admires was dangerous. He is constantly turning over, in his quiet way, nicely arranged apple-carts . . . If civilization is to endure it will be because of men like Michael Scott.' Scott's attempt to answer 'the question' of how to square a Christian faith with the ugliness and injustice manifest in the world was seen as one of the book's great strengths.[1]

The reviews of *A Time to Speak* by British writers tended to be more hedged with reservation but were, on the whole, highly complimentary. Anthony Sampson, who had edited *Drum* magazine in Johannesburg for several years, perceptively fastened on one of Scott's more popular sayings – 'the trouble with moderates is that they are only moderately against evil'– seeing it as the key to his determined character. Sampson's article in the *Saturday Review* commended Scott for his 'practical patience' and observed: 'again and again in this book we see Scott not as a passionate saint, but as the methodical strategist . . . the Africa Bureau, to which visitors troop with their troubles and delegations, is becoming one of the crucial links between the West and the new Africa.' Drawing on his direct knowledge of Johannesburg, Sampson also favourably reviewed the man as well as the book:

> Since Scott began campaigning in South Africa, alone and abused, much of what he publicized has become taken for granted by liberal opinion in Britain and America, and other courageous fighters have appeared on the battlefront: but the great work of people like Father Huddleston and the Bishop of Johannesburg (Ambrose Reeves), could not have happened without the first break through the colour bar by Michael Scott.

The Times Literary Supplement thought that Scott's narrative was 'untidy', but rated the book 'an astonishing and illuminating document'. The left-wing newspaper *Tribune* called it 'a great story, one of the greatest of our time', while the *Oxford Times* deemed it 'profound, and lit with a Christian zeal rare in our times'. There was even an accolade of sorts from the outside right. Peregrine Worsthorne, writing in the *Daily Telegraph*, commented, 'not since the days of Newman's *Apologia* has a priest wrestled with his conscience in print with such sincerity and frankness. A reader's doubts about the crusade are soon lost in the fascinating study of the crusader.'

Trevor Huddleston in the *New Statesman* would use his review of the book to reiterate his apology to Scott:

> I confess it, there were times when Michael seemed to me to be precisely the 'rather eccentric clergyman'; who made such futile gestures as going voluntarily to prison, prying into evil labour conditions to no purpose, and eventually getting himself excluded from South Africa as an undesirable alien. In other words Michael was ten years ahead of us in vision and in achievement.[2]

Despite all this excellent coverage, *A Time to Speak* never came close to achieving the level of popular success enjoyed by Alan Paton's *Cry, The Beloved Country* or Trevor Huddleston's *Naught for Your Comfort*. And with hindsight, it is not difficult to perceive why this was the case. Both Paton and Huddleston, in their radically different ways, were able to convey worlds that totally involved the reader's emotions and imagination, and held them fast throughout. *A Time to Speak*, though capably and sometimes wittily written, was a much less accessible book, partly because its subject-matter was more complex but mainly because of the constraints the author imposed on himself. While his battles with the powers of injustice, and with his own doubt-filled conscience, were unflinchingly described, Scott was austerely reticent about people. Indeed, one of the book's chief characteristics was the avoidance of expressions of personal feelings about significant characters in the author's life. This can be construed as charitable restraint, but in what purported to be autobiography, it was a major drawback. It was likely to give a reader the impression that he or she was not getting the full story, and such an impression would not have been incorrect.

Among those not mentioned in Scott's life story were Michael Carritt, the Communist agent he worked closely with in India before the war; Jack Harris, the ex-OSS secret agent who guided Scott's steps on the way to his first triumph at the UN in New York; Bishop Geoffrey Clayton, his main clerical antagonist in South Africa; Bishop Ambrose Reeves, who withdrew Scott's licence to preach in South Africa; Trevor Huddleston, his intimate as a friend and later his critic in South Africa; and Canon John Collins, the bane of his London existence. These were all people who affected Scott's life, sometimes in very dramatic ways, yet Scott could not bring himself even to name them, let alone characterize them. In the case of Clayton the precise reason is known. When Cyril Dunn was planning to write his biography in the mid-1970s, he specifically asked Scott why he had omitted direct mention of such an outstandingly important character as Geoffrey Clayton from *A Time to Speak*. Scott had replied, 'I had a sort of revulsion against Clayton. I didn't mention him in my autobiography because I didn't like to admit this feeling about him even to myself, let alone in a book that other people would read.'[3]

Scott's reluctance to acknowledge the intensity of his personal feelings in print was by no means confined to those who he felt were hostile to him, or who might have crossed him, or who represented an association he no longer wished to admit. It also applied to those he felt were his nearest and dearest. Thus, of Mary Benson, the reader of *A Time to Speak* learned that she worked for the Africa Bureau, 'in the most selfless way in place of the fame and fortune she had been tempted to seek in the film world', and that she 'spent herself to the utmost, typing far into the night, and seriously affected her own health', but there was not the remotest hint of his long pursuit of an 'ideal relationship' with her nor that this attachment had had near-catastrophic consequences for his own health. The treatment of David Astor is similar. By the time *A Time to Speak* was published, Astor had been Scott's primary provider of income and support for almost six years, quite apart from being the man who extricated him from the dire potential consequences of the Oxford incident. Astor is mentioned once in Scott's story – as a co-contributor to the Penguin Special, *Attitude to Africa*.[4]

Reticence on this scale does not imply Scott was an unemotional character. From many other sources and indeed from Scott himself, at least when he was not specifically writing about himself, we know the reverse was the case. What his reticence does imply is his extreme difficulty in evaluating his feelings about other people as individuals (as opposed to allies in a cause), particularly those who might be classified as his peers. This level of distrust of his own emotions may have been connected with ambivalent, unresolved feelings about his parents through the peculiar circumstances of his abuse as a child. But this of course was in the 'bottled-up' area that could not be disclosed, though *A Time to Speak* does go so far as to criticize 'excessive use of corporal punishment' in schools.[5]

The most insightful review of Scott's book was the one written by Elizabeth Pakenham in *Socialist Commentary*. Lady Pakenham, who, as a member of the Africa Bureau executive, was acquainted with the book's long gestation, had this to say: 'To those who know the Reverend Michael Scott, it is clear that nothing would have induced him to write about himself at all had he not felt that his life's-work could be made more effective if people understood his personal story.' It was, therefore, the autobiography of a man whose preference was for keeping himself to himself, a highly uncommon combination not likely to be conducive to maximum disclosure. According to Lady Pakenham, who was in a position to know, Scott's main motives for breaching his personal privacy to the extent that he did was the need 'to awaken the West to its duties [in Africa]' and the wish 'to set his quasi-communist past in perspective so that false accounts may no longer hamper his work'.[6]

These twin objectives, which were of course not strictly autobio-graphical at all but much more concerned with the public-relations aspect of his cause, were reasonably well achieved. Most of the reviews, particularly those in America, focused on Scott's accom-plishments in Africa, seeing them as the harbinger of further change on that continent where the process of decolonization had already broken from a trot into a gallop. And the American Committee on Africa, run by Scott's friend George M. Houser, was more than happy to have further literary ammunition to fire off in support of its liberation message.

On the matter of his 'quasi-communist past', Scott's book did volunteer information that was not on the record, some of it quite humorous. His pre-war days as a Communist agent in India and the Far East were recalled in a mildly farcical way from the perspective of a mature man looking back on the eccentricities of his youth. There were, nonetheless, limits to Scott's retrospective frankness. Nothing was mentioned concerning his close association with Michael Carritt, whose service to the British Raj was combined with the provision of positive operational intelligence to the Indian Communist Party. As it was, Scott was able to portray his 'quasi-communism' as part of a learning curve that led him back to a more profound appreciation of Western values.

Even Scott's edited reminiscence was deemed startling by Roger Baldwin of the International League for the Rights of Man (ILRM), who acted as Scott's guarantor for his multiple US visa applications throughout the 1950s. Baldwin never believed the allegations of a Communist connection levelled against Scott by his opponents in South Africa and by the visa authorities, that is until he read *A Time to Speak*, when 'it was a surprise to find they had so much substance'.

Baldwin, however, was philosophical on the subject. He would later tell Cyril Dunn that the ILRM would have stood by Scott even if it had been told of his 'Communist associations' from the outset, though he confessed himself somewhat taken aback by Scott's degree of reticence on the issue: 'I never asked him why he had not been frank with us from the beginning, but it was characteristic of him to be close-mouthed about his personal affairs and views.'[7]

Scott's public repentance for his previous Communist affiliation in *A Time to Speak* did not have much impact on his white supremacist critics in southern Africa. They continued to regard him as an indissoluble part of the 'red menace'. But it did have the immediately beneficial consequence of easing his, and Baldwin's, interminable problems over his access to the United Nations. Instead of getting into a regular tangle with the US visa authorities for not being prepared to answer questions about past Communist connections, Scott just directed their attention to the relevant pages in his book.

T HE WIND of change that was gusting through Africa when *A Time to Speak* was published never amounted to more than a light zephyr as far as the Hereros were concerned. Despite its established place in the UN calendar, South-West Africa remained firmly trapped under the heel of its powerful neighbour. In January 1956 Scott wrote to the South African High Commissioner in London formally requesting permission to visit Chief Hosea Kutako to inform him of developments at the UN. The request was routinely denied in a letter signed, apparently without irony: 'Your obedient servant'.

Obedience or, more precisely, the lack of it was now central to South Africa's relationship with the UN. For ten years South Africa had failed to comply with regular two-thirds majority resolutions of the General Assembly designed to bring its stewardship into line. Instead, South Africa had proceeded with its plan to absorb South-West Africa into the political system of the Union and to extend its network of discriminatory legislation against its inhabitants. South Africa's only significant sop to world opinion was to refrain from calling this process 'incorporation', though it was just that in all but name.

In an attempt to strengthen its hand, the UN made further recourse to the International Court at the Hague for more advisory opinions on its powers. To some radicals, Scott among them, this seemed like the political equivalent of treading water, as South Africa had already demonstrated its readiness to ignore advisory opinions, but it did inch matters forward. In 1955 the court advised that although South Africa exercised its authority in the Territory under the Mandate of the old League of Nations, the UN General Assembly was acting within its competence in passing resolutions on South Africa by a two-thirds majority. Under the pre-war League, a unanimous vote had been necessary. This opinion had the effect of reaffirming all the UN's previous decisions, but hardly touched on the question of South African compliance in the future. However, a subsequent advisory opinion, delivered in June 1956, did provide a positive response to one of Scott's more assiduous campaigns at the UN.

The court accepted that the UN could receive oral petitions by individuals who could provide information on the administration of South-West Africa. This deviation from the norm had been strenuously opposed by the British government, which had gone to the lengths of sending its attorney-general, Sir Reginald Manningham-Buller, to the Hague to plead for its rejection. Even so, the court's decision was unanimous, and Scott was able to begin the trawl for suitable petitioners. Effectively, South Africa's stranglehold on information coming out of the Territory had been broken. In the first two years after this reform was introduced, the number of petitions to the UN, both written and oral, increased sharply. Among them were several from leaders of the Ovambos, the dominant tribe in the north of the Territory. The Hereros and the smaller tribes were no longer isolated in their opposition.

Despite this welcome advance, Scott was becoming ever more convinced that only a compulsory adjudication by the court, empowering the UN to apply sanctions, could bring South Africa into compliance. In 1957 he returned to this theme again in a statement to the Fourth (Trusteeship) Committee, and was rewarded with a more positive echo, followed by a big surprise. Twelve member states put their signatures to a resolution referring to the possibility of recourse to the International Court for a compulsory judgment, only to be deflected by an unanticipated proposal from the chair of the Fourth Committee, Thonat Khoman of Thailand. Clearly by pre-arrangement, he introduced a resolution for the setting-up of a small but high-powered Good Offices Committee, with Britain and the United States as its leading members. It was suggested that this arrangement could sort out the whole thorny South-West Africa problem once and for all. Impressed by the apparent readiness of the great powers to get involved, the Fourth Committee decided, on reflection, to give this unexpected initiative a chance.

The Good Offices Committee consulted closely with South Africa and surfaced a year later with a plan. It envisaged a neat form of partition of the Territory, allocating UN Trusteeship status to the poor north, while the south, which contained the good ranching land and most of the mineral wealth, was deemed suitable for annexation by South Africa. Among those granted hearings by the Fourth Committee to comment on the plan were Michael Scott and Mburumba Kerina, a handsome young petitioner who had been accorded representative status to work with Scott by the Herero Chief Hosea Kutako. Scott and Kerina were quizzed for four days by a Committee that was already unimpressed by the plan. The notion of partition soon withered away, and the old battle stations were resumed.[8]

Although Scott and Kerina had combined effectively in seeing off the threat of partition, it was not generally a happy association. Kerina, still only in his middle twenties, was impetuous and inclined to overstatement. At one point, he was seized with the idea of inviting the UN to explore a charge of genocide against South Africa. Scott was able to persuade him that this might prove counter-productive. He was too late, however, to head off an embarrassing misunderstanding over scholarships. Learning that Scott had some influence over scholarship placements in the New York area, Kerina vastly exaggerated its extent in messages back to the Territory. As a result, a hopeful group of would-be students, among them several leading Hereros, left the country illegally, landing up in a small Bechuanaland town to await further instructions. Kerina met them there and cabled the UN to say that the scholarship candidates were all assembled, awaiting official support and transportation. Eventually, a member of the UN Secretary-General's staff had to be sent out with the thankless task of telling them that no actual scholarships had been arranged, and that they should return home.[9]

Relations between Scott and Kerina became a bit easier when they were joined in New York by Fanuel Kozonguizi, another young petitioner who enjoyed Chief Kutako's support. Kozonguizi, a graduate of Fort Hare University, was politically more sophisticated than Kerina. Scott got on well with him but even Kozonguizi could present problems. In a desperate attempt to move matters along more quickly, Kozonguizi went to China in 1960 where his attack on colonialism and imperialism was broadcast on Peking radio. At the UN the South African delegation jumped at the chance to attack Kozonguizi and to rake up Scott's earlier link with the Communists. Scott was dismayed by Kozonguizi's action but defended his UN colleague vigorously in public.

While all three men derived their ultimate authority from Chief Kutako and his Council, their interests did not wholly coincide. Scott naturally saw the UN as being the prime focus for potential advance, whereas both Kerina and Kozonguizi saw it as being supplementary to the effort of raising political consciousness across tribal lines throughout the Territory. To the young men in a hurry, Scott sometimes gave the appearance of being too tolerant of the UN's delays and evasions. At such times Kerina and Kozonguizi were prone to see themselves as prime candidates for supplanting Scott rather than supporting him.

Chief Kutako, who was approaching ninety, had to work hard keeping his UN petitioners in line. At one stage he wrote to Kerina in New York telling him to curb actions designed to build up his own image, and reminded him that Scott was still the chief spokesman for the Hereros at the UN.[10] A few months later he wrote to Kozonguizi in precisely the same vein. He never allowed Scott to doubt his undeviating loyalty. Kutako wrote to him in November 1958: 'I am unable to explain to you in a letter the love the people of this country feel for you.'[11]

UNDER THE apartheid laws that applied to South-West Africa, all 'native' locations had to be at least 500 yards from any European-inhabited area. This created problems in the Windhoek Old Location, close to where Scott had pitched his tent back in 1948 when assembling his early evidence for the UN. Since those days, the neighbouring European area had expanded to the point where the

Old Location was deemed to be in violation of the segregationist law. Accordingly, the authorities ordained that its 16,000 inhabitants should move to a site three miles out of town. The new township was called Katutura by the local white officialdom, apparently unaware that its meaning in Herero was 'No place of our own'.

On 10 December 1959, there was a large demonstration against the forced removals. The police ordered the demonstrators off the streets. When the crowd did not disperse quickly enough, the police fired into it. By the evening forty-four Africans had been wounded and eleven killed, one of them a brother of Mburumba Kerina.[12] Although the Windhoek Old Location shootings would soon be eclipsed by a much larger atrocity – the Sharpeville massacre in South Africa four months later, in which sixty-nine were killed and hundreds wounded – it had the effect of solidifying political opposition in the Territory, further radicalizing the Ovambos. Their party, soon to become the South-West African People's Organization (SWAPO), would draw the Namas and many of the Hereros into a united campaign against South African occupation.

The Windhoek shootings also accelerated events at the UN where the Assembly finally invited legally qualified states to undertake constructive proceedings against the Union of South Africa in the International Court to achieve a 'binding' judgment. The best legally qualified states, as Scott had indicated some years earlier, were Ethiopia and Liberia.

On 4 November 1960, Ethiopia and Liberia, with the backing of the Conference of Independent African States and the UN's South-West Africa Committee, formally launched their action against South Africa in the Hague Court. It was, Michael Scott said, 'a matter of profound satisfaction'.

There was a counter-attack of sorts at the UN. In an attempt to make the best of a bad job, Eric Louw argued that further discussion of his country's mandate in South-West Africa should be suspended on the grounds that it was now *sub judice*. This, given the snail's pace of the Court's deliberations thus far, amounted to a request for the UN to keep quiet for some years to come. But, in the wake of Sharpeville and after the fiasco of the Good Office's partition proposal, patience with South Africa had all but expired. The *sub-judice* proposal was overwhelmingly defeated.[13]

The mood of the UN had changed, as had its composition. In the course of 1960, African membership of the UN rose from nine to twenty-five, mainly as a consequence of General de Gaulle's readiness to shed France's imperial possessions. The new arrivals had the effect of bringing the Afro-Asian block up to forty-six out of a total UN membership of ninety-nine. In her book *South West Africa*, Ruth First wrote of 1960 as the year that 'Africa swept into New York's Forty-Second Street', marking the emergence of a new spirit of African militancy that 'charged old issues with a new fury'.[14]

There were still large areas of Africa under colonial rule, but even in Kenya and the Central African Federation, which seemed to have the most intractable problems, the end was deemed to be in sight. And now even South-West Africa appeared to be in with a chance of catching up in the race for independence. For a while at least, Scott could turn his attention to other matters.

CHAPTER TWENTY

DOING TIME IN ENGLAND

THE FIRST Aldermaston March, in April 1958, bore only a modest resemblance to the huge Ban-the-Bomb processional jamborees that came later and which would end in London's Trafalgar Square in a festive atmosphere of blazing banners and blistered feet. For one thing, the marchers trudged the 52 miles the other way: from London to the bleak spectacle of the Aldermaston Atomic Research Establishment in the Berkshire countryside. For another, they were not that numerous – around 1000 through the four marching days of Easter, though swelling to several thousand more at the close. And for yet another, it caused only mild public excitement.

Press coverage varied from the modest, and that sometimes mildly scornful, to the minimal, though the *Evening Standard* carried a downpage item from Reading Town Hall where the marchers paused to make speeches. It reported that 'the longest and most prolonged applause' was accorded to a remark made by a priest, quoting the Reverend Michael Scott, who told his fellow marchers: 'It may be the time will come in this country when we have to resort to passive resistance.'[1]

Once in Aldermaston the marchers passed a peremptory but impeccably even-handed resolution calling on Britain, the United States and the Soviet Union to 'stop testing, manufacturing and storing nuclear weapons immediately'.[2] After the march, Scott took part in the deputations that delivered this message personally to No. 10 Downing Street and the US and Soviet Embassies in London.

Within the Africa Bureau, it was hoped that this would be the full extent of Scott's commitment to what seemed, on the surface, a peripheral cause as far as Africa was concerned. David Astor shared many of Scott's concerns about the arms race, but he could not bring himself to endorse a campaign that could lead to Britain's voluntarily renouncing its nuclear weapons. The Bureau's chairman, Lord Hemingford, had similar reservations, coupled with the fact that he felt that Scott was already overextended with his existing commitments in Africa and at the UN. Nor did he approve of passive resistance in a democratic society.

On the other hand, given the temper of the times it was recognized that asking Scott to steer clear of anti-nuclear issues was akin to urging a fish to abjure water. Hemingford's disapproval was therefore limited to an insistence that when engaged on Ban-the-Bomb issues, Scott should always make it plain that he was acting in his capacity as a private citizen, and not as the Hon. Director of the Africa Bureau.[3] The distinction would come under considerable pressure in the ensuing years, particularly when Scott's activities in his private capacity led him to jail on three occasions, but it managed to survive.

Scott's life between 1958 and 1962 was a blur of intercontinental events, taking in many trips to Africa to attend independence celebrations and Pan-African conferences of the new states, wearing the same dog collar but a variety of hats (Africa Bureau Director, official Herero representative, sometimes simply 'honoured guest') and regular visits to the UN each year to denounce South Africa and keep the Herero issue alive. Yet through it all he kept the nuclear issue in Britain in sharp focus.

In an age grown resigned to the existence of weapons of mass destruction, it is hard to appreciate the degree of fervour aroused by the Campaign for Nuclear Disarmament (CND). It was without question the most remarkable grass-roots movement in post-war Britain, forcing itself on the attention of a sceptical press and ultimately of the country's politicians. James Cameron of the *News Chronicle* was one of the few journalists who took the movement seriously from the beginning – he had witnessed the effect of the atom bomb on Hiroshima. In his combative autobiography, *Point of Departure*, Cameron would write of the campaign in the late 1950s: 'All over the country new groups arose; meetings sprang up everywhere; young people in Britain found in CND something unprovided by either politics or the church, which was a rationale for hope and sanity.'[4]

And not only the young. The opportunity for some release from the fears built up by the development of the H-bomb and the aggressive posturing of the Great Powers was something that appealed across the generational and class lines. While nobody imagined that nuclear weapons could be uninvented, the idea that Britain should lead the way by renouncing them seemed to many to make logical as well as moral sense. In the event of a nuclear showdown Britain, with its large implants of American military bases, was a prime target for obliteration.

From the beginning, there was friction between those who believed in direct action, encompassing techniques of civil disobedience, and those who believed that all forms of protest should stay within the bounds of the law. Those of the latter persuasion accepted the leadership of the CND's executive under the chairmanship of the ubiquitous Canon John Collins. His committee organized most of the big demonstrations and marches, though it would also 'coordinate' with other groups ready to adopt more radical methods, in particular the Direct Action Committee Against Nuclear War (DAC). Aside from the first Aldermaston March, which the DAC had organized before CND took it over as its showpiece annual event, Collins was never a fan of the DAC's activities. Like Lord Hemingford, Collins did not believe that a strategy based on civil disobedience could be justified in a country that enjoyed full democratic rights.

Other CND luminaries, such as the novelist J.B. Priestley and the left-wing journalists Kingsley Martin (*New Statesman*) and Michael Foot (*Tribune*), shared this outlook. The objective, as they saw it, was to win over the opposition Labour Party so that it would implement anti-nuclear policies, if and when it formed the government after the next general election. To the radicals in the DAC, obsessed with the imminent threat and the moral iniquity of any policy based on nuclear weaponry, this approach seemed too slow. Michael Scott shared their view.

In the course of 1958 Scott accepted an invitation to serve on the executive of the DAC, which, as most of its activists were in their early twenties, had the effect of hugely increasing the committee's average age. Scott established an instant rapport with Michael Randle, the son of a conscientious objector, raised as a Catholic, who had spent most of his formative years working on a farm in Ireland. Randle, aged twenty-four, combined chairmanship of the DAC with reporting for *Peace News*. Scott also worked closely with April Carter, who had given up an Oxford scholarship to become the DAC's secretary, and with the committee's formidable young Field Officer, Pat Arrowsmith, already embarked on a career in protest that would lead to her serving eleven terms in jail and to championing lesbianism long before gayness became publicly acceptable. Arrowsmith, like Scott, had a clergyman father, though she described her own upbringing as being at the 'low' end of the Anglican spectrum.[5]

At the Africa Bureau there were raised eyebrows at the company their Director was keeping; though for Jane Symonds, Mary Benson's successor as the Bureau's secretary, there were also consolations. She detected a positive lightening of Scott's general mood; he was 'invigorated' by his contact with the young radicals, and this made him happier in his other work.[6]

Scott spent the Christmas of 1958 in jail. His route there had its origins in the picketing of a ballistic missile site under construction near Swaffham in Norfolk. A group of about fifty DAC demonstrators were deemed to be obstructing work in progress. There was a fracas, though it appeared to be more a consequence of the Irish labourers fearing that their concrete-mixer was under threat than of any ideological divide. Returning from an All-African People's Conference in Ghana, Scott arrived on the scene late, but in time to get himself arrested as 'a disturber of the peace and not a person of good behaviour inasmuch as he on divers days between 10th and 20th days of December 1958 organized and took part in trespassing on Air Ministry Property . . .' Of the thirty-six arrested, fourteen gave assurances not to repeat the offence and were released on payment of a small fine. Scott, among the refusers, was imprisoned in Norwich jail along with Michael Randle, who later confessed to being mildly awestruck by having Scott as a cell-mate: 'it was like sharing a cell with Nelson Mandela'.[7] Pat Arrowsmith and April Carter were accommodated in Holloway prison.

The events at Swaffham, whatever the gradualists in CND might say, had the effect of reaching parts of the newspaper business that had proved untouchable by more pacific means. From the perspective of the popular press, the disarmers' tale now offered colour and drama, and their headlines showed a degree of appreciation. The *Sunday Dispatch* enticed its readers with 'Pacifist Parson Flies in for Rocket-Base Protest', while the *People* bannered its main story:

'Twenty-one follow "The Saint" to prison'. The more serious Sundays also gave it extensive coverage, and dutifully quoted Scott's appeal to the Swaffham magistrates: 'We have to discover', he had told them, 'techniques of non-violent resistance to injustice which is what the Africans are trying to do.'[8]

The magistrates, however, were more intent on discovering techniques of returning Swaffham to its former status as a quiet country town. On 29 December, the protesters were summoned back to court, and ordered to agree to keep the peace for a year or go back to jail for a further fourteen days. 'Nobody', said the chairman of the magistrates, 'wants to make martyrs of you.' He released them from custody and gave them seven days to make up their minds, which, in most cases, had already been made up.

Scott was working at his desk at the Africa Bureau in Denison House when the police arrived on the morning of 8 January 1959 with a warrant for his arrest. It was a good-humoured, even light-hearted, proceeding. A *News Chronicle* reporter who was on the premises at the time observed that the policemen were extremely polite: 'I am sorry Sir, but you are under arrest.' As he slipped on his duffel coat, the Director's parting words to Jane Symonds were, 'Keep the home fires burning.'[9] On emerging from Brixton jail two weeks later, Scott was asked his opinion of the British prison system. He said it was preferable to the one in South Africa.

Canon Collins's response to Swaffham was a blunt reaffirmation of the line that CND was not in favour of civil disobedience, though he later issued a softer, if still grudging, statement expressing the movement's 'sympathy and admiration' for those who went to prison. There was, however, the hint of a larger problem to come in the remarks of CND's president, Bertrand Russell, the venerable philosopher who, in his eighty-eighth year, showed no sign of regarding his post as merely honorific. Swaffham, Russell said, was 'abundantly justified' on the grounds that, 'The Press, with very few exceptions, has boycotted news of peaceful and orderly activities, by those who hope to prevent nuclear warfare . . . it is only by such methods (as those deployed in Swaffham), that public opinion can be made aware of the fact that our population is being led blindfold towards mass extinction.'[10]

The momentum of DAC's activities, directed mainly at nuclear establishments, factories and bases, began to pick up again, providing a newsworthy adjunct to the stately advance of the overall CND campaign. In an effort to fend off a planned demonstration at the Harrington Ballistic Missile Base near Northampton, summonses were issued against the entire DAC leadership for producing inflammatory leaflets 'inciting the public to commit a breach of the peace'. Pat Arrowsmith, April Carter, Allen Skinner, Frances Edwards, Will Warren and Hugh Brock, Michael Randle's Quaker editor on *Peace News*, all veterans of Swaffham, were imprisoned for two months for refusing to be bound over to keep the peace. Scott and Randle escaped the same fate only by being out of the country on other business – in Africa, where they were hoping to stop France's first atomic weapons test in the Sahara desert.

Of all Scott's campaigning activities, the mission attempting to head off France's pursuit of a *force de frappe* was probably the one that afforded the most personal satisfaction. In the first place, the Sahara Project, as it was called, was a manifestation of genuinely international radicalism, with a sponsorship that included Martin Luther King Jr and the Nobel Prizewinning chemist Linus Pauling, along with Lord Russell and A.J. Muste. Its working committee included close friends from New York, Bayard Rustin, one of King's closest associates in the American civil rights movement, and Bill Sutherland, who now worked in Ghana's Ministry of Finance. In the second place, it advanced the cause and authority of the United Nations. In November 1959 the General Assembly passed with a two-thirds majority a resolution calling on France to drop plans for atomic testing in the Sahara (Britain and the United States were among the abstainers). Third, and most relevantly for Scott, it married the cause of international peace with the rise in political consciousness of black Africa. The Sahara Project had the public support of Ghana's President Kwame Nkrumah from the outset, while his country's Council for Nuclear Disarmament had indicated a readiness to supply most of the volunteers.

The plan was for a motorized expedition from Accra, heading north into Upper Volta, then under French control, before proceeding through the French Sudan to the test site near Reggan, a distance of 2100 miles. At the site they would set up a camp with the objective, according to the Project's official fact sheet, of remaining 'until the test is called off'. If it was not called off, the expedition team proposed to 'place their lives in the way of the nuclear instrument'.

There were seventeen volunteers for the long, dusty trek into the valley of the shadow of death. Three were English: Scott, Randle and Francis Hoyland (a young Quaker art teacher from west London); and two were Americans: Bayard Rustin and Bill Sutherland. Ghana supplied two journalists, S.C. Ablorh and P. Marshall, two clerks, B.M. Akita and P.A. Dornu, two drivers, F.A. Koteye and K.M. Arkhurst, a businessman, K. Frimpong-Manso, and a musician, George Asante. From southern Africa came Ntsu Mokhehle, the President of the Basutoland National Party. H. Arinze, a Nigerian student, and Esther Peters, a Frenchwoman, completed the team. At fifty-two, Scott was the oldest, followed by Rustin, forty-nine, and Sutherland and Mokhehle, both forty; the rest were in their mid-twenties to early thirties.

Scott was greeted by a huge crowd at Accra airport when he arrived with news of the UN's thumbs down to the French nuclear test. The *Accra Daily Graphic* of 18 November headlined its story: 'A Hero's Welcome' and carried a photograph of a smiling Michael Scott precariously balanced on shoulders of his well-wishers in the midst of a cheering, arm-waving throng.

The expedition set off from Accra in a convoy of three heavily loaded landrovers, with extra supplies of sugar and tobacco for use as currency along the way. As the team crossed Ghana there were several stops for impromptu rallies with enthusiastic crowds, most of whom appeared to have heard Scott's broadcast on Radio Ghana announcing that their journey was 'the start of a holy war against war'. By 12 December, the expedition had covered the 554 miles to the Upper Volta border, and there it more or less stayed.[11]

The French border police confiscated their passports and warned them that any attempt to cross the frontier would result in their immediate arrest. The contingency then was to set up a protest camp on the border in the hope that the Ghanaian authorities would be able to bring pressure to bear to have the route opened through Upper Volta. Despite the fierce heat by day, and the cold at night, the waiting time was not entirely disagreeable. Bill Sutherland, the joker in the group, coined the team's watchword 'Goya', a shortening in deference to Scott of 'Get Off Your Arse'. Sutherland also derived great amusement from Scott and Randle's pedantry over how to brew the tea – always carry the teapot to the kettle.[12] Bayard Rustin led the singing of Negro spirituals, accompanied by Scott who exhibited a firm grasp of the lyrics. Randle played guitar. The general mood was upbeat, though Scott was mildly afflicted by thoughts of neglecting affairs back at the Bureau. He wrote to David Astor:

> Up before light – a wonderful African morning. We have four songs we sing and a dance . . . Please let me know what would be best for the executive and my position on it – as of course I should want to do what is best for the work of the Africa Bureau, but I can't knock off this action in the middle. It has been a wonderful experience and the best experiment in racial cooperation I have known.[13]

The border stayed closed, and when a further attempt was made to cross it the French police took the precaution of impounding the expedition's vehicles and its loud-hailer.

On 15 January 1960, the two Michaels, Scott and Randle, and five other team members set off across the border on foot on 'a symbolic march' towards their objective. They were sixty-six miles inside French territory when they accepted a lift from a passing truck, which turned out to be on official business. Instead of being taken to the next town, they found themselves being driven back to the border post where they were warmly greeted by a French official with the words, 'Bonjour. Good to see you again.'

Nothing daunted, Scott raced back to Accra and got on a plane for Tunis where the second All-African People's Conference was being held. He hoped to improvise an alternative expedition to the test site, proceeding from the direction of Morocco. On 13 February, France effectively cut off this option by detonating its first nuclear device in the Sahara. Back in Accra, Scott and Randle organized a Positive Action Conference for Peace and Security in Africa, designed to coordinate action against further French tests. It attracted 300 delegates from newly independent African states, and proved to be a vociferous and popular three-day event.

The Sahara Project had its elements of high farce, but it also successfully caught the mood of black Africa's rising exasperation with the white man's use of their continent as a convenience. Scott and the rest of the team were accorded high praise in black newspapers throughout the continent. The fact the expedition had fallen short of its stated objective by some 1500 miles was not regarded as significant. As *Drum* magazine put it, 'in spite of rebuffs, they spotlighted their cause and ideas'.[14]

IN BRITAIN, meanwhile, the issue of how best to spotlight the nuclear disarmers' cause had reached a delicate stage. A hugely successful Aldermaston March marked the movement's entry into mainstream politics. The big unions were starting to take the campaign seriously, as was a large section of the Labour Party. At the party's Scarborough conference in October, two of the biggest union bosses, Jack Jones of the transport workers (TGWU) and Hughie Scanlon of the engineers (AEU), used their block votes in favour of resolutions supporting unilateral nuclear disarmament. The resolutions were passed and, in theory at least, it was now official Labour policy. The edge of this victory was to some extent blunted by the Labour leader, Hugh Gaitskell, announcing that he would 'fight, fight and fight again' to get the decision reversed. But it was a stupendous achievement for a campaign that had existed in an organized form for less than three years.[15]

'Just at that moment of potential triumph,' James Cameron would write ruefully in *Point of Departure*, 'the campaign began to destroy itself, and to fall to bits under the pressure of its internal divisions.'[16]

Cameron, like other veterans in the movement, was persuaded that the open feud between Bertrand Russell and Canon John Collins that surfaced immediately after the conference was the major reason for CND's collapse as a popular movement. There are good grounds for doubting that this was the case. However, there was never any doubt about which side of the argument most engaged Scott's sympathies. He was a member of the group that planned and shaped the Committee of 100, which was committed to the mass civil disobedience techniques that Collins found so upsetting.

The original contriver was Ralph Schoenman, a remarkable twenty-four-year-old Brooklyn-born American, who was studying political theory at the London School of Economics. To some, his level of hyperactivity was off-putting, but he was undeniably full of ideas. In his autobiography, Russell recalled that Schoenman was the 'catalyst' for the idea that could energize CND while avoiding the pitfalls of the DAC, which, to the philosopher's way of thinking, seemed 'too often concerned with individual testimony by way of salving individual consciences'. They would talk at great length at Russell's home in Plas Penrhyn in North Wales. Russell then discussed the notion of mass civil disobedience with other young activists:

> Inspired by the enthusiasm of Ralph Schoenman, this company had grown to a large and steadily expanding group. Early in September he [Schoenman] had brought the Reverend Michael Scott to see me. Scott was an active member of the Direct Action Committee and became one of the most stalwart members of the Committee of 100. I saw him as well as Schoenman almost daily and he and I published under our joint names *Act or Perish* which presents the nucleus of the policy of the Committee.[17]

As luck would have it, a letter co-signed by Russell and Scott outlining the aims of the Committee of 100 in its prelaunch phase was sent to the wrong person. Instead of landing on the desk of John Connell, an official of the Noise Abatement Society and a presumed sympathizer, it found its way into the postbox of a right-wing journalist of the same name, who gleefully blew the gaff on the operation in the columns of the *Evening Standard*.[18] Collins, who had no prior knowledge from his president of what was being incubated inside the CND, was not surprisingly upset. It was always Russell's contention, and indeed Scott's, that they were only in the process of taking 'soundings' in the movement without any view to splitting it, and that it was Collins's obtuseness and overreaction that created the actual division. This, they claimed, was why Russell angrily resigned as president, declaring that Collins was 'impossible to work with'[19] and the reason for the emergence of the Committee of 100 as a separate, and apparently competing, entity (with Russell its president and Scott vice-president).

There was something in this, but not a great deal. Collins's heavy-handedness may well have marginally affected the timing of the split but its occurrence was unavoidable. There was no way the text of *Act or Perish* coupled with the Committee of 100's stated aims could be endorsed by Collins or indeed by anyone else wishing to maintain the movement as part of the political mainstream.

The core of the Russell–Scott analysis was: 'We are told that in a democracy only lawful methods of persuasion should be used. Unfortunately, the opposition to sanity on the part of those who have the power is such as to make persuasion by ordinary methods difficult and slow, with the result that if such methods alone are employed we shall all be dead before our purpose can be achieved.'[20] This combined with a Committee of 100 policy to the effect that at least 2000 demonstrators had to be mobilized for any single civil disobedience demonstration. This represented a massive expansion of potentially disruptive activity. Up to that point the numbers involved in the DAC's direct action initiatives had rarely exceeded a hundred. There seemed no reason to doubt that such a policy would maximise public attention, but it also seemed to be a sure-fire way of losing voters, assuming they survived to the next election. Collins would claim that his campaign had been derailed by 'some Iagos knocking about', presumably with Scott and Schoenman cast in the roles. His more considered view of the launching of the Committee of 100, expressed in his autobiography, *Faith Under Fire*, was that it was 'underhanded, amateurish and silly'.[21]

Russell and Scott were right in perceiving that there was a high level of discontent in CND with Collins's cautious leadership, but wrong in their appreciation of the potential legions they could muster. But in the heady beginning all things seemed possible. As a concept the Committee of 100 demonstrated almost instant appeal to many of the liveliest creative young minds in the country. In his book *The Disarmers*, Christopher Driver would write: 'During the high noon of the Committee of 100, it almost seemed that the entire younger generation in the theatre – John Osborne, Arnold Wesker, Robert Bolt, Shelagh Delaney, Vanessa Redgrave and others – were strewn around the pavements of London in flat rejection of everything which the political leadership of the country was trying to do.'[22]

The first major 'sit-in' was outside the Ministry of Defence in Whitehall in February 1961. Several thousand demonstrators watched Russell and Scott make their approach to the Ministry equipped with hammer and nails and of a mind to follow Martin Luther's example at Wittenberg by nailing their proclamation to the front door. After some discussion they resorted to sticky tape for affixing the Committee's demands which were, nonetheless, bold. They required 'the complete rejection by our country of nuclear weapons and all policies and alliances that depend on them' and 'the immediate scrapping of the agreement to base Polaris (missile)-carrying submarines in Britain'. The turn-out was deemed impressive but the police managed to defuse the event to a large extent by taking no action. Russell said afterwards, 'we do not want forever to be tolerated' and was echoed by Schoenman, more luridly: 'We want the government to be put in the position of jailing thousands of people or abdicating.'[23]

By the spring, the policy of trying to asphyxiate the Committee of 100 with kindness was changing. In April another mass 'sit-in' in Parliament Square ended with 826 arrests being made, though the consequences were still not grave. The majority were fined £1 and given seven days to pay. Vanessa Redgrave accepted bail in time to appear in the matinee performance of *The Lady from the Sea*, while a person unknown paid Michael Scott's fine, presumably to deny him the opportunity of another day in court for refusing to pay.

As far as possible, CND and the Committee of 100 did try to dovetail their activities but, with Russell and Collins not on speaking terms, it was never easy. There had to be some commingling of the rank and file on the Aldermaston March and when Russell and Collins were obliged to share the same speaker's platform at Trafalgar Square. But there was no handshake to bridge the divide. Collins was also adversely affected by a number of conspicuous placards in the crowd bearing the unflattering slogan 'Fire the Canon'.

Scott's last public service to the Committee of 100 took place in September when, with Russell and thirty-four other presumed Committee leaders, he was arrested for refusing to be bound over to keep the peace in connection with another projected 'sit-in' rally in Trafalgar Square. They were sentenced to a month in prison, reduced to a week in Russell's case, on medical grounds. After emerging from prison, Scott took leave of absence from the Committee, pleading pressure of business in Africa.

This was not a diplomatic exit. Scott had promised his friend Julius Nyerere that he would attend Tanganyika's independence celebrations. On the other hand, Scott's absence from the scene at this stage probably prevented further splintering in the splinter group. He always professed the most profound admiration for Russell. Some years later in an essay entitled *Civil Disobedience and Morals*, he would write of the philosopher: 'to me he appears as a giant among mental and spiritual dwarfs'.[24] But Scott was at odds with Schoenman. And when Schoenman joined Russell's personal staff, giving the fast-talking young American even more influence, the internal councils of the Committee of 100 became increasingly fractious.

Scott felt that it was most important that all actions should exhibit fidelity to the Gandhian principles of disciplined non-violence; that objectives should be clearly defined, with the demonstrators carefully prepared for likely eventualities and that any disruption caused should be clearly mitigated by dignified evidence of readiness to suffer any legal consequences. Schoenman, on the other hand, at least to Scott's way of thinking, seemed prepared to settle for more opportunistic methods that took the police and sometimes the Committee's own foot soldiers by surprise. After the Aldermaston March, Schoenman unilaterally led 600 people a further mile to the American Embassy in Grosvenor Square, and invited them to sit down. Unprepared for this challenge, some did and some did not. The result was a confused and, in some sectors, bad-tempered mêlée which inspired many arrests, but provided little evidence of dignified moral witness. Scott saw this kind of action as disruption without the mitigation of satyagraha. It was not something of which he could approve.

It can also be assumed that Russell and Scott, despite their fulsome protestations of esteem and admiration for each other, did not see eye to eye on matters of rhetorical style. In an address to a Youth CND conference, Russell had vilified the Western world's leaders in the following terms:

> We used to call Hitler wicked for killing Jews, but Kennedy and Macmillan are much more wicked than Hitler . . . We cannot obey the murderers. They are wicked, they are abominable. They are the wickedest people in the story of man and it is our duty to do what we can against them.[25]

In his public statements, Scott's policy was to indict the sin but not the sinner. Indeed, he always maintained that highly personalized attacks were almost certain to prove counter-productive. More specifically, he did not share Russell's nightmarish view of Harold

Macmillan. In the previous year the British premier had made his famous 'Wind of Change' speech to the South African parliament in Cape Town, and Scott had been much encouraged. He regarded Macmillan as a leader with the capacity to listen. This much was manifest in the letter Jane Symonds wrote on his behalf while he was in prison. Dated 16 September 1961, it ran:

> Dear Mr Prime Minister,
>
> As I think you will know Michael Scott is at present serving a sentence of one month's imprisonment for his part in a non-violent protest against nuclear weapons. I have today received a letter from him, in prison, asking me to write to you and express some of his thoughts at this time.
>
> He says that their use of a non-violent means of protest on the great issue of nuclear disarmament is 'one of the positive results of Britain's association with India from whom we learned the values of civil disobedience'.
>
> Michael Scott . . . says how greatly he values the effort which you are making for peace and understanding between East and West. The hope of Michael Scott and his colleagues is that their Movement will contribute to your great efforts and that Britain may be persuaded to renounce nuclear arms and follow India's example by joining the unaligned nations of the world.
>
> Their resort to civil disobedience is not only as a protest but, they hope, an example of a means of effective resistance which India demonstrated many years ago but which the world has been slow to follow. His hope is that their movement may be an example to people who have taken up arms against one another in any part of the world.
>
> I fear this is an inadequate statement of the views which Mr Scott asked me to express to you, but you will be able to supplement it through your own knowledge of him and his ideas. It is above all a message of support and thanks to you and your people. Yours sincerely. Jane Symonds. Secretary.[26]

As the letter appears to have gone unanswered it is not known whether Harold Macmillan was beguiled by the parallels between Gandhian passive resistance in India and the disorder on the streets close to his own front doorstep. One suspects not. There was, after all, a clear distinction between passive resistance to advance the cause of a downtrodden, subject nation, and passive resistance to advance a minority cause (albeit a large one) in a democratic society. In the latter case its use was bound to give rise to the accusation that it was a form of blackmail by the minority of the majority, and carried with it the risks of hardening opposition and alienating the uncommitted who might have been susceptible to gentler forms of persuasion. In the case of the Committee of 100 neither of these risks was avoided.

The central problem for the Committee of 100 was that the big 'sit-ins', though impressive to begin with, suffered from the law of diminishing returns in public relations terms. Uncommitted Londoners soon began to express exasperation with having the centre of their city tied up by demonstrators who seemed to be having an agreeable time experiencing, and inflicting, mild discomfort for a cause, but hardly suffering for it. It also became clear that the large demonstrations, however non-violently conceived, were a magnet for other groups more interested in combative confrontations with the police, and their activities inevitably claimed much of the publicity. This was in evidence at the Trafalgar Square demonstration in September 1961, which, partly as a consequence of the imprisoning of Russell and Scott in the days before the event, attracted record numbers, estimated at 12,000, of mixed Committee of 100 and CND supporters with a mingling of hard left and anarchist groups. More than 1000 people were arrested, among them an indignant Canon John Collins.

Unfortunately, given the nature of its support, there was not much else the Committee of 100 had to offer. Its hastily improvised structure had worked against the development of a strong organization in the large provincial cities, and the pledges of support nationally had been disappointing. Scott himself later wrote in an essay analysing the campaign's decline: 'Where the Committee miscalculated was in believing that once the movement caught on, it would grow and spread automatically.'[27] Scott also criticized aspects of the campaign's tactics and discipline but, as one of the founders, he was hardly in a position to question its original conception.

It was also quickly realized that the pool of committed civil disobeyers was shallower than originally imagined, even after the DAC had been merged into the Committee of 100 to avoid duplication of effort. It was one thing to get several thousand people, including a good sprinkling of showbiz and other celebrities, out on the streets of the West End with a good chance of getting off with a light fine or even of walking home free. It was quite another to get the faithful to spend weeks outside bleak nuclear establishments, with a near certainty of going to jail. That side of the operation was still heavily dependent on Randle and Arrowsmith and all the usual suspects in the narrow orbit of *Peace News*.

The friction caused by the split between CND and the Committee of 100 put a brake on the movement's conventional political advance. The Labour Party fell back into line behind Hugh Gaitskell, reversing its unilateralist decision at the next conference. If not the end, it was the beginning of the end. With a sense that public opinion was edging back in their direction, the authorities became more unforgiving. In December 1961, a Committee of 100 action directed against the American airbase at Wethersfield in Essex resulted in the arrests of Michael Randle[28] and five other activists, who were charged under the draconian terms of the Official Secrets Act. They were sentenced to eighteen months' imprisonment.

The legal battering of the Wethersfield demonstrators had the effect of impoverishing the Committee of 100. This would be accompanied by a perception in the wider CND that the big demonstrations had had their day, while mounting smaller ones seemed like advertising evidence of decline. There was no clear way out of this bind, and the sixth Aldermaston March, in 1963, would be the last.

Recrimination between veterans of CND and the Committee of 100 survives in muted form to this day, with each side blaming the other for deploying tactics that contributed to the movement's drastic loss of momentum. In truth, the effective undermining of the Ban-the-Bomb movement had little to do with Scott or Collins or Russell or Schoenman. The key factor in the nuclear protest story was entirely out of their hands. In a chilling week of October 1961 the world looked on impotently as Russia and America played out a game of 'nuclear chicken' over Soviet nuclear bases in Cuba. On the surface, the events of the missile crisis seemed to justify the work of the anti-nuclear movement; and for a few short weeks they did provide the impetus for a fresh spasm of protest demonstrations. With hindsight, this can be seen as the movement's death throe.

The deeper impact of the missile crisis was that it provided an unexpected reassurance. It demonstrated that the superpowers could go to the nuclear brink, peer over its edge into the abyss, and then manage to retreat in a way that suggested that they would not be at all eager to go back. The nuclear age, it seemed, might not be so uncontrollable after all. Some might describe this as the dawning of a new realism, though it could still turn out to be a delusion. Either way, it defeated the efforts of both Michael Scott and John Collins to ban the bomb.

TWENTY-ONE

GUNNING FOR
THE CANON

I N CLERICAL PARTNERSHIPS, as in most others, it is often easier to gauge the unvarnished extent of a man's animosities through the utterances of his spouse. This aspect lent a special interest to Diana Collins's lively book *Partners in Protest*, in which she reminisced about her campaigns with her husband, Canon John Collins, in the course of which she dwelt on the personality of the Reverend Michael Scott: 'A very strange character,' she wrote, 'and I cannot profess to understand him.' Nevertheless, she did elaborate:

> I have known people sympathetic to the cause of African freedom who thought Michael a dangerous troublemaker and a somewhat inhuman and insensitive character . . . I have known others who have worked with Michael, who regard him with love and admiration, and speak of his pastoral feeling as well as his dedication. And, at first, John and I were disposed to be among the friends and admirers.[1]

Mrs Collins made it clear that her admiration for Scott never wholly expired, but that her disposition to regard him as a friend was extinguished by events in the early 1960s. The cessation of amiable feeling had little to do with the Ban-the-Bomb controversy, in which the differences between Scott and John Collins were, for the most part, articulated in public. Of much greater significance was an unreported conflict over South African appeal funds that was waged in parallel with their nuclear quarrel. Some of the murkier details of this episode, which involved Scott's Africa Bureau and Collins's Christian Action, are detailed in Diana Collins's book, in a chapter entitled 'The Rift'. But some are not, largely because they were hidden even from the leading participants in the drama.

In the spring of 1960 the Africa Bureau was facing a cash crisis. Despite efforts to raise money through appeals and subscriptions, the Bureau had never been self-supporting. In the early days it had been heavily dependent on David Astor's generosity, but over the years it had managed to secure a more regular income from a variety of charitable foundations in Britain and the United States. Through the late 1950s one of the most dependable sources of finance was the Farfield Foundation, based in New York. One of Jane Symonds's routine tasks, as Scott's secretary, was to write quarterly reports for Farfield on how its money was being spent. The Foundation had made it clear that its commitment could only be short-term, but as the funds were renewed quarterly for almost four years there was no real expectation of the supply drying up. By 1960 it was providing £3300 a year (£50,000 in today's money), a third of the Africa Bureau's annual budget. Then suddenly, seemingly inexplicably, Farfield turned off the tap.

It would be another seven years before Scott and the rest of the Africa Bureau's personnel were in a position to appreciate that Farfield was a conduit for funds provided by the American Central Intelligence Agency (CIA). It was revealed as such in a 1967 Congressional inquiry, following disclosures in *Ramparts* magazine about the CIA's covert funding activities. Further details of Farfield's activities have been more recently provided by the English author Frances Stonor Saunders in her able investigative book *Who Paid the Piper? The CIA and the Cultural Cold War*, published in 1999.

At the time Farfield was channelling CIA money into the Africa Bureau, its executive director was John 'Jack' Thompson, a former English teacher at Columbia University. Thompson had been recruited into the CIA by Cord Meyer, one of the secret world's legendary figures who would eventually be put out to grass as the agency's front man in London. Meyer and Thompson had known each other since 1945, when both were assistants to the US delegation at the San Francisco Conference where the structure of the United Nations was established. According to a close friend, quoted by Stonor Saunders, Thompson became 'obsessed with saving Africans from the Russians'.[2]

It is easy to perceive why such a character should look favourably upon the Africa Bureau as being worthy of Farfield's largesse. Thompson may have appreciated the piquancy of supplying CIA funds to assist a priest who had also once been a Communist agent. The real mystery is not so much why the money was handed over in the first place, but why it stopped when it did, with decolonization in Africa still some way from realization.

There is no direct evidence on this point, but a plausible explanation could be that it was caused by Scott's high-profile advocacy of nuclear disarmament. The Farfield connection was severed soon after his return to London from Ghana where he had been attempting to coordinate international anti-nuclear feeling through the Sahara Project. Covertly allocating CIA money to foster the West's interests in Africa was one thing, but deploying its funds in a way likely to impair the West's nuclear arsenal might have seemed less felicitous.

When Farfield's support evaporated the Bureau faced some painful belt-tightening in order to survive. At the same time, Canon Collins's Christian Action operation seemed to be awash with funds. In the month after the Sharpeville massacre, on 21 March 1960, Christian Action's Defence and Aid Fund, originally established to assist the Treason Trialists in South Africa, logged nearly £40,000 (£600,000 in today's money) in donations, and the cascade of money continued in the following months.

It was probably inevitable, under the circumstances, that somebody would put two and two together to make five, though the arithmetic was unlikely to have originated with Michael Scott. In his autobiography, *A Time to Speak*, published two years earlier, Scott placed great emphasis on the importance of the Africa Bureau maintaining its independent status, especially in relation to Christian Action. Yet by the summer of 1960 the two organizations were locked in secret negotiations: effectively to fuse their South African operations. The strongest impetus for this development, unwelcome to Collins and formerly unwelcome to Scott, came from David Astor.

In a long and intelligent career, one of Astor's least adroit moves was this attempt to engineer a close working relationship between Scott and Collins, two men with a natural gift for rubbing each other up the wrong way. It would have the effect of propelling Scott's mistrust of Collins to the brink of paranoia, and very nearly drive Collins out of the business of raising money for South African liberation.

Astor's basic idea was that Britain should unify its approach to the problem of how best to oppose apartheid and that Collins, the acknowledged fund-raising genius, had a key role to play. He wrote to Collins on 28 May 1960, rather severely: 'the anti-apartheid sentiment in this country could achieve a new unity or could be divided irrevocably by what we do now, and by "we" I really mean "you!" . . . It would be a big thing to do if you shared with others on equal terms the power and the money you have at your disposal.'[3]

As Collins was beholden to the *Observer* for its support of Defence and Aid's public appeals, he was bound to explore any idea coming from Astor, even if he did not relish its content. Reluctantly, he entered into negotiations with the Africa Bureau's chairman Lord Hemingford on possible 'unification' procedures. These proved extremely complicated. Diana Collins wrote in her memoir:

> At one stage in these troublesome and time-consuming negotiations, John was ill, so I had to represent him in a meeting with the Africa Bureau. Someone protested that under a proposed arrangement the Bureau members would not have their 'proper rights'. I replied sharply that they had no rights, it was Christian Action that proposed to offer them some; the point was taken.[4]

Later, when Lord Hemingford seemed ready to make a concession to Christian Action's case, he was deterred by Jane Symonds who thought he was giving too much away. Symonds wrote to Scott, who was abroad, to say that she thought she had been able to assist Hemingford to a better understanding of his (Scott's) conviction on the matter of Christian Action's 'unreliability' and proneness to manipulation by 'undesirable elements'.[5]

The gap in understanding widened with Trevor Huddleston's disappearance from the scene. As a member of the Africa Bureau executive, Huddleston could be counted on to cool matters when the Scott–Collins relationship turned stormy. But in the autumn of 1960 he was appointed Bishop of Masasi in Southern Tanganyika. When it was most needed, his moderating influence was far away.

One of the problems besetting the power-sharing idea was that Collins was never as flush with funds as he seemed, though he liked to give the impression he was doing better than was actually the case, on the principle that the appearance of success was likely to breed success. Scott, and indeed Astor, had a poor grasp of the importance of showmanship in the enterprise, assuming the money rolled in just because the cause was 'good'. The corollary of this assumption was that control of its disbursement should not be limited to Collins and his Christian Action advisers, but shared by others in the anti-apartheid cause. They presumed that they were entitled to influence, even dictate, how the money Collins raised should be spent.

There were, to be sure, large amounts of cash flowing into the Defence and Aid office in the basement of the Collins's Amen Court home, round the corner from St Paul's. But it never stayed there long. Between December 1956 and 1960 Collins raised almost £180,000 (close to £3 million in today's money) but at several times along the way came close to observing the bottom of the barrel. The reason for this was that the outlay of funds, mainly for the Treason Trialists' defence and the welfare of their families, was regular (until March 1961, when the last of the 156 Trialists was acquitted), while the incoming money was subject to extreme fluctuations, depending on the success or otherwise of Collins's campaigns and how well they caught the unpredictable tides of public concern about South Africa. In 1960, moreover, the Collins operation accepted responsibility for funding a range of satellite Defence and Aid committees that sprang up in the major South African cities in response to the State of Emergency declared by the apartheid regime after Sharpeville. This created the need to move the money around even more swiftly and Collins found it difficult to comprehend how this could be done if, as the 'unification' process implied, another level of bureaucracy was superimposed on his operation.

Collins got on well with Hemingford, the Bureau's negotiator-in-chief, but his own manifest foot-dragging in the 'unification' talks began to arouse Scott's darkest suspicions. Scott's exasperation with Collins would feed into a series of damaging rumours about the Defence and Aid operation to the effect that it was a) misapplying welfare funds, b) less than above-board in its financial dealings, and c) soft on Communism. As they soured relationships in all that was to come, each rumour merits examination.

Most damaging was the suggestion that Collins was misapplying Defence and Aid funds which, under the terms of its charitable status, had to be disbursed on an equitable basis. Scott promoted the suspicion that Defence and Aid's welfare programme in South Africa favoured the African National Congress (ANC) at the expense of the

Pan-Africanist Congress (PAC). At the time Robert Sobukwe's recently formed PAC was deemed to be the rising force of black nationalism in South Africa, and it was a PAC positive action campaign against the pass laws that led to the bloody Sharpeville confrontation. The PAC would in time virtually self-destruct, as a consequence of internecine violence inside its leadership, but it enjoyed a wide measure of popular support in 1960 – within South Africa and without. 'Because of the PAC's anti-communism,' Nelson Mandela wrote in his autobiography, 'it became the darling of the Western press and the American State Department, which hailed its birth as a dagger in the heart of the African left.'[6]

Both Astor and Scott favoured the PAC because it was anti-Communist, though it was already exhibiting a disturbing propensity for recklessness and making wild claims. In articulating the complaints made by PAC exiles in London, Scott was reporting their disaffection accurately but with no direct knowledge of what was actually happening on the ground. In fact, in the three months after Sharpeville more than 80 per cent of Defence and Aid's welfare funding was allocated to PAC families, while throughout 1961 the smaller PAC received more of Amen Court's money than did the ANC.

The rumour that there was something shifty about Collins's financial arrangements also appears to have emanated from Scott, though it was first aired by Bertrand Russell, in the edgy period shortly before the CND and Committee of 100 split. Russell was one of the sponsors of Defence and Aid. According to Diana Collins, the philosopher 'began to question John suspiciously about the administration of the Fund's finances. John could think of no source for these suspicions other than Michael Scott.'[7] The short answer to such suspicions was that there was nothing in the Fund's audited, up-to-date accounts which were available for public inspection that suggested any irregularity. And the money could hardly be more closely watched; George Hamilton, Christian Action's treasurer, formerly of Hambros, practically lived in Amen Court. Even so, there were aspects of the Collins operation that might have been open to criticism. Some disbursements, particularly those made to exiled South Africans living in London, were borderline in charitable terms. And there had to be question marks over some of the Canon's better salaried appointments. One senior Defence and Aid figure, who was handling significant funds, was discreetly allowed to go after it was discovered that he had been struck off as an attorney in the Transvaal over a £7000 shortfall in a widow's trust fund. Very likely, Collins was sensitive to having these matters too closely scrutinized. On the other hand, there were no skeletons in his financial closet that could be deemed comparable to the receipt of CIA funds.

The rumour that Collins was 'soft on Communism' was probably the most securely founded, at least in the sense that he had become a lot softer than Scott. Although there was no trace of a Communist affiliation in Collins's past – he was still a Tory, when Scott was first attracted to Communism – he was often characterized as 'the Red Canon'. Collins made no secret of his support for the ANC, even though it was moving closer to the South African Communist Party as they jointly edged towards the concept of 'armed struggle'. He was also ready to employ two Communists at Amen Court on the grounds that they shared the same liberation objectives in South Africa as his own. The Africa Bureau was reckoned to be more high-minded in this regard. It did not approve of working with Communists, collectively or individually.

Given the nature of these rumours, the likelihood of Collins and Scott working effectively together did not seem great, but Astor maintained the pressure, writing to Collins in December 1960 with a plea for the discipline of cooperation. To Collins, however, it appeared as if the discipline of submission was being requested. Scott clearly had a keen interest in shaping the way Christian Action went about its business, while Collins had no particular interest in influencing the work of the Africa Bureau in any way. And the power-sharing prospect seemed even less appealing to him when Scott, with Astor's support, began to nurture the dream of a new freedom fund.

The new fund, it was argued, would be more empowering for Africans. The idea was that money should be raised in Britain and then put at the disposal of responsible African liberation leaders who were better equipped to make the appropriate disbursements. It was a high-minded concept, in theory, but problematic in practical terms. It was assumed that in Britain significant funds could only be raised for essentially peaceful purposes, but there was no way of guaranteeing the money would not end up in parts of the African continent prone to insurrection and violence. Scott, nonetheless, persisted in trying to solve the conundrum of how a Southern African Freedom Fund could be created in consultation with Astor's friend Dingle Foot and a number of senior figures in the Labour and Liberal parties. They held meetings at the House of Commons, widening the circle of those inclined to view Collins as awkward and uncooperative.

Irritated by what seemed an impractical scheme which, very probably, would call on his fund-raising skills and eat into potential funds for his tightly targeted Defence and Aid operation, Collins's resistance to the 'unification' idea moved abruptly from passive to active. In May 1961 he announced that he proposed establishing a new Christian Action political fund designed to supplement the existing legal and welfare commitment of the Defence and Aid Fund. This caused affront to the dignified proponents of Scott's Southern African Freedom Fund, which it seemed to pre-empt. Then Collins added aggravation to insult by proposing a structure for his new fund that would clearly favour the ANC over the PAC. Even Diana Collins's account of this initiative would describe it as 'a bad mistake',[8] needlessly offering ammunition to his opponents.

Collins later maintained that he had been 'not aware' of how advanced plans were for a South African Freedom Fund. This was a serious economy with the truth, but coming from a man who felt he was being persistently slandered by his co-warriors in the liberation cause, it was perhaps understandable. In any event, he paid a high price for the mistake a few days later, when the insalubrious private row went public in the columns of David Astor's *Observer*.

Under the heading 'Canon Jumps the Gun', the newspaper reported: 'The accusation that Canon L.J. Collins of St Paul's is so keen on championing various causes that he sometimes takes actions which are hasty and perhaps injurious to those causes is one that has often been heard in pro-African and antibomb circles.' The article commented censoriously on Collins's proposed political fund, and went on to say, 'Those who have suffered from the Canon's spirit of competitiveness are groaning, "There he goes again."'

This was an accurate reflection of how things looked to Scott and Astor, but there cannot have been more disagreeable reading for

Collins. The first consequence was a blazing row in the *Observer* editor's office between Astor and an enraged Collins, though, as Astor remembered it later, 'there was some laughter'. Collins's anger was also expressed in the minutes of Christian Action's executive council, which recorded the chairman's 'grave concern at the public loss of confidence caused by Mr David Astor through the medium of the *Observer*', described as 'the culmination of a long period of hostility, not just an isolated incident'. But Collins was dispirited as well as angry. In *Partners in Protest*, Diana Collins said that her husband was so distressed 'by this whole wounding business, that he contemplated winding-up Defence and Aid altogether'.[9] He was deterred from doing so by appeals from Albert Luthuli, the ANC's Nobel Prizewinner, and from other African leaders.

In the meantime, both Collins's controversial political fund and Scott's projected Southern African Freedom Fund remained stalled for lack of funds. But matters were coming to a head, principally because the parties to the dispute were now aware that any further outbreak of open conflict could so undermine public confidence that nobody would be in a position to raise any funds. In the wake of the *Observer* article the Trades Union Congress had withdrawn its support from the Defence and Aid Fund, while the fund's fresh contributions had tapered almost to vanishing point.

In the autumn of 1961, 'in spite of hostility and unpleasantness'[10] wrote Diana Collins, a formula was finally agreed for the creation of a joint board of management linking the South African interests of the Africa Bureau and Christian Action. The chairman of the board was Frank Pakenham (soon to become Lord Longford), a man who enjoyed the confidence of both Scott and Collins. This seemed like a victory for Scott and Astor but, given the attitudes brought by both sides to the union, it could only be Pyrrhic.

Propinquity in the boardroom failed to ease the mutual incomprehension felt by Scott and Collins. Both were, by common consent, 'bad in committee', but the real problem was that they were bad in radically different ways. Africa Bureau executive meetings took the form of long-running seminars often with nobody quite knowing what had been decided until Scott, after 'inner disquisition', made a positive move, frequently after the event. At Christian Action the most common complaint about Collins's brusque style of management was that he tended to use his committees as a 'rubber-stamp' for decisions arrived at in great haste, sometimes without consultation, before the event. Each organization of course had to accommodate itself to the foibles of its boss, and both did so with considerable efficiency, but this was no help when the bosses themselves were obliged to sit down and commune together.

After the first meeting of the new board of management, Collins wrote to his friend Sir Kenneth Grubb of the Church Missionary Society, 'Plenty of goodwill but very little direction or leadership' and complained that 'most of the time was wasted' by Scott's discursive approach to the issues. Scott was unable to attend the second meeting in December 1961, as he was away attending a conference in Beirut. But he would pen his pre-meeting cautionary thoughts in a letter to Frank Longford that bristled with suspicion of Collins's actions and motives.[11]

Longford soon realized that he was presiding over a farce. The yoking together of two antipathetic organizations, with one required to come up with most of the money, was clearly demotivating to the money-raiser to the point where both were likely to wind up impoverished. On Longford's initiative, the arrangement was quietly dissolved a few months later, and Collins and Scott went back to paddling their own canoes.

Although its life was short, the legacy of bitterness produced by the failure of the 'unification' idea was long. Scott rarely lost an opportunity to snipe at Collins's efforts, while Astor bore the scars of his disappointment into old age. He would describe Collins as a man 'who showed no respect for anyone who disagreed with him' and 'an operator not hindered by a sensitive conscience'.[12] But it does appear that Collins was only using what power he had to defend a valuable organization with a proven record of achievement (and which would later go on to even greater achievements).

However one looks at the episode, it cannot be regarded as Scott or Astor's finest hour. In Scott's case it is probably best regarded as a narrow escape from a level of administrative slog that was outside his area of competence. His genius was for throwing up illuminating and creative ideas, and for dramatising many of them in action, but in terms of consistently exercising bureaucratic power he was no match for Collins, and never could be.

One of the more interesting ideas Scott had during the stand-off with Collins concerned a generally unrecognized peril at the heart of the decolonization process. As early as 1960, Scott would write in the *Observer*, 'as formerly dependent peoples achieve sovereignty and a seat in the United Nations, they, in turn, acquire the sovereign nation's ability to discriminate against minorities with impunity'. Scott made the point that, in this situation, minorities could find themselves more prone to persecution than in the past. One consequence of this article was the establishment of the Minority Rights Group, set up by David Astor, with a view to prodding the United Nations into a better appreciation of the danger of neglecting 'minority issues' in Africa and other parts of the world.[13] The subsequent history of Africa from the Congo, through Biafra, Uganda and Rwanda, to the Sudan, amply demonstrates that early warning systems in isolation are not enough. But they have to be a starting point for effective action. And the first organized moves to achieve such a starting point can fairly be ascribed to Michael Scott and David Astor. It was one of their finer hours.

CHAPTER TWENTY-TWO
POSITIVE RESISTANCE

THE IDEA OF mobilizing a 'non-violent army' to head off the possibility of more open conflict was almost as old as the century. Gandhi had first broached it in South Africa back in 1906. In later life he returned to the idea when considering the formation of a Shanti Sena (Peace Brigade) to help deal with the problems of a nascent, independent India. But progress in this direction was halting and eventually cut short by Gandhi's assassination. Michael Scott seems to have first encountered the concept at Sevagram in 1950, and it clearly influenced his thinking in relation to the demonstrations in Nyasaland and later to the Ban-the-Bomb dissent on the streets of London. But in both these cases his responses, of necessity, were largely conditioned by the need to adjust to campaigns that were already under way. The difference in 1962 was that he would suddenly find himself, for the first time, in a position to assemble and command a non-violent army working from scratch. And, not unlike Gandhi, Scott found it more problematic than it looked, though he had given the matter considerable forethought.

As early as August 1957 Scott had outlined this vision in an address to a conference of theologians and religious leaders in France assembled by the Mouvement Chrétien Pour La Paix:

What seems to be urgently needed by our world is a peace force drawn from people of every country and race and colour, and from every religion and none who will be the pioneers of a new undiscovered country. It will not be an army of bigots and fanatics. But it will have a divine enthusiasm for tolerance and forgiveness. It will glory in the maximum of uncertainty and doubt on many matters of doctrine, definition and name-calling. It will have no loyalty oath to any race or nation or tribe, to any earthly boundaries or arbitrary limitations, because it will be an army more like a religious order with its citizenship in heaven. It will seek its inspiration from the source of beauty, truth and goodness in the created order of things. It will learn the hard art of appreciating the infinite variety of colour and shade and contrast in the drama of creation. Its loyalty will be to the things that belong to peace. Its members will be skilful and trained in the tasks of devising laws and constitutions which will enable people to work together to create and construct and to differ from one another by civilized techniques. Such an army will not be afraid of breaking laws that are unjust, or of the methods of boycott and non-cooperation where laws and customs prevent people living in peace and friendship with one another and, where they wish to, worshipping with one another.[1]

In short, Scott envisaged an army composed of people very much like himself who, almost by definition, were not in large supply. Even so, they were sufficiently numerous to bring a new international organization into existence.

The World Peace Brigade, as it was called, was founded at a conference in Beirut, Lebanon, on 1 January 1962 with the benefit of a support system that girdled the globe.[2] Its three elective co-chairmen were Michael Scott representing Europe, A.J. Muste, the veteran radical pacifist, representing the Americas, and Gandhian socialist Jayaprakash Narayan representing Asia. Sponsors of the enterprise included notables from every continent, among them Martin Buber of Israel, Martin Luther King Jnr of the United States, Danilo Dolce of Sicily, Vinoba Bhave of India, Martin Niemoller of Germany and Julius Nyerere, the president of newly independent Tanganyika.

Financial assistance for the enterprise was pledged from North America, mainly by Quaker supporters of the pacifist War Resisters International, which had first mooted the idea of a peace brigade, and closer to home by Anthony Brooke, one of Scott's more exotic acquaintances. Brooke, who was the descendant of the extraordinary Englishman James Brooke, who became the Raja of Sarawak in 1841, devoted much of his considerable inheritance to peace and anti-colonial causes. The intention, from the outset, was to make it a high-profile operation. Scott, who would discuss the WPB's options with the UN's Secretary-General, U Thant, saw the initiative as something that could point the way to more creative peacekeeping by the United Nations, the precursor of what might be a standing non-violent army.

All the omens indicated that the most propitious start for the

WPB would be in Africa, where localized forms of peaceful protest seemed to be unequal to the challenge presented by the last, and most obdurate, elements of the British Empire. After two spectacular years, the 'wind of change' pace set by the British premier Harold Macmillan, with the assistance of his liberal Colonial Secretary, Iain Macleod, appeared to be blowing itself out.

The process of decolonization up to this point had been impressive. Sierra Leone, like Tanganyika, had been granted its independence in 1961, and Uganda had already been accorded a constitutional conference in London, the normal preliminary to independence, in the same year. Even Kenya, with Jomo Kenyatta finally released from prison and restored to leadership of his party, could be seen to be in a state of rapid transition, though there were still reminders of its grim past. When Kenyatta came to London in November 1961, the press conference Scott organized for him was disrupted by a man intent on splattering the African leader with a bag of chicken entrails.[3]

The real sticking point, for African nationalists and the British government alike, was the Central Africa Federation, under the leadership of its bull-like premier Roy Welensky. The Welensky administration, openly sympathetic to the apartheid government to the south, was opposed to any moves towards independence in the federation, or in any of its component parts, that seemed capable of threatening white political supremacy. It had also equipped itself with a sophisticated public relations organization in London that deftly manipulated sentiment on the Tory backbenches against any dis-memberment of the federation.[4] Welensky could be brought to resign himself to the loss of Nyasaland, which was both poor and over-whelmingly black. But the idea of allowing Northern Rhodesia, which had a substantial white population and even more substantial mineral reserves, to detach itself in the same way was not one he could entertain.

Against Welensky in Northern Rhodesia the main black oppo-sition was vested in the United National Independence Party (UNIP) led by Kenneth Kaunda, a Christian and friend of Michael Scott. Kaunda, having served his term in jail for political activity, was fast running out of patience. At one point in 1961 when it appeared that Welensky's Westminster PR lobby was getting the better of

Macleod's Whitehall liberalism, Kaunda warned of a dangerous situation developing in the territory that 'would make Mau Mau look like a child's picnic'.[5] He later modified this observation and reaffirmed his movement's non-violent aims, but of the rising level of African anger there could be no shadow of doubt.

It seemed to Scott like a near-perfect case for what he described as 'positive resistance', which had become almost the theme message of his talks to the Pan-African gatherings over the previous four years. In essence, it could be defined as the proactive version of passive resistance, designed to take the fight to the opposition purposefully, but always non-violently. It was a message that commanded respect, though many in his audiences were already persuaded that effacement of the last traces of the empire could not be accomplished without some resort to violence.

With Kaunda's cooperation Scott was able to establish a strategy that would both develop 'positive resistance' and provide a major role for the World Peace Brigade. The plan was that Kaunda would call a general strike in Northern Rhodesia to advance its claims for independence. This would be accompanied by a Freedom March over the border from neighbouring Tanganyika (soon to become Tanzania), with the World Peace Brigade as its most conspicuous component. The reasoning behind the strategy was that, as the marchers proceeded into Northern Rhodesian territory, the British government would come under increasing international pressure to bring Welensky into line. Alternatively, the marchers' very probable arrest at the border could have much the same effect.

In February 1962, the strategy was further refined at a Pan-African Freedom conference in Addis Ababa, which elected Kenneth Kaunda as its chairman. Among the WPB people there were Scott and the two black American radicals who had been his companions in the Sahara Project against the French nuclear test, Bayard Rustin and Bill Sutherland. These three old comrades, along with the Gandhian Siddharaj Dhadda, constituted the WPB's East African high command.

Scott also unexpectedly met up again with Nelson Mandela, then going the rounds of the Africa conference circuit, talking up the case for the ANC. Back in South Africa, where he was wanted by the police, Mandela had already acquired the nickname of 'the Black

Pimpernel'. According to Anthony Sampson, Mandela's authorised biographer, the Addis Ababa encounter had the genuine warmth of a meeting of old friends, with Mandela deriving encouragement from the fact that Scott appeared to be less enamoured with the PAC than he had been in the past. However, their intimacies must to some extent have been limited by the fact Mandela was now the secret commander-in-chief of MK, the armed wing of the ANC, which had recently embarked on a campaign of sabotage in South Africa. For Mandela at least, 'positive resistance' had ceased to be an option. Mandela may well have been aware of the irony of finding Scott and himself simultaneously heading 'armies' with radically different tactical approaches, but he does not appear to have mentioned it at the time.[6]

By the end of February Scott's volunteer marchers were starting to arrive at the mustering point in Dar es Salaam, where an impromptu training camp had been set up. Scott's goal was to achieve a WPB contingent with a mix of at least ten different nationalities. Each country was expected to provide a minimum of three people of which, it was hoped, at least one would be a well-known personality to guarantee worldwide news coverage. Two of the WPB's co-chairmen, Scott and Narayan, were set to go on the march, as were Rustin and Sutherland, and further recruits were promptly forthcoming from India, Canada, Italy, France and Germany. By mid-March there was a sufficient number of experienced civil disobedience campaigners assembled to ensure a presentable international display. The assembling of the main body of marchers, some 5000 Africans, was seen as being no problem. All, effectively, was in a state of readiness, waiting for Kaunda's signal.

Apprehension began to set in by April, when it became clear that Kaunda's UNIP was not wholly united in support of the plan. On 8 April, Scott wrote anxiously to a friend in London: 'We cannot switch people's enthusiasm and activities on and off. And to bring people from Europe and America on a venture that may cost them their liberty and perhaps their lives demands a lot of organization and effort at both ends, and the people who come may have to give up jobs and in some cases make provision for their families, and have budgeted for a spell in jail or being physically out of action . . . (all) for an as yet unspecified date.'[7]

There was no specific date in May either, though Kaunda did write to Scott from Lusaka on 2 May in mollifying terms: 'I must say at once that I admire your courage and determination to stand up to so many things. I do know that your waiting patiently for us to move in Northern Rhodesia takes a lot of courage and energy. I do hope, however, that you will not have long to wait now before we decide one way or the other.'[8]

UNIP never did bring Scott's WPB contingent into play, and by July most of its members had demobilized themselves. In political terms its existence had not been entirely fruitless. The threat of the march, coupled with a general strike, was almost certainly among the pressures that finally persuaded the British government to impose more drastic terms on Welensky, insisting that future elections should provide for majority rule. This, at least, was Kaunda's firm impression. In 1964, when his country – rechristened Zambia – finally achieved its independence, Kaunda invited Scott and Bill Sutherland to flank him on the speaker's rostrum, in recognition of the WPB's contribution to its struggle.[9]

Even so, there was no concealing the fact that the march-that-never-was amounted to a frightful body blow to the WPB. Like most armies, non-violent ones are expensive to maintain even when they are not marching. And most of the WPB's projected budget had effectively been dissipated without the organization experiencing a whiff of the precious oxygen of publicity. It was not quite the end of its endeavours, though its subsequent efforts, under Scott's co-chairmanship, were on a more limited scale. These included a sponsored voyage from London to Leningrad to protest against Soviet nuclear testing; one of the earliest marches against the Vietnam War in Washington; and a Peace March from Delhi to Peking, led off by Scott in its early stages, but which never managed to cross the Chinese border.

It was soon realized that such projects were rendered more cumbersome, and a lot more expensive, by having to be answerable to an international infrastructure. And that, realistically, any funds that became available were probably better spent on more traditional avenues of protest. After a lifespan of two years, the World Peace Brigade was quietly interred in the graveyard of brave ideas whose time had not come, though, given the advances in communications technology since then, it might be worth trying to exhume.[10]

To the bitter disappointment of the East African march project, Scott was also able to add the discomfort of a serious rupture in his relations with the higher command of the Africa Bureau. His chairman, Lord Hemingford, was of the opinion that the Hon. Director had taken on a demonstration too far, and one that did not remotely justify his absence from the London office for almost five months. It seemed to Hemingford that Scott was no longer maintaining a distinction between Bureau affairs and what now seemed like an evangelical commitment to civil disobedience. Scott, in his own defence, argued that his efforts in East Africa were wholly in line with Bureau policy, which had been fiercely critical of the Central African Federation since its creation.

At one stage it was suggested that Scott should resign from the Hon. Director's post, but continue to serve in a lower-profile role as an ordinary member of the executive.[11] However, it was recognized that this would not in itself ease matters, because it was Scott who actually epitomized the organization. In Africa and at the United Nations in New York Scott *was* the Africa Bureau, and was likely to be regarded in the same light even if he was demoted to the rank of receptionist. In the end, there was a resignation, but it was Hemingford who walked away.

CHAPTER TWENTY-THREE
INDUSTRIAL WARFARE

I T SOMETIMES APPEARED to Scott's critics that he had a powerful addiction to lost causes. This was not the case. Like most people, Scott had a distinct preference for winning, though, at the same time, he recognized that pursuit of the art of the impossible, which he saw as being a Christian's duty, was unlikely to result in a string of easy victories. The only true defeat, in his eyes, was refusing to engage in the struggle. He could conjure up a long theological explanation for this attitude, but acknowledged that it came down in the end to his favourite, most-quoted four lines from T.S. Eliot's poem, *East Coker*:

> There is only the fight to recover what has been lost
> And found and lost again: and now, under conditions
> That seem unpropitious. But perhaps neither gain nor loss.
> For us, there is only the trying. The rest is not our business.

The trying in Scott's case was to find the avenues most likely to advance the cause of peace and justice, and if he seemed to be blocked in one direction he would try another, and then another. To those accustomed to pursuing more conventional political, or indeed religious, agendas, this would give his career a bewildering aspect. In intellectual (and often geographical) terms, nobody quite knew where he would crop up next, or where exactly he was coming from. He was immersed in the processes of politics, but was clearly not a politician. He dressed and talked in a priestly manner, but had no discernible parish. He would listen with apparent intensity to advice, and almost invariably act on his own inner prompting. He would start enterprises on what seemed like the spur of the moment, and sometimes, almost as abruptly, fade from the scene. Even David Astor, the man most appreciative of Scott's method, would sometimes confess himself baffled by what he termed the 'tangential' quality of his friend's thoughts and actions.[1] Very often they would agree to differ, but Astor's faith in Scott's central purpose remained constant.

Scott's own faith was the clue to his extraordinary resilience through all the flights and drops in his progress. His interpretation of his religion would allow him to be disappointed, disheartened even, but never demoralized. Advancing years failed to diminish this capacity for bouncing back after a reverse. Indeed, throughout most of his fifties, when his Crohn's condition eased, he seemed able to call on even greater reserves of energy, although a part of the explanation may have been that he lived more sensibly. Instead of doing the rounds of B. & B.s and cheap hotels, he accepted an invitation from Robert and Deborah Carter, two supporters of the Africa Bureau, to live in the small top-floor flat of their house in Keats Grove, Hampstead, close to the Heath. For relaxation, away from it all, there was still Astor's country home.

In New York too, where he spent up to three months of every year, his living conditions improved. This was due to his ripening friendship with the businessman-cum-philanthropist Daniel Bernstein, with whom Scott established a relationship that paralleled the one he had with David Astor in England. Bernstein made his money as a stockbroker but spent much of it on radical causes through his own foundation.[2] One of his most successful campaigns highlighted the horror of napalm use in Vietnam, but his main interest was in Africa. In the early 1960s, Oliver Tambo – the ANC's peripatetic president-in-exile – was a frequent visitor to the Bernsteins' comfortable home in Scarsdale outside New York. So too was Michael Scott as soon as his visas granted him some latitude of movement outside the limits of Manhattan. Scott still lodged through the week at the General Theological Seminary, but spent most weekends with Bernstein and his wife Carol in green and pleasant surroundings with an amiable profusion of children and dogs, an ambience not unlike Astor's Sutton Courtenay.

Through Bernstein, Scott encountered a wider range of radical secular acquaintance that decisively influenced his approach at the United Nations. A member of the Bernstein circle, who also became a close friend of Scott's, was W.H. 'Ping' Ferry, then the second in command at the Centre for the Study of Democratic Institutions, a progressive 'think-tank' in Santa Barbara, California. Ferry's thinking was on Scott's wavelength. He was the author of a celebrated academic paper outlining the case for unilateral disarmament, not from the traditional religious pacifist position, but from that of a twentieth-century man who had found himself in a lunatic asylum and was looking for an escape hatch. Most of Ferry's writing, however, was concerned with the problems caused by advanced capitalism and its tendency to produce too many goods and too little real work. He was also critical of the dangerous imbalances created by the arms industry.[3] Scott was not tempted to re-embrace Communism as a result of such influences, but they gave a harder edge to his criticism of capitalist enterprise in Africa. Exposing what he called the continent's 'military-industrial complex' became his major preoccupation.

Much of the ammunition for his criticisms was provided by another American academic, Alvin W. Wolfe, Professor of Social Anthropology at Washington University, St Louis, Missouri. Wolfe's dry studies of the interlocking interests of the West's industrial concerns in Africa had excited little beyond academic interest, until Scott gave them prominence at the UN in a series of submissions to the Fourth Committee and its Committee on Colonialism. From the latter part of 1962 into the early months of 1964, Scott's most important contribution to the UN's proceedings was a trenchant indictment of Western industry in Africa, particularly mining, which he saw as an accomplice of repression in southern Africa spreading 'the evil of migrant labour', and as insensitively manipulating the vulnerable newly independent states to the north. It touched a nerve.

In a widely reported speech to the Africa Affairs Society of America in April 1963, Clarence B. Randall, the former chairman of the Inland Steel Company, described Wolfe and Scott as:

> loosing a stream of invective against these great corporations. Using every means at their command, they have endeavoured to whip up animosity against them in the United Nations. Wolfe does the writing, Reverend Scott distributes the materials to the delegates, and appears before the committees . . . What these gentlemen have done seems to me to have been highly irresponsible.[4]

Scott's UN assault made a similar impression on his own Africa Bureau. Colin Legum, in his capacity as Astor's liaison man, wrote a memo to his boss complaining about 'the new bee in his [Scott's] bonnet about the role of big business in Southern Africa'. Peter Calvocoressi, who succeeded Lord Hemingford as Bureau chairman, was also sternly critical, warning Scott in a private letter against associating himself with 'rather indiscriminate and misdirected mud-slinging'.[5] But the most serious opposition came from a new executive member, Sir Jock Campbell, the chairman of the *New Statesman*, who had been recruited to improve the Bureau's level of business expertise.

Campbell was an outgoing character, listing his recreations in *Who's Who* as 'reading, hitting balls and painting', but he had experience of commerce in a racially charged environment. He was chairman of Booker McConnell and proud of his modernising achievement in its main business, sugar from the West Indies which had its origin in the slave trade. His extensive commercial network as head of the Commonwealth Sugar Exporters Association meant that he was on friendly terms with several of the captains of industry who figured in Scott's indictment. Among them was Sir Ronald Prain, head of the mining conglomerate Rhodesian Selection Trust, who wrote to Campbell to complain of Scott's 'wild charges and imaginings' at the United Nations. Prain went on to say:

> It is generally assumed in America that the forthcoming investigation at the UN of the mining industry, with all its political overtones and opportunities for the Communist countries and other troublemakers to damage corporate and personal reputations, can be ascribed to the single personal influence and recommendation of Michael Scott. We have been through hundreds of pages of the record of the recent hearings and there is no substantial request for any such investigation from any other source.[6]

Jock Campbell was also disposed to see the benign side of the gigantic Anglo-American Corporation, known as 'the Octopus', which, from its base in gold mining, spread its tentacles through all aspects of business life in South Africa. He said of Anglo's boss, Harry Oppenheimer, that he, like Sir Ronald Prain, was 'able, liberal and progressive – struggling to bridge the awful chasm between the desirable and the possible'.[7] By this time South Africa's fiercely ideological premier, Hendrik Verwoerd, had succeeded in removing more than a million Africans to Bantustans ('homelands') in pursuit of the country's segregationist aims. But operations of this type were seen as being beyond the control of big business which, through its public relations apparatus, still contrived to portray itself in a progressive light.

A great deal of money was deployed to suggest that industry had an essentially benevolent role in Africa. What was known as the 'Oppenheimer Thesis' advanced the proposition that economic growth would ensure the eventual demise of apartheid, as Africans were inexorably drawn into skilled jobs and middle-class existence. This was supported by historical analysis of a sort. In 1964, one of Oppenheimer's executives, Michael O'Dowd, produced a paper arguing that South Africa's degree of social development was not abnormal for a country emerging from the first stage of industrial development, comparing it to Mexico or Britain in the 1850s. American and British businessmen seeking to develop opportunities in the country were impressed with such thinking. Some worked closely with the South African Foundation, a well-funded lobby, established with the encouragement of the apartheid government to enhance the country's image overseas.

Oppenheimer was its most charismatic figure, but the Foundation's first president, Sir Francis de Guingand, was also well regarded in Britain as the former Chief of Staff to Field Marshal Montgomery, the hero of El Alamein. Lord Montgomery himself was one of many distinguished guests of the Foundation who accepted its hospitality in South Africa and pronounced themselves impressed with the country's efforts. American companies which subscribed to the South African Foundation included General Motors, Union Carbide, Mobil and Chrysler.

Against this weight of ostensibly authoritative opinion, Scott's presentations at the UN sounded shrill. He also, to some extent, hampered his own case by trying to link the mining industry with the events surrounding the death of Dag Hammarskjold, the previous UN Secretary-General. Hammarskjold, on a mission to head off the secession of copper-rich Katanga from the Congo, died in a plane crash near Ndola in Northern Rhodesia in 1961. This provided a field day for conspiracy theorists, among whom Scott could certainly be included. Scott admired Hammarskjold, whose comment that the United Nations was created not to bring mankind to heaven, but to save it from hell, was close to his own appreciation of its function. He felt that the circumstances of the Secretary-General's death had been inadequately investigated.[8] But no positive evidence of foul play by the multiple suspects, ranging from the mining colossus Union Minière, through the CIA, the KGB and MI5, to the mercenaries who swarmed over Katanga, was ever clearly established.

On a less conspiratorial level, Scott inspired a number of studies both by the UN, where Enuga Reddy, his highly placed Indian friend in the Secretariat, was inclined to take his charges seriously, and by George Houser's New York-based American Committee on Africa. They painted a less glowing picture of industry in Africa than that peddled by its public relations men. Noteworthy was the fact that Britain and the United States, the countries which appeared most resistant to arms and oil sanctions against South Africa, were by a long way the biggest investors in apartheid (Britain with 60 per cent of the total foreign investment, America with 11 per cent). Mining accounted for the larger part of this investment and the widely held notion that African miners in South Africa were better off than those working elsewhere was a fallacy. In fact, the income differential between blacks and whites in the South African mining industry had markedly increased. At the end of the war the average wage of black mineworkers had been a tenth of that of white miners. By the early 1960s it was a fifteenth, and still falling. In the country's leading industry there was, in reality, no indication of Africans ascending into the skilled middle class via the route suggested by the 'Oppenheimer Thesis'. Looking back on that period in *Black and Gold*, his book analysing the impact of Western industry on Africa, Anthony Sampson wrote: 'Many industrialists suggested they were discreetly persuading Pretoria to modify its policies; but there was no real evidence of it, and the trade lobbies almost imperceptibly turned into lobbies to defend apartheid.'[9]

Scott's prescience in this area added weight to the arguments for sanctions against South Africa and the UN managed to promote a limited embargo on the sale of arms to that country in 1964. His efforts also provided much of the basic information for the 'disinvestment' campaigns mobilized by anti-apartheid movements around the world in later years, and which led enterprises like Barclays Bank to pull out of South Africa. Indeed, most of the economic pressures that would eventually combine to bring down the apartheid regime can be traced to origins in Scott's UN speeches in this period. There was also a more immediate consequence. Scott recalled that in his early years at the UN, he was reproved by members of the British delegation for daring to suggest that economic considerations were at all relevant to Britain's voting habits. After 1963, he was not troubled by this particular reproach.

Scott's one concession to Campbell, Calvocoressi and his other critics in the Africa Bureau would be to temper his criticisms of Sir Ronald Prain's Rhodesia Selection Trust by portraying it as one of the fairer players in the 'Cape to Katanga' mining team in his later submissions to the UN. But they never managed to rein in Scott from his general indictment.

Much of the heat generated inside the Bureau by Scott's UN activities was due to the fact that it was running out of better things to do. Its prime original function of offering backdoor diplomatic access to the British government for emergent African nationalists was now almost a thing of the past. The range of post-colonial African leaders who owed a debt of gratitude to the Bureau or to Scott personally was impressive. Nkrumah in Ghana, Kenyatta in Kenya, Hastings Banda in Nyasaland (soon to be Malawi), Nyerere in Tanganyika (in the process of merging with Zanzibar as Tanzania), and Kaunda (in Northern Rhodesia, later Zambia), were in this category. But the new leaders had either established, or were in the process of setting up, their own diplomatic arrangements. They were sentimentally attached to the Africa Bureau, but they no longer had need of it.

Meanwhile, little of real significance was happening on the South-West Africa front. Constitutional progress there now seemed to depend on the interminable deliberations of the International Court of Justice at the Hague. A UN mission sent to explore conditions in the Territory in 1962 had ended in farce. Led by the Filipino Victorio Carpio, it concluded its ten-day visit with a joint communiqué, ostensibly emanating from Carpio and the South African premier, Dr Verwoerd, which implied that there was no grave cause for concern about the administration of the territory. Carpio, who was indisposed in hospital at the time the communiqué was released, later maintained that he had no part in its drafting. At the UN there was a high level of recrimination about the episode, but the internal inquiry that followed failed to establish much beyond the fact that Scott and his fellow South-West Africa representative, Mburumba Kerina, were still at odds. Kerina had alleged that Carpio's inept performance was a result of his being led astray by a female member of the UN secretariat who accompanied the mission. Scott did not agree, and pointedly defended the UN official at the inquiry. He thought she had been made a scapegoat.[10]

Scott's most potent fantasy in this doldrum period was of airlifting a group of World Peace Brigade activists into the Windhoek area. His idea was that they should establish a non-violent beachhead in the Territory in defiance of its South African masters. But volunteers proved hard to find. Bill Sutherland, who had been with Scott on the Sahara Project and as his co-general on the East African march enterprise, remembers him being animated on the subject when visiting him in Hampstead in 1963. Sutherland liked to tell the story about when he and Scott went down to the fairground on Hampstead Heath and bought themselves a ride on a whirling machine equipped with capsules on long extended arms. Scott, as the former aviator, took the controls but failed to notice the stick that levered their capsule into the air. 'Do you think', Sutherland remembers saying, 'I'd be fool enough to fly on a secret mission with you into Windhoek, when you can't even get this thing off the ground?' Operation Windhoek was always a non-starter as far as Sutherland was concerned, but he was impressed by his old friend's undiminished appetite for further outdoors adventure.[11]

There was no real prospect of its being provided by the Africa Bureau. South Africa was still the towering problem for all those concerned with liberation prospects south of the Zambezi, but Scott's Bureau could no longer be considered in the van of protest on that subject. Apartheid was now one of the dominating issues at the UN, and was ascending the policy agendas of the major powers. Even on the campaigning front in Britain, the Africa Bureau's role could only be regarded as marginal. The Anti-Apartheid Movement, established in 1960, had become the magnet for creative enterprise by the disaffected, exiled South Africans who were arriving in Britain in increasing numbers. Its efforts were also complemented by Canon Collins's Defence and Aid Fund, which experienced a revival after the collapse of the misguided attempt to link its destiny with that of the Bureau. The Collins fund raised all the money required for the defence of Nelson Mandela and the other ANC leaders charged with sabotage at the Rivonia Trial in 1964. Most were sent down for long terms of imprisonment on Robben Island, but their escaping the death penalty was attributed, in some measure, to the sophistication of their defence strategy.

None of this implied that the Africa Bureau was obsolete, but by 1964 the need to rethink its aims and policies was powerfully evident. For a while Scott seems to have envisaged its future in a more specialist research capacity, actively monitoring industry's role in Africa in a way that supplemented his efforts at the United Nations. But to do that he needed to win over the doubters on his own executive, which was sure to be an uphill task. There were problems too about how the Bureau should position itself in relation to the new Africa. A consequence of liberation was that black politicians could, if they felt inclined, abuse power as much as the whites. This was progress, but it represented difficult new terrain for an Africa Bureau hoping to maintain its relevance. In the event of any deviation from democratic standards in the newly independent states, should the Bureau be assertively supportive of old African friends, frankly critical or keep quiet? There were no easy answers but it was hard to avoid the questions.

Scott did give some thought to these issues, but not for long. In March 1964, tangential as ever, he departed for the north-easternmost corner of India on an enterprise that would, as it turned out, remove him from the concerns of the Africa Bureau for the next two years.

CHAPTER TWENTY-FOUR
AN INDIAN EVICTION

MICHAEL SCOTT's relationship with India had always been close. He not only looked on the country as a source of spiritual nourishment through the example of Gandhi and his disciples, but he had come to rely on it for practical assistance. At the United Nations the Indian delegation had long been his most steadfast supporter on matters affecting southern Africa. As a result of this affinity, Scott became better acquainted than most outsiders with one of the Indian nation's most painful domestic concerns.

Scott was already well versed in the history of the Naga people's struggle against Indian rule. There was, nonetheless, a degree of culture shock when, in April 1964, he first encountered its contemporary reality. As soon as he arrived in Kohima, Nagaland's modest capital, he was instructed to proceed by jeep to a point fifteen miles away in the jungle. The arrangement was that someone would meet him outside Ndunglua village. These were among his first impressions:

> The country is like a concertina – a series of steep-sided ravines covered with thick jungle tropical trees, wild bananas and bamboos. We were met at the roadside by an underground contact man in Naga dress – a hand-woven cloth worn over the shoulders and an apron hanging down in front. He had a knife-blade across his back and two enormous bracelets made out of elephant tusks on his arms. His hair was cut all-round as if a basin had been used . . . Our guide led us on foot for four or five miles and we took narrow paths uphill and down dale. We came to a valley with a great torrent running through it. Across this torrent they had built for us a swaying suspension bridge from bamboo, with an archway with the word 'Welcome'. The river was about 150 feet wide; the bamboo bridge swung frighteningly. It really was a wild torrent. If anyone had fallen in his number would have been up. I remember rather profanely thinking that just as nothing less than Almighty God could have started me on this enterprise, so I should only have the Almighty to thank if I reached the

other side of the River Teipu. All along the road there were men with light machine-guns . . . There were about 200 troops on parade. They had a beautifully made camp – huts with walls made of split bamboo and with a thatch of rushes. The troops were very proud of their weapons – mostly rifles, with a few light machine-guns and hand grenades around their belts. One or two things that looked like rockets. I inspected the guard.[1]

Scott was welcome in these martial surroundings as the lone European member of a mission aiming to bring peace to Nagaland, where a brutal civil conflict had been raging, almost imperceptibly to the outside world, for a decade. Scattered in remote villages in the tangled jungle-covered mountains of a territory 70 miles wide and almost 200 miles long on India's north-east frontier, most of the 350,000 inhabitants had been touched, in many cases bereaved, by the war. Scott's mission had been set up by the Baptist Church, which had evangelized the Naga Hills in the late nineteenth century in a way that had moderated some of the more ferocious local customs; converts who could not be induced to give up headhunting were excommunicated.[2]

There had, however, been no significant diminution of the Nagas' independence of spirit. As the colonial power, Britain had administered the region with the loosest of reins, essentially allowing the fourteen Naga tribes to conduct their own affairs, though it sometimes tapped into their warlike skills. Nagas had fought on the Western Front in the First World War, and alongside British troops in the action that repelled Japanese invaders at Kohima in 1944. But the Nagas, who were of Mongolian descent, felt little affinity with their closest Indian neighbours in the plains of Assam below. Shortly after the war, a delegation of Naga leaders had met with Mahatma Gandhi, who told them that they could not be forced into a union with India, and famously assured them, 'I will ask them to shoot me first before one Naga is shot.'[3] Gandhi did not live long enough to test this pledge.

The outrage of the Naga nationalists had its origin in 1947 when the British granted India independence with the territory of Nagaland as part of the overall consignment. Under new Indian masters, concerned about the integrity of the new country's borders, the Nagas' sense of grievance rapidly escalated. By the mid-1950s a full-scale civil war had developed, with 40,000 Indian troops deployed to suppress some 3000 hit-and-run guerrilla fighters. With the non-combatant population caught up in a situation where military reprisals often took the form of village and crop burning, civilians were often the worst casualties. Nagas suspected of 'collaborating' with the troops were frequently shot.

In 1963 Nagaland was recognized as the sixteenth state of the Indian Union, a measure designed to appease moderate Naga opinion. But the Indian troops stayed, and hostilities continued unabated. In 1964 the Nagaland Baptist Convention secured the support of the Indian government for its peace initiative, which involved the appointment of three commissioners. Two of them were Gandhians: Jayaprakash Narayan, who had worked with Scott as a co-chairman of the World Peace Brigade, and Bimala Prasad Chaliha, the Chief Minister of Assam. The third was Michael Scott. The veteran Naga church leader, the Reverend Longri Ao, said of Scott's appointment that it was made 'not because he is a known world leader but because he is a servant of Jesus Christ'.[4]

There were other good reasons for the appointment. Scott was seen as a friend of India, with connections at the highest level. He had worked closely with Mrs Pandit, the sister of the Indian Prime Minister Jawaharlal Nehru, during his early days at the United Nations and, as recently as 1963, after his visit to India to launch the World Peace Brigade's Delhi-Peking March, had held private talks with Nehru himself. Nagaland was the main subject of their discussions. Scott did not have to be told about India's sensitivities over its land frontiers (Nagaland's border was with Burma, but China was close), and its abiding worries about secession based on ethnic or religious differences, which dictated the conventional wisdom that liberties granted to the Nagas might lead to demands for larger ones among the Punjabis and Tamils. Scott knew of these concerns as well as any Indian politician. But he also knew a great deal about Naga grievances and aspirations, albeit without ever having been to Nagaland – the exiled nationalist leader of the Nagas, Angami Zapu Phizo, had for some time worked at a desk in the Africa Bureau's office on the Vauxhall Bridge Road.

One of history's more peculiar associations had come about when an American-based nephew of the Naga leader wrote to Scott in 1960 urging him to look out for his distressed uncle who was then in Zurich. Scott consulted Mrs Pandit in London's India House to find out more about Phizo. After speaking to her advisers, Mrs Pandit came back with the information that Phizo was a man with a high price on his head and wanted for murder. She advised Scott to have nothing to do with him. 'But somehow,' Scott recalled, 'I couldn't quite accept the story as it was given to me by India House, and I eventually succumbed to another letter begging me to go to Zurich, where Phizo was thought to be in danger of being arrested.'[5] The upshot was Scott's returning to London with Phizo as his travelling companion.

The relationship between Scott and Phizo was never smooth. The Naga leader was a prickly character, prone to irascible outbursts and easily offended. With his customary reticence, in terms of character assessment, Scott described him as 'not personable'. He was also, in a specifically British context, not well suited to a heroic role. During the war Phizo had been among the small group of Nagas who sided with the Japanese invaders, believing their promise of early independence for Nagaland. Scott's decision to allow him work space in the Africa Bureau was not applauded by every member of staff. Some saw Phizo as a distraction, and the time Scott spent with him was dismissively described as 'Phizzy business'.[6]

Nevertheless, Scott and, to a large extent, David Astor came to the view that Phizo's testimony on the subject of Nagaland's 'long night of terror', while possibly exaggerated, was not unfounded. This impression was strengthened by Astor's sending Gavin Young, one of the *Observer*'s ablest foreign correspondents, to Nagaland. Trekking overland to avoid the Indian blackout on information from the region, Young gathered material for a series of three articles under the heading 'An Unknown War'. In the article published on 14 May 1961, Young reported:

> The tenor of Naga civilian complaints of Indian injustice was unvarying. Villagers jostled their way forwards to describe personal sufferings in vivid detail. The stories of burnt rice-stores and houses seemed endless. Individuals told how they had been beaten and tied up for hours without water; how they had been bound and hung head

downwards from trees to be flogged; how sons, brothers and fathers had been bayoneted to death.

Refugee women described how Indian troops arrived in the village last year . . . 'We were about 120 men and women before the Indian patrol arrived. There are thirty survivors, only three of them men.'[7]

Gavin Young's dispatches brought the Nagaland conflict out of the shadows, but offered no immediate prospect of any relief. In international terms it was India's domestic concern, beyond legitimate interference by other powers. Astor came to regard it as 'a test case' that illustrated the problems that can arise for awkward ethnic minorities under newly independent regimes. Both he and Scott agreed that the Nagas should provide a prime focus for the new Minority Rights Group organization which they had already discussed in principle. In the meantime, they wrote letters – Scott to Nehru, Astor to influential friends in Britain – calling for a peace process in Nagaland, and publicized this aim, losing friends as a result.

In an article entitled, 'A People in Danger', published in the *Observer* in August 1963, Scott wrote: 'Those who have tried to help the Nagas make their voices heard have been accused, as I was by a member of the Quaker Peace Committee, of encouraging their recalcitrance. Thus do peacemakers, for fear of being contaminated by violence, range themselves on the sides of the big battalions.'[8]

In answer to a question about Scott in the Lok Sabha (Lower House), Nehru had defended him vigorously, describing him as 'an Englishman, who had played a very notable part in exposing South Africa and South-West Africa. Indeed he was very much opposed to racialism and apartheid, and we have all admired his activities in that matter.'[9] Nehru's public regard, however, would be accompanied by a rising level of private concern. Eventually he offered Scott something like a deal: if Scott could find a way of ending hostilities against the troops in Nagaland, he would personally involve the prime minister's office in the quest for a lasting settlement.

Despite his deepening involvement, Scott had been hopeful that when, and if, a peace process was implemented there would be other suitably qualified people available to do the more detailed work. He had originally resisted the idea of taking on another affair comparable in complexity to that of the Hereros, thinking he did not have the physical or mental stamina for the job.[10] But when the Naga Baptists, with the discreet support of the Indian government, formally requested his presence, it had the force of an invitation that could not be refused.

Scott was the first peace commissioner to arrive on the scene and, as it turned out, the one required to do most of the peacemaking. The commissioners had been allocated a small fleet of white-painted jeeps to go about their business, but the terrain and the concealed nature of many of the underground hideouts dictated many miles of trudging on foot. The agreed first objective of the Peace Commission was the achievement of a ceasefire as the essential preliminary to concrete negotiations. In pursuit of this, it soon became apparent that Scott was able to penetrate more deeply into hostile areas than Narayan and Chaliha, as Indian nationals, could ever hope to reach. Even Nehru's Foreign Secretary, Y.D. Gundevia, who would emerge as one of Scott's sharpest critics, acknowledged that the ceasefire was essentially Scott's accomplishment. In his book, *War and Peace in Nagaland*, Gundevia wrote:

> From April to August [1964], Scott played a hero's role in these wild difficult hills. For a while, the leaders of the hostile groups refused to meet Chaliha and Narayan: they talked to Scott only. More than fifty-seven years of age, he was not physically the strongest European that the Nagas had set eyes on, by any means, but his friends did not seem to spare him. Tall, lean, pale, with deep-set eyes, he carried his frail frame all over the jungles, often walking miles through the thick forests . . . He met the underground leaders at numerous rendezvous, never in the same place twice . . . [11]

On a visit to the border village of Konyak, a rebel stronghold, Scott was impressed by the longhouse, which featured a display of forty human skulls. He was not sure if they were of recent vintage, but confessed to finding them 'very eerie'. In these settings, Scott's main protection would often be positive news of Phizo's recent welfare. This could be coupled with the assurance that the Nagas' exiled leader wanted them to give ceasefire a chance. As confidence in him grew, many village chiefs ventured into Kohima to see Scott at the Baptist mission house. He was touched by the directness of their Christian faith, and their solicitude for him. When he went down with a severe case of dysentery, they advised against his checking into a hospital where, he was warned, there was a higher risk of his being assassinated.[12] Scott was also sustained by the extraordinary beauty of the country. On clear days he could see as far as the jagged outlines of the Himalayas far to the north changing from golden to rose in the evening and rose to gold in the morning.

The agreement to end hostilities, ratified on 6 September 1964, brought almost instant relief for the civilian population. Gundevia, commenting on the situation in mid-1965, wrote:

> After September 1964 not a shot had been fired in the jungles of Nagaland and in the three northern subdivisions of Manipuri [the territory to the south with many Naga inhabitants]; the people did not want bloodshed and the reign of terror to start all over again. There had been no political settlement, true – but there were no murders, either, for eight months. At the going rate of a hundred and fifty kills a month, they had been saved twelve hundred lives.[13]

Under the terms of the ceasefire the Indian Army agreed to suspend jungle operations, raiding of rebel camps, searching of villages, arrests and the imposition of forced labour as a punishment, and aerial actions. They also accepted a proposal that armed troop movements should be limited to no more than 1000 yards from their outposts. For their part the underground guerrillas undertook to refrain from sniping, sabotage, kidnapping, imposing fines on villages, marching with arms and/or in uniform in populated areas, and to avoid operating within 1000 yards of any security posts. In the event of accidental encounters between the two sides, the guidance was 'no firing unless first fired on'. It was not peace so much as a heavily armed truce, and Scott was well aware of its limitations. But as it was Nagaland's first significant turn in a pacific direction for ten years, it represented a genuine cause for hope.

Despite his success in bringing about the ceasefire, Scott was concerned by the loss of the man he regarded as the ultimate patron of the enterprise. Prime Minister Nehru had died on 27 May, only three days after a ceasefire had been agreed in principle, though it would take another three months to hammer out its details. In Scott's view, the enmities engendered by the long conflict made it difficult, perhaps impossible, to achieve any lasting settlement. Nehru had grasped the point and expressed a willingness to set up a Commission of Inquiry as a way of exposing and then binding old wounds. In embryo form Scott's idea resembled the one that informed the Truth and Reconciliation Commission which was instituted in South Africa after apartheid. Now Scott found himself having to go about persuading the new incumbent, Lal Bahadur Shastri, of the merits of his ideas.

On a trip to Delhi, Scott delivered a package of documents to Shastri's office. These detailed alleged atrocities committed against the Nagas which Scott felt should be investigated in a formal inquiry. In a covering letter which was, by Scott's standards, unusually blunt, he wrote: 'the whole story of Nagaland has not been told . . . I'm convinced that Jawaharlal Nehru was never given the true picture of the tragedy that was being enacted here in all these years.' He urged the new premier to make a priority of attending to a situation that constituted 'a mockery of everything India stood for and Britain and the West aim to defend'.[14]

Shastri made no immediate response to the Commission of Inquiry idea but soon displayed a commitment to the peace process comparable to that shown by Nehru. Within three weeks of the ceasefire coming into force, the Indian authorities established a custom-built peace camp at Chedema, five miles from Kohima. The camp consisted of a collection of huts, four of which were allocated to the Indian delegation, four to the Peace Commission and four to the political representatives of the underground who styled themselves 'The Nagaland Federal Government'. The Indian government disapproved of this appellation, originally assumed by the Naga nationalists back in 1956, but it was deemed acceptable in the peace talks. Movement between the delegations was designed to be as free as possible; if bilateral talks between the Naga and Indian delegations proved too difficult, they were encouraged to communicate through the Peace Commissioners. The importance placed on talks by the Indian government was evidenced by the fact that its delegation was led by the experienced Foreign Secretary, Y.D. Gundevia. The early indications were that he and Scott would get along. Scott said of Gundevia that he was 'full of banter, but he hasn't the awful contempt for the Nagas that some Indians have'. Gundevia, though distrustful of the Phizo connection, said complimentary things about Scott, describing one of his Kohima sermons as being as good 'as any I have heard anywhere in my life'.[15]

The slow progress of the talks would erode these areas of mutual esteem. An attempt to transform the ceasefire into a more meaningful disarmament agreement, with arms actually being surrendered, broke down as it was evidently beyond the capacity of one side to trust the other. It did, however, have the useful by-product of strengthening the mechanism for keeping the uncertain peace. The Peace Commission had a new group of Peace Observers grafted onto its operation, with the task of monitoring the ceasefire. Based in Kohima, its role was to provide an instant investigation service for reported infractions. The original members of the new group included Noba Krishna Choudhury, the former Chief Minister of Orissa, Marjorie Sykes, an English Quaker teacher who became a naturalized Indian citizen, and Dr M. Aram, a studious young Gandhian who became one of Scott's closest allies and later wrote the most authoritative account of Nagaland's peace process. As the ceasefire had to be renewed on a monthly basis, the activities of the Peace Observers' team proved welcome to both sides.[16] But on the main political front there seemed no way ahead.

With the protagonists seemingly irreconcilable, the Peace Commissioners came up with an imaginative proposal document. Its key suggestion, inspired by Narayan and endorsed by both his colleagues, ran as follows:

> On the one hand, the Naga Federal Government could, *of their own volition*, decide to participate in the Union of India and mutually settle the terms and conditions for that purpose. On the other hand, the government of India could consider to what extent the pattern and structure of the relationship between Nagaland and the government of India should be adapted and recast so as to satisfy the political aspirations of all sections of Naga opinion . . . [17]

The assumption was that if the Nagas could be guaranteed the highest degree of autonomy, they might be persuaded to renounce their inconvenient claim to sovereignty. This would provide the bedrock for an agreement that would accord honour to both sides. There was a pleasing symmetry to the concept, but also a serious catch. Which side would be the first to make the commitment? The Nagas, for their part, were unlikely to renounce their claim to independence in advance of knowing India's full 'package' of concessions. The Indians were naturally reluctant to make significant concessions without being assured that the Nagas would indeed 'of their own volition' be sure to renounce claims to sovereignty, especially after being allowed a glimpse of this long-desired status. The problem of trust in the other side's motives remained. This was compounded by problems of interpretation even among the authors of the idea.

Scott was inclined to see the formulation as representing something that might be accomplished after a long period of reconciliation and reconstruction. The other two Peace Commissioners saw it as a potential deal capable of fairly rapid ratification. More importantly, Gundevia, fatigued by the need to commute regularly between Delhi and the peace camp in Nagaland, also saw it in that light. The delays irritated him, and he let the irritation show. Frustration with the intractable nature of the talks soured his relationship with Scott, though a surface politeness was preserved. In his book, *War and Peace in Nagaland*, the flattering references to Scott as the 'hero' of the ceasefire are followed by scathing descriptions of him as 'a zealot', possessed of 'a one-track partiality' and unable to differentiate between 'the truth, the whole truth and less than half the truth'.

On his journeys into the jungle Scott, like Gavin Young before him, found himself besieged by villagers with stories of distress and disfigurements suffered in the war. He took notes, an activity which Gundevia seemed to find reprehensible: 'No man', Gundevia wrote, 'so obsessed with the day before can see what is happening today; he cannot therefore really help in shaping the future of an unsophisticated people.' But Scott's real offence in Gundevia's eyes was that he did not appear to be exerting his undoubted influence with the underground to bring about compliance with the 'of their own volition' formula. Instead, according to Gundevia, he functioned as 'the advocate of the underground'.[18]

This was not an accurate reading of Scott's position. Scott never declared himself unreservedly in favour of an independent Nagaland, but he also did not feel that it was his role to exert undue pressure on those who did, or at least not until some of the bitterness had been bled out of the conflict. The guidance papers he circulated among the delegates, with titles like *A Time to Kill and a Time to Heal* and *For Law, not War in Nagaland,* were essentially about reconciliation, not about a predetermined political end. Indeed, one paper written for the benefit of the underground outlined the economic advantages of the connection with India. Where Scott parted company with Gundevia, and to a lesser extent with his co-Commissioners, was in seeing the stalled talks as having a positive value, almost regardless of content: 'Time', he wrote, 'is needed for healing and there is therapeutic value in the talks and negotiations themselves.' With the guns finally silent, he felt that the main enemy of any peace process was not unbridled extremism but any exhibition of impatience in the quest for a long-term political settlement. Scott told the Peace Observer, Dr Aram, 'the pressure from Gundevia for a reply appears to the Federal [underground] side as if the Peace Commission proposals are being used as an ultimatum to force acceptance of the government's position.'

In counselling the benefits of procrastination and avoiding the real point at issue, Scott was in some ways ahead of his time. The concept of a peace process that appears to be going absolutely nowhere, but still has merit, is something thoroughly familiar in modern Britain after its long painful experience of trying to resolve conflict in Northern Ireland. But it did not play outstandingly well in India in those days. As the talks dragged on deep into 1965, they began to attract adverse comment from Indian politicians and observers who thought the Nagas only responded to the traditional stern measures.

In May 1965 Scott wrote to Astor explaining his difficulties, some of which were physical: 'It is now fourteen months since I have been here and I reckon to have travelled about 5000 miles on very rough roads which a jeep cannot manage 10 or 12 mph over.' His stay had been more prolonged than he expected, because of the slow progress in building confidence where 'there is so much mistrust on both sides'. The best hope, Scott thought, would be mutual acceptance of 'a truce period' during which the sovereignty question could be kept in abeyance while reconstruction had a chance to begin. Scott's letter also emphasized his determination to see the thing through – 'I feel it personally almost more of a "sacred trust" than South-West Africa because I was asked to come here for a purpose that has not yet been achieved.' It did, however, hint at a possible impediment. He had recently consulted Dr Arthur Hughes at the Welsh Mission Hospital in Shillong, in Assam, and been advised to have another operation for his Crohn's condition, which had started to flare up again: 'But he can keep me going (with antibiotics) as long as necessary to complete this effort.'[19]

Dr Hughes, however, became more insistent. And in August 1965 Scott returned to England for another resection operation at the Middlesex Hospital. During his convalescence, Scott wrote to the UN Secretary-General, U Thant, asking him to consider ways of placing the Nagaland issue on the UN's agenda. This letter, when it became public, would further excite Gundevia and Scott's other critics in India; they saw it as trying to 'internationalize' a domestic problem.[20] David Astor was among the friends who advised Scott to regard his mission in Nagaland as being at an end, but to no avail. Scott returned in November.

The talks were still deadlocked. India continued to contend that the Nagas' underground leadership should guarantee its willingness to commit to the Indian Union. The 'Federal Government' continued to refuse any commitment without more clearly defined terms of association. It was clear that any further progress required some outside impetus or form of mediation. Scott hoped this would be provided by Prime Minister Shastri, who, already engaged on reaching a new settlement with Pakistan, seemed anxious to turn his attention to Nagaland. Then Shastri died suddenly, in January 1966, and India found itself making the acquaintance of its third Prime Minister in less than two years, Mrs Indira Gandhi. She too, however, was quickly convinced of the gravity of the situation on her north-east frontier.

On 18 February 1966, in what was seen as the high point of the peace process, Mrs Gandhi received a deputation consisting of the three Peace Commissioners, the Nagaland Federal Prime Minister Kughato Sukhai and four other members of his underground nego-tiating team. At Mrs Gandhi's request, Scott opened the proceedings with a prayer. The press reported Sukhai applauding the fresh start being made to 'India–Naga political negotiations', while Mrs Gandhi was quoted as being impressed by 'the sincerity and earnestness' of the Naga leaders. The *Observer*'s Delhi-based correspondent, Cyril

Dunn, commented in his report on the occasion, 'Cordiality seems to have vanquished the handicaps.'[21]

This appearance was deceptive. The meeting had indeed been friendly, although this was partly because there was a deliberate avoidance of any areas of substantive disagreement. Such matters, it was thought, could be deferred to subsequent meetings when Mrs Gandhi planned to meet the Naga leaders alone. In the meantime, the new Prime Minister found herself coming under attack in Parliament for exhibiting softness towards the Naga 'hostiles'.[22]

Scott's position also became much more delicate. His ready intimacy with the underground leaders, once the chief asset of the ceasefire initiative, was now interpreted as stiffening Naga resistance, and giving the underground leaders ideas above their station. The unalterable facts of Scott's being white and a foreigner made it easier to characterize him as a meddlesome intruder. Already suspect for trying to 'internationalize' the conflict, Scott became the main focus of hostility towards the Peace Commission. The ultranationalist press claimed that it had become a shield which the Naga underground hid behind while building up arms dumps on the Burmese side of the border. These, it was suggested, were to be used in another round of hostilities. The ceasefire was still holding inside Nagaland, but between February and May 1966 there were four bomb incidents on trains in northern India, near the Nagaland border, that resulted in large-scale casualties with 147 people killed. The identity of the saboteurs was not clear, but the popular presumption was that the explosions were caused by an extreme nationalist wing of the Nagas hoping to disrupt the peace talks, though the possibility of their being the work of *agents provocateurs* with a similar motive could not be discounted. In an atmosphere of rising tension the Peace Commission disintegrated. First Narayan resigned, then Chaliha.

Scott's exposed position as the only surviving Peace Commissioner lasted only a few hours. On 3 May 1966, while receiving treatment at the Mission Hospital in Shillong, he was served with an order from the Indian Ministry of External Affairs requiring his immediate departure from the country. The order stated that in view of his 'partisan' attitude, his presence 'was no longer considered helpful to talks that are going on with the underground Nagas'. An armed squad of the Assam Rifles escorted him to a Circuit House and watched over him for the night in order, Scott was told, 'to protect him from tigers and elephants'. He left India the following day after being subjected to a strip-search at the airport. Cyril Dunn's report on Scott's deportation in the *Observer* was headlined, 'India Turns on Their Hero'.[23] Mrs Gandhi resumed her talks with the Naga leaders in the mistaken hope that they would prove more pliant with Scott out of the picture. The talks were broken off a year later, still irresolvably deadlocked on the issue of sovereignty.

In his summary of Scott's odyssey through Nagaland, Y.D. Gundevia would write in *War and Peace in Nagaland* in a way that combined exasperation with a backhanded compliment:

> I have only too frequently been accused of having been far too polite – 'soft' is the word – to Reverend Michael Scott. I was polite (surely you have to be polite to anybody) because the zealot was doing and did a job in Nagaland in 1964, which neither he nor anyone else could have done without being a zealot. But when he went 'out of bounds' and his fanaticism ran away with him, we had to tell him enough was enough. And that is what happened.[24]

Dr Aram in his book *Peace in Nagaland*, published in 1975, was more struck by 'the wave of anguish' that swept over Nagaland after Scott's deportation, though he was happy to record that the instinct for peace had by then been implanted deeply enough not to be obliterated, as many had feared would be the case. He wrote: 'With the ceasefire in 1964 came peace. When the talks broke down in 1967, the ceasefire did not break down. When the ceasefire ended in 1972, peace did not cease.' There would be sporadic violent clashes between the security forces and the underground, 'but no return to the widespread trouble and large-scale violence'. Aram's account describes Scott's 'innocence' as sometimes giving rise to 'unnecessary complications', but on the whole he thought Nagaland – and India – had much to thank him for.[25]

CHAPTER TWENTY-FIVE

LOSING TOUCH

T HE MOST VISIBLE consequence of Scott's two years in Nagaland was that his hair, previously only streaked at the temples, had gone iron grey. Less detectable was the fact that his habitually individualistic judgement had begun to harden into eccentricity.

In one sense his heroic story was over. Scott's ejection from India represented the last of his deportations from another country, and he would not see the inside of another prison cell. The special quality that invested his witness, from Tobruk to Nagaland, was his ability to dramatize a cause through personal action. His capacity to influence the thinking of others, and indeed shape his own, was largely due to the bravery he displayed in leading from the front. Given the complications of his health, the remarkable feature of his story was his managing to sustain this quality for so long. But with the onset of old age it inevitably began to wind down.

During Scott's two-year absence, the Africa Bureau had been kept going by the diligence of its chairman, Peter Calvocoressi, and the dedication of its long-time secretary Jane Symonds, who ensured that issues of its regular publication, *Africa Digest*, still rolled off the presses. The operation had been obliged to downsize to smaller premises in Great Smith Street, handily close to the House of Commons, though meetings of the executive were customarily held in the *Observer* building in Blackfriars. Scott's stock with his executive was still high but some of its members were naturally getting fretful about the Hon. Director's degree of focus on their chosen continent of interest.

The African issues that confronted the Bureau in 1966 were more formidable than ever. The apartheid regime in South Africa had recovered from the shock of Sharpeville and was going economically from strength to strength, with most of the ANC's leadership securely behind bars. In Rhodesia, the white settler minority was busy consolidating its dominant position after Ian Smith's Unilateral

Declaration of Independence (UDI) from British overlordship. The prospects for South-West Africa, which had seemed moderately bright when Scott left for Nagaland, were now bleak.

After ruminating for six years, the International Court at the Hague had failed to produce a judgment. By eight votes to seven, with the President using his casting vote, the Court dismissed any case against South Africa on the grounds that the applicants – Ethiopia and Liberia – had not established any 'legal right or interest appertaining to them in the subject-matter of the claims'. It spelled an end to the peaceful, legal route to a solution of the country's problems, which Scott had championed for so many years. The Court's decision finally prompted the UN General Assembly to assert that South Africa had forfeited its mandate, and the territory would be taken into UN 'administration'.[1] However, given South Africa's defiance and clear determination to maintain the territory as its own fifth province, nobody was at all clear about how this could be done. Meanwhile, SWAPO, the strongest of the liberation groups, declared its intention to take up arms.

Scott touched base with these African issues in London and New York but by the end of the year was off again, tangentially as it seemed, to the Far East. At short notice he accepted an invitation to join a peace group with the objective of entering Vietnam, where it intended to place itself conspicuously at risk from American bombing of that country. The expedition's obvious attraction was that it aped to some extent the 'valley of the shadow of death' tactics of the Sahara Project, which Scott had pioneered and regarded as having been highly successful. It also offered the prospect of again combining his talents with those of Pat Arrowsmith, whose record of multiple imprisonments for anti-war and anti-nuclear protest activity surpassed even that of Scott himself.

Scott and Arrowsmith's association in the peace movement went back a long way, and though prickly at times, was seen as creative. The most intriguing of their previous associations concerned the occasion when the picket outside the Aldermaston Weapons Establishment was trying to undermine the allegiance of the workers by subversive leafleting. Responding to the idea that one leaflet should specifically appeal to Christian sentiment, Scott drafted a document. To the dismay of the activists, it was strong on human rights and humanitarian concerns but virtually devoid of any specifically Christian reference. It was Arrowsmith, an atheist but with the natural vocabulary of a vicar's daughter, who supplied the deficiency. Under her influence, cogent references to how Jesus Christ, as a skilled carpenter, would have reacted in an environment dedicated to the perfection of H-bombs, found their way into the leaflet. The result was a punchy document, which actually did persuade two Christians to stop working at Aldermaston.[2]

However, any hopes for a similar dovetailing of their talents in what was called the Non-Violent Action in Vietnam (NVAV) were soon dashed. As the most famous activist in the group, Scott was deputed to go on ahead to Phnom Penh, the capital of Cambodia, to help pave the way for the rest of the protestors, now around twenty-five strong and most of them still in their twenties. Scott flew out shortly before Christmas, only to return, to everyone's astonishment, four days later. His explanation was that he had picked up rumours about a possible invasion of Cambodia by the Americans, seeking to wipe out the North Vietnamese troops alleged to be hiding there. He felt impelled to return to London to warn the British government, which had previously indicated that it would no longer support American policy over the Vietnam war if Cambodia was invaded. As it appeared probable that the Foreign Office could have gleaned this intelligence by more conventional means, it seemed a dotty explanation to the protest group, and Scott lost some popularity as a result. In her account of the expedition, *To Asia in Peace*, Arrowsmith sternly records that even at this early stage, 'Our confidence in him [Scott] was somewhat shaken.'

After Christmas, the group met to decide whether Scott was sufficiently 'with' them. Scott was dispatched for a long walk round Highgate, while Arrowsmith and the rest of the team debated whether or not he should stay as part of the operation. The majority, in the end, felt that his eminence and great experience, combined with the possibility of losing sponsored funds if he was rejected, dictated his continued presence.

In Phnom Penh, where the group assembled in January 1967, things only got worse. They never did make it to neighbouring North Vietnam to risk their lives there, as Ho Chi Minh, on reflection, proved disinclined to let them in. Obliged to kick their heels in

Phnom Penh, Scott aroused further resentment by busying himself with assiduous lobbying of Prince Sihanouk, with a view to organizing outside mediation between India and the Nagas, vainly as it turned out. Once again the issue of how far Scott was identified with group interests, and how far he was using the expedition to pursue his own particular initiatives, became the talking point. Arrowsmith, in the process of leading a quest for alternative forms of protest in Cambodia, became more sharply critical of Scott for 'the way he evaded coming to grips with our ideas'.[3]

In Scott's mind there was apparently no contradiction between pursuing his objectives as a whistle-blowing political reporter, an international mediator on behalf of the Nagas and a peace protester as part of the same operation. He would later describe the early collapse of the whole NVAV operation as something that 'used up a lot of money and made a lot of us look rather ridiculous', but he would not accord much blame to himself. He seemed mildly shocked that Arrowsmith should characterize his motives on the trip as 'devious'.[4] Scott was of course certain of the rectitude of his own actions. But his ability to convey that certainty to others was evidently in decline.

Soon after Scott's return from Cambodia, he was obliged to digest the unpalatable information that the Africa Bureau had once been funded by the CIA. The revelation that the Farfield Foundation, the Bureau's main funding source through the late 1950s, had been a CIA conduit emerged among a host of other disclosures by *Ramparts Magazine* and subsequent Congressional inquiries into the Agency's undercover funding activities.[5] Publicly, it was not immediately embarrassing to the Africa Bureau. Nobody outside those most closely associated with its activities knew about any Farfield–Bureau connection. The British press focused almost entirely on the disclosures about the CIA's connection with the Congress for Cultural Freedom and the prestigious magazine, *Encounter*, which featured the work of many leading pundits of the day.

Privately, however, the revelation must have been traumatic for Scott. One aspect of his governance of the Bureau had always been that it should not accept money from what might be deemed tainted sources. This had led him to refuse offers of help from industrialists with South African interests, though he had often been advised to do just that by executive members hoping to ease the Bureau's recurrent funding crises. The public posture of the Bureau had always been one of being poor but strait-laced.

There appears to be no record of how Scott initially reacted to the news of the CIA's unwanted involvement in his secular ministry, but it soon prompted another campaign. By the end of 1967 Scott had mounted a strenuous personal attack on secret funding through the Fourth Committee at the UN, in a series of long letters to highly placed members of the Secretariat (including the Secretary-General) and subsequently through the UN's Special Committee on Apartheid. He did not neglect to declare an interest. In his sub-mission to the Special Committee, Scott noted:

> for the information of the Committee the Africa Bureau was for three years up to 1960 in receipt of a grant of $3,000 from the Farfield Foundation which several years later was reported in a Committee of Congress to be a 'conduit' of the CIA. (I can vouch for the fact that no 'strings' were attached to this support which was very inconsiderable in proportion to the amounts channelled to other organizations.)

This understated the extent of Farfield's support, though it was to Scott's credit that he mentioned it at all, as there had been no previous public report of any connection between his Bureau and the CIA. However, Scott's UN admission, appearing as it did in the latter stages of a long, convoluted document, entirely escaped the attention of the mainstream British press, though it was gleefully picked up by *People's News Service*, an alternative publication, some years later.[6]

The main plank of Scott's anti-secrecy case was unexceptionable. His opposition was, he said, 'to ways in which Government funds were being channelled through voluntary organizations concerned with Africa through government-financed trusts and foundations, and the widespread damage that is being done to the work of voluntary organizations through their being used for the purposes of strategy, counter-intelligence and counter-insurgency.' His appeal for more openness and transparency was illustrated by a diagram of 'The CIA wheel',[7] with spokes from the centre extending to a rim of numerous activities in the fields of education, law, culture and media. There was much in this that met with general approval, but Scott encountered a deep frostiness in the Secretariat when, to its way of thinking, he recklessly extended his argument against secrecy to include Canon Collins's Defence and Aid operation.

Up to this point the role of Collins's operation had only been imperfectly understood, and the UN was anxious to keep it that way. It had become, in effect, the UN's very own subversive operation against apartheid, underpinning the work of resisters in the ANC and the PAC, both of which had been banned in the wake of Sharpeville. Most of the key developments in Defence and Aid had occurred while Scott was away in Nagaland, and they were hugely significant. Working closely with Enuga Reddy, the Secretary to the Special Committee on Apartheid, who had previously assisted Scott on his campaign against big business in South Africa, Collins had transformed his operation. At Reddy's behest he had devised an international base for his outfit, redubbing it the International Defence and Aid Fund (IDAF). As such it became the conduit for a huge volume of funds, eventually amounting to many millions of pounds, from a UN fund established to finance action against apartheid. Reddy wanted to preserve secrecy on just how much money was going from the UN to IDAF. He also wanted, even more fervently, to preserve secrecy on how the funds were actually being disbursed inside South Africa.

This consideration became even more vital in 1966, when the South African government banned Defence and Aid altogether. In reality, Collins and IDAF were still getting the money into the country to assist the defence of resisters in political trials and to help support the families of those in jail. However, this could only be done through a series of espionage-style cut-outs, concealing the real source of the money. Part of the deception in relation to trial expenses involved laying a false paper-trail for the South African authorities, suggesting that the money was coming from rich liberal benefactors in Britain, and not, as was mainly the case, from the UN via IDAF. And thus far the security of this elaborate arrangement had not been breached by South Africa's diligent secret police.

Scott's attack on secrecy in the UN, however, constituted a threat. From where Collins, and much more importantly, Reddy, were standing, he had become a dangerously loose cannon in the secretly organized fight against apartheid. Reddy recalls eventually having to bring the delicate aspects of IDAF's operation privately to Scott's attention and was gratified to note that it resulted in some abatement of his 'campaign of criticism'.[8]

Meanwhile, Scott was experiencing more problems on the home front with members of his executive who felt the Africa Bureau was in danger of losing its way. One of them, Rita Hinden, the long-time editor of *Socialist Commentary*, took her exasperation to the point of resignation. In a letter to Scott, dated 29 March 1968, she explained the reasons for her departure:

> It was one thing for us all to work together on African problems when the 'enemies' were Western imperialism and S. African racialism – if we could get rid of those all would be well, so we hoped, and worked happily together to that end. But since almost all the colonies have become independent, all sorts of other problems are rampant in Africa, but the Bureau has never really wanted to face up to any of them. It has concentrated on fighting its rather hopeless battle against S. African (and Rhodesian) racialism, over which we are knocking our heads against various stonewalls and say nothing about what is going on in the rest of Africa – some of it pretty bad. Yet public opinion knows that the African independent states are not exactly bastions of peace and light, and it has obviously lost respect for an organization which criticizes fiercely the wrong-doings of white men and says nothing about wrong-doings of men who are black.[9]

Hinden's letter did encapsulate a popular perception of the Africa Bureau's presumed bias. But it also implied a defeatism in relation to white supremacy that could not possibly be shared by Scott, and indeed was not shared by most of the committee. However, even executive members who disagreed with Ruth Hinden's analysis were concerned about what seemed to be a lack of coherence in its policy-making.

The composition of the executive had changed over the years but it still contained a range of eminent and energetic characters. The line-up in 1968 included two former Tory MPs, Charles Longbottom and the maverick Humphry Berkeley, who switched to Labour, and one sitting Conservative MP, Richard Hornby. Their efforts were supplemented by E.J.B. Rose, a distinguished publisher, Richard Kershaw, a talented broadcaster who had previously worked in the Foreign and Commonwealth Office, Peter Parker, an able businessman who went on to become boss of British Rail, and Jock Campbell, Scott's old sparring partner on industrial issues, recently ennobled as Lord Campbell of Eskan. Colin Legum still provided the Bureau's liaison with his editor David Astor, though Astor himself, immersed in a desperate circulation battle with a renascent *Sunday Times* and plagued by problems with the print unions, was less frequently in evidence.

Through 1968 a strong consensus emerged that the Bureau would be better served by having more stability at its helm. There was no coup d'état. Scott had already spoken to Jock Campbell and his chairman, Peter Calvocoressi, of being ready to move on if a suitable younger director could be found.[10] In October 1968 Scott, aged sixty-one, formally resigned his position as Hon. Director, and Guy Arnold, aged thirty-six, moved into Great Smith Street as the Africa Bureau's first full-time paid Director. In his announcement of the change in leadership, Peter Calvocoressi emphasized that Scott's unique experience would not be lost to the enterprise. He would remain on the executive and therefore in a position to provide guidance for his successor.[11]

Guy Arnold was an adventurous young man who had travelled widely in the Americas, the Far East and in Africa, where he had shown considerable administrative capacity in developing Kenneth Kaunda's Youth Service scheme in the year before Zambian independence. He was an able speaker, a good writer and inclined to the left on most issues. It was generally thought that Arnold's youthful energy would combine well with Scott's seasoned wisdom. However, things turned out differently.

CHAPTER TWENTY-SIX

SCOTT VERSUS THE
AFRICA BUREAU

AFTER SIXTEEN YEARS of steering the Africa Bureau creatively, if sometimes erratically, from the front, Michael Scott could hardly be expected to exhibit an immediate talent for his newly assigned role as a back-seat driver. Even so, some of the early portents were quite promising. Shortly after Guy Arnold took over as Director, Scott made a point of coming around to pledge his personal support. He told his young successor that he had no intention of interfering or doing anything that might compromise his leadership, though he would help out if he could. Scott also indicated that, in the short term at least, his scope for hands-on helpfulness had to be limited as he wanted to spend much more of his time in East Africa where interesting developments were taking place.

With Scott out of the country, Arnold commenced his stewardship by trying to establish more amicable working relationships with other groups involved in the anti-apartheid cause. Over the years the Africa Bureau had developed a stand-offish reputation, partly as a consequence of Scott's long absences but also because of his preference for operating alone. One of Arnold's first meetings was with Ethel de Keyser and Abdul Minty, the two leading figures in the Anti-Apartheid Movement, which had developed a strong populist following. They discussed how they might cooperate on future campaigns. Some time later Arnold also seized what seemed an opportunity to improve relations with Defence and Aid, which Scott had always viewed with great suspicion. Arnold met Canon Collins at a conference and extended a fraternal hand, only to be cut dead when Collins realized he was from the Africa Bureau. Despite the snub, Arnold felt he had learned something. He would later comment ruefully, 'At least I knew then that enmity between Scott and Collins went both ways.'[1]

Meanwhile, in East Africa, Scott became involved in a scheme that Arnold thought risked enmity for the Bureau from all directions. Scott had initiated discussions of a highly delicate and secret nature with two powerful friends: Kenneth Kaunda, the President of Zambia, and Julius Nyerere, the President of Tanzania. Of the two presidents, Scott was probably closer to Kaunda, who awarded him one of Zambia's highest honours by enrolling him as a member of the Order of Companionship of Freedom. But his connection with Nyerere was also strong, with communication between them facilitated by Nyerere's long-time personal assistant, Joan Wicken, who had once accompanied Scott on an Aldermaston March and worked in his Africa Educational Trust.

Scott's idea was that they should sponsor a 'dialogue' with the apartheid regime in South Africa, which had been under the rough-hewn leadership of Balthazar Johannes Vorster since Hendrik Verwoerd's assassination two years earlier. This was an immensely risky undertaking in that it was bound to be anathema to the ANC and SWAPO and to the liberation movements operating in Rhodesia. After the years of effort designed to ensure South Africa's pariah status at the United Nations and elsewhere, it was sure to be seen as a reactionary move, however well intentioned. In a private letter to Scott, dated 22 January 1969, Kaunda described the problems posed by the idea as 'very difficult and rather explosive'.[2]

Scott still thought it a risk worth taking. In a paper sent to Kaunda and which Kaunda passed on privately to other East African leaders, Scott spelled out an apocalyptic vision of civil war in South Africa. He saw this as being the likely consequence of the failure by the UN and the Great Powers to promote any meaningful change there. And 'in addition to the horror of civil war, there is the real danger of the conflict spreading far beyond the borders of South Africa, and the Big Powers being drawn into the war on opposite sides. This could lead to world war.' He also made it clear that he envisaged a 'dialogue' without preconditions. In the most controversial section of the paper Scott argued that 'intractable problems' had too often been approached by concepts of 'Use Force' or 'Sanctions' or 'One Man, One Vote' or 'Majority Rule'. In the end, wrote Scott, these solutions 'precisely because they evoke strong Nationalist enthusiasm and dedication to the cause by a too long oppressed people, will bring war to Africa on an ever-increasing scale – a war that has already begun on the borders of Zambia, Angola, Rhodesia and Mozambique'.[3]

Scott also had what he considered the perfect venue for the proposed talks. While in Zambia, he normally stayed in the Kitwe area of the Copper Belt at the Mindolo Ecumenical Centre, which had a record of interracial initiatives going back to 1958. Funded by the Anglican Church, it had already – since Zambian independence – acted as a discreet host for meetings of churchmen north and south of the South African border. Scott enjoyed a good relationship with Mindolo's English director, Wilfrid Grenville-Grey, and found him receptive to the idea of giving his centre's conference arrangements a more directly political complexion, as long as meetings were held 'without publicity'.[4] Having laid the foundations for his idea, Scott communicated with the Africa Bureau in London asking for an endorsement of his scheme and active support. After consulting with his chairman, Peter Calvocoressi, Arnold wrote back, on 26 February 1969, in careful terms:

> I fully appreciate your reasons for making these proposals but, with due respect Michael, I disagree. It seems to me for example that the moment Prime Minister Wilson initiated talks with Ian Smith [the leader of Rhodesia's UDI] in revolt he conceded half of Smith's case and things have gone from bad to worse ever since. To sit down with the representatives of apartheid is, in diplomatic terms, the equivalent of granting them recognition and I imagine if they agreed to such a meeting they would only do so because they believed that they could obtain maximum propaganda out of it to their own advantage. In other words, I could see South Africa putting out propaganda along the following lines:
>
> 'After years of denigrating our efforts in South Africa, now even people like Michael Scott have recognized that apartheid is here to stay and that there is justice in our cause and, indeed, are willing to sit at a table with us and talk. This is very sensible of them. We did not believe the time would ever come that they would admit how wrong they had been in the past to oppose us. Of course we are reasonable people and we are willing to talk with anyone provided – as these people have now done – that they concede we have a reasonable case.'
>
> Again Michael, I hesitate to disagree with you on an issue over

which you have clearly thought very deeply but I do feel from the Bureau's point of view to sponsor, or indeed take part in, any such kind of confrontation could possibly compromise us politically beyond repair with those of our African friends and allies who would not show the understanding that President Kaunda does.[5]

For a few weeks what Guy Arnold saw as 'the Mindolo threat' seemed to recede, as Scott's attention was diverted to another item on the East African political agenda, in which he acted in an advisory capacity. The main fruit of this was the Lusaka Manifesto of April 1969. Fourteen East and Central African states were represented at an occasion that affirmed disapproval of racialism, but agreed to recognize South Africa as an independent state like themselves. The governments represented at Lusaka refused to abandon their support for those seeking freedom in South Africa, but they expressed a desire to do this by peaceful means rather than war. The Lusaka Manifesto would be adopted by the Organization of African Unity (OAU) and subsequently by the United Nations. It was predictably not approved by South Africa and not wholly pleasing to the ANC, though for other reasons. The ANC was worried by what seemed to be an implication that the goal in South Africa was not full 'liberation' as it had been in the former colonial territories. However, as the ANC in exile was heavily dependent on Zambian hospitality it could not afford the luxury of much public dissent, though the Algiers office of the ANC did issue a statement of criticism.[6]

In the wake of the Lusaka Manifesto, Scott stayed on in Zambia with Arnold, back in London, becoming increasingly apprehensive. Although Nyerere, after further consideration, had backed off from the notion of any 'dialogue' or 'confrontation' with Vorster's regime, Kaunda evidently had not. Mindolo was still on the agenda, and Scott was still actively canvassing its benefits. In September 1969 Arnold undertook his own tour of East Africa, ostensibly to improve his contacts in the area, but also with the idea of deterring Scott as his main objective. After a long inconclusive session at Mindolo, Arnold returned to London and wrote to Scott in Kitwe reiterating his old objections and adding a few new ones:

Dear Michael,

I am glad we had the opportunity to talk for most of the Tuesday I was at Kitwe. I go on thinking about your proposed confrontation with people from South Africa and I go on getting more and more disturbed by it . . . I know you say the confrontation is being managed by Wilfrid [Grenville-Grey] and Mindolo and that you are merely in the background giving advice. With due respect to Wilfrid, this is simply not how it will appear to Africans, to South Africans or, indeed, anybody else. You are far too well known for anybody seriously to believe that you are merely advising and that Wilfrid is masterminding the whole thing. I had direct evidence of this in Dar es Salaam. I went to lunch with Nathan Shamuyarira. [At that time Shamuyarira was the representative of the Zimbabwe African National Union in Tanzania. ZANU along with Joshua Nkomo's Zimbabwe National People's Union (ZAPU) constituted the main opposition to Ian Smith's rebel regime. After independence Shamuyarira became Zimbabwe's first Minister of Information.] On the way he said to me: 'What is Michael Scott doing?' I replied somewhat evasively that you were currently at Mindolo helping with seminars, etc. He then said, 'What is this new line Michael has on South Africa?' to which I again said, slightly evasively, you were thinking of the possibility of a new break-through in terms of the whole question of Southern Africa. To which he replied that you are now collaborating with South Africa. At this point in the conversation I realised of course that he knew a good deal more than I had suspected when we started talking. I of course denied that you were collaborating and we then discussed your proposals fully, since he already appeared to know a great deal about them . . .

The point here, Michael, is this: if at this stage in the proceedings Africans of his calibre are using the word collaborate about your activities in Mindolo, I would suggest this could do both you and the Bureau a lot of damage. Anyway, I would ask you to go on thinking about the points I made as I am very worried about the whole thing.[7]

Scott was not a man to be intimidated by the notion of unpopularity, even with erstwhile friends. But it was Arnold who eventually won their battle of wills, mainly because he took the precaution of carrying the Africa Bureau executive and its advisers with him. David Astor and Colin Legum were among those who wrote to Scott warning that it was too soon to bring off the dialogue he envisaged, believing that it could only create distrust in the current circumstances. With Scott finding himself unable to deliver the Africa Bureau, which was perceived by Africans as his own personal organization, Kaunda's enthusiasm for the project declined.

Scott reluctantly backed off and would later speak of Mindolo as an opportunity lost. More objectively, it appears to have been a major embarrassment that was narrowly avoided. Two years later Vorster tried to undermine Kaunda with a crude attempt to smear him in African eyes by alleging that he had entered into secret negotiations with the South African government. Kaunda was obliged to defend himself by publishing all the official correspondence between the two governments, which showed that he had exercised extreme caution.[8] However, if Mindolo had gone ahead, there seems no reason to doubt that Vorster would have used it as an even bigger stick with which to club Kaunda, and cause division in the ranks of black African nationalists.

In Scott's defence, the Mindolo episode can be seen as a valiant response to what he perceived as 'another Vietnam' developing in Africa. It can also be argued that he anticipated the means by which the carnage would be brought to a close. In the end apartheid was indeed dismantled by a process of dialogue between white supremacists and black nationalists (though the nationalists were the long-termers incarcerated in South Africa's prisons, rather than the leaders of Africa's independent nations). Nevertheless, their ability to be on speaking terms was to a large extent due to minds being concentrated by thirty years of civil conflict and the South African economy, under the impact of financial sanctions, being close to collapse. Even then it was touch and go. In political terms, the most that can be said for Scott's initiative is that it was an idea some considerable way ahead of its time.

Wilfrid Grenville-Grey, the director of Mindolo, later remembered Scott as being in favour of 'dialogue', precisely because it was against the prevailing conventional wisdom, adding, 'He was rather like that.' Grenville-Grey also remembered Scott as being entertaining company, with a store of jingles and rhymes that he would recite from time to time to keep their spirits up. One that particularly came to mind was a verse from 'Heroes', the long poem by Menella Bute Smedley, a cousin of Lewis Carroll, which went:

> A glorious gift is prudence
> And they are useful friends
> Who never make beginnings
> Lest they can see the ends.
> But give us now and then a man
> That we may make him king.
> Just to scorn the consequences
> And just to do the thing![9]

Scott regretted the failure of his Mindolo initiative, but never exhibited regret for having made it.[10] As was the case with many of his actions that seemed puzzling to others, he was inclined to say, 'People tend to forget that I'm a clergyman.' It certainly came within the terms of T.S. Eliot's interpretation of Christian witness that Scott most esteemed: 'for us there is only the trying. The rest is not our business.' This interpretation was his strength when it came to operating outside the limits of conventional opinion. But it could also be a serious weakness, particularly when Scott projected himself into the role of mediator, which required specifically political skills rather than those of a protestor against injustice. Politics, even for clergymen, has its rules, though many are unwritten. The cardinal one is that anyone who deliberately flouts the conventions, and does not emerge with some degree of success, automatically forfeits credibility. Scott's heroic early record ensured that he never lost the affection and respect of African nationalists, but with Mindolo he lost credibility in a way that would never be retrieved.

DESPITE THEIR differences, relations between Scott and Arnold were by no means all bad. In one particular area there was actual improvement. There would be no repeat of the problem back in the early 1960s when Scott found himself in hot water with his committee for, as they saw it, going too far in his UN attacks on big business and the mining combines. On assuming office, Arnold had made it plain that he would not seek to curb anything Scott might say at the UN as long as it was clear that Scott was speaking on his own behalf, and not on behalf of the Bureau. With that proviso, Scott could take whatever line he wished. This understanding held firm, though there were other factors that sharply diminished Scott's authority in the world forum, particularly in relation to South-West Africa, his main area of expertise.

After the farce of the 1966 International Court decision, or more accurately lack of decision, South-West Africa became a front-line issue at the UN, with a succession of resolutions that dramatically changed its status along with its name. UN Resolution 2145 of 27 October 1966 formally placed the territory under the direct responsibility of the United Nations. The UN Council for South-West Africa was established in 1967 as the administrative body which would, in theory at least, govern until independence was achieved. A UN Commissioner for the territory was appointed. In December 1967 Resolution 2145 was deemed to have been violated by South Africa when it took thirty-seven SWAPO fighters out of the territory for trial in Pretoria. In 1968 the UN renamed the territory as Namibia. In 1969 South Africa was formally required to vacate Namibia, which it refused to do. As a result the Security Council endorsed the termination of the Mandate and South Africa's continued presence became illegal. Two years later the International Court finally managed to come to a decision which was that South Africa's occupation of Namibia was indeed illegal.[11]

Scott approved most of these actions but his role, now that the big decision-making machinery of the UN was engaged, was essentially marginal. There was no humiliation in this. Indeed, it can be seen as a mark of his success in having finally, and irrevocably, involved the UN directly in alleviating the plight of the Hereros and other tribes of what was now Namibia. Nevertheless, it did mean that Scott was no longer looked to as a source for ultimate guidance on what should happen there. This loss of status was compounded by the fact that Scott was clearly not in tune with Sam Nujoma's SWAPO, which had emerged as the leading liberation organization, committed to armed struggle against South Africa.

Scott's relationship with the liberation movements who felt obliged to resort to violence had always been somewhat equivocal. He did not condemn armed struggle but enthusiasts for armed struggle made him uneasy. Emotionally and philosophically, his attitude to violence was shaped by his own wartime experience. He could defend the right to hit back for victims of violence and oppression, but it had to be a last resort, and to be avoided if there was any glimmer of a non-violent option. Hence his eternal quest for peaceful alternatives. However, this did mean that when the die was cast Scott could seem like an uncertain ally. He had wavered in his support for the ANC in the past and SWAPO clearly felt Scott was not unreservedly on its side. According to the UN's Enuga Reddy, who carefully monitored the power-shifts in the liberation struggle, 'The ANC and the Anti-Apartheid Movement began to support SWAPO from about 1965. Michael was slower; while SWAPO respected Michael, their relations were not very warm.'[12]

In simple power terms, the UN, having finally locked horns with South Africa, had to be more concerned with what SWAPO wanted than with what Michael Scott thought was for the best. Scott still enjoyed a highly respected status as the authentic voice of the Herero interest. But when Chief Hosea Kutako died at the age of a hundred in 1970 even this area of influence was threatened.

The connection between Scott and Kutako had always been close. At one point Scott had precipitated the UN's smallest crisis by presenting a sculpture of Kutako's head to the Fourth Committee. The procedural debate on whether the Committee could accept the gift and 'own' property eventually had to be referred to the Secretary-General for adjudication, who decided that it could in this instance.[13] Scott and Kutako were never able to meet again after Scott's banning from South Africa, but they maintained their intimacy through regular correspondence about events at the UN. And the old chief could always ultimately be relied on to back Scott in any crisis. Whether his successor as chief of the Hereros would see Scott in the same benign light was not immediately apparent.

In this uncertain period the long-running tension between Scott and his co-petitioner Mburumba Kerina erupted into open hostility over a new issue. The problem arose as the UN was sympathetically considering a proposal that Finland should host an international conference on Namibia, which would feature a wide range of experts. Scott was in favour, and Kerina against. Kerina wanted the conference to be in Zambia, and was opposed to inviting any 'European experts'. In the war of words that followed, Scott accused Kerina of applying 'an apartheid concept of nationalism'. Scott viewed Kerina's proposal as a form of discrimination that could only antagonize people sympathetic to the Namibian cause. He also retrospectively criticized Kerina's role in the infamous Carpio affair of some years earlier.[14]

On 2 November 1970, Scott himself came under ferocious attack for what were termed his 'despicable allegations' against Kerina. Two supporters of Kerina, Kohepwe Mbaka and Kai Ma Riruako, describing themselves as 'sons of those very people who originally authorized Michael Scott to present their early petition to the UN', delivered an open letter to the chairman of the Fourth Committee calling for Scott to 'take leave of our affairs'. Scott, it claimed, had 'created confusion, division and distrust among dedicated Namibians and their liberation movements with a view to safeguarding his status of a chosen "Big White Father" liberator of Namibians'. The Fourth Committee was urged to ascertain 'who Michael Scott really speaks for. His credentials for either the World (Peace) Brigade, Africa Bureau, International League for the Rights of Man, the World Council of Churches, or his "Big White Father Mission" do not qualify him as a spokesman for the Namibian people.'[15]

The language in the letter was over the top, but not without significance. At some point in most racially orientated struggles there came a stage at which black people were likely to exhibit resentment of white liberals shouldering their burden. It had happened some years earlier in the American civil rights movement with the rise of Stokely Carmichael and was happening in South Africa with the emergence of Steve Biko's Black Consciousness Movement. In some ways the evidence that young Namibians were perceiving a destiny that did not include Michael Scott was a mark of progress, albeit a painful one. In the short term, however, it was treated as a manifestation of impudence by their Herero elders. On 30 November, Clemens Kapuuo, Kutako's successor as chief of the Hereros, wrote to the chair of the UN's Fourth Committee firmly asserting, 'We have confidence in the Reverend Michael Scott and it is our earnest wish that he should continue to represent us at the United Nations.'[16] With this endorsement, order, though scarcely harmony, was restored to the ranks of the feuding Namibian petitioners at the United Nations.

Despite its lurid nature, there was one passage in the offending document that could not reasonably be contested. This ran: 'during the period from 1964–1966 Michael Scott absented himself from our struggles for other missions in Asia'. It was clear that the authors' dissatisfaction with Scott stemmed mainly from his lack of involvement in that period. Scott's detour to Nagaland can rightly be considered one of his pinnacles of achievement, but it was also an indication of the fact that there is often a penalty to be paid for trying to do too much.

The Nagaland interlude was also disruptive on a more prosaic level. The flat in Hampstead, which had provided some stability for his London existence, was no longer an accommodation option on his return to England. He therefore resumed his no fixed abode style of living in a series of cheap bed and breakfast establishments. Although this would be interspersed with long absences in New York and in Zambia, his living conditions became a matter of concern to his London acquaintances. A possible solution to the problem was found when John and Faith Raven, two of the Bureau's wealthier supporters, announced that they had a small cottage, currently unoccupied, on their estate near Royston in Hertfordshire. Scott moved in but only increased the alarm of his friends when he acquired a motorbike for commuting to London. It also became apparent that the appetite for speed that had almost killed him as a young man in India was still intact.

One of his closest friends at the time was Lorna Richmond. Her connection with Scott went back to the late 1950s, when she had been taken on by the Africa Bureau to help Jane Symonds with the extra work created by Mary Benson's departure. She had to stop working there when the sudden expiration of the Farfield/CIA funding dictated some belt-tightening in the operation. But Richmond's friendship with Scott continued to flourish, maintained by occasional visits to the theatre and restaurant meals. She was more than twenty years younger than Scott, and deeply in love with him but without entertaining any great hopes. Her relationship with Scott naturally inspired comparisons between her and Mary Benson but beyond the fact of their both being tall and attractive they did not appear to have much in common. Richmond, who had never been to Africa, showed no inclination to become Scott's equal in terms of his various causes, though she was invariably supportive of his aims. Benson could radiate dynamism and confidence as a speaker on African issues, while Richmond was shy and diffident and uncomfortable when, as sometimes happened, her work at the Bureau required her to make public speeches. It was Richmond, however, who exhibited the greater wisdom when it came to the complex business of loving Michael Scott.

Although she later entertained thoughts that Scott might marry her, she never pressed the point and became reconciled to their occasional visits to the theatre marking the full extent of any relationship. However, when Scott became a commuting motorcyclist she thought it proper, if only in the interests of his self-preservation, to acquaint him with a safer option. The lodger in her top-floor flat in King Henry's Road, a short step from Primrose Hill, had just moved out, leaving the spare room vacant. Aside from being in familiar territory, close to where Scott had previously lived in Hampstead, it was central and the other occupants of the property were known to be friendly. The house was owned by Jim Green, whose wife Jan organized the Africa Bureau's fund-raising concerts, and the Green family lived downstairs.

Scott duly sold his motorbike and moved in. Scott and Lorna Richmond lived together in King Henry's Road for the last thirteen years of his life, far and away the longest time he spent in any one place. Scott maintained the privacy of his own room, but they cohabited on terms of great affection, with Scott exhibiting a talent for domesticity that could not have been predicted during his vagabond earlier existence. This much is clear from the touching, but clear-eyed, memoir Lorna Richmond wrote at Anne Yates's request some years after Scott's death:

> All these years later, I find it hard to write about Michael and fear giving an over sentimental impression of our life together. The fact remains it was a very special, caring relationship . . .
>
> Despite all the outward pressures and his inner doubts and worries, I found him very restful to be with. There was always the sense of deep inner strength and a keen sense of humour that never deserted him, even in the darkest hours. Both a subtle sophisticated humour and then, at times, a mischievous 'childlike' one, enjoying little practical jokes of the ink blob, sham spider variety.

At times, especially when overtired, Michael could be diffuse in speech and sometimes downright exasperating, but there was never a time my heart didn't lift at the sound of his step on the stair, and his key in the door. Never a time I wasn't conscious of how lucky I was to have him part of all the little caring, sharing things of everyday life. The flat had become a real home.

He could be surprisingly domesticated. If I was returning late from work, often a meal would be waiting – put together from a very limited range of cooking skills or, if I was really lucky, from the Indian takeaway.

Almost always, he tackled the dishes, despite the frequent 'Why is it when there are only two of us, I seem to be washing-up for six.' Realising cleaning the cooker to be my least favourite chore, he became proficient, besides being a dab hand at restoring burnt pans.

Similarly, when at the typewriter inspiration failed, he would have bouts of DIY. Some oddly successful, others not so, as when he glued a formica top to a small table rescued from a skip, in the process transferring the glue to practically everything else, including, as I dramatically discovered on going to wash my hair, the bathroom basin.

We spent hours putting together a so-called 'easy to assemble' mail order set of drawers, but I wasn't allowed to forget that was my idea.

I could write a comedy series based on Michael's enthusiasm for rooting in skips, though I have to admit the odd success, such as an excellent pram, completely cleaned by him with disinfectant before presentation to someone we knew who could not afford such an article.

He never lost a sense of wonder over small things which, childlike, he immediately wanted to share. Come and see this – flower, sunset, mysterious object, whatever. Often Martha-like, I would say, 'I can't come now, I'm too busy,' though, thankfully, not always.

He could be extremely observant at times, despite constant preoccupation with weighty matters. He was quick to sense a change of mood and showed such concern if he thought something was worrying me (particularly if he feared he might be the cause), or if I wasn't well. Luckily, the latter didn't happen often.

Flowers, or pot plants, were frequent gifts at any time, or funny little inexpensive things, such as quite useful gadgets for the kitchen. When it came to proper birthday and Christmas presents he would tease, 'I paid good money for that, so don't turn up your nose as if I'd got it off the skip.'[17]

CHAPTER TWENTY-SEVEN

A SUSPICIOUS NATURE

ICHAEL SCOTT never gave up the fight. On the occasion of his seventieth birthday, David Astor penned a generous portrait of him in the *Observer* under the heading of 'The Man in the Crumpled Suit'. Describing him as 'the first crusader against apartheid', Astor also provided a snapshot of his friend in contemporary action: 'His tall figure and elderly clothes, with papers bulging from the pockets and a general air of having been slept in, will still often be seen in the Members' Lobby of the House of Commons and at the United Nations, and in the less popular demos, apparently ageless and tireless.'[1]

The portrait of Scott as a resolute, still itinerant, lobbyist for the causes of peace and justice in Africa was not inaccurate. It was, however, benevolently incomplete. Through the 1970s Scott's wanderings were mainly confined to his regular end-of-the-year visits to the United Nations in New York. He was therefore able to spend much more time attending to the day-to-day concerns of the various organizations that had been spawned by his career: the Africa Bureau and its closely related Africa Publications Trust, which published *Africa Digest*, the Africa Educational Trust (AET), and the Minority Rights Group. They were, as a result, very often in serious turmoil.

Scott proved to be almost uniquely ill equipped for the emeritus role of providing background support. Administration had never been his strong point, so he had little to pass on in terms of expertise in that area. On the other hand, his restlessness meant he had no gift for leaving things well alone, and allowing people to get on with their work unimpeded. And while he could make clarion calls at the UN calling for 'transparency' in financial matters, his own grasp of accountancy methods was highly idiosyncratic. But his main drawback in what was now essentially an advisory capacity was his inability to break the habit of avoiding confrontation or argument in committee and coming up later with ideas for urgent action in his own particular time after 'inner disquisition'. Though a handicap during his long period of leadership it was never a disabling one because the administration existed to serve his ends and to fit in with what he might ultimately decide. However, it was a habit that could only cause disruption when others had direct responsibility for setting the main agenda. Indeed, even minor matters of business tended to dissolve into confusion when Scott was intimately involved.

An early case in point was provided by a surprise inheritance of $10,000 from the estate of Daniel Bernstein, who had been Scott's main benefactor in New York. Bernstein's widow, Carol, told Scott that the money was his to do with as he wished, though she recommended a world cruise. Scott naturally rejected this notion, and pledged its use in one or other of the causes he was involved in. As a result of this windfall, Scott promptly donated £500 to the Africa Bureau which, strapped for cash, was downsizing again to premises in Grafton Street, near the Tottenham Court Road. The Bureau's Director Guy Arnold was naturally delighted to receive additional funds. But his gratitude was soon moderated by Scott's chosen method of payment which seemed, if only unconsciously, to usurp the notion of his being in charge. Hence this passage in Arnold's painstaking letter to Scott of 3 June 1971:

> The question of your £500. I am sorry to revert to this, but I do want to get the record straight. You say in this paper: 'A sum of five hundred pounds has already been given to the Africa Bureau in support of its policy pamphlet "SW Africa: Proposals for Action".' This is not my understanding at all. First, you have in fact given a cheque for £350 and you say that £150 was 'spent on discharging debts to AB members'. This was not in fact the case. You spent the money to help K____ visit Holland. You asked us to issue him with a cheque which we did and you paid the Bureau back, but it was your decision to help him. Had he come to the Bureau I neither had the money nor, in policy terms, would I have helped him in any case. Secondly, you used money to pay back Jan [Green] because she had lent a sum of money to B____ M____. In fact Jan had asked me if the Bureau could lend him money and I had told her, first, that we could not and, second, that in fact he was a bad risk and she should not either. Jan chose to do so. You chose to repay Jan because B____ M____ turned out, as I had predicted, to be a bad risk. There was a third person, L____, as well.

The point I want to make here is in no sense critical of your actions. It was your money and you have every right to use it any way you chose, but these three people are not as a matter of fact Africa Bureau members and nor were these debts the responsibility of the Africa Bureau. Nor would I have been willing, as Director, to undertake responsibility for them.[2]

A higher degree of umbrage was demonstrated by Mrs Pat Herbert, the Director of the Africa Educational Trust, when it made a long-planned move to new premises in the Africa Centre, near Covent Garden. Shortly before the scheduled move, Scott had advised against it on the grounds of a rumour he had heard to the effect that the Centre had been in receipt of a hidden £400,000 from the Foreign Office. This appears to have been a lurid amplification of the fact the Centre had once applied for, and received, a £40,000 interest-free loan for renovation work from a minor government department. Scott warned Mrs Herbert of the danger of 'infiltration' at the new address. In a letter, dated 15 August 1973, to Kenneth Kirkwood, Professor of Race Relations at St Antony's College, Oxford, and one of AET's senior trustees, Mrs Herbert confessed to having felt 'some hesitation about expressing my growing unease about him [Scott] and his apparent wish to undermine (to put it mildly) the activities of others'. However, the Africa Centre experience enabled her to let rip:

> I was amused but furious. At three separate meetings I have announced the unofficial offer of accommodation available at the Africa Centre, at the last making it definite. He was present at all these, said nothing, viewed the offices with me and reserved one space for himself plus part-time secretary. Then two weeks before the actual move he decides to express doubts and fears about being considered agents of the Foreign Office . . . I have always taken Michael 'on trust' as I am not equipped to judge the vast store of experience and knowledge he possesses . . . But I'm fairly impatient with him and his way of ignoring committee decisions when it suits him.[3]

In the aftermath of this experience Mrs Herbert indicated her displeasure by pointedly reducing Scott's chosen square footage of space to make him 'a less welcome visitor'. Meanwhile, back at the

Africa Bureau, much of the old momentum had been lost. Peter Calvocoressi, who had held the enterprise together through Scott's long absences in the 1960s, retired in 1971, and Guy Arnold left a few months later. Jane Symonds, the Bureau's able long-term secretary, had already resigned some time earlier to get married. She would soldier on, as Mrs Kellock, on a spare-time basis, ensuring regular publication of the *Africa Digest* (until it finally expired in 1975), but her particular skill in divining Scott's true intentions was lost to the administration. One of her successors, Christine Troughton, showed glimpses of her capacity but she soon emigrated to Canada.

After Arnold's departure there never was another full-time Director. Calvocoressi, however, was replaced as chairman by Sir Bernard de Bunsen, who had been Principal of Makerere College in Uganda. Sir Bernard was a distinguished figure and a capable administrator, though less than dynamic. Soon after taking over, he began comparing notes with AET's Mrs Herbert about the difficulties of dealing with their mutual founding father. Scott was inclined to give him a hard time over seemingly insignificant matters, like the precise wording of the minutes.[4]

Scott also ran into problems with the Minority Rights Group (MRG) though these were of a slightly different order. After an uncertain start the MRG had achieved a modest level of distinction under the chairmanship of Jo Grimond, the former leader of the Liberal Party. Scott, however, saw it as being insufficiently proactive, too much given to issuing formal academic reports and not, as he had hoped, actively involving itself in the advocacy of minority concerns, as he had been – and indeed still was – in relation to the Hereros and the Nagas. But the serious difference between him and Grimond opened over what was essentially a domestic issue, though it had minority group implications.

In the spring of 1971, with East Pakistan in a state of civil war, dozens of Bangladesh Action committees sprang up in England, dedicated to raising funds for refugees. To oversee the efforts of the Bangladesh Fund three trustees were appointed: Donald Chesworth, then chairman of War on Want, Syed Chowdhury, the representative in Britain of the first Bangladesh government-in-exile, and John Stonehouse, a Labour MP with radical credentials. According to Fazlul Huq, the legal adviser to the Bangladesh Welfare Association, a large proportion of the funds raised, possibly as much as £1 million, went astray.

Although the evidence for this was decidedly sketchy, Scott became a determined advocate of the need to investigate Fazlul Huq's allegation, bringing it to the attention of a wide range of powerful figures up to, and including, the new Labour Prime Minister Harold Wilson. Further suspicion was caused by John Stonehouse's flight followed by his well-advertised fake suicide and his eventual extradition from Australia. He was brought back to England to face charges under the Fraud and Theft Act in relation to his activities in another enterprise, the Bangladesh Trust, and on conviction sentenced to seven years. However, the authorities after investigation could find no positive evidence of criminality by Stonehouse, or indeed anyone else, in relation to the separate Bangladesh Fund, the object of Scott's and Huq's suspicions. Undeterred, Scott pressed on. Grimond, meanwhile, who from the outset had disapproved of Scott's attempt to involve the MRG in his campaign, quietly resigned from its chairmanship.

With Stonehouse behind bars, Scott transferred his attentions to the other English trustee of the Bangladesh Fund, Donald Chesworth, who through his work at War on Want also happened to be a close friend of Trevor Huddleston, then Bishop of Stepney. This would lead to a stormy encounter at the bishop's home in the East End that concluded with Huddleston ordering Scott and Fazlul Huq out of his house for daring to imply that his friend was 'a swindler'. Scott later claimed there had been a misunderstanding, but as an example of how to lose friends and not influence people to any marked degree the Bangladesh Fund story could hardly be excelled. The line between tenacity and a Canute-like refusal to acknowledge reality is not always easy to detect, but in this case Scott seems to have crossed it.[5]

The other line that Scott crossed with increasing frequency was the one between reasonable and unreasonable suspicion of other people's motives. Many of Scott's unwelcome interventions in the affairs of the various organizations he had created can be traced back to what had become a rampant concern about security, which seemed to him to be constantly under threat from both sides of the ideological divide. This concern was maximised by Scott achieving the unusual feat of becoming both more anti-capitalist and more anti-Communist in his old age. In his paper, 'A World Problem Needs a World Strategy', written in 1976, he affirmed: 'The Communists have an irrational almost apocalyptic urge to take over control of organizations considered to be progressive and, by infiltration, to influence policy-making in voluntary bodies which spring up in response to the need to oppose apartheid.'[6] However, if anything, he appeared to be even more alarmed by undercover activity coming from capitalist directions, with the CIA and South Africa's Bureau of State Security (BOSS) highest on the list of suspects.

Scott's attitude may have been a reaction to his discovery that the Africa Bureau had been subsidized by the CIA. Once bitten, he was more than likely to be twice shy. But the range of Scott's suspicions, sensing corruption on all sides, suggested a more general cause. He had always had a highly distrustful nature but for the most part it had been able to fasten on areas where distrust was a valuable asset, most notably on relations between nation states and in particular on Britain in its relations with southern Africa. But late in life the force of the distrustful element in his personality became more concentrated on the everyday workings of comparatively small organizational structures. In this circumstance, colleagues and friends, even old ones, could find themselves suspected of subversive activity.

The word 'paranoid', which had occasionally been attached to Scott's thought processes in the past, most notably by Mary Benson, was more frequently on the lips of his acquaintances. And Scott himself was not at all slow to pick up on the fact. In a letter to David Astor, in April 1972, Scott bemoaned the fact that the *Observer*, once his strongest press supporter, no longer seemed to be interested in running articles from him, and went on to ask, 'Is this what you could call "paranoid" or is it something to do with the way newspapers are run?'[7]

There is no record of a specific reply from Astor, but a frank one would have said that to survive commercially newspapers are obliged to be essentially about news. And Scott, rendered marginal by major developments in Namibia – and to an even larger degree by his Mindolo initiative – no longer had anything remotely like the news value that attached to him in the past. This could change if he did what he did best, actually create news through the force of his own courageous personal example in action. But without this prime ingredient Scott could no longer expect much in the way of mainstream press coverage.

As it happened, at around this time Scott was contemplating another head-in-the-lion's mouth type of operation that would have guaranteed a return to the headlines. His idea was that he should lead a mission to Uganda to advise the fearsome Idi Amin against persecuting the Asians in his country, and then proceed to Malawi (formerly Nyasaland) to counsel Hastings Banda against his persistent use of detention without trial to silence dissidents. But the Foreign Office got wind of the idea and succeeded in deterring him.[8]

CHAPTER TWENTY-EIGHT

MAVERICK STATUS

Aside from his frustration with events in politics and the media, Scott's life as an old-age pensioner showed many signs of improvement. Lorna Richmond was able to establish a more regular pattern to his eating habits, even managing to curb his appetite for sweets and cake. The hammerings to his health caused by Crohn's Disease eased almost completely. He had recurring bouts of sleeplessness but there were consolations to be found even in insomnia. On still nights, he wandered up Primrose Hill, where he could hear the lions roaring in Regent's Park Zoo, a comforting sound, Scott told his friends, that reminded him of Africa.

Another nearby resource was provided by the spacious residence of the Vicar of Hampstead, the Reverend Graham Dowell. Scott had previously met Graham and Susan Dowell in Lusaka where Dowell had been the university chaplain. After they returned to England, Susan Dowell recalled, 'Scott shambled back into our lives. There was room in the vicarage for a saint.'[1] Scott used the room to accommodate the massive overflow of papers and filing cabinets that threatened to engulf his and Lorna's living arrangements in King Henry's Road. The Hampstead vicarage was also equipped with a staircase leading up to the roof, where Scott could sunbathe in undisturbed privacy on summer days, though the Vicar did once have to field a call from a parishioner politely inquiring if he knew that he had a naked man on his roof.

He was also better off than he had been at any previous stage in his life. David Astor showed no inclination to stop his annuity, which had risen by degrees to £2000 a year, and this, combined with his state pension, guaranteed Scott a new level of economic stability that was not compromised by conspicuous consumption beyond his indulgence of a taste for brightly coloured woolly hats and scarves in the winter months. He paid the £4 a week rent for his room regularly and found himself in the mildly surprising position of being able to save, though only for planned future projects in the field of human rights.

Even the disruption of Scott's American support system caused by the death of Daniel Bernstein proved only temporary. Bernstein's widow, Carol, married another old American friend of Scott's, W.H. 'Ping' Ferry, recently retired from California's Centre for the Study of Democratic Institutions. Ferry, who had supplied some of the ideas for Scott's UN assault on big business in Africa, was keen to keep up the connection. With the agreement of his new wife, Ferry opened an account in London on which Scott could draw to further his various campaigns and initiatives. Both Carol and 'Ping' Ferry corresponded with Scott regularly in a way that was always supportive of his efforts, though not invariably uncritical.[2]

Scott also became involved in the disbursement of serious funds as an executive committee member of what was termed the Study Project on External Investment in South Africa and Namibia. With the benefit of a Ford Foundation grant of $200,000 the Study Project was established under the joint sponsorship of Scott's Africa Publications Trust, the Institute for the Study of International Organization at Sussex University, the Graduate School of International Studies at Denver University in Colorado, the Scandinavian Institute of African Studies at Uppsala University and the African Politics Research Unit at the Free University of Berlin. Despite the respectability of this line-up the Study Project encountered flak from the outset.

To the main anti-apartheid movements calling for complete economic disengagement from South Africa the exercise seemed like a waste of money and time. In defence of the enterprise Scott argued, with some validity, that there was still much that needed to be known, and much that South Africa's defenders and supporters around the world wanted to keep under wraps. At the United Nations as recently as 1970 Scott had been foiled in his attempt to place on record a list of British cabinet ministers and British companies with interests in South Africa. The British delegate to the UN had objected on a point of order, and was supported in the view that such information was a matter of 'domestic jurisdiction'.

Unfortunately for Scott's argument, the elephantine nature of the project provided its critics with further ammunition. First mooted in the late 1960s, the problems of coordinating the huge undertaking, which had equipped itself with an international Board of Governors as well as an Executive Committee, ensured that it did not seriously get going until 1972, by which time it was already arousing suspicions of being a roundabout way of promoting 'dialogue' with South Africa. Then came a spate of revelations in the British press, suggesting that journalism had already accomplished what the Study Project had set out to do. The *Sunday Times* ran an article by Denis Herbstein about discriminatory business practices in South Africa that added impetus to the disinvestment campaign. Then, on 12 March 1973, the *Guardian* carried the front-page headline 'British Firms Pay Africans Starvation Rate'. In the series of articles that followed Adam Raphael brilliantly delineated how major British companies benefited from apartheid's low wage economy. In the wake of the newspaper revelations a Parliamentary inquiry was established, which used its authority to extract testimony from British firms that had previously refused to cooperate with the Study Project. The issue of what Scott's Study Project was actually for became even more sharply focused.

In an article entitled 'South Africa's Frail Friends' in the *New Statesman*, the left-wing writer Suzanne Cronje poured scorn on the enterprise for reinforcing the status quo and 'providing the comforting illusion that "something is being done" while South African profits roll in'. She maintained that further research was not required 'to prove that South Africa is running a slave labour system for the benefit of investors'. Scott defended the Study Project in a letter to the *New Statesman*, but in a way that lacked his customary thoroughgoing conviction. In fact, he was himself entertaining serious reservations and privately looking for conspiratorial explanations for the project's delays and ambiguities. He confided these worries in a letter to 'Ping' Ferry, who was then in the process of quietly resigning from the Project's Board of Governors on the grounds that it was becoming an exercise in 'academic needlepoint'. Ferry replied to Scott in a way that managed to be simultaneously both calming and dismaying. He said he could perceive no evidence of 'conspiring men' being in any way involved. On the other hand, he saw much evidence to suggest 'the folly of trying to deal with political issues with sedulously accumulated data'. In a handwritten postscript to her husband's typed text, Carol Ferry wrote that the whole thing looked like a potential 'snow job', adding: 'I'm sorry, because my loyalty to you (like Ping's too) is as strong as ever. I hate to leave you in what I very much fear is a serious lurch.'[3]

The Study Project lumbered on for another two years, producing five volumes of evidence and research, which Scott formally commended to the attention of the UN's Fourth Committee on 14 October 1975. Its impact was minimal, primarily because of the absence of a sixth volume: the one that was supposed to detail the external arrangements of South Africa with Britain, by far the most important overseas investor. This crucial study, which clearly should have been the main point of the enterprise, had never been completed because its assigned author had backed out at a late stage just before the money ran out. Scott put a brave face on things at the UN, but privately he was furious.[4]

Much of the odium for this omission was incurred by Colin Legum, who had been drafted in at a late stage to usher the chaotic venture to some kind of conclusion. This would have the side-effect of promoting Legum close to the top of Scott's list of suspected subversive characters.

Of all the people Scott had dealt with in the Africa Bureau, Scott had known Legum the longest. When Scott had made his witness at the Tobruk shantytown back in 1947, Legum had been a closely interested observer in his capacity as a Johannesburg city councillor concerned with housing. At the Africa Bureau Legum's more worldly pragmatic approach to problems had sometimes conflicted with Scott's moral stance on the issues, but they were much more often in agreement. Even so, the differences became hugely magnified in a lengthy document Scott prepared some time later to illustrate what he described as Legum's 'seemingly devious record'. Once his darkest suspicions had been committed to paper, Scott showed the document to David Astor, who promptly advised, 'Tear it up.'[5]

Scott was always intensely busy, but many of his efforts, like the Study Project, were destined to end in anticlimax. He established another mini-organization, the Mandate Trust, to add to his campaigning range.[6] One of its first publications was entitled 'Namibia'. Written by Leonard Lazar, a friend of Scott's who taught comparative law at the London School of Economics, it usefully summarized the now dauntingly complex legal status of the territory. The main purpose of the Mandate Trust, however, was to seek redress through the courts for black citizens in Southern Rhodesia who had been dispossessed by Ian Smith's rebel regime. Legal bills would eventually eat through a large proportion of the funds provided by the Ferrys, but Scott failed to get the British courts to acknowledge jurisdiction in the matter. Another court action, launched with the intention of highlighting the actions of British mining companies operating in Namibia in a way that appeared to flout the UN's authority and enrich South Africa, had to be abandoned for lack of funds. It is possible to argue that much of Scott's effort in this period seemed to confuse activity with real action. On the other hand, opportunities for real action of the type Scott most admired, principled non-violent protest, were virtually nil on the African continent through most of the 1970s.

In both South Africa and Namibia, the degree of repression exerted by the apartheid authorities cut off any chance of organized non-violent protest, though the tradition of Anglican radicalism which Scott had done so much to establish in Namibia still flourished. In the course of the decade, three churchmen, bishops Colin Winter and Richard Wood and the Reverend Edward Morrow, were all deported by the South African overlords for establishing too close an acquaintance with those resisting their rule. In Southern Rhodesia, where the British government's ineffectual sanctions policy was failing, the country's destiny was clearly going to be determined by force of guerrilla arms. The border areas of the front-line states were all mini battle zones. Some optimism was induced by the end of the Portuguese empire in Africa in 1974, but this would rapidly be dissolved by manifestations of civil war in both Angola and Mozambique, with the combative mixtures being stirred by Vorster's South Africa. Meanwhile, in much of independent black Africa civil liberties had effectively been suspended as one regime succeeded another, usually as a result of coups d'état.

There seemed to be no part of the continent that could be described as immediately receptive to Scott's basic Gandhian message. Had he been a lesser man, Scott could, after Mindolo, have enjoyed a leisurely old age as a Grand Old Man of Peace, pontificating serenely about the violence of the times in an above-it-all manner. Some of his friends, concerned for his health, did urge him to take this route and there can be little doubt that, if he had followed their advice, his legend in public relations terms would have been infinitely more secure. However, he chose to continue with the daunting business of grappling with the problems of the day. It is hardly surprising that his reward was frustration and serial disappointment, par for the course for most of those aiming to solve Africa's problems.

Ironically, one of the few anti-apartheid organizations that flourished continuously, albeit covertly, through the entire decade was Canon Collins's International Defence and Aid Fund, which attracted heavy funding not just from the UN but directly from Scandinavia, then emerging as a heavy investor in the liberation cause, and from a wide range of other countries. And it enjoyed great success in getting the money through to defence lawyers in South Africa and to the families of imprisoned resisters, though the full extent of this success could not be revealed until many years later, most capably in Denis Herbstein's book *White Lies: Canon Collins and the Secret War against Apartheid*.

Scott's animosity towards Collins, however, still burned bright. While he respected the warning of the UN's Enuga Reddy against saying anything that might jeopardize IDAF's complex security arrangements, he felt free to criticize the operation in general terms. To his way of thinking, Collins's IDAF formed part of what he described as a dangerous 'declination to the Left' in the liberation movement. With most of those actually engaged in armed struggle looking to the Communist bloc, mainly the Soviet Union and China, for arms and military training, Scott argued that the West should seek out other avenues for its funding efforts. As it was, much of the West's funding, channelled through IDAF, which included Communists in its organization, and going principally to supporters of the ANC, which had come to merge its interests almost completely with those of the South African Communist Party, had the effect of enhancing the Communist position in a way that seemed almost to justify the apartheid regime's anti-Communist rhetoric. In his 1976 paper, 'A World Problem Needs a World Strategy', Scott asserted, 'it is true to say that the whole front against apartheid has been narrowed to a left wing confrontation'.

There was logic in this analysis, but it was not easy to perceive an alternative. South Africa's repressive apparatus dictated that any kind of internal opposition had to be subversive, or simply not exist. The inescapable problem posed by BOSS and its vigilant surveillance of any untoward tendencies was that it would be necessary to find cover for even the most moderate and benevolent activities. So it was South Africa, rather than any function of choice by the West, that shaped the nature of its opposition. Scott had clearly identified a problem, but was not able to propose a credible alternative solution. Ultimately, of course, a solution emerged from a direction that neither Scott, nor indeed anyone else, was able to predict: the collapse of the Soviet empire in Europe, which effectively drew the teeth of any Communist menace in Africa.

At the time, Scott's criticisms of IDAF effectively cut him off from the mainstream of the anti-apartheid movement. And he drifted even further away when, following his own logic, he decided to endorse a relatively short-lived breakaway ANC faction, which rejected the idea of serving alongside Communists. Similar considerations seem to have dictated his distancing himself from SWAPO, accepted by the UN as 'sole authentic spokesmen' of the Namibian people. Scott was a patron of Friends of Namibia, a British support group established in 1969, but when it became clear that the focus of its support was on SWAPO and much less concerned with the smaller nationalist groups, Scott wrote a letter to *The Times* criticizing its role. Although Scott's actions in relation to both the ANC and SWAPO can be seen as an aspect of his instinct for siding with the underdog, they also unquestionably further marginalized him as a political figure. Aside from a small group who were devoted to him personally, Scott no longer had anything resembling a constituency of political support. He still enjoyed a maverick status as a poser of awkward questions but ideologically he was seen as an almost complete loner.

Among Scott's closer acquaintance there was a fairly distinct cleavage in perceptions of his role. Those who might reasonably be classed as having a disciple relationship, old Quaker friends like Ernest and Beth Morton, and sympathetic church people, like the Dowells in Hampstead, saw him as a man still intent on applying simple Christian truths, and that the complexities he encountered proceeded from the recalcitrant nature of the times. In contrast, newer and generally less religious-minded acquaintances were more likely to see him as a man whose interpretation of his faith led him to complicate what seemed relatively simple secular issues to a quite extraordinary degree. In some cases this perception could lead to antipathy, in others to a kind of baffled admiration.

The experience of Jo Morris, a young woman who left the Foreign Office Research Department to work closely with Scott, was not untypical. Scott assigned her the task of looking into the activities of the multinationals in Southern Africa and researching the condition of black workers in Namibia as part of the Study Project. Recalling her working association with Scott over a period of eighteen months, Morris remembered him as being 'kindly', 'shambolic and disorganized', 'compulsive', 'indecisive' and 'enveloped in his own world': aside from being 'doggedly determined', 'a man with a mission', 'often funny in a self-deprecating sort of way' and someone who 'on occasions showed great insight in going straight to the heart of a matter'. She thought it was near impossible for anyone to work with him for a great length of time, 'because he was so demanding', with a disturbing tendency to ring up late at night to discuss projects that were churning in his brain. Despite these complications, Morris liked and admired him a lot, though she could understand how others might find Scott difficult.[7]

By the mid-1970s Scott had also become a puzzling figure as far as the press was concerned, and not a particularly popular one. His position on issues no longer had anything like the clarity of his earlier protest years. Whereas once he could be identified with popular, albeit minority, movements, he was now seen as someone more inclined to work with Establishments – both black and white – in pursuit of change. And there was considerable confusion even in the minds of his admirers over when Scott was adopting the role of a mediator, as he had in the context of Nagaland and Mindolo, and when he was acting in his more traditional role as a vigorous apologist for human rights. The one thing about Scott that remained totally unchanged was the impressive strength of his conviction on any subject or course of action after his mind was made up after 'inner disquisition', though this could in itself be a bit off-putting. The broadcaster Richard Kershaw was generally supportive of Scott's initiatives on the Africa Bureau's executive but also inclined to the view that 'somehow the mantle of righteousness was worn with too much confidence'.[8]

Scott's public visibility was further reduced by a major shift in

David Astor's life. In 1975 Astor resigned as editor of the *Observer* which was losing out in its circulation war with the *Sunday Times* and becoming increasingly unprofitable. Some months later he sold the newspaper to Atlantic Richfield, an American oil company. The new proprietors pledged themselves to maintain the paper's liberal tradition, and kept Colin Legum on as the Africa correspondent, but the change of ownership effectively severed Scott's personal connection with his most sympathetic ally in the press. By now, Legum and Scott were regularly at odds. Before selling the newspaper, however, Astor devised what he thought was a creative outlet for Scott's restless energy – work on his biography.

CHAPTER TWENTY-NINE

A PLACE FOR PARANOIA

THE CHOSEN BIOGRAPHER was Cyril Dunn, a long-time *Observer* staff writer on the verge of retirement, who had reported ably, sometimes brilliantly, from all Scott's main overseas locations in Africa, India and the United States. The author of a book about Southern Rhodesia, *Central African Witness*, Dunn had a reputation for diligence and earnestness that was reflected in a popular description of him as 'the last of the puritan reporters'.[1] He admired Mahatma Gandhi and thought Scott's early witness against racism in South Africa and his efforts on behalf of the Hereros at the United Nations both ranked as stupendous achievements. Indeed, Dunn seemed in every way perfect for the job and he got off to a promising start.

In a long series of conversations Scott opened up, seemingly for the first time, on some of the details of his abuse as a child. He also revealed that part of his distaste for Bishop Clayton in South Africa had been occasioned by what he saw as some resemblance between the bishop and his abusing headmaster. Dunn hoped he would be able to fill in some of the emotional areas that had been left blank in *A Time to Speak*. But there were still problems.

Scott's memory of the stages in his various campaigns was good. He could recall significant statements and documents at the United Nations, sometimes with their file reference numbers, going back twenty years and more. But his memory of associates and allies, once they had disappeared from his campaigning orbit, tended to be hazy. Whenever possible, Scott tried to steer their conversations in the direction of his current campaigns. On the more personal level, Scott seemed resistant to exploring the psychological consequences of the abuse, which he talked about, Dunn noted, 'in a kind of trance'. As their conversations progressed, Dunn found himself more and more baffled by the intricacies of his subject's personality and motivation, and what seemed to him 'Scott's terrible lack of harmony with himself'.

Even Scott's Christianity failed to provide a fixed point of reference, though Dunn was intrigued by what Scott described as the 'religion of doubt'. Doubt, it seemed to Scott, was a positive good, as those who espoused certainty were inclined to lack any sense of wonder. He felt that science, rather than the Church, had a greater apprehension of the world's mystery. The Church, like any other institution, could have an imprisoning effect on people's minds. He told Dunn at an early stage of their conversations, 'I think that on the whole, over the centuries, the Church has done more harm than good.' At a later stage, Dunn learned that Scott had, quite recently, applied for an official church post as an assistant priest, only to be turned down on age grounds. He also observed that Scott still wore his dog collar on formal occasions. It was hard for a layman, and very likely would have been for a theologian, to grasp a line of consistency running through it all. As for Scripture, Scott had no time for dogma or what seemed like superstition in either of the Biblical testaments, though it was clear that the example of Christ was all-important. But it was Christ as a militant figure rather than as gentle Jesus meek and mild. When Dunn broached the subject of 'turning the other cheek', he felt he was losing Scott's interest and attention.

Dunn's growing puzzlement with his subject was conveyed in a letter to David Astor on 4 March 1975 reporting on his progress. On the one hand, Dunn described Scott as being 'so obviously kind and gentle by nature'. On the other hand, Dunn said that he could not help but be disconcerted by 'the way he seems to scarcely remember people who've broken their back to help him, the way he distrusts and suspects people and above all by the way he seems never to have thought anyone really capable of helping him and certainly not replacing him. It's also dismaying to find how many of our friends, who ought to be his friends, actually dislike him.' But the central problem for Dunn was not so much what Scott said, or what anyone said about him, but the business of coming to terms with Scott's extraordinary absent-mindedness, which sometimes seemed like imperviousness to other people's concerns. By way of illustrating his difficulty on this score, Dunn wrote to another friend telling of his experience of interviewing Scott over dinner at David Astor's country home in Sutton Courtenay:

He spilt a boatful of rich chicken gravy all over the rich Astorian carpet and not only tramped to and fro through the appalling mess repeatedly while elaborating on some nice procedural point cropping up at the UN Fourth Committee in 1953 but left me housemaiding on my knees for an hour while he went off to listen to some radio chat programme dimly related to the Work.[2]

Dunn saw the humour in the situation but the problem of relating the manifest humanity of Scott's high purpose to his seeming oblivious-ness to his immediate human surroundings began to seem almost insuperable. He wrote to the same friend, saying of his assignment, 'I feel almost a year of unremitting effort has got me no more than 100 feet up the North face of this literary Eiger.' And on another occasion, more colloquially, 'What I've got is worse than an albatross. I'm beginning to howl like a dog.'

The problem for Dunn was compounded by the fact that some of Scott's contemporary campaigns, like those involving the Mandate Trust and the attempt to expose an alleged Bangladesh Fund fraud, did not seem to warrant the obsessive energy Scott was devoting to them, since they appeared sure to fail. These misjudgements, as they seemed to Dunn, led to his writing to Scott, in October 1976, with the advice: 'Stop battering your grey old head against the brick walls of the world . . . Rest now on your shining laurels – or should it be shining oars? The one good thing in Hinduism is the right it confers on old gentlemen like you and me to devote these last few years to an agreeable renunciation of the world.'

By 1977 Dunn had interviewed most of Scott's closest friends. His carefully cross-indexed interview notes ran to some 300 pages, almost a book in itself. But he was still baffled by the problem of how to explain the connection between his subject's extraordinarily diverse adventures. Eventually, he wrote to Scott seeking written clarification of his precise aims and motivation in the various causes he pursued. He also suggested that overall coherence might be achieved by entitling the book, 'The Losing Battle'. In his reply, dated 27 January 1977, Scott wrote back:

My dear Cyril,
    . . . I had not really thought of you wanting to pursue the 'inward-

ness' of the matters which have engaged me so much as to pursue a true record of what actually happened.

I can see now that you have posed the question in such a direct way that it may be difficult for you to make head or tail of my part in it without looking into the personal factors much as I might like these to be taken for granted or kept to a minimum. What I will have to say about this aspect will sound dreadful when put on paper and I would much rather not if we could have talked but since that is not easy and since it seems important that a record of events and interplay of personal factors should be made I will try to do something about it . . .

Sceptical as you have every reason to be I do believe that the most powerful weapon in pursuit of truth and justice and the causes you are concerned with is selflessness – what Eliot and the Bhagavad Gita refer to as not desiring the fruits of action. Once that comes powerfully in as it so often does in politics, nationalism and of course religion the twists of corruption begin to take over . . .

If one acts disinterestedly something 'miraculously' comes out of it. The Nagas do get a bit of respite. South Africa does have to begin to change. It is not miraculous as is usually understood. It is the normal process of creation and if one cooperates with it something good or something of beauty or of truth comes out of it. But it is not a losing battle. A seed must fall into the ground and die but what a 'wonder' if it comes up. 'For us there is only the trying, the rest is not our business' says TSE [T.S. Eliot]. So why call it the 'Losing Battle'?

Scott's thoughts did not appear at all 'dreadful' to Dunn, who was not expecting anything remotely conventional, but they did seem to beg another question. In relation to Scott's actions, particularly in later life, it could almost be argued that he was actually trying too much, in too many directions, in ways that came to limit the overall effectiveness of his witness. So was 'only the trying' in itself enough? Or should Man, as well as God, make it his business to judge its consequences, if only to improve its efficiency? Dunn wrote back to Scott requesting further elucidation, but with a note of levity that suggested the enterprise was getting beyond him: 'I'm sorry you don't like "The Losing Battle"; you evidently don't agree with my enlightened view that the way to win battles is to lose them! What about: "The Apostle Michael and His Religion of Doubt"? (I'm joking).'

Scott and Dunn preserved an amiable, mildly joking relationship but the battle to keep the biography on track proved to be a losing one. After wrestling with the project for almost three years, Dunn finally gave up. The riddle of Scott's personality and motivation remained intact as far as Dunn was concerned, though he later wrote to a friend that of all the political priests he had known personally, a pantheon that included Trevor Huddleston, John Collins, and Ambrose Reeves, 'None of the others were in Michael's class for originality, nerve, human interest and sheer uniqueness.'

Public appreciation of these qualities was not entirely lost. After Dunn withdrew from the biographical enterprise, two academics stepped in with a much simpler proposition. Professor Paul Hare, an American Quaker who then held a chair in Sociology at the University of Cape Town, and Dr Herbert Blumberg on the staff of the University of London's Goldsmith College, had the idea of taking Scott through the various campaigns in his life on a verbatim question and answer basis. This required a tape recorder and some editing skill but not much in the way of psychological insight. The result was *A Search for Peace and Justice*, a book that still qualifies as an excellent introduction to anyone contemplating a non-violent course of political action. At the time, however, it seemed to provide the epilogue to Scott's active career.

The Africa Bureau had already closed its doors in 1978. During its final years, it had only been fitfully active though one of its last publications, *The Great White Hoax*, had usefully illuminated the murky world of secret funding of overseas publications and organizations by the apartheid regime. Its disclosures were soon after validated by what was known as the 'Muldergate crisis', which led to the fall of Vorster and several of his ministers for their part in administering a clandestine fund that had fuelled 138 'secret project' propaganda operations throughout the Western world.

The Minority Rights Group survived with Ben Whitaker, the former Labour MP for Hampstead, as its Executive Director, but without Michael Scott and David Astor, who both resigned from the organization after forming the opinion that it had become 'a virtual quango'.[3] The Africa Publications Trust lost much of its impetus with the end of the Study Project and the lapse in publication of the *Africa Digest*. By the end of the decade talks were in progress to merge what remained of its activities with the Africa Educational Trust. The AET was still modestly in business, but felt itself cramped by Scott's abiding preoccupation with security.

Scott's seeming paranoia on this point, however, came to be viewed in a more appreciative light only a few weeks into the new decade. In January 1980, it was revealed that a similar organization, the International University Exchange Fund (IUEF), based in Geneva, had been penetrated by a South African police agent, Craig Williamson. He had risen to the rank of deputy director of the IUEF and been in a position to manipulate its activities for several years. In the cascade of public disclosures that followed, the IUEF effectively disintegrated, while Williamson went back to South Africa hailed as 'a master spy' before progressing further in its security world as an underground killer. The victims of his letter bombs included Ruth First, who had worked with Scott in Bethal as a young woman and later married the ANC's Joe Slovo, and Jennifer and Katryn Schoon, the wife and six-year-old daughter of the ANC's Marius Schoon in Angola. Subsequently, Williamson was also reputed to have been involved in the assassination of the Swedish Prime Minister, Olaf Palme, in February 1986, though this allegation was never proven.[4]

In 1981 the AET tripled its allocation of full scholarship awards. The reason for this great leap forward was new funding from Sweden and other Scandinavian countries, which had previously channelled their largesse into IUEF. The new appeal of AET to the Scandinavians was based on its being seen as subversion-free, thanks in no small measure to the alarums of Michael Scott.

CHAPTER THIRTY

MOVING MOUNTAINS

AVID ASTOR claimed to have known three truly heroic figures in his life. The first was Adam von Trott, a close friend at university, who moved on to a career in the German Foreign Ministry, where his activities led to his execution in 1944 for his part in the plot to assassinate Hitler. The second was George Orwell, who shaped many of Astor's early policies at the *Observer*, and who wrestled with the attraction of Communism before going on to write *1984* and *Animal Farm*, two of the greatest anti-totalitarian tracts of his time. The third was Michael Scott.[1]

It can fairly be deduced from this that Astor particularly esteemed heroes who struggled with divided loyalties. And of the three he cited, the most divided of all seems to have been Michael Scott, whose inclinations took him in and out of Communist allegiance, in and out of the Church – at least in career terms – and in and out of popular celebrity. Scott also appears to be the most difficult to grasp in terms of personality. Hence the widely different perceptions of him even among those who knew him best. Sometimes they appeared to be describing entirely different people.

To Cyril Dunn, Scott appeared to exhibit 'a terrible lack of harmony with himself'. Yet to Lorna Richmond, who lived closest to Scott, he seemed 'restful to be with' and possessed of a calming 'deep sense of inner strength'. Dunn expressed surprise at the number of potential friends of Scott who actually disliked him. Richmond, on the other hand, testified to the solidity of Scott's old friendships with the people who came and went at King Henry's Road, a long list headed by Ernest and Beth Morton, Jane Kellock (formerly Symonds), Graham Dowell, Len Lazar, Guy and Molly Clutton-Brock after their eviction from Rhodesia, the doctors Anthony and Maggie Barker, who returned from their mission hospice in Zululand to work in the casualty department of a London hospital, and the American activists Bill Sutherland and Bill Johnston, whenever they were in town. Scott clearly had no difficulty maintaining the affection of sterling old friends.

However, it is probable that Dunn and Lorna Richmond were both right. Dunn was essentially a contemporary witness to Scott's life in furtherance of The Work which, on Scott's own definition, involved exploring 'the art of the impossible', an exceptionally complicated proceeding even with Jesus Christ as a guide. Some of Scott's greatest achievements came from this exploration, but it also led, especially in old age when he was unable to dramatise his aims through personal action, to his greatest frustrations. This may have exacerbated the distrustful aspect of his personality as he found others unable to live up to his high expectations. In reality, the art of the impossible was never as contagious as Scott had hoped. Indeed, it often made those cast in a less heroic mould feel uncomfortable or even hostile. Either way, the consequences tended to be inharmonious and to make Scott appear as, for want of a better word, impossible.

In contrast, Lorna Richmond and Scott's older friends were able to witness him with his engine of attack on the sins of the world switched off, or at least in neutral. With them he could relax and, for a while at least, exhibit a self that did not feel the need to be supercharged. This was the one that made playful jokes, rummaged in skips, fixed up old perambulators, entertained Jan Green's children downstairs by dropping sweets through the banisters, and did the washing-up. In short, this side of Scott manifested all the attributes of a man with a capacity for undemanding companionship. There was a tangible difference between Scott as a destabilizing crusader and Scott as a man at ease, though the demands of the former almost invariably took precedence over the latter.

The problem of inserting Scott into any of the conventional pigeon-holes, either sacred or secular, undoubtedly contributed to the comparative lack of public appreciation of his life's work. Even so, the honours that did come his way were by no means inconsiderable. In 1972 the General Theological Seminary in New York awarded him an honorary Doctorate in Theology, which complemented the Zambian Order of the Grand Companion of Freedom bestowed on him by Kenneth Kaunda in 1968. In 1975 Colin Winter, the exiled Bishop of Damaraland, as the Namibian diocese was then still called, appointed Scott as a canon *in absentia*.

Scott was never in a position to officiate in the cathedral, but it did entitle him to sign himself with the distinguished appellation, 'Honorary Canon, St George's Cathedral, Windhoek'. He rarely seems to have done so other than in correspondence with the Secretary-General of the United Nations, but he was pleased with the appointment. He also felt honoured in 1979, when he was approached by the International Fellowship of Reconciliation (IFOR), the prestigious interfaith pacifist organization, which had grown since the First World War to achieve a worldwide membership of more than 100,000 that included Christians, Jews, Hindus, Buddhists and Muslims. IFOR asked Scott to represent its human rights interests at the United Nations. Scott did so, combining it with his regular duties as the representative of the Hereros.

No actual awards came Scott's way from the liberation movement, but the absence of hard feelings about past differences was demonstrated at a Friends International Centre meeting at which Moses Garoeb, the Secretary-General of SWAPO, went out of his way to praise Scott from the platform as being the man who first took his country's plight to the UN and brought its struggle to the attention of the world. According to a report of the meeting, Scott, who was at the back of the hall, 'stood and received tremendous applause'. There was no similar occasion for a public display by the ANC, but there was no doubting the brightness in its memory of Scott's early crusading efforts, particularly at Tobruk. In Nelson Mandela's *Long Walk to Freedom*, published many year later, Scott figured as 'a great fighter for African rights'[2] while John Collins, whose IDAF had contributed to the ANC's cause more constantly that Scott had ever done, was not favoured with a mention. Of the four leading white clergymen most associated with the nationalist struggle in South Africa it appears that Collins and Ambrose Reeves enjoyed the respect of Africans, while Huddleston and Scott, who were seen as not merely supporting but as actually identifying with their cause, excited something more akin to love.

No prizes were awarded to Scott by the British, which in a way was an honour in that it demonstrated that Scott's prickly opposition to Britain's official policy in southern Africa remained intact until the end. He never became an extinct radical of the type that can often qualify for sentimental honours in old age. To Scott the early 1980s seemed a desperate time. With Margaret Thatcher and Ronald Reagan conjoined as the major figures in the West, Africa appeared destined for further polarisation. Both leaders were more favourable than their predecessors had been to white supremacy and white business interests in Africa. The Soviet bloc, implacable as ever, continued to pour money and arms into the continent's numerous trouble-spots. In South Africa and Namibia the armed struggle was escalating, as was the brutality of the repression imposed by Vorster's successor as president, P.W. Botha. Rhodesia, having achieved its independence as Zimbabwe, soon resumed its status as a battle-ground when its new prime minister Robert Mugabe sent in troops to crush a Matabele uprising. As was the case throughout the 1970s, the margin of opportunity for non-violent political change was not readily apparent.

Scott's combative energy in old age was mainly expressed through his battered typewriter, which churned out personal appeals for constructive interventions in the concerns of Africa to dignitaries as diverse as Queen Elizabeth II and Helmut Schmidt, the Chancellor of the Federal German Republic. He also composed a succession of position papers on subjects close to his heart, ranging from religion to the correct spelling of the name of the royal yacht. Scott's convoluted prose style and his reluctance to indulge in personalities sometimes made it hard to locate a publisher, but he usually found a way. In the spring of 1981, he had a triple success, placing his theological treatise, 'No Faith Without Doubt' in the Quaker magazine, *The Seeker*; a long article on the perils of Africa's 'declination to the Left' in *Chronicle*, the organ of the Dag Hammarskjold Centre for the Study of Peace and Violence;[3] while his thoughts on the royal yacht ran in the *Daily Mirror*'s 'Old Codgers' column, edited down but to the point: 'My father was the vicar of Northam on the River Itchen where they serviced George V's vessel and I have a brass plate worded Brittannia. You say the current yacht is Britannia. Please settle.' The *Mirror*'s scholarly finding was that there had been some 'fooling' with the spelling of the word since 1716 but that weight of custom and practice favoured a single 't'.

Scott also exercised his playful side in correspondence with a patent agency in Blackfriars seeking advice on the possible commercial application for his design of a chair with a V-shaped back and two shoulder height armrests, which, he claimed, facilitated 'reading and writing while also viewing a TV screen'. The structure had suggested itself during one of Scott's late bouts of DIY enthusiasm. With an instinct for modernity, he called his chair 'The TV Easee', but he undermined his own creation with an excess of honesty, revealing that a seating arrangement of similar design had flourished in the eighteenth century to accommodate gentlemen in long-tailed coats. The agency good-humouredly, but firmly, advised that it was unlikely to qualify for patent status as 'in its broad concept the arrangement is not novel'.[4] Most of Scott's correspondence, however, had the serious intent of exploring alternatives to violence, in Africa particularly but also throughout the world. Distant friends in Canada and the United States and in northern Europe found themselves regularly urged to set up 'unaligned groups' to provide an alternative voice to the Cold War bellowing of the Great Powers.

Occasionally, when his closest sympathies and antipathies were engaged, Scott allowed himself a note of asperity in his letter-writing. One his longer running mini-campaigns was the protection of Bertrand Russell's posthumous reputation against those inclined to denigrate the great philosopher's memory. He was upset by a BBC documentary which appeared to downplay Russell's role in the peace movement while elevating that of Canon Collins who had provided the main on-camera interview. 'I do hope,' Scott wrote severely to Alan Dobson, the programme's producer, in May 1981, 'it may be possible for you to present a rather more generous appreciation of the role of Bertrand Russell in the CND movement than was elicited from the interview with Canon John Collins. It is an occupational hazard of preachers to clothe the subject of one's discourse with the same limitations that one has oneself, particularly if one is not aware of them.'[5]

In 1982 Scott tried to enlist the support of Sue MacGregor on BBC's *Woman's Hour* for his concept of 'a new reformation', which he felt had to come from women as they were 'less entrenched in the deeply channelled vested interests of institutional religion'. Scott maintained that all 'the religions of The Book' – Christianity, Judaism and Islam – suffered from an irrational overemphasis on the past, failing to distinguish between historical fact and primitive speculation in ways that were sometimes 'positively vicious'. He wanted *Woman's Hour* to take on the challenge of infusing the myth-encrusted areas of the traditional faiths 'with present-day values and knowledge of the universe'.[6] This challenge was not accepted, though Scott was still posing new ones for himself. He discussed with David Astor the feasibility of developing Rights and Justice, a tiny organization they had founded some years earlier, into a major international enterprise that would be free of the impediments of the other organizations he felt had failed him in the past. Although the AET was now on a more solid footing, Scott continued to fret about its vulnerability to 'infiltration'. Both of Scott's older brothers, Nigel and Roy, had died and Scott's modest savings had been enhanced by the inheritance of some family money. So he could fund the expansion of Rights and Justice from his own financial resources. His physical resources, however, were fast running down.

Scott made his last appearance at the United Nations as the representative of the Herero interest and IFOR in the winter of 1982 at the age of seventy-five. He stayed in Scarsdale with Carol and 'Ping' Ferry, who became concerned about the swelling in his legs. He needed a wheelchair to navigate his way through the airport on the homecoming journey. The bursitis that caused the swelling eased on his return to Primrose Hill but was soon superseded by a larger problem. In the spring of 1983 he was diagnosed as having cancer of the liver. It was made clear to Scott that he had only a few months, probably no more than six, to live. The cancer diagnosis effectively closed off the Rights and Justice development option but Scott maintained his flow of forward-looking correspondence, writing to, among many others, the UN's Secretary-General, Javier Perez de Cuellar, proposing the imposition of a new Indemnity Tax on those trading with apartheid; Michael Dummett, Wykeham Professor of Logic at Oxford University, seeking his assistance in organizing a symposium on 'the West's attitude to Communism and the East'; and the Greenham women, whose peace protest camp outside the US nuclear missile base near Newbury was causing major offence to Mrs Thatcher's government and reviving the long dormant spirit of CND.

Scott's 'Letter to The Women of Greenham Common' was the most revelatory, possibly because they, rather like Scott himself at Tobruk, were establishing a point of principle by living in what the authorities perceived as the wrong place at the wrong time. It had been many years since Scott had been able to draw attention to himself and his causes through public protest and there were some who felt that Scott's militancy had lost its edge. His public preoccupation for some time past had been not so much with protest but with finding formulas that could provide alternatives to violence and with getting people to talk to one another across hostile divides, as had been the case in Nagaland and as he hoped would eventually be the case in Namibia and South Africa. However, Scott's letter to the Greenham women, dated 1 June 1983, indicated that age had not withered his basic radicalism in relation to either church or state:

> The women of Greenham Common have started or restarted something that will never end – unless it be the end of the world when all life on this planet is brought to an end. For they have, at this particular juncture, and on that particular spot, determined, of their own free will, to resist the great evil of our time. And, by doing so by non-violent means, they have joined the ceaseless struggle against evil which will not be vanquished . . . They have raised the question to which it is imperative to find the answer now. For time is of the essence in this matter. And so, as one of England's philosophers of this century, Bertrand Russell, has shown us, by example, is courage. And, for women, the courage to question is especially required. It needs courage to challenge the power of the State in the modern world, with its claim to be the exclusive arbiter of Right and Justice, and with the destiny of men and women under its control. But it also requires courage to question the authority and truth of Holy Scripture. Through centuries of belief in the infallibility of the Bible, the three great monotheistic religions have perpetuated the slander that it was through Woman's thirst for knowledge about the meaning and origin of good and evil, that evil gained entry into the scheme of things on earth.
>
> Perhaps we are standing at the threshold of a new reformation. But if there is to be a new renascence of learning for humanity, it will require women to play their part, both within and without the Churches, in helping to dispel the obscurantism on which some very powerful religious institutions have thrived for too long.[7]

The Greenham women may well have been mildly surprised to find themselves seen as being in the front-line of resistance to the institutional church as well as the power of the state, but Scott was probably keen to cover all contingencies in what proved to be his last campaigning document. Three weeks later he wrote the letter to Astor in which he documented his abuse as a child. Scott said that he felt the need to be more explicit about this area of his experience: 'For it is about one of the "hidden influences" in the make-up of some of my generation and some of the generation still growing up, and because it may help to explain a defect or deficiency that makes for a distrustful disposition, and which some women friends have called "something mysterious about you" probably not wanting to sound slighting.'[8] Scott clearly obtained some relief from being able to confess 'the bottled dread' that he felt had permanently damaged his interior life, but there was no staying the course of his illness.

In the few weeks he had left to live, Scott was able to put his affairs in order. He had no property to dispose of, but £65,000 had been assembled in the bank against the expense of the Rights and Justice venture. His friends, Ernest Morton and the Barkers, agreed to act as his executors and to ensure the money went towards causes in the field of human rights. Scott was also visited by other old friends, and on one occasion by Mary Benson. The most regular visitor was David Astor whose London home in St John's Wood was only a short walk from King Henry's Road. He often took a light lunch with Scott and they would talk for an hour or so afterwards. Scott's conversation was quite lucid but mainly wedded to a particular theme.

He thought his life had been a failure. For all his talk about planting seeds from which miracles might grow, he felt there had been little sign of germination. Though possessed of a faith said to be capable of moving mountains, nothing much in the political landscape had changed, as far as Scott could see, except, possibly, for the worse. To his way of thinking, his and Astor's joint effort to inspire peaceful change in Africa had made very little difference. Astor remembered Scott reciting these thoughts without any sign of bitterness, as if they were simple matters of fact. He also remembered trying to temper his friend's pessimism by saying that there had been one major change: Scott's attitude to the race question, originally horrifying to his Church, was now the orthodoxy of the Anglican hierarchy, and this represented a fundamental alteration in people's attitudes that could yet produce fruitful results.[9] On the issue of

Africa itself, Astor found himself less able to console. He, like Scott, could perceive no immediate peaceful outcome to the violent torments of that continent.

Michael Scott died in his room on 14 September 1983. Lorna Richmond, who had nursed him through each stage of his final illness, was with him to the end. His funeral was conducted at Hampstead parish church, though his ashes would later be transferred to the parish church in the village of Kingston in East Sussex, where Lorna moved after Scott's death. At his memorial service in St Martin-in-the-Fields, on 17 November, Trevor Huddleston recalled how Scott's original perception of South Africa's racial crisis had been far more acute than his own, and paid tribute to 'the sheer complexity of Michael's causes and the fantastic energy of the man in following them through'. In his letter of condolence to Lorna Richmond, George Houser, the founder of the American Committee on Africa, spoke of Scott's 'untold contribution to the cause of freedom, to world peace and justice and I think the preservation of the Christian gospel'. The CND's organizer, Bruce Kent, a Catholic priest, also wrote to her, commending Scott as 'a great man, wider and bigger than any dozen Bishops or Popes'.[10]

But the finest testimonial to Scott and the seeds his life had planted would be seen in the public events that occurred seven years after his death. In the space of a few months the Berlin Wall came down in a way that dramatised the collapse of Communism, Nelson Mandela was released from jail in circumstances that opened the bright prospect of a negotiated end to apartheid, and the Hereros[11] and other citizens of a newly independent Namibia went to the polls to vote in their country's first free elections. Despite the pessimism of Scott's last days, the mountains had moved.

In 1992 a group of Michael Scott's friends assembled in the Sussex village church where his ashes are kept. Archbishop Desmond Tutu officiated at the ceremonial unveiling of a stained-glass window dedicated to Scott's memory with the inscription: 'He spoke for the oppressed.' It still provides an iconic focus for those inclined to venerate Scott as a saint, and, for those not so inclined, a useful reminder of one of the strangest and bravest Englishmen of his time.

NOTES AND SOURCES

INTERVIEWS SINCE the year 2000 were conducted by Lewis Chester, unless otherwise stated. The extensive interviews carried out by Cyril Dunn during Scott's lifetime are located among the Scott Papers in Rhodes House in Box 5C. The handwritten index to these interviews is in Box 78. Anne Yates also interviewed a wide range of Scott's friends and acquaintances after his death. Many of her interview notes are also located among the Scott Papers but dates for them are not in all cases available.

INTRODUCTION

1. Lord Tweedsmuir writing from the UN General Assembly session in Paris to the Commonwealth Relations Office (CRO) in London. National Archives: Commonwealth Relations papers in class DO35/3820, 16 January 1952.
2. Homer Jack reviewing Michael Scott's book A Time to Speak in *The Progressive*, December 1958.
3. Bruce Kent, letter to Lorna Richmond, 1983, (Scott Papers (SP), Box 9).
4. David Astor speaking on BBC radio, circa 1958. Quotation from a BBC Recording Services tape transcript, undated (SP, unnumbered box).
5. Cyril Dunn, letter to Anne Yates, 8 February 1985 (SP, unnumbered box).

CHAPTER ONE
IN THE END

1. David Astor, interview, June 2001.
2. Michael Scott to Astor, 21 June 1983 (Scott Papers (SP), Box 65).
3. Astor to Scott, 24 June 1983 (SP, Box 81).

CHAPTER TWO
IN THE BEGINNING

1. Scott, *A Time to Speak* (London: Faber and Faber, 1958), pp. 19–20.
2. Scott, interview with Cyril Dunn, June 1974.
3. Scott, *A Time to Speak*, p. 19.
4. Ibid.

5. Ibid. p. 14.
6. Ibid. p. 27.
7. Ibid. p. 1.
8. Ibid.
9. David Astor, interview, June 2001. Scott's main theological treatise, published in *The Seeker*, a Quaker magazine, in 1981, was entitled 'No Faith Without Doubt'.
10. Scott, *A Time to Speak*, p. 21.
11. Ibid. p. 26.
12. Ibid. p. 29.
13. Ibid. pp. 29–30. Also details of Scott's secondary school days supplied by Michael Rogers, archivist at King's College, Taunton, by e-mail, February 2005.

CHAPTER THREE
IRRESOLUTE IN AFRICA

1. Scott, *A Time to Speak*, p. 31.
2. Ibid. pp. 30–1.
3. Scott, interview with Cyril Dunn, June 1974.
4. Scott, *A Time to Speak*, pp. 32–6.
5. Ibid. p. 37.
6. Ibid. p. 38.
7. Ibid. p. 97.
8. Ibid. pp. 40–1.
9. Scott, interview with Dunn, June 1974 and *A Time to Speak*, pp. 41–3.
10. Scott, *A Time to Speak*, pp. 44–5.
11. Ibid. p. 45.
12. Ibid. pp. 46–7.
13. Ibid. p. 47.
14. Ibid. p. 50.

CHAPTER FOUR
COMMUNIST COMMITMENT

1. Mary Benson, *A Far Cry: The Making of a South African* (London: Penguin, 1989), p. 64.
2. Scott, *A Time to Speak*, p. 53.
3. Scott, interview with Cyril Dunn, June 1974.
4. Scott, *A Time to Speak*, pp 55–6. Scott's problem with a homosexual priest in Kensington is referred to in the notes of Dunn's interview with him, June 1974.
5. Scott, *A Time to Speak*, p. 55.
6. Scott, interview with Dunn, June 1974.
7. *News Chronicle*, 27 March 1947, article by Jane Orme entitled 'Portrait of Michael Scott'.
8. Scott, interview with Dunn, February 1975.
9. Scott's contact with Harry Pollitt in his interview with Cyril Dunn, June 1974. Details of Emile Burns' background were supplied to Dunn in an interview with Tristan Jones, August 1974. Burns is not mentioned in *A Time to Speak*, though

the book does furnish information about the origins of Scott's Communist commitment. The quote urging 'the inseparability of prayer and action' appears on page 60.

10. Scott, *A Time to Speak*, p. 62.
11. Jane Orme, interview with Dunn, October 1974.
12. Scott, *A Time to Speak*, p. 64.

CHAPTER FIVE

A PASSAGE TO INDIA

1. Scott, *A Time to Speak*, p. 67.
2. Ibid. p. 73.
3. Ibid. p. 75.
4. Ibid. pp, 69–71 and Scott interview with Cyril Dunn, June 1974.
5. Nigel West, *Mask* (London: Routledge, 2005), p. 37.
6. Michael Carritt, *A Mole in the Crown* (London: published privately by Michael Carritt, distributed by Central Books, 1985) pp. 131–5.
7. Ibid. p. 143.
8. Ibid. p. 132.
9. Michael Carritt, interview with Anne Yates, January 1987 (SP, unnumbered box).
10. Scott, *A Time to Speak*, p. 76.
11. Carritt, interview with Yates, January 1987.
12. Scott, *A Time to Speak*, p. 78.
13. Ibid. pp. 67–8.
14. Ibid. pp. 79–82.
15. Bishop Foss Westcott writing from Calcutta on 8 August 1939 to the Co-operating Committee for the International Student Service in London. The letter was in the form of a reference for Scott, who had offered to work with Jewish refugee students before he was incapacitated by illness (SP, unnumbered box).
16. Scott, *A Time to Speak*, p. 64.

CHAPTER SIX

WARTIME

1. Scott, *A Time to Speak*, pp. 83–4 and his interview with Cyril Dunn, February 1975.
2. Carritt, *A Mole in the Crown*, p. 132 and Michael Carritt's interview with Anne Yates, January 1987 (SP, unnumbered box).
3. Scott, interview with Dunn, February 1975.
4. Ibid.
5. Scott, *A Time to Speak*, p. 88.
6. Ibid. pp. 85 and 88.
7. Ibid. pp. 85 and 89.
8. Ibid. pp. 90–1.
9. Ibid. p. 93.
10. National Archives: MI5 documents relating to Michael Scott, released in September 2005, in KV2/2052.
11. Scott, *A Time to Speak*, p. 94.

CHAPTER SEVEN

BETRAYAL

1. Trevor Huddleston's address at the memorial service for Michael Scott held in St Martin-in-the-Fields on 17 November 1983. Subsequently published as a commemorative brochure (SP, Box 9).
2. Scott, *A Time to Speak*, p. 98.
3. Sir Alfred Milner, quoted in *The Scramble for Africa* by Thomas Pakenham (London: Abacus, 1992), p. 667.
4. General Jan Smuts quoted in *South Africa: An Historical Introduction* by Freda Levson Troup (London: Eyre Methuen, 1972), p. 285.
5. Scott, *A Time to Speak*, pp. 100–3.
6. Adrian Hastings, *A History of African Christianity 1950–1975* (Cambridge University Press, 1979), p. 23.
7. Scott to Geoffrey Clayton, 8 September 1943 (SP, Box 88); Clayton reply to Scott, 16 September 1943 (SP, Box 71).
8. Scott, *A Time to Speak*, pp. 113–15.
9. Clayton to Scott, 21 October 1943 (SP, Box 71). Scott's prickly relationship with Clayton is the main topic of his interview with Cyril Dunn, June 1974.
10. Alan Paton, *Apartheid and the Archbishop: The Life and Times of Geoffrey Clayton* (London: Jonathan Cape, 1974), pp. 118 and 120.
11. Scott to Clayton, 10 November 1943 (SP, Box 88).
12. Scott, *A Time to Speak*, p. 115.
13. Ibid. p. 117.
14. Lewis Mumford, *The Culture of Cities* (New York: Harcourt Brace 1938).
15. Scott, *A Time to Speak*, p. 119.
16. 'The Afrikaner-Broederbond: A State within a State' would eventually be published as part of a pamphlet by Michael Scott's Mandate Trust in London, November 1976. The full pamphlet was entitled *Mandate for Right and Justice 1946–76*.
17. Ibid. p. 9.
18. Scott, *A Time to Speak*, p. 121.
19. Ibid. pp. 121 and 123.

CHAPTER EIGHT

DOING TIME IN AFRICA

1. Trevor Huddleston, interview with Cyril Dunn, January 1975.
2. Scott, letter to J.H. Hofmeyr, 6 May 1946 (SP, Box 83).
3. H.R. Raikes to Scott, 14 May 1946; Scott to Raikes, 19 May 1946 (SP, Box 83).
4. Scott, *A Time to Speak*, p. 135.
5. Ibid. p. 138
6. Bettie du Toit, interview with Dunn, 1975.
7. Clayton to Scott, 13 July 1946 (SP, Box 88)
8. Scott's address to the Durban magistrate's court published in *The Leader*, the Indian Congress paper, 27 July 1946.
9. Yusuf Kat's cartoon first appeared in *The Leader* illustrating an article entitled 'The Padre Passive Resister' in July 1946. It was subsequently featured in several

other publications. *Indian Opinion* ran its supplement on the Durban demonstrations on 5 July 1946.

10. Telegrams of support to Scott in Durban jail (SP, Box 40).
11. *Sunday Express*, 28 July 1946.
12. Harry Leach, quoted in the *Sunday Express*, 28 July 1946.
13. Scott on prison life in *A Time to Speak*, pp. 142, 143 and 145.
14. Ibid. p. 149.
15. Tom Comber to Scott, 15 December 1982 (Lorna Richmond collection).

CHAPTER NINE
TOBRUK

1. Freda Levson Troup, interview, 28 August 2003. The epic lunch also featured in her interview with Cyril Dunn, September 1974.
2. Scott to Clayton, 8 January 1947 (SP, Box 88).
3. Nelson Mandela, *Long Walk to Freedom* (London: Abacus, 1995), p. 121.
4. Freda Levson Troup, interview, August 2003.
5. Margaret Becklake, interview with Elizabeth Welsh, September 2005
6. Ismail Meer, interview with Anne Yates, 13 June 1993 (SP, unnumbered box).
7. Bill Sutherland's posthumous tribute to Scott 'I Remember Michael', written in Dar es Salaam, April 1986 (SP, Box 15).
8. Scott, *A Time to Speak*, pp. 280–1.
9. Nicholas Monsarrat, *Life Is a Four Letter Word*, vol. II, *Breaking Out* (London: Cassell, 1970), pp. 244–5.
10. Scott, *A Time to Speak*, p. 154.
11. Mandela, *Long Walk to Freedom*, pp. 121–2.
12. Clayton to Scott, 28 April 1947 (SP, Box 88).
13. *Ebony*, November 1947; *Sunday Express*, 13 April 1947; *Rand Daily Mail*, 22 April 1947; *Inkululeko*, No. 111, April 1947.
14. The film *Civilization on Trial* with commentary by Scott was used to supplement his lobbying efforts at the House of Commons and at the United Nations. The original rough cuts would later, through Mary Benson's cinematic connections, be professionally edited by Clive Donner.
15. Letter from Scott's mother, 29 April 1947 (SP, Box 78).
16. Clayton to Scott, 28 April 1947 (SP, Box 88).
17. Scott/Huddleston correspondence from 18 May to 20 June 1947 (SP, Box 88).
18. Scott, *A Time to Speak*, pp. 176–7.
19. A typescript version of Scott's interrupted address to the angry Bethal farmers survives (SP, Box 29).
20. Trevor Huddleston, *Naught for Your Comfort* (Glasgow: William Collins, 1956), p. 44.

CHAPTER TEN
THE HERERO CONNECTION

1. Paul Rohrbach, quoted in Freda Levson Troup's early biography of Scott, *In Face of Fear* (London: Faber and Faber, 1952), p. 55. Also discussed by Scott in his

pamphlet *Orphans' Heritage* (London: Africa Bureau, 1958), p. 7.

2. General Lothar von Trotha's Extermination Order quoted by Jon M. Bridgman in *The Revolt of the Hereros* (University of California Press, 1981), pp. 127–8.
3. Pakenham, *The Scramble for Africa*, p. 614.
4. Troup, *In Face of Fear*, p. 58.
5. Scott recollected Tshekedi Khama's words in his interview with Cyril Dunn, July 1974.
6. Quoted by Scott in *A Time to Speak*, p. 219.
7. Verses from 'Lines Penned to Commemorate a Gallant Episode in the year MCMXLVIII'. Typed copy of the full version, with the initials of Freda Levson and Anthony and Margaret Barker, among the Scott Papers (Box 87).
8. Scott, interview with Dunn, February 1975.
9. Scott, *A Time to Speak*, p. 221.
10. Petition in the records of the UN General Assembly Second Session, Fourth Committee, 16 September–6 November, 1947, pp. 139–95. Copy in SP, Box 1.
11. Scott, *A Time to Speak*, p. 226.
12. Clayton's reference for Scott, 17 September 1947 (SP, Box 88).
13. National Archives, Washington, D.C. Search conducted by Linda Melvern for a book about the United Nations. Her findings in relation to Michael Scott's status were published in a letter to the *Guardian*, 27 March 1990.
14. Scott, *A Time to Speak*, p. 233.
15. Ibid. pp 232–3.
16. Scott to Leon and Freda Levson, 27 December 1947 (SP, Box 40).
17. The South African police dossier is appended as Annex B to Scott's report for the Council of Asiatic Rights, Transvaal, and the Council for Human Rights, Natal, after his return from the United Nations in New York. The report is dated February 1948 (SP, Box 30).
18. *New York Post*, 30 December 1947, article by Henry Beckett headlined 'More Saint than Sinner'.

CHAPTER ELEVEN

FROG VERSUS BULL

1. Scott, *A Time to Speak*, p. 235.
2. Ibid. p. 245.
3. Troup, *In Face of Fear*, pp. 175–6, summarizes the press campaign against Scott.
4. Scott to Mrs Lavoirpierre, organizer of the Council for Human Rights in Durban, 25 March 1948 (SP, Box 40).
5. Scott, *A Time to Speak*, p. 245.
6. Ibid. p. 236.
7. Ibid. p. 239.
8. The Votes for All Conference was held on 22 May 1948. The text of Scott's address to the conference was published in *The Passive Resister*, 28 May 1948 (SP, Box 84).
9. Scott to Chief Luthuli, 22 June 1948. There is a handwritten copy of this letter among the Scott Papers (unnumbered box).
10. Scott, *A Time to Speak*, pp. 201–4.

11. Ritual murder is the main topic of 'Black Magic', chapter 12 in *A Time to Speak*, pp. 194–207. Scott also returned to the subject in an article, entitled 'A Plea to Parliament', for *Time and Tide*, 24 January 1959. The quote, 'whole affair is beyond me', is from *A Time to Speak* p. 203, as is the 'Good Samaritan' quote, p. 195.

12. Scott letter to the Archdeacon of Johannesburg, 5 August 1948 (SP, Box 71).

13. Esther Levitan, interview with Anne Yates, August 1999.

14. Rusty Bernstein, *Memory Against Forgetting* (London: Viking, 1999), p. 105.

15. Scott to Malan, 13 October 1948 (SP, Box 30).

16. Troup, *In Face of Fear*, pp. 188–91.

17. George Norton to Leon and Freda Levson, 26 November 1948 (SP, unnumbered box).

18. *Manchester Guardian*, 9 November 1948.

19. Mrs Pandit's response reported by Ruth First in *South West Africa* (Harmondsworth: Penguin, 1963), p. 183.

CHAPTER TWELVE

HOMECOMING

1. Scott described his connection with the Quaker 'musketeers' in his interview with Cyril Dunn, February 1975. Other sources among the Scott papers (in an unnumbered box) include Esther Muirhead's 'Notes on Michael Scott' prepared for Anne Yates in 1990; a long Muirhead letter to Yates, 2 October 1993; and an unpublished paper entitled, 'Memories of the Quaker International Centre at 32 Tavistock Square', written by Keith Irvine, the son of Fred and Dorothy Irvine, who were the wardens at the Centre during Scott's time there.

2. Keith Irvine, 'Memories of the Quaker International Centre', p. 4.

3. Agatha Harrison's support for Scott commented on in Muirhead's letter to Yates, 2 October 1993, and in Scott's interview with Dunn, February 1975.

4. Meeting with the Commonwealth Relations Minister referred to in Scott's pamphlet *Christianity Must Overcome Racialism*, May 1949, p. 2 (SP, Box 82).

5. Scott's letter to forty-one bishops seeking to 'rouse to conscience of Christendom', 19 February 1949 (SP, Box 22).

6. The disappointing response from South Africa is commented on in Scott's letter to the Christian Council of South Africa (CCSA), 20 February 1949 (SP, Box 22).

7. Clayton to Scott, 9 May 1949 (SP, Box 22).

8. Scott, *Christianity Must Overcome Racialism*, p. 3.

9. Scott, *A Time to Speak*, p. 247.

10. Newsletter headed: 'News of the Rev. Michael Scott, as contained in recent letters.' August 1949 (SP, Box 50).

11. Ambrose Reeve's letter withdrawing Scott's general licence to preach in South Africa, 19 October 1949 (SC, Box 71).

12. Scott, *A Time to Speak*, pp. 252–4.

13. Mexico delegate quoted in Stanley Burch's news dispatch to the *News Chronicle*, 29 November 1949. Delegates for Haiti and Belgium quoted in Burch's draft notes for feature article, November 1949 (SP, Box 91).

14. Stanley Burch's notes (SP, Box 91).

15. Scott's first UN speech referred to in *A Time to Speak*, pp 257–9. The full text was reproduced in a transcript of the 138th meeting of the Fourth Committee of the United Nations, 26 November 1949, made by the UN archives recording unit. There is a copy among the Scott Papers (Box 1).
16. Burch, *News Chronicle*, 29 November 1949.
17. Ibid.
18. Scott, interview with Dunn, July 1974.
19. Malan's statement reported in *The Times*, 29 November 1949.
20. Scott, interview with Dunn, February 1975.

CHAPTER THIRTEEN
CELEBRITY STATUS

1. Horace Alexander, article in *The Statesman*, 9 January 1950.
2. Scott, *A Time to Speak*, p. 298.
3. Ibid. p. 256.
4. Clayton's perception of Scott as 'a freelance' was reported in a letter to Scott from the Rev. G.C. Streatfield, director of the South African Church Institute, 10 October 1950 (SP, Box 71). The comment on Reeves's 'cold caution' is expressed in Sister Geraldine Mary's letter to Scott, 1 March 1951 (SP, Box 71). The indication that Reeves was subsequently 'sorry' is in Scott's interview with Dunn, July 1974.
5. The National Peace conference on racialism in Africa was held in London, 8–10 June 1950. This would inspire the creation of an autonomous African Relations Council which held its first meeting in August 1950.
6. *The Times*, 18 April 1950.
7. Guy Ramsey, *Daily Mail*, 18 April 1950.
8. Scott's enthusiasm for damming the Okavango river to irrigate the Kalahari desert is expressed in *A Time to Speak* pp. 216–18 and explained more fully in his essay, 'Britain's Responsibilities in Southern Africa', published in *Attitude to Africa* (London: Penguin Special, 1951), pp. 124–8.
9. National Archives: MI5 documents relating to Michael Scott, released in September 2005, in KV2/2052 and KV2/2053.
10. Fletcher's comment on Scott features in a 1952 letter to Freda Levson, of which part of the text survives (SP, unnumbered box). Esther Muirhead estimate of Scott as a 'holy man' is in her letter to Anne Yates, 2 October 1993.
11. Mary Benson, *A Far Cry* and her interview with Cyril Dunn, July 1974.
12. Principal sources on Canon John Collins: his autobiography, *Faith Under Fire* (London: Leslie Frewin, 1966); the account written by his wife, Diana, *Partners in Protest* (London: Victor Gollancz, 1992); and Denis Herbstein's book, *White Lies: Canon Collins and the Secret War Against Apartheid* (Oxford: James Currey, 2004).
13. Collins, *Faith Under Fire*, p. 181.
14. Ibid. pp. 181–2.
15. BBC (radio) Recording Services tape transcript, undated. Broadcast as part of a programme about Bloomsbury (SP, unnumbered box).
16. Richard Cockett, *David Astor and the Observer* (London: André Deutsch, 1991) provides the most authoritative source. Astor's problem with the superspy Kim Philby is recounted pp. 155–6. Other insights into Astor's character and methods

provided by ex-*Observer* employees, Peter Dunn, interviewed January 2005, and Roger Law, interviewed April 2005.

17. Astor to Patrick Gordon Walker, 7 July 1950 (SP, Box 15).
18. Scott to Benson, 1 April 1951 (SP, unnumbered box).
19. National Archives: Commonwealth Relations papers in class DO 35/3820, 16 January 1952.
20. Margery Perham to Scott, 20 November 1951 (SP, Box 40).
21. Refusal of passports to the chiefs described in Ruth First's *South West Africa*, pp. 187–8.
22. National Archives: Commonwealth Relations papers in class DO 35/3820, 22 January 1952.

CHAPTER FOURTEEN

EVICTION FROM AFRICA

1. Quoted in the magazine *Africa Today*, June 1963. Scott is described as having made the remark in a talk given at the *Catholic Worker* (SP, Box 66).
2. David Astor, interview, June 2001.
3. Scott commented on George Norton's 'great sense of humour' in his interview with Cyril Dunn, February 1975.
4. Report on the Africa Bureau 1952–1954, p. 7.
5. Scott, *A Time to Speak* , p. 270.
6. Scott et al. *Attitude to Africa*, pp. 11–12.
7. Quoted in a letter from Jane Kellock to Anne Yates, undated (SP, unnumbered box).
8. Scott, *A Time to Speak*, pp. 276–9.
9. Ibid. p. 281. Mary Benson's reservation about Scott's advocacy in Nyasaland in her interview with Cyril Dunn, July 1974.
10. *African Episode* by Michael Scott, originally published in *Nimbus*, a magazine of literature, the arts and new ideas, Vol 2: No. 2, Autumn 1953. Later reprinted as an Africa Bureau pamphlet (SP, Box 65). Also quoted in part in *A Time to Speak*, pp. 282–4.
11. The Minutes for the year 1953 are in the General Administration section of the Africa Bureau files (ref. Minutes, Box 1, file 2). These files are kept separately from the actual Scott Papers but housed in the same location.
12. Margery Perham to Scott, 30 June 1953 (SP, Box 40).
13. Africa Bureau files (ref. Minutes, Box 1, file 2).
14. National Archives: MI5 documents relating to Michael Scott, released in September 2005, in KV2/2053 and KV2/2055.
15. Lord Hudson's remarks at the United Nations reported in the *News Chronicle*, 27 October 1953.
16. Scott's press statement was issued on his behalf in New York by the International League for the Rights of Man (ILRM), 17 November 1953 (SP, Box 79).
17. Huggins to Scott, 13 January 1954 and 21 June 1954 (SP, Box 79).
18. Quoted in *The First Dance of Freedom* by Martin Meredith (London: Hamish Hamilton, 1984), p. 77.
19. Scott, *A Time to Speak*, pp. 289–93.

20. Neil Parsons, *Intelligence Reporting in Colonial Botswana 1895–1965* (University of Botswana History Department, 1999), p. 3.
21. Alan Seager, *The Shadow of a Great Rock*, an illuminating account of the Seretse Khama crisis from the perspective of an English missionary working in Bechuanaland at the time. Published privately in arrangement with ID Books, Flintshire, 2004.
22. Mary Benson, *Tshekedi Khama* (London: Faber, 1960), p. 231.
23. Meredith, *The First Dance of Freedom* p. 330.
24. Scott's article in the *Observer*, 9 March 1952. Reference to setting-up of African Development Trust in *A Time to Speak*, pp. 287–8.
25. African Protectorates Trust, *A Time to Speak*, p. 286. This developed into the Africa Educational Trust (AET), described in *A Search for Peace and Justice: Reflections of Michael Scott* edited by A. Paul Hare and Herbert H. Blumberg (London: Rex Collings, 1980), p. 100.
26. Scott, *A Search for Peace and Justice*, p. 104.
27. M.K. Gandhi, *The Story of My Experiments with Truth* (London: Penguin, 1982), p. 318.
28. Benson, *A Far Cry*, p. 88.
29. David Astor, interview, June 2001.

CHAPTER FIFTEEN

MAN ABOUT MANHATTAN

1. Scott, statement issued to the New York press, 1 October 1952 (SP, unnumbered box).
2. Ibid.
3. Linda Melvern, *The Ultimate Crime* (London: Allison and Busby, 1995), p. 75.
4. Stanley Burch to Cyril Dunn, 6 November 1974 (SP, Box 5c).
5. Scott to Mary Benson, 19 October 1952 (SP, Box 82).
6. Scott, interview with Dunn, July 1974.
7. Bill Johnston, interview with Anne Yates, January 1987 (SP, unnumbered box).
8. John Gunther, *Inside Africa* (New York: Harper, 1955), pp. 551–2. The Greta Garbo story was related by Colin Legum, interview, July 2001.
9. Scott, interview with Dunn, July 1974.
10. George M. Houser, *No One Can Stop the Rain* (New York: Pilgrim Press, 1989), p. 111.
11. Allard Lowenstein, *Brutal Mandate* (New York: Macmillan, 1962), p. 7.
12. *Time*, 14 April 1952; *Christian Century*, November 1950. Another profile of Scott, comparing him to Schweizer and Gandhi, was published in *Christian Century*, July 1952. The *World Christian Digest* wrote about Scott in a similar vein under the heading 'Brother to All Africans' in its issue of October 1952.
13. *Chicago Defender* to Scott, enclosing a certificate placing him on its Honour Roll of Democracy, May 1953 (SP, Box 37).
14. Scott paper, 'Free Africa, Apartheid and the Politics of Public Relations', 26 July 1968, pp. 8–9 (SP, Box 18).
15. Melvern, *The Ultimate Crime*, p. 55.
16. Jack Harris letter to Anne Yates, 23 November 1993. Further details about

Harris's role at the United Nations in Melvern, *The Ultimate Crime* pp. 51–5.

17. Harris to 'Pixie' Benson, 6 September 1953 (SP, Box 40).
18. Scott, *A Time to Speak*, p. 10.
19. Scott, interview with Dunn, July 1974.
20. Scott, interviews with Dunn, July 1974 and February 1975. Lauterpacht's legal advice also described in 'The Rise of Nationalism in Namibia and its International Dimensions', a D.Phil. thesis by Peter H. Katjavivi (St Antony's College, Oxford 1986) p. 175.
21. Mary Benson, extracts from her diary notes and letters, December 1954 (SP, Box 78).

CHAPTER SIXTEEN

'MADE FOR EACH OTHER'

1. Mary Benson, *A Far Cry*, pp. 58–9.
2. Ibid. p. 60.
3. Ibid. p. 61.
4. Ibid. p. 81.
5. Ibid. p. 63.
6. David Astor, interview, June 2001.
7. Benson, interview with Cyril Dunn, June 1974.
8. Benson, *A Far Cry*, p. 90.
9. Ibid. pp. 89–90.
10. Benson letter to P. Rasmussen, partially reproduced in extracts from her diary notes and letters, January 1954 (SP, Box 78).
11. Benson to Scott, 4 December 1955 (SP, unnumbered box).
12. Benson, *A Far Cry*, p. 89.
13. Benson, extracts from her diary notes and letters, January 1955 (SP, Box 78).
14. Ibid.
15. Ibid.
16. Benson, interview with Dunn, June 1974 and extracts from her diary notes and letters, March 1955 (SP, Box 78).
17. Benson to Scott, 1 April 1955 (SP, unnumbered box).

CHAPTER SEVENTEEN

CRISIS IN OXFORD

1. Parson's Pleasure described by David Horan in *Oxford* (Oxford: Signal Books, 2002), p. 112.
2. David Astor, interview, June 2001. Also his interview with Anne Yates, December 1992 (SP, unnumbered box). Documents concerning Astor's contacts with hospitals and an Oxford law firm on Scott's behalf are among the Scott Papers (Box 15).
3. Nigel Scott to Mary Benson, 29 July 1955; Benson to Nigel Scott, 31 July 1955; Nigel Scott to Benson, 4 August 1955 (SP, unnumbered box).
4. New York appeal 'To Friends of Michael Scott', June 1955 (SP, Box 30).
5. Mary Benson to Anne Yates, undated (SP, unnumbered box).

6. Benson, *A Far Cry*, pp. 213–18.
7. David Astor, interview, June 2001.
8. Mary Benson, interview with Cyril Dunn, June 1974.
9. Scott to Astor, 21 June 1983 (SP, Box 65).
10. Nigel Scott to Mary Benson, 4 August 1955 (SP, unnumbered box).
11. Esther Muirhead to Anne Yates, 2 October 1993 (SP, unnumbered box).
12. Scott, interview with Dunn, February 1975.

CHAPTER EIGHTEEN

CAMPAIGNING CLERICS

1. A church council in the Archdeaconry of Kota Kota would later, in 1961, formally petition for the appointment of Scott as a bishop on the grounds that 'his life does not differ with that of an African'. (SP, Box 83).
2. This version of 'Mau Mau Boogie' is from Lorna Richmond's collection of Scott's papers. However, other versions were current in white supremacist Africa at the time and later. Barbara Trapido in *Frankie and Stankie* (London: Bloomsbury, 2003), p. 238, recalls a variation on the same theme featuring in a freshers' song and rugger chorus at the University of Natal in the early 1960s. The last verse ran: 'Look, said Mama Muntu/ Look who we've shot/ We've shot the Reverend Michael Scott.'
3. Africa Bureau background sources: Jane Kellock, interview, July 2001, and Lorna Richmond, interviews, August 2003 and November 2004.
4. Scott, *A Search for Peace and Justice*, pp. 96–7.
5. Herbstein, *White Lies*, p. 53.
6. D. Collins, *Partners in Protest*, p. 184.
7. Herbstein, *White Lies*, p.54.
8. Ibid. p. 25.
9. Scott upstaged by Collins: in his interview with Cyril Dunn, February 1975, Scott maintained that he, not Collins, had the original idea of inviting Chief Hosea Kutako to preach at St Paul's Cathedral in 1952.
10. Africa Bureau and Christian Action at odds: over fund-raising, Herbstein, *White Lies*, p. 55; over Bantu Education appeal, Collins, *Faith Under Fire*, pp. 216–17; and over Tshekedi Khama, *White Lies*, p. 56.
11. Robin Denniston, *Trevor Huddleston: A Life* (London: Macmillan, 1999), p. 69. Also Collins letter to Scott, 8 March 1956 (SP, Box 63).
12. House of Lords meeting in Mary Benson's *Far Cry*, p. 88.
13. Huddleston on Scott in *Naught for Your Comfort*, p. 44. Scott on Huddleston, interview with Cyril Dunn, June 1974. David Astor's 'peace conference' designed to bring Scott, Huddleston and Collins closer together is described in Herbstein, *White Lies*, pp. 57–8.
14. Colin Legum, interview, July 2001.
15. Scott letter in *Manchester Guardian*, 12 November 1956. Astor's prominent role in the Suez Affair described in Richard Cockett's *David Astor and the Observer*, pp. 212–20.
16. Pakenham, *The Scramble for Africa*, p. 675.
17. Scott, *A Time to Speak*, p. 295.
18. Ibid. p. 303.

CHAPTER NINETEEN

'A TIME TO SPEAK'

1. American reviews of *A Time to Speak* in 1958: *St Louis Post Dispatch*, September, *New York Herald Tribune*, 9 November, *Progressive*, December.
2. Reviews of *A Time to Speak* by British writers in 1958: *Saturday Review*, 27 September; *New Statesman*, 18 October; *Daily Telegraph*, 24 October; *Oxford Times*, 24 October; *Tribune*, 14 November; *Times Literary Supplement*, 28 November.
3. Scott, interview with Cyril Dunn, June 1974.
4. Scott, *A Time to Speak*, pp. 271 and 275 Scott on Benson, p. 271 Scott on Astor.
5. Ibid. p.20.
6. *Socialist Commentary*, February 1959.
7. Roger N. Baldwin memo to Cyril Dunn, May 1975, and follow-up letter, 2 June 1975 (SP, Box 5C).
8. Ruth First, *South West Africa*, pp. 190–92.
9. Kerina's role in the scholarship fiasco described in Scott's interview with Dunn, February 1975.
10. Houser, *No One Can Stop the Rain*, p. 114.
11. Kutako to Scott, 16 November 1958 (SP, unnumbered box).
12. Old Location forced removals described in First, *South West Africa*, pp. 209–11.
13. Ibid. p. 215.
14. Ibid. p. 212.

CHAPTER TWENTY

DOING TIME IN ENGLAND

1. *Evening Standard*, 7 April 1958.
2. Reported in *The Times*, 9 April 1958.
3. David Astor, interview, April 2001.
4. James Cameron, *Point of Departure* (London: Panther, 1969), p. 292.
5. Pat Arrowsmith, *I Should Have Been a Hornby Train* (London: Heretic Books, 1995), p. 20. The youthful composition of the Direct Action Committee is described in Christopher Driver's *The Disarmers: A Study in Protest* (London: Hodder and Stoughton, 1964), pp. 49–50. Scott on his role in the ban the bomb campaign, *A Search for Peace and Justice*, pp. 186–204.
6. Jane Symonds, letter to Anne Yates, undated (SP, unnumbered box).
7. Michael Randle, interview, January 2005. Also interviewed by Anne Yates, November 1991 (SP, unnumbered box).
8. *Sunday Dispatch*, *People* and *Observer* of 21 December 1958.
9. Scott's arrest reported in the *News Chronicle*, 9 January 1959.
10. Driver, *The Disarmers*, p. 108.
11. Scott's anti-nuclear campaign in Africa is detailed in 'The Sahara Protest Team', an article by April Carter published in *Liberation without Violence: A Third Party Approach* edited by A. Paul Hare and Herbert H. Blumberg (London: Rex Collings, 1977), pp. 126–56. Additional sources: interviews with April Carter and Michael Randle, January 2005. The Sahara Project Fact Sheet is among the Scott

Papers (unnumbered box).

12. Bill Sutherland, memorial paper 'I Remember Michael' (SP, Box 15).

13. Scott to Astor, 18 December 1959 (SP, Box 15).

14. *Drum* magazine, March 1960. On the general impact of the Sahara protest, Carter, *Liberation without Violence*, pp. 143–6.

15. Cameron, *Point of Departure*, pp. 292–3.

16. Ibid. p. 293.

17. *The Autobiography of Bertrand Russell: 1944–1967*, Vol. III (London: Allen and Unwin, 1969), pp. 605–6.

18. *Evening Standard*, 28 September 1960.

19. *The Times*, 25 October 1960.

20. *Act or Perish: a call to non-violent action by Earl Russell and Rev. Michael Scott* issued by Committee of 100, Goodwin Street, London (SP, Box 8). Also reproduced in Hare and Blumberg (eds), *A Search for Peace and Justice*, pp 194–5, and *The Autobiography of Bertrand Russell*, pp. 632–4.

21. John Collins's 'some Iagos' quote appears in Caroline Moorhead's *Bertrand Russell* (London: Sinclair-Stevenson 1992), p. 507. His strictures on the Committee of 100 in Collins, *Faith Under Fire*, p. 334.

22. Driver, *The Disarmers*, p. 218.

23. Ibid. p. 118.

24. Scott's essay 'Civil Disobedience and Morals' published in *Bertrand Russell: Philosopher of the Century* edited by Ralph Shoenman (London: Allen and Unwin 1967), pp. 63–6. Scott's poor opinion of Schoenman in *A Search for Peace and Justice*, pp. 212 and 215.

25. Driver, *The Disarmers*, p. 120 and the *Observer*, 16 April 1961.

26. Jane Symonds to Harold Macmillan, 15 September 1961 (SP, unnumbered box).

27. Scott's essay 'Pacifism is not enough' in *20th Century* (London) Spring issue, 1964, p. 146.

28. Michael Randle would later become famous for helping the double agent George Blake to make a successful escape from Wormwood Scrubs. He was assisted by Pat Pottle, another Committee of 100 activist. In 1991 both men were prosecuted at the Old Bailey. In a show trial atmosphere, Randle presented a 'defence of necessity', arguing that it was sometimes right to disobey the letter of the law for a greater good, and alleged that Blake's unprecedented forty-two-year sentence was a violation of the 1688 Bill of Rights which forbade 'cruel and inhuman' punishment. The main facts in the case were not in dispute, but both Randle and Pottle were acquitted. The jury's verdict, according to the *Guardian* report on the trial, qualified as 'the most contrary in modern English history'.

CHAPTER TWENTY-ONE

GUNNING FOR THE CANON

1. D. Collins, *Partners in Protest*, p. 285.

2. Farfield Foundation documents are among the Africa Bureau Papers in Rhodes House, Box 56, file 4. Other sources: interview with Mrs Jane Kellock, formerly Jane Symonds, July 2001, and Francis Stonor Saunders book, *Who Paid the Piper? The CIA and the Cultural Cold War* (London: Granta Books, 1999), p. 426.

3. David Astor to John Collins, 28 May 1960 (SP, unnumbered box). Further information on the attempt to bring Scott and Collins together in Herbstein, *White Lies*, pp. 57–60. Christian Action's cash flow in Collins, *Faith Under Fire*, p. 234.

4. D. Collins, *Partners in Protest*, pp. 283–4.

5. Jane Symonds to Scott, 23 November 1961 (SP, Box 40).

6. Mandela, *Long Walk to Freedom*, p. 268.

7. D. Collins, *Partners in Protest*, p. 247.

8. Ibid. p. 284.

9. John Collins's clash with David Astor in Herbstein, *White Lies*, p. 65. Collins's thoughts of giving up fund-raising for Southern African causes in D. Collins, *Partners in Protest*, p. 284.

10. D. Collins, *Partners in Protest*, p. 284.

11. John Collins letter to Sir Kenneth Grubb quoted in Herbstein, *White Lies*, p. 66. Scott to Frank Pakenham, 24 December 1961 (SP, unnumbered box).

12. Astor on Collins in Herbstein, *White Lies*, p. 66.

13. Scott article, 'How We Might Lead – A Fair Hearing for Minorities' in the *Observer*, 30 October 1960. Formation of the Minority Rights Group described in *David Astor and the Observer*, p. 205.

TWENTY-TWO

POSITIVE RESISTANCE

1. Text of speech delivered by Scott to the Mouvement Chrétien Pour La Paix at the Chateau de Boissy, 17 August 1957 (SP, Box 5).

2. World Peace Brigade background: Charles C. Walker article, 'Nonviolence in Eastern Africa 1962–4: The World Peace Brigade and Zambian Independence' in Hare and Blumberg (eds.) *Liberation without Violence*, pp. 157–77; Barbara Denning article, entitled 'International Peace Brigade' in *The Nation*, 7 April 1962; Aubrey Hodes, *Encounter with Martin Buber* (London: Penguin, 1971), pp. 72–3; and Joan Wicken interview with Anne Yates, June 1993.

3. Scott, interview with Cyril Dunn, March 1974.

4. Richard Kish, *The Private Life of Public Relations* (London: MacGibbon and Kee, 1964), pp. 63–4.

5. John Hatch, *Two African Statesmen: Kaunda of Zambia and Nyerere of Tanzania* (London: Secker and Warburg, 1976), p. 165.

6. Anthony Sampson, *Mandela* (London: HarperCollins, 1999) p. 164.

7. Letter from Scott to Bayard Rustin in London, 8 April 1962, quoted in Walker, *Liberation without Violence*, p. 166. Rustin had visited London briefly in an effort to stiffen the morale of Africa Bureau executive, which was split on the merits of Scott's involvement in another civil disobedience campaign.

8. Kaunda to Scott, 2 May 1962, quoted in Walker, *Liberation without Violence*, p. 166.

9. Walker, *Liberation without Violence*, p. 175.

10. Ibid. pp. 174–5.

11. Scott to Hemingford, 27 June 1962 (SP, Box 68).

CHAPTER TWENTY-THREE

INDUSTRIAL WARFARE

1. David Astor, interview, April 2001.
2. Scott, interview with Cyril Dunn, February 1975.
3. 'One of the Great Gadflies', obituary article on W.H. 'Ping' Ferry in *The Nonviolent Activist*, Jan–Feb 1996 (SP, unnumbered box).
4. Clarence B. Randall, address entitled 'Winds out of Africa', 3 April 1963 (SP, Box 66).
5. Colin Legum memo to Astor, 14 March 1964; Peter Calvocoressi letter to Scott, 3 March 1964 (SP, both Box 66).
6. Sir Ronald Prain to Sir Jock Campbell, 20 February 1964 (SP, Box 66).
7. Campbell's original remarks about Oppenheimer which Scott found upsetting were made in November 1962 as part of his address to Africa Bureau members entitled, 'The New Africa – Pride and Prejudice: Sense and Sensibility'. The 'Oppenheimer Thesis' and the role of the South African Foundation are discussed in Anthony Sampson's *Black and Gold: Tycoons, Revolutionaries and Apartheid* (London: Hodder and Stoughton, 1987), pp. 90–6.
8. Scott statement to the UN Fourth Committee, 8 November 1963, calling for a Commission of Inquiry into the mining industry and into the circumstances surrounding Dag Hammarskjold's death (SP, unnumbered box).
9. Sampson, *Black and Gold*, p. 89.
10. Scott, interview with Dunn, February 1975. Ruth First also describes what she calls 'the Carpio fiasco' in *South West Africa*, pp. 221–3 and 240.
11. Bill Sutherland, memorial paper 'I Remember Michael' (SP, Box 15).

TWENTY-FOUR

AN INDIAN EVICTION

1. Scott's first impressions of Nagaland in his typewritten account of his adventures written in Shillong, 1966, pp. 6–7 (SP, Box 5). Similar versions also feature in Hare and Bloomberg (eds) *A Search for Peace and Justice*, pp. 157–8 and in Scott's pamphlet *The Nagas: India's Problem or the World's? The Search for Peace* (London: 1966).
2. M. Aram, *Peace in Nagaland* (New Delhi: Arnold Heinemann, 1974), pp. 308.
3. Ibid., pp. 83–4.
4. Ibid., pp. 20–21 and 49–50.
5. Scott, *A Search for Peace and Justice*, p. 153.
6. Jane Kellock, interview, July 2001 and Scott's impression of Phizo in his typewritten account, p.2 (SP, Box 5).
7. Gavin Young, his series of articles in the *Observer* appeared on 30 April, 7 May and 14 May 1961 under the headings: 'An Unknown War', 'Jungle Baptists fight it out with India' and 'Charges of Atrocity on Nehru's Doorstep'.
8. *Observer*, 25 August 1963.
9. *The India News*, 13 August 1960. Scott's understanding with Nehru in *A Search for Peace and Justice*, p. 154.
10. Scott, *A Search for Peace and Justice*, p. 152.

11. Y.D. Gundevia, *War and Peace in Nagaland* (New Delhi: Palit and Palit, 1975), p. 113.
12. Scott's hospital avoidance advice in his typewritten account, p. 15 (SP, Box 5).
13. Gundevia, *War and Peace in Nagaland*, p. 163; terms of ceasefire, pp. 116–17.
14. Scott to Shastri, 3 July 1964 (SP, Box 72).
15. Gundevia, *War and Peace in Nagaland*, p. 121. Scott on Gundevia: his typewritten account, p. 18 (Box 5).
16. Aram, *Peace in Nagaland*, pp. 51–2.
17. Ibid. p. 38.
18. Gundevia criticisms of Scott in *War and Peace in Nagaland*, pp 79, 103, 137, 142–143, and 179.
19. Scott to Astor, May 1965 (SP, unnumbered box contains an abridged version of this letter).
20. Scott to U Thant, 26 October 1965 (SP, Box 28). Criticism of Scott for trying to 'internationalize' the Naga issue, Gundevia, *War and Peace in Nagaland*, pp. 178–80.
21. *Observer*, 20 February 1966. Source on the deputation to Mrs Gandhi, Aram, *Peace in Nagaland*, p. 92.
22. Gundevia, p. 174 and Aram, pp. 102–3 on criticisms of the Indian government.
23. *Observer*, 8 May 1966 and Aram, p. 112.
24. Gundevia, *War and Peace in Nagaland*, p. 104.
25. Aram, *Peace in Nagaland*, pp. 113, 67 and 315.

CHAPTER TWENTY-FIVE

LOSING TOUCH

1. Colin Legum, *The United Nations and Southern Africa*, published by the Institute for the Study of International Organization, University of Sussex, Brighton, 1970 (ISIO Monographs, First series, no. 3).
2. Pat Arrowsmith, interview, January 2005.
3. Pat Arrowsmith, *To Asia in Peace* (London: Sidgwick and Jackson, 1972), pp. 44 and 79.
4. Scott, *A Search for Peace and Justice*, pp. 163–4.
5. *Ramparts* magazine, April 1967. For impact of the magazine's disclosures about CIA covert funding Frances Stonor Saunders, *Who Paid the Piper?* p. 382.
6. Scott paper on 'The UN, NGOs and Southern Africa' submitted to the UN Special Committee on Apartheid, June 1968, pp. 6–7 (SP, Box 18). The alternative publication which picked up on the CIA/Farfield/Africa Bureau link was *People's News Service*, London, in its issue of 10 April 1978 (SP, Box 79).
7. Scott's correspondence with UN officials about the CIA summarized in his paper, 'Free Africa, Apartheid and the Politics of Public Relations', 26 July 1968, p. 7 (SP, Box 18). His 'CIA wheel' was submitted to the Secretariat's Special Political and Trusteeship Division (SP, Box 9).
8. Enuga Reddy, interviewed by e-mail, December 2004.
9. Rita Hinden to Scott, 29 March 1968 (SP, Box 68).
10. Scott to Campbell, 24 June 1967 (SP, Box 66).
11. Peter Calvocoressi emphasized the dovetailing of Scott's and Arnold's talents in his chairman's address to the Africa Bureau executive, 11 November 1968.

CHAPTER TWENTY-SIX

SCOTT VERSUS THE AFRICA BUREAU

1. Guy Arnold, interview, January 2005 and Ethel de Keyser, interview, January 2001.
2. Kenneth Kaunda to Scott, 22 January 1969 (SP, Box 39).
3. Scott paper, 'Alternative to Apartheid – Alternative to War?', Mindolo, January 1969 (SP, Box 39).
4. Mindolo paper, 'Proposal for Southern African Consultations', April 1969 (SP, Box 81).
5. Arnold to Scott, 26 February 1969 (SP, unnumbered box).
6. Lusaka Manifesto described by John Hatch in *Two African Statesmen*, p. 255. Its impact on the ANC described by Enuga Reddy, interview, December 2004.
7. Arnold to Scott, 11 September 1969 (SP, Box 68).
8. *Dear Mr Vorster... details of exchanges between President Kaunda of Zambia and Prime Minister Vorster of South Africa*, pamphlet published by Zambia Information Services, 1971 (SP, Box 13). Also Hatch, *Two African Statesmen*, p. 255.
9. Wilfrid Grenville-Grey, interview, August 2003.
10. Scott's Mindolo regrets recounted in his paper, 'Aid to Africa', 24 June 1979 (SP, Box 79). Also his interview with Cyril Dunn, February 1975.
11. Peter H. Katjavivi, D.Phil. thesis 'The Rise of Nationalism in Namibia and its International Dimensions', pp. 387–9.
12. Reddy, interview, December 2004.
13. Scott presented the bust of Herero Chief Hosea Kutako, sculpted by F.E. McWilliam, R.A., to the UN's Fourth Committee in 1962. McWilliam's work on the commission was described in the *Observer*, 30 July 1961.
14. Scott to chairman of the UN Fourth Committee, 11 October 1970 (SP, Box 2).
15. Open letter to the UN Fourth Committee criticizing Scott's role, 2 November 1970 (SP, Box 2).
16. Chief Clemens Kapuuo to chairman of UN Fourth Committee supporting Scott, 30 November 1970 (SP, Box 2).
17. Lorna Richmond, interviews August 2003 and November 2004. Her memoir, composed at the request of Anne Yates, was written in October 1987.

CHAPTER TWENTY-SEVEN

A SUSPICIOUS NATURE

1. *Observer*, 31 July 1977.
2. Guy Arnold to Scott, 3 June 1971 (SP, Box 39).
3. Pat Herbert to Kenneth Kirkwood, 15 August 1973 (SP, unnumbered box).
4. Problems over the Africa Bureau minutes featured in Scott's letter to Sir Bernard de Bunsen, 24 December 1971, and in de Bunsen's letter back to Scott, 29 December 1971 (SP, both Box 51).
5. Scott and Fazlul Huq, *Traffic in Charity, Britain Bangladesh* (London: Mandate Trust, 1976). The Bangladesh Fund also features in Hare and Blumberg (eds), *A Search for Peace and Justice*, pp. 229–30. Letters from Jo Grimond to Scott

expressing disquiet about his campaign, 1 August 1974 and 13 October 1976 (SP, both Box 27). The 'swindler' reference by Trevor Huddleston was made in an interview with Anne Yates, February 1987.

6. Scott paper, 'A World Problem Needs a World Strategy', 1976. Originally composed as a private memorandum for David Astor but later distributed more generally (SP, Box 81).

7. Scott to Astor, 10 April 1972 (SP, Box 81).

8. Lord Caradon broke news of the Foreign Office's lack of enthusiasm for the proposed visit to Idi Amin in a letter to Scott, 9 September 1972 (SP, Box 56). Scott's disappointment was later expressed in a letter to Colin Legum, 7 June 1974 (SP, unnumbered box).

CHAPTER TWENTY-EIGHT

MAVERICK STATUS

1. Susan Dowell, interview with Anne Yates, November 1999.

2. Scott correspondence with Carol and W.H. 'Ping' Ferry (SP, Box 79 and some letters in unnumbered boxes).

3. Denis Herbstein, *Sunday Times* , 18 April 1971, article posing the question: 'South Africa: Do British companies set a good example or just collect the profits?'; Suzanne Cronje, *New Statesman*, 30 March 1973. Letter to Scott from W.H. Ferry with postscript by Carol Ferry, 9 July 1973 (SP, unnumbered box).

4. Scott paper, 'Aid to Africa', 24 June 1979, laments the inadequacies of the Study Project (SP, Box 79).

5. Scott paper, 20 July 1979 (SP, unnumbered box).

6. Scott in Hare and Bloomberg (eds) *A Search for Peace and Justice*, on the Mandate Trust and its initiatives, pp. 101–2, 109–10, 173–85.

7. Jo Morris, interview with Margaret Lipscomb, August 2000. Also interviewed February 2005.

8. Richard Kershaw, interview with Anne Yates, undated.

CHAPTER TWENTY-NINE

A PLACE FOR PARANOIA

1. Peter Dunn, Cyril Dunn's son, who worked with his father as a journalist on the *Observer* before moving to the *Sunday Times*. Interview, January 2005.

2. While working on the Scott biography Cyril Dunn corresponded regularly with Jack Woolley, a family friend who worked as a schoolmaster in Wimborne, Dorset. Known in the family as 'the Wimborne Letters', these convey the contemporary highs and lows of Dunn's association with Scott. This chapter features quotations from these letters dated 8 July, 10 October and 14 November 1974 and 26 February and 14 October 1975.
Other correspondence referred to includes:
Dunn to Astor, 4 March 1975 (SP, Box 78)
Dunn to Scott, 18 October 1976 (SP, Box 78)

Dunn to Scott, proposing 'The Losing Battle' as a title, 20 January 1977 (SP, Box 78)
Scott to Dunn, commenting on this proposal, 27 January 1977 (SP, Box 78)
Dunn to Scott, 11 February 1977 (SP, Box 78)
Dunn's letter commenting on Scott's 'sheer uniqueness' was written to Anne Yates, 8 February 1985 (SP, unnumbered box).
3. Scott to David Astor, 20 December 1982 (SP, unnumbered box).
4. Herbstein, *White Lies*, pp. 217–19.

CHAPTER THIRTY

MOVING MOUNTAINS

1. David Astor, interview, April 2001.
2. Nelson Mandela, *Long Walk to Freedom*, p. 121.
3. Scott's theological article 'No Faith Without Doubt' in Spring 1981 issue of *The Seeker*, magazine of the Seekers Association, a Quaker group. His article, 'Apartheid in the Developing World – Need for a Reappraisal' appeared in *The Chronicle*, publication of the Dag Hammarskjold Information Centre on the Study of Violence and Peace, Vol. 2. No. 1, May 1981.
4. Scott to Kings Patent Agency, London EC4, 10 September 1975; Kings Patent Agency to Scott, 9 October 1975 (Lorna Richmond collection).
5. Scott to Alan Dobson, 21 May 1981 (SP, Box 53).
6. Scott to Sue MacGregor, 15 September 1982; letter from BBC *Woman's Hour* correspondence section turning down Scott's programme idea, 8 November 1982 (Both SP, Box 53).
7. Scott to Greenham women, 1 June 1983 (SP, Box 9).
8. Scott to Astor, 21 June 1983 (SP, Box 65).
9. Astor, interview, June 2001.
10. Trevor Huddleston, memorial service address, St Martin-in-the-Fields, 17 November 1983 (SP, Box 9); George Houser letter to Lorna Richmond, 19 September 1983 (Lorna Richmond collection); Bruce Kent letter to Lorna Richmond, undated (SP, Box 9).
11. The legacy of von Trotha's massacre of the Hereros still remains unresolved despite Germany's emergence since independence as Namibia's biggest donor country providing aid for a number of development projects. In 2005 the German government announced a reparation fund of 20 million Euros after expressing 'regret' for the killings. This was deemed inadequate by Herero leaders, who claimed that a more appropriate compensation figure would be in the region of 4 billion dollars.

BIBLIOGRAPHY

Abel, Elie, *The Missile Crisis*, Lippincott, Phildelphia, 1966
Aram, M., *Peace in Nagaland*, Arnold Heinemann, New Delhi, 1974
Arrowsmith, Pat, *To Asia in Peace*, Sidgwick and Jackson, London, 1972
—— *I Should Have Been a Hornby Train*, Heretic Books, London, 1995
Bailey, Martin, *Oilgate: The Sanctions Scandal*, Coronet, London, 1979
Behr, Edward, *The Algerian Problem*, Penguin, Harmondsworth, 1961
Benson, Mary, *Tshekedi Khama*, Faber, London, 1960
—— *The African Patriots: The Story of the African National Congress of South Africa*, Faber, London, 1963
—— *Chief Albert Luthuli of South Africa*, Oxford University Press, 1963
—— *South Africa: The Struggle for a Birthright*, Penguin, Harmondsworth, 1966
—— *Nelson Mandela: The Man and the Movement*, Penguin, London, 1986
—— *A Far Cry: The Making of a South African*, Penguin, London, 1989
Bernstein, Rusty, *Memory Against Forgetting*, Viking, London, 1999
Biko, Steve, *I Write What I Like*, Picador Africa, Johannesburg, 2004
Bingham, T.H. and S.M. Gray, *Report on the Supply of Petroleum and Petroleum Products to Rhodesia*, HMSO (Foreign and Commonwealth Office), London, 1978
Bower, Ursula Graham, *Naga Path*, Murray, London, 1950
—— *The Hidden Land*, John Murray, London, 1953
Bowra, C.M., *Memories*, Harvard University Press, 1967
Bridgman, Jon M., *The Revolt of the Hereros*, University of California Press, 1981
Cameron, James, *Point of Departure*, Panther, London, 1969
Carritt, Michael, *A Mole in the Crown*, privately published, distributed by Central Books, London, 1985
Chater, Patricia, *Grass Roots*, Hodder and Stoughton, London, 1962
Chester, Lewis, *Martin Luther King*, Heron Books, London, 1971
Clark, Ronald W., *The Life of Bertrand Russell*, Jonathan Cape, London, 1975
Clutton-Brock, Guy and Molly, *Cold Comfort Confronted*, Mowbray, Oxford, 1972
Cockett, Richard, *David Astor and the Observer*, Andre Deutsch, London, 1991
Collins, Diana, *Partners in Protest: Life with Canon Collins*, Gollancz, London, 1992
Collins, John, *Faith Under Fire*, Frewin, London, 1966
Creech Jones, Arthur, *Africa Challenge: The Fallacy of Federation*, Africa Bureau, 1952
Cronjé, Suzanne (with Margaret Ling and Gillian Cronjé), *Lonrho: Portrait of a Multinational*, Friedmann, London, 1976
Crossman, Richard (ed.), *The God that Failed*, Harper and Row, New York, 1950
Davenport, T.R.H., *South Africa: A Modern History*, Macmillan South Africa, Johannesburg, 1977
Deenadayalan, E. (ed.), *Naga Resistance and the Peace Process*, Other Media Communications, New Delhi, 2001
Denniston, Robin, *Trevor Huddleston: A Life*, Macmillan, London, 1999

Driver, Christopher, *The Disarmers: A Study in Protest*, Hodder and Stoughton, London, 1964

—— *Patrick Duncan: South African and Pan African*, Heinemann, London, 1980

Dunn, Cyril, *Central African Witness*, Gollancz, London, 1959

Fanon, Frantz, *Black Skin White Masks*, Grove Press, New York, 1967

—— *Toward the African Revolution*, Grove Press, New York, 1967

Ferry, Wilbur H., *What Price Peace*, Centre for the Study of Democratic Institutions, Santa Barbara, California, 1963

First, Ruth, *South West Africa*, Penguin, Harmondsworth, 1963

—— (with Jonathan Steele and Christobel Gurney), *The South African Connection: Western Investment in Apartheid*, Temple Smith, London, 1972

Fischer, Louis, *The Life of Mahatma Gandhi*, Jonathan Cape, London, 1951

Forsyth, Frederick, *The Biafra Story*, Penguin, Harmondsworth, 1969

Fürer-Haimendorf, Christoph von, *Return to the Naked Nagas*, Murray, London, 1976

Gandhi, M.K., *The Story of My Experiments with Truth*, Penguin, London, 1982

Gundevia, Y.D., *War and Peace in Nagaland*, Palit and Palit, New Delhi, 1975

Gunther, John, *Inside Africa*, Harper Bros, New York, 1955

Hailey, Lord, *The Republic of South Africa and the High Commission Territories*, Oxford University Press, 1963

Hare, A. Paul and Herbert H. Blumberg (eds.), *Liberation without Violence: A Third Party Approach*, Rex Collings, London, 1977

—— *A Search for Peace and Justice: Reflections of Michael Scott*, Rex Collings, London, 1980

Harvey, Rosemary and others, *The Great White Hoax: South Africa's International Propaganda Machine*, Africa Bureau, London, 1977

Hastings, Adrian, *The Church in Africa 1450–1950*, Clarendon Press, Oxford, 1954

—— *A History of African Christianity 1950–1975*, Cambridge University Press, 1979

Hatch, John, *Two African Statesmen: Kaunda of Zambia and Nyerere of Tanzania*, Secker and Warburg, London, 1976

Hazzard, Shirley, *Defeat of an Ideal: A Study of the Self-destruction of the United Nations*, Macmillan, London, 1973

—— *Countenance of Truth: The United Nations and the Waldheim Case*, New York, Viking, 1992

Henderson, I. (ed.), *Man of Christian Action, Canon John Collins: The Man and His Work*, Lutterworth Press, Cambridge, 1976

Herbstein, Denis, *White Lies: Canon Collins and the Secret War against Apartheid*, Currey, Oxford, 2004

Herbstein, Denis and John Evenson, *The Devils are Among Us*, Zed Books, London, 1989

Hodes, Aubrey, *Encounter with Martin Buber*, Penguin, Harmondsworth, 1971

Hofstadter, Richard, *The Paranoid Style in American Politics and Other Essays*, Knopf, New York, 1965

Horan, David, *Oxford*, Signal Books, Oxford, 2002

Houser, George M., *No One Can Stop the Rain*, Pilgrim Press, New York, 1989

Huddleston, Trevor, *Naught for Your Comfort*, William Collins, Glasgow, 1956

Irvine, Keith, *The Rise of the Coloured Races*, Allen and Unwin, London, 1972

Johnson, Richard W., *How Long Will South Africa Survive*, Macmillan, London, 1977

Kabaka of Buganda, *Desecration of My Kingdom*, Constable, London, 1967

Katjavivi, Peter, *A History of Resistance in Namibia*, Currey, Oxford, 2004

Kaunda, Kenneth and Colin Morris, *Black Government?*, United Society for Christian Literature, Lusaka, 1960

Kish, Richard, *The Private Life of Public Relations*, MacGibbon and Kee, London, 1964

Knightley, Phillip, *The First Casualty*, Harcourt Brace, New York, 1975

—— *The Second Oldest Profession*, André Deutsch, London, 1986

Lazar, Leonard, *Namibia*, Mandate Trust, London, 1972

Legum, Colin, *Must We Lose Africa*, W.H. Allen, London, 1954

—— *Pan-Africanism: A Short Political Guide*, Praeger, New York, 1962

—— *Africa Since Independence*, Indiana University Press, 1999

Lewis, David L., *Martin Luther King*, Praeger, New York, 1970

Lodge, Tom, *Black Politics in South Africa since 1945*, Ravan Press, Johannesburg, 1983

Lowenstein, Allard, *Brutal Mandate*, Macmillan, New York, 1962

Luthuli, Albert, *Let My People Go*, Collins, London, 1962

Mandela, Nelson, *Long Walk to Freedom*, Abacus, London, 1995

Martin, David, *General Amin*, Faber, London, 1974

Meli, Francis, *South Africa Belongs to Us: A History of the ANC*, Zimbabwe Publishing House, Harare, 1988

Melvern, Linda, *The Ultimate Crime*, Allison and Busby, London, 1995

Meredith, Martin, *The First Dance of Freedom*, Hamish Hamilton, London, 1984

Monsarrat, Nicholas, *Life Is a Four Letter Word*, vol. II, *Breaking Out*, Cassell, London, 1970

Moorhead, Caroline, *Bertrand Russell*, Sinclair-Stevenson, London, 1992

Mumford, Lewis, *The Culture of Cities*, Harcourt Brace, 1938

Nujoma, Sam, *Where Others Wavered: the Autobiography of Sam Nujoma*, Panaf Books, London, 2001

Pakenham, Thomas, *The Scramble for Africa*, Abacus, London, 1992

Paton, Alan, *Cry, The Beloved Country*, Charles Scribner, New York, 1948

—— *The Long View*, Pall Mall Press, London, 1968

—— *Apartheid and the Archbishop: The Life and Times of Geoffrey Clayton*, Jonathan Cape, London, 1974

—— *Journey Continued*, Oxford University Press, 1989

Peart-Binns, John S., *Ambrose Reeves*, Gollancz, London, 1973

Perham, Margery, *Africans and British Rule*, Oxford University Press, 1941

Post, Ken, *The New States of West Africa*, Penguin, Harmondsworth, 1964

Reeves, Ambrose, *South Africa Yesterday and Tomorrow: A Challenge to Christians*, Gollancz, 1962

Rosie, George, *The Directory of International Terrorism*, Mainstream Publishing, Edinburgh, 1986

Russell, Bertrand, *The Autobiography of Bertrand Russell: 1944–1967*, vol. III, Allen and Unwin, London, 1969

Sampson, Anthony, *The Money-Lenders*, Hodder and Stoughton, London, 1981

—— *Black and Gold: Tycoons, Revolutionaries and Apartheid*, Hodder and Stoughton, London, 1987

—— *Mandela: The Authorised Biography*, Harper Collins, London, 1999

Saunders, Frances Stonor, *Who Paid the Piper? The CIA and the Cultural Cold War*, Granta Books, London, 1999

Schoenman, Ralph (ed.), *Bertrand Russell: Philosopher of the Century*, Allen and Unwin, London, 1967

Schumacher, Ernst F., *Economic Development and Poverty*, Africa Bureau, London, 1966
—— *Small is Beautiful: Economics as if People Mattered*, Blond and Brigg, London, 1973
Scott, Michael, *Shadow Over Africa*, Union of Democratic Control, London, 1950
—— (with Arthur Lewis, Martin Wight and Colin Legum), *Attitude to Africa*, Penguin, Harmondsworth, 1951
—— *A Time to Speak*, Faber, London, 1958
—— (with Fazlul Huq) *Traffic in Charity: Britain Bangladesh*, Mandate Trust, London, 1976
Seager, Alan, *The Shadow of a Great Rock*, ID Books, Flintshire, 2004
Segal, Ronald, *African Profiles*, Penguin, Harmondsworth, 1962
—— (ed. with Ruth First), *South West Africa: Travesty of Trust*, André Deutsch, London, 1967
Smith, William Edgett, *Nyerere of Tanzania*, Zimbabwe Publishing House, Harare, 1981
Sykes, Christopher, *Nancy: The Life of Lady Astor*, Collins, London, 1972
Thayer, George, *The British Political Fringe*, Blond, London, 1965
Thomas, Hugh, *The Suez Affair*, Weidenfeld and Nicolson, London, 1966
Trapido, Barbara, *Frankie and Stankie*, Bloomsbury, London, 2003
Troup, Freda Levson, *In Face of Fear*, Faber, London, 1952
—— *South Africa: A Historical Introduction*, Eyre Methuen, London, 1972
Urquhart, Brian, *Hammarskjold*, Bodley Head, London, 1972
—— *A Life in Peace and War*, Weidenfeld and Nicolson, London, 1987
—— *Ralph Bunche: An American Life*, Norton, New York, 1993
Verrier, Elwin, *The Nagas in the 19th Century*, Oxford University Press, 1969
Welsh, Frank, *A History of South Africa*, Harper Collins, London, 1998
West, Nigel, *MI5*, Triad/Panther, London, 1983
—— *Mask*, Routledge, London, 2005
Wheatcroft, Geoffrey, *The Randlords*, Athenaeum, London, 1985
Wilson, Monica and Leonard Thompson (eds), *The Oxford History of South Africa*, vol. I, Clarendon, Oxford, 1969; vol. II, 1971
Winter, Gordon, *Inside BOSS: South Africa's Secret Police*, Penguin, Harmondsworth, 1981
Worsnip, Michael E., *Between the Two Fires: The Anglican Church and Apartheid*, University of Natal Press, 1991

INDEX

Ablorh, S.C. 203
Africa Bureau 131, 139, 157, 158, 177–8,
    184, 214–16, 217, 220, 235, 239–40,
    255, 261–2, 278–9, 297
    and MS 127–30, 133, 140–1, 142–4, 148,
    197–8, 216, 258–60, 263–74, 269–70
Africa Educational Trust 279–80, 298
African Development Trust 142–3
African National Congress (ANC) 58,
    92, 138, 139, 172, 221, 229, 240
African Protectorates Trust 143
African Relations Council 115
Akita, B.M. 203
American Committee on Africa
    (ACOA) 151, 170, 190, 237
Amin, Idi 142, 283
Andrews, Charles 29
Angoni tribe 132
Ao, Longri 243
Aram, Dr M. 249, 251, 254
Arinze, H. 203
Arkhurst, K.M. 203
Arnold, Guy 263, 265–8, 269–70, 278,
    280
Arrowsmith, Pat 200, 256, 257
Astor, Bridget 169
Astor, David 130, 136, 142, 144, 157, 161,
    162, 215, 216–17, 219, 221–2, 244, 292
    and MS 1, 2, 3, 121–3, 127, 129, 166–8,
    177, 189, 232, 252, 284, 306
Astor, Waldorf 122
Attitude to Africa (Astor) 130
Attlee, Clement 100–1
Attlee, Mary 128
Auden, John 28

Baille, John 128
Baldwin, Roger 105, 150, 151, 152, 190–1
Bamangwato tribe 78, 141
Banda, Hastings 135, 283
Bangladesh 280–1
Barker, Anthony 79, 299, 306
Barker, Margaret 79, 299, 306
Basutoland 92–4
Bechuanaland 78–9, 80, 123
Becklake, Margaret 59
Bell, George 33, 103, 114, 160, 161
Bengal Flying Club 28–9

Benson, Mary 126, 128, 131–2, 136, 142,
    143, 144, 154
    and MS 118–20, 156, 157–64, 169–72,
    176, 189
Berg Damara tribe 89
Berkeley, Humphry 261
Bernstein, Carol 278, 285
Bernstein, Daniel 149, 233, 278–9
Bernstein, Rusty 95
Bethal (Eastern Transvaal) 70–2
Bhave, Vinoba 226
Blaxall, Arthur 60
Blumberg, Herbert 297
Bolt, Robert 207
Bonham Carter, Lady Violet 184
Boshoff, Frans 93, 95
Botha, P.W. 302
Bowra, Maurice 128,165
Boyle, Edward 184
Bradley, Ben 24
Braun, Loswell 59
British Film Institute 119, 157
Brock, Hugh 202
Broederbond 45
Brooke, Anthony 226
Bruwer, Andre 44
Buber, Martin 226
Bunche, Ralph 153
Bunsen, Bernard de 280
Burch, Stanley 110, 147
Burns, Emile 18, 19, 35
Byers, Frank 103

Cachilia, Yusuf 50
Calvocoressi, Peter 235, 255, 262, 265,
    280
Cambodia 258
Cameron, James 198, 205
Campaign for Nuclear Disarmament
    (CND) 197–202, 205–8, 209–13
Campaign for Right and Justice 41–2,
    43–7, 95
Campaign for the Defiance of Unjust
    Laws 138, 139, 181
Campbell, Jock 235
Carpio, Victorio 238–9
Carr-Saunders, Alexander 143
Carritt, Michael 23–8, 32, 188, 190

Carter, April 199–200
Carter, Deborah 233
Carter, Henry 115
Carter, Robert 233
Central African Federation 130–8, 177, 227–8
Central Intelligence Agency (CIA) 215, 258–60
Chaliha, Bimala Prasad 243, 253
Chesworth, Donald 280
Choudhury, Noba Krishna 249
Chowdhury, Syed 280
Christian Council of South Africa 103–4
civil rights movement 148, 150
Clack, Maurice 47, 52
Clayton, Geoffrey 72, 103–4, 106
and MS 37, 40–1, 42–3, 47, 48, 52, 57–8, 65, 83, 114, 188, 293
Clutton-Brock, Guy 142
Cohn, Roy 146
Cole, G.D.H. 27
Collins, Diana 214, 217, 219, 221, 222
Collins, John 128, 158, 171, 199, 201, 206, 211, 260, 263, 301
and MS 120–1, 179–81, 182, 214, 216–24
Comber, Tom 48, 55–6
Commission of Churches on International Affairs 84
Committee of 100: 205–8, 209–13
Communist Party (Great Britain) 17–20, 24, 31–3
Communist Party (India) 23–8
Communist Party (South Africa) 46, 92, 95, 117, 190–1, 220, 289
Connell, John 206
Council for Human Rights 50, 90
Courtney, Winifred 171
Crawford, James 128
Cripps, Lady 102
Cry, the Beloved Country (Paton) 120
Cullen, Archibald 12, 13

Dadoo, Yusuf 50, 53, 92
DeKeuper, Ethel 263
Defence and Aid 216, 217, 218–20, 239–40, 260, 263
Delaney, Shelagh 207
Dhadda, Siddharaj 228
Direct Action Committee Against Nuclear War (DAC) 199–200, 201–2, 206
Dobson, Alan 303

Dolce, Danilo 226
Donner, Clive 119
Dony, Francoise 152–3
Dornu, P.A. 203
Doshi, P.C. 26
Dowell, Graham 284, 299
Dowell, Susan 284
Driberg, Tom 103, 104–5
Driver, Christopher 207
du Toit, Bettie 50, 52, 138
Dummett, Michael 304
Dunn, Cyril 6, 18, 80, 155, 176, 188, 190, 252–3, 254, 293–8, 300
Dutt, R. Palme 18

Eden, Anthony 183
Edwards, Frances 202
Engleheart, Henry 10
Ethiopia 155

Farfield Foundation 215–16, 258–9
Far Cry, A (Benson) 157
Ferry, W.H. 233–4, 285
First Dance of Freedom, The (Meredith) 142
First, Ruth 70, 95
Fletcher, John 101, 115, 118, 119, 121, 128
Foot, Dingle 183, 221
Foot, Isaac 128
Foot, Michael 199
Frimpong-Manso, K. 203

Gaitskell, Hugh 212
Gandhi, Indira 252, 253, 254
Gandhi, Mahatma 22, 29, 50, 51, 88, 225
Garoeb, Moses 301
General Strike 9
Geraldine Mary, Mother 47, 114, 161
Ghana 184–5, 203
Ghetto Act (1946) 50–3
Gilmour, Ian 184
Gluckman, Dr Henry 46
Gomani, Philip 132–3
Good Offices Committee 193
Green, Jan 143, 274
Green, Jim 274
Greenham Common peace camp 304–6
Greenidge, George 128
Grenville-Grey, Wilfrid 265, 268
Grigg, John 180, 184
Grimond, Jo 184, 280–1
Grubb, Kenneth 223
Guingand, Francis de 236
Gundevia, Y.D. 246, 247, 248–9, 251, 254

Gunther, John 149–50

Hammarskjold, Dag 236–7
Hamilton, George 219
Hare, Paul 297
Harold Oram Organization 152
Harrington, Donald 171
Harris, Jack 153–4, 188
Harrison, Agatha 29, 102, 124–5
Hastings, Adrian 40–1, 140
Hemingford, Lord 127–8, 134, 197–8,
    218, 231, 235
Herbert, Pat 279–80
Herbstein, Denis 286
Herero tribe 74–87, 88, 89, 96–9, 102–4,
    105–11, 124–6, 157, 192
Himumuine, Berthold 80, 143
Hinden, Rita 261
Hofmeyr, J.H. 48
Hornby, Richard 261
House, Humphrey 28
Houser, George 150–1, 190, 237, 307
Hoveka, Nikankor 125
Hoyland, Francis 203
Huddleston, Trevor 72, 161, 217, 281
    and MS 37, 47, 67–9, 73, 181–3, 187,
    307
Hudson, Lord 135
Huggins, Godfrey 136–8
Hughes, Arthur 252
Hunter, Father 67
Huq, Fazlul 280–1

In Face of Fear (Levson) 116–17, 143
India
    and Nagaland 241–54
    MS in 21–30, 113–14, 241–54
    and Peace Commission 248, 249, 250,
    253
Indians
    in South Africa 50–1, 53, 83, 90–1
Intermediate Technology Group 143
International Defence and Aid Fund
    (IDAF) 260–1, 289–90
International League for the Rights of
    Man 105, 146, 150, 170, 190–1
International University Exchange
    Fund (IUEF) 298
Irvine, Dorothy 101, 102
Irvine, Fred 101

Jack, Homer 186
Jacobs, Julius 19–20
Johnston, Bill 149

Jones, Arthur Creech 133
Jones, Jack 205
Jooste, Gerhard 108

Kabaka 141, 142
Kat, Yusuf 53
Kapuuo, Clemens 272
Katjiuongua, Theophilias 125
Kaunda, Kenneth 227, 228, 230, 262,
    264, 268
Kent, Bruce xi, 307
Kenyatta, Jomo 178, 227, 238
Kenya 140, 178, 227
Kerina, Mburumba 193–4, 239, 271–2
Kershaw, Richard 261, 291
Khama, Seretse 141–2
Khama, Tshekedi 78, 80, 82, 123, 141,
    142, 172
Khoman, Thonat 192
Kilmartin, Terry 112
King, Martin Luther 148, 226
King-Hall, Stephen 184
King's College (Taunton) 8
Kirkwood, Kenneth 279
Komo, Samuel 62–4
Koteye, F.A. 203
Kozonguizi, Fanuel 194
Krause, F.E.T. 43
Kutako, Hosea 80–1, 82, 89, 102, 109,
    125, 126, 181, 191, 194, 271

Labour Party 101–2, 205, 212
Landis, Elizabeth 149
Laski, Harold 27
Lazar, Leonard 287, 299
Lauterpacht, Sir Herscht 155
Leach, Harry 52, 54
League of Nations 76–7, 125
Lean, David 118, 119
Legum, Colin 128, 130, 161, 183, 234, 287,
    292
Lekhotla la Bafo (Council of
    Commoners) 92, 93
Levitan, Jack 93–4, 95
Levson, Freda 57, 58–9, 60, 79–80, 94,
    101, 116–17, 138, 143
Levson, Leon 57, 58–9, 60, 94, 101
Lewis, Arthur 128
Lewis, C.S. 165
Liberia 155
Lie, Trygve 154
Livingstone, David 112,140
Longbottom, Charles 261
Longford, Frank 223

Louw, Eric 97, 98, 195
Lowenstein, Allard 151
Lusaka Manifesto 266
Luthuli, Albert 92, 172
Lyttelton, Oliver 130, 131

McCallam Scott, John 128, 133
McCarran, Patrick 145
McCarthy, Joe 145
MacGregor, Sue 303
Macleod, Iain 227
Macmillan, Harold 209–10
Mahareru, Frederick 78, 80, 82
Malan, D.F. 96–7, 103, 110–11, 181
Mandela, Nelson 58, 60, 64, 138, 172,
    219, 228–9, 240, 301
Manningham-Buller, Reginald 192
Marlowe, Lovina 171
Marshall, P. 203
Martin, Kingsley 115
Mask (West) 23
Mau Mau rebellion 129–30
Mboya, Tom 178
Meer, Ismail 60
Melvern, Linda 146
Meredith, Martin 142
Meyer, Cord 215
MI5, 35, 117, 134–5,
MI6, 122, 123
Michael Scott Committee 101, 105,
    118–20
Milner, Alfred 38
Mindolo 265–9
Minority Rights Group (MRG) 280,
    297
Minty, Abdul 263
Mokhehle, Ntsu 203
Monsarrat, Nicholas 61, 141
Montgomery, Bernard Law, Viscount
    Montgomery of Alamein 236
Moroka 65
Morrow, Edward 288
Morton, Beth 143, 290, 299
Morton, Ernest 143, 290, 299
Mtembu, Theophilus 63, 64, 67
Mugabe, Robert 302
Muirhead, Esther 101, 103, 115, 118, 119,
    128
Muirhead, Gordon 101, 119, 128
Mumford, Lewis 44
Muste, A.J. 150

Nagaland 241–54
Naicker, Dr 92

Nama tribe 77, 82, 89
Namibia *see* South-West Africa
Nasser, Gamal Abdel 183
National Association for the
    Advancement of Coloured People
    (NAACP) 150
National Peace Council 115
Narayan, Jayaprakash 226, 243, 253
Naught for Your Comfort (Huddleston)
    181
Nazi-Soviet pact 32, 95
Nehru, Pandit 247–8
Niemoller, Martin 226
Nigeria 185
Nkomo, Joshua 267
Nkrumah, Kwame 185, 202
Noel-Baker, Philip 102
Northam 4–6, 8
Northern Rhodesia 227, 228
Norton, George 60, 64–5, 98, 99, 101,
    119, 128
Nyasaland 130–5, 227
Nyerere, Julius 208, 264

Obote, Milton 142
Observer (newspaper) 112, 122–3
O'Dowd, Michael 236
Okahandja 82
Oppenheimer, Harry 235, 236
Orme, Jane 19–20
Orwell, George 122, 299
Osborne, John 207
Ovambo tribe 89, 192

Pakenham, Elizabeth 128, 159, 189–90
Pakenham, Thomas 184
Palme, Olaf 298
Pan-Africanist Congress (PAC) 218–19,
    221
Pandit, Mrs 243, 244
Parker, Peter 261–2
Parson's Pleasure (Oxford) 165–6
Paton, Alan 120, 158
Pauling, Linus 202
Perez de Cuellar, Javier 304
Perham, Margery 126, 128, 134, 142, 143,
    160
Peters, Esther 203
Philby, Kim 122–3
Phizo, Angami Zapu 243–4
Pike, James 171
Pollitt, Harry 19, 24, 35
Prain, Ronald 235
Prentice, Sartell 84, 106, 109

press
  reactions to MS 89–90, 101, 151,
    186–91, 286, 291–2
Priestley, J.B. 199

Quakers
  and MS 101–2, 123, 127

Raikes, H.R. 49–50
Ramsey, Guy 115
Randall, Clarence B. 234
Randle, Michael 199, 200, 204
Raphael, Adam 286
Raven, C.E. 128
Raven, Faith 273
Raven, John 273
Reddy, Enuga S. 153, 237, 260–1, 271
Redgrave, Vanessa 207-8
Reeves, Ambrose 106, 114, 161, 171, 188
Reith, Lord 124
Rhodesia 255–6, 287–8
Richmond, Lorna 143, 273–6, 284,
    299–300, 307
Robeson, Paul 104, 150
Rohrbach, Paul 74–5
Roma Mission College fire 92–3
Rose, E.J.B. 261
Royal Air Force:
  MS enlists in 33–4
Russell, Bertrand 3, 201, 205, 206–7,
    209–10, 219, 303
Rustin, Bayard 150, 202–3, 228

Sahara Project 202–5
St Paul's College 12, 13
St Raphael's leper colony 10–11
Sampson, Anthony 186–7, 237
Sangster, W.F. 128
Satchell, Father 53
Scanlon, Hughie 205
Schoenman, Ralph 205–6, 209
Schoon, Jennifer 298
Schoon, Katryn 298
Schoon, Marius 298
Schumacher, E.F. 143
Schweitzer, Albert 112
Scott, Ethel (mother) 4, 66, 112–13,
    174–5
Scott, John 5
Scott, Michael
  and the Africa Bureau 127–30, 133,
    140–1, 142–4, 148, 197–8, 216,
    258–60, 263–74, 269–70
  and the Africa Educational Trust

    279–80
  and Agatha Harrison 102
  and Ambrose Reeves 106, 114
  as anti-apartheid campaigner 115–17,
    179–82
  anti-fascism 32, 33
  arrested 166–9, 200–1, 208
  in Basutoland 92–4
  in Bethal (Eastern Transvaal) 70–2
  and the Campaign for Nuclear
    Disarmament (CND) 197–202,
    207–8, 209–13
  and the Campaign for Right and
    Justice 41–2, 43–7
  chaplain in England 15–18
  childhood 1–8
  and Communist Party (Great
    Britain) 17–20, 31–3, 35
  and Communist Party (India) 190
  and Communist Party (South Africa)
    46, 95, 117, 190–1, 289
  and Crohn's Disease 32–3, 123, 233
  criticism of African economies 234–8
  and Cyril Dunn's planned
    biography 293–8
  and David Astor 1, 2, 3, 121–3, 127,
    129, 166–8, 177, 189, 232, 252, 284,
    306
  death 1–3, 306–7
  depression 166–9
  in East Africa 263–9
  enlists in the RAF 33–4
  and Freda Levson 116–17
  and Gandhi/Gandhism 29, 50, 88,
    113, 186, 209, 225–6, 288–9
  and Geoffrey Clayton 37, 40–3, 47,
    48, 52, 57–8, 65, 83, 114, 188, 293
  and Godfrey Huggins 136–8
  and H.R. Raikes 49–50
  and the Herero tribe 77–87, 88, 89,
    96–9, 102–4, 105–11, 124–6
  illnesses 9–10, 31, 32–3, 34–5, 123–4,
    169–70, 304
  imprisonment 50–6
  and In Face of Fear (Levson) 116–17
  in India 21–30, 113–14, 241–54
  and the International Defence and
    Aid Fund (IDAF) 289–90
  and Jan Smuts 90
  and John Collins 120–1, 179–181, 182,
    214, 216–24
  lifestyle 118, 232–3, 273, 275, 284
  and Lorna Richmond 273–6, 284
  and McCarthyism 145–6

and the Mandate Trust 287–8
marriage proposals 59, 161–2
and Mary Benson 118–20, 156, 157–64,
    169–72, 176, 189
and Mburumba Kerina 193–4
and MI5 117, 134–5
and Michael Carritt 23–8, 32, 188, 190
move to South Africa 10–13
in New York 145–6, 149, 233–4
and Nelson Mandela 64, 228–9
and Nyasaland 130–5
Observer profile of 112
ordination 12, 15
in Oxford 165–7, 168–9
paranoia of 281–2
and the peace movement 256–7,
    304–6
and Philip Gomani 132–3
political action in South Africa 48–53,
    90–1
political influences 6, 17, 18–20, 50, 88
press reactions to 89–90, 101, 151,
    186–91, 286, 291–2
in psychoanalysis 172–3
psychological profile of 173–6, 293–6,
    299–300
and Quakers 101–2, 123
relationship with parents 6–7, 173–5
religious ideas of 7, 12, 290–1, 294,
    303–4
returns to England (1948) 101–2
returns to South Africa (1943) 35–8
and Rhodesia 287–8
and Roma Mission College fire 92–3
and the Sahara Project 202–5
and Samuel Komo 62–3
school 1–3, 8, 173
and Seretse Khama 141–2
at Sevagram 113–14
and South-West Africa 77–87, 88, 89,
    96–9, 102–4, 105–11, 124–6, 154–6,
    269–72
and the Study Project on External
    Investment in South Africa and
    Namibia 285–7
and the Suez Crisis 183–4
in Tobruk 60–3, 64–7
travels in South Africa 12–13
and Trevor Huddleston 37, 47, 67–9,
    73, 181–3, 187, 307
and the United Nations 82–7, 146–8,
    152–6
and the United Party 45
in United States of America 145–52,
    156
and Vietnam 257–8
and the 'Votes for All' People's
    Assembly 91–2
and women 59
and World War II 31–6
writes *A Time to Speak* 113
Scott, Nigel (brother) 8, 15, 169–70
Scott, Perceval (father) 4, 34, 174
Scott, Richard 184
Scott, Roy (brother) 8, 15
Scott, Thomas (grandfather) 5
Selassie, Haile 155
Sevagram 113–14, 225
Shamuyarira, Nathan 267
Shastri, Lal Bahadur 248
Sierra Leone 227
Singh, Maharaj 83–4
Skinner, Allen 202
Slovo, Joe 298
Smuts, Jan 38–9, 44, 51
    and MS 90
South Africa
    and the Broederbond 45
    and the Campaign for Right and
        Justice 41–2, 43–7
    and Central African Federation
        130–8
    and Christian Council of South
        Africa 103–4
    disinvesting from 285–7
    election (1948) 95–7
    and farm working conditions 70–1
    and the Ghetto Act (1946) 50–3
    and Indian population 50–1, 53, 83,
        90–1
    and the mining industry 44, 234–8
    MS criticises 115–17
    MS moves to 10–13
    MS returns in 1943 35–8
    MS travels in 12–13
    political action of MS 48–53
    press reactions to MS 89–90
    prison conditions in 54–5
    protests in 138–9
    and South-West Africa 74, 77–8,
        85–6, 88–90, 96–9, 105–11, 124–6,
        152
    and the United Nations 152, 154–6,
        191–4, 255–6, 260–1
    and the World Peace Brigade 226–7,
        228–31, 239
South African Foundation 236
South-West Africa 74–8, 85–6, 88–90,

152, 192–6, 238–9, 271–2
and MS 77–87, 88, 89, 96–9, 102–4,
    105–11, 124–6, 154–6, 269–72, 288
South West African People's
    Organisation (SWAPO) 195,
    270–1
Southampton 4–6, 8
Southern African Freedom Fund 220–1,
    222
Springbok Legion 62
Stafford-Clark, David 167–8
Stephens, Bob 121
Steyn, Dr Colin 46
Steyn, Marais 45
Stonehouse, John 281
Stonor Saunders, Frances 215
Study Project on External Investment
    in South Africa and Namibia
    285–7
Suez Crisis 183–4
Sukhai, Kughato 252
Sutherland, Bill 150, 151, 203–4, 239
Swaffham 200–1
Sykes, Marjorie 249
Symonds, Jane 143, 215, 280

Thomas, Norman 150
Thompson, John 215
Time to Speak, A (Scott) 113, 186–91
Tobruk (shantytown) 60–3, 64–7
Transvaal 90–1
Treason Trial Defence Fund 171
Trotha, Lothar von 75–6, 109
Troughton, Christine 280
Tubman, William 155
Tucker, Henry 45
Tutu, Desmond 307
Tweedsmuir, Lord 124–5, 126
Tyerman, Donald 184

U Thant 252
Uganda 141, 142
United National Independence Party
    (UNIP) 227–8, 229, 230
United Nations 146–7
    and the Central African Federation
        135–6
    and the Herero tribe 82–7, 88, 89,
        105–11
    and MS 146–8, 152–6

and South Africa 152, 154–6, 191–4,
    236–8, 260–1
and South-West Africa 90, 96–9,
    125–6, 154–6, 192–4, 238–9, 270,
    271–2
and the United States of America
    153–4
United Party (South Africa) 45
United States of America
    civil rights movement 148, 150
    MS in 145–52, 156
    and the United Nations 153–4
Upper Volta 202, 203

Verwoerd, Hendrik 235, 238
Vietnam 257–8
Vorster, Balthazar Johannes 264
'Votes for All' People's Assembly 91–2

Waddams, H.M. 184
Walker, Patrick Gordon 123
Warren, Will 202
Waterson, Sydney 46
Welensky, Roy 227, 228
Wesker, Arnold 207
Westcott, Foss 30
Whitaker, Ben 297
White, Walter 150
Wicken, Joan 264
Williams, Ruth 141
Williamson, Craig 298
Wilson, Harold 281
Wilson, J.L. 128
Windhoek shootings 195
Winter, Colin 288, 300
Witbooi, David 82, 125
Wolfe, Alvin W. 234
women
    and MS 59
Wood, Richard 300
World Peace Brigade 226–7, 228–31, 239
World War II 31–6
Worsthorne, Peregrine 187
Wraige, H.E. 43, 45

Young, Gavin 244–5, 250

Zambia 230, 262, 264–9
Zemba, Lydia 171
Zimbabwe 302